Women of Color in Leadership

Taking Their Rightful Place

Edited by
Richard Greggory Johnson III
G.L.A Harris

Birkdale Publishers

San Diego

ISBN 978-0-9724419-6-4
Library of Congress Control Number: 2010922002

Cover Design: Richard Greggory Johnson III and Sidney Shiroma

Sixteen of the contributors to this volume provided photographs of themselves to be used on the cover.

Top row, left to right
Karin Pleasant, Olga Welch, Fayneese Miller, Phyllis Wise

Second row from top, left to right
Yolanda Flores, Teresa Kaimanu, Melba Boyd, Shakuntala Rao

Third row from top, left to right
Carolyn Lewis, Vidu Soni, Martha Bárcenas-Mooradian, Kathleen Bergquist

Bottom row, left to right
Chris Robinson-Easley, Gloria Cuadráz, G.L.A. Harris, Renée Sanders-Lawson

Birkdale Publishers, Inc.
P.O. Box 270261
San Diego CA 92198-0261
website www.Birkdalepublishers.com
telephone 858 774 6075

Women of Color in Leadership

Taking Their Rightful Place

Contents

Part III   Medicine and the Natural Sciences

Part IV   International Scholars

Part V   The Practitioners

Forward

Women of Color in Leadership: Taking Their Rightful Place is a moving collection of narratives that demonstrate the contributions of leaders of different races, genders, sexual orientation, social class, and nationality. The broad scope of the book makes it a major contribution to this important topic. In fact, I have not read a book with a goal of presenting such a breadth of issues through the writing of authors who have such a wide spectrum of personal and professional life experiences. Their narratives are inspirational and troubling.

Despite major progress in the last century towards equal rights for all people, we still face challenges. What is made exquisitely clear in this book is that inequality of opportunity still persists, though it may be more subtle. The authors beautifully portray narratives of triumph, frustration, and perseverance. The strength of this book is that most of the chapters are written by accomplished women of color, women who are considered successful. It illustrates different strategies that they use to overcome persisting prejudice. They also offer hope that by working together, progress will be made. It reaffirms for me that diversity and excellence go hand in hand. It reminds me how much we benefit from embracing people with different perspectives (in everything that we do), that derive from their race, gender, sexual orientation, social class, and nationality. This book is a poignant reminder of the importance of the principles of inclusion. As we approach the greatest and most complex challenges of our time, it is essential that we hear all voices so that we work toward the best solutions.

Phyllis M. Wise
Provost and Executive Vice President
University of Washington
March 2010

Preface

In 1988, I was a twenty-one year old master's degree student in leadership studies at DePaul University in Chicago with plans of going on for a doctorate in public policy. I studied such key figures as Niccolo Machiavelli, Plato, Peter Drucker, Max Weber, and Frederick Taylor to name only a few theorists in leadership studies. It never occurred to me that leadership perspectives from diverse groups, including from women, more specifically women of color, were missing from the reading list in many if not all of my classes. Many of my classes centered on leadership from a white man's perspective. Since this was the perspective I was exposed to, I came away believing that to be an organizational leader meant being a tall, heterosexual white man from privilege.

I did not have the language or the confidence to criticize my professor's choice of texts for their classes. Before arriving at DePaul, I attended a HBCU (Historically Black University/College) in the South. There we revered our professors as gods and did not question their selection of course materials. Perhaps to some extent, my deference was a function of being an undergraduate student, especially one at a more traditional college.

Despite not having read literature in graduate school on women of color and other diverse groups, I knew something was missing. I grew up with a strong mother and all through my years of graduate school I wondered where her narrative was in the literature. The daughter of Hillary Clinton would not have this issue because her mother is well documented in gender studies. Indeed, for my mother, and millions of other women of color, this is not the case, and their voices often go unnoticed and unappreciated.

My experiences were good at DePaul overall, but they would have been better had professors supplied us with readings on leadership that may have altered our perceptions to be more inclusive. Now, as a professor in an Educational Leadership and Policy Studies masters and doctoral program myself, I take my responsibilities seriously and ensure that my graduate students receive a diverse array of readings that touch upon gender, race, sexual orientation and social class. I believe that a rich subject literature draws from many aspects of the academic and practitioner community.

Leadership Program Data

The findings of a sample content analysis of leadership doctoral programs are presented in the table below. All leadership programs in the sample offer either the D.P.A. (Doctor of Public Administration), Ed.D. (Doctor of Education), or Ph.D (Doctor of Philosophy) degree. The doctorate was used as the unit of analysis as it is a terminal degree, and the assumption is that students might have the opportunity to engage in diverse leadership literature and discussions before completing their degree. Each program is currently a campus-based program, providing full-time and/or part-time doctoral instruction. This study did not intentionally seek to exclude online doctoral leadership programs, such as Antioch University's Ph.D. Program in Leadership and Change. However, the data would be unreliable, as many online programs have classes such as Independent Studies or "Contracts" that do not lend themselves well to content analysis. Each program in the sample has its curriculum clearly posted to its website and is current. Additional efforts were made to contact individual programs when content information on the Website was not clear. Programs that offered only a concentration or specialization in leadership were not included in the sample. The purpose of the content analysis was to demonstrate the limited amount of leadership doctoral programs integrating courses in women and leadership courses.

Table 1 demonstrates a number of interesting findings. First, none of the programs require that students take a course that touch on women's issues. However, several sample programs offer one or more courses in diversity as part of their core requirements. This is a step in the right direction, as many diversity courses address gender, sexual orientation, social class and race (see R.G. Johnson, 2009, Adams et. al., 2000). In courses offered on diversity there is no guarantee that any specific topic would make it into the class content, specifically women of color issues and other gender related issues each time the course is taught.

Table 1

University & Program	Course Name – required / elective
Gonzaga University Ph.D. Program Leadership Studies	1) Leadership and Feminist Ethics – Elective 2) Leadership & Social Justice – Elective 3) Leadership & Diversity – Elective 4) Leadership & Culture – Elective
University of Victoria Ed.D in Leadership Studies	1) Leadership, Learning & Social Justice – Elective 2) Leadership Education & Diversity – Elective
University of Vermont Ed.D Program in Educational Leadership and Policy Studies	1) Women & Leadership – Elective 2) Challenges of Multicultural Education – Elective
University of San Diego Ph.D. Leadership Studies	1) Multicultural & Philosophical Foundations of Education – Elective
Bowling Green State University Ed.D. Leadership Studies	1) Diversity & Cultural Leadership – Core 2) Diversity of School Communities & Political Dynamics – Elective
University of Baltimore D.P.A. Program	none offered
Hamline University D.P.A. Program	none offered
Regent University Ph.D. in Organizational Leadership	none offered
University of Nevada, Las Vegas Ed.D in Educational Leadership	1) Leading for Social Justice
San Fransisco State University Ed.D Educational Leadership	1) Qualitative Analysis of Race, Class, Gender in Society and Education – Required 2) Quantitative Analysis of Structural Inequality in Education – Required 3) Transformational Strategies to Address Inequality in Education & Society – Required

Source: Doctoral Program Websites, Spring 2010.

Secondly, Table 1 demonstrates a lack of integration between leadership studies and issues addressing women of color. This is evident since none of the sample programs offer the two topics together. Marsh Dowling's chapter on intersectional analysis persuasively argues that women of color face discrimination and marginalization on multiple levels because of a combination of their gender and their status as racial/ethnic minorities. Unfortunately, despite the optimists, the United States is not living in a post-racial society since President Obama's election, and women of color are more often than not, still last on the ladder of success. Table 1. reveals that although leadership doctoral programs all have core requirements and electives, there is little if any commitment to a much needed area of study that integrates issues of diversity, women of color, and leadership.

It is not evident whether individual faculty in leadership programs research issues about women of color, leadership and social justice. This was not the intent of the research in Table 1. However, based upon the lack of information contained in peer-reviewed books and journal articles on the topic, it is doubtful that such research is occurring.

Book Design

This book is divided into four parts Higher Education Senior Administrators, The Faculty, Medicine and the Natural Sciences, International Scholar, and The Practitioners. Authors who are considered senior administrators such as deans and provosts are included in Part I: Higher Education Senior Administrators. Authors Fayneese Miller and Olga Welch are among the few women of color who are senior administrators currently serving at Predominately White Institutions within the United States. Both of their chapters go to the heart of this volume in terms of exploring issues of leadership, social justice and what it means to be a woman of color in the academy. Miller opens her chapter with an analysis of the media's coverage of Michelle Obama and her sense of fashion. Is the media's reaction to her preference for sleeveless dresses "colored" by the fact that Michelle Obama is a Black woman? To some, Michelle Obama's preference for sleeveless dresses indicates that she is *out of place* as first lady. Do women of color face the same kind of judgement in the academy?

Part II: The Faculty, comprises scholars whose role is primarily research and teaching. Many of these individuals also hold administrative positions such as Program Director or Program Coordinator (e.g., Susan Gooden and Adriana Katzew). Part II is subdivided into three disciplines: education, humanities, and social sciences. Authors in this section include Theresa Julnes Kamainu (public administration and policy), Amy Kirschke (art), Yolanda Flores (romance languages), and Marsha J. Tyson Darling (history). This section is by far the largest section of the volume and is meant to provide the reader with insights into what life can be like as a women of color in a space still greatly inhabited by individuals who are white and often male.

Part III contains chapters addressing women of color in medicine and the natural sciences. As editors of this volume, we were adamant tabout including such a section. We thank Fayneese Miller, Regina Toolin, and Robert Biral for their insightful chapter on the challenges facing women of color in the sciences, as well as Drs. Cynthia Macri and Evelyn Lewis for sharing their unique journeys on becoming medical officers in the armed forces. Each chapter in this section gives an account that indicates a desire for the author to do something uncommon, but in the end, so very rewarding.

Part IV: International Scholars is one of the smaller sections of the volume, but it nonetheless packs a huge punch with scholars such as Shakuntala Rao and Martha Bárcenas-Mooradian. Rao gives a haunting account of life in the academy as an Indian women, while Bárcenas-Mooradian provides an intimate portrayal of the life of indigenous women in a poor rural village in Mexico.

The last section of this volume, Part V: The Practitioners, contains chapters written by practitioners in their various professional fields. For example Karin Pleasant is the Co-Executive Director of a nonprofit organization for the performing arts in Southern California. Pleasant's narrative gives the reader an account of life for a women of color, executive in a male-dominated industry. Her chapter provides the reader with an account of her journey and ultimately what she hopes to accomplish.

Diversity of Book Content

This book is diverse in authorship (race/ethnicity, sexual orientation, partner status, etc.), and interdisciplinary in scope, nature, and practitioner orientated. Each chapter is either theoretical, narrative or mix methods. My coeditor and I received almost one hundred submissions and inquiries about our volume resulting from the Call For Proposals distributed in fall 2008. We were pleased with the response, which clearly demonstrates a gap in the literature. Chapters for the volume were selected based upon, scholarship, uniqueness of topic. I am pleased that individuals who were not women of color were eager to contribute a chapter to our collection. We have a chapter co-authored by Fred Bonner and a chapter on African American women artists written by Amy Kirschke, a non-African American woman. My coeditor, publisher and I believe that having contributors who were not women of color would add to the richness of the volume. We believe this is the case.

Finally, this volume speaks to the strength and will of women of color. We feel privileged to be able to provide a stage from which their voices can ring loudly. It is our hope that women of color, women, men, graduate and undergraduate students will read these chapters and understand that a segment of the U.S. population has historically been left out of the conversation on leadership. This volume celebrates the successes of our unsung population and provides them a place at the table where they can take their rightful places.

Richard Greggory Johnson III
Associate Professor
University of Vermont
March 2010

Part I

Senior Administrators in Higher Education

Untangling the Ivy Vines:
A Perspective on Women of Color in Higher Education

Fayneese Sheryl Miller
University of Vermont

Life can only be understood backwards; but it must be lived forwards.
—Søren Kierkegaard

Ivy vines. Thorny thicket. Briar patch. Dilemmas. Higher education. Women of color. What possible combination of conjunctions could ever connect them all? Not blessed with more than normal ability to read minds, I suspect that many of you reading this paper both anticipate what I am about to say and will be able to add your own stories.

Within all spheres of society, women of color have had to deal with what Dr. Anna Julia Cooper, a Black woman intellectual, educator, and feminist, called both the "woman question" and the "race question." Cooper, born into slavery in 1858, the child of an enslaved African woman and her white master, died in Washington, D.C. in 1964, not far from where Martin Luther King, Jr. had given his "I Have a Dream" speech the year before. According to one chronicler (Rashidi, 2002) of her long life, she "possessed an unrelenting passion for learning and a sincere conviction that Black women were equipped to follow intellectual pursuits." Cooper is little remembered today as are other towering Black women intellectuals born during the 19th century, whose legacy we keep alive at present in the efforts we make to affirm Cooper's belief in the deservingness of Black women.

We have risen to the rank of First Lady of the United States, Secretary of State, University President, Provost, and CEO. Yet the histories for most if not all of these women contain narrative threads that do not always follow the neat chronologies paraded forth in the laudatory press releases or glowing hiring announcements detailing their particular accomplishments. For every one who rises, many do not, which seems reasonable under our meritocracy that rewards ability rather than wealth. Still, for women of color, the notion that the meritocracy exists on a level playing field where leaders are chosen and advance on the basis of ability and achievements alone is illusory. Too much evidence exists to the contrary, whether in our own personal stories or in the tabloid and mainstream press that questions at every turn our deservingness for the positions we either aspire to or attain.

Emotional Responses and Deservingness

Soon after her husband's inauguration, the spotlight shone brightly on Michelle Obama. She was feted in public, photographed at civic and family events, and featured in numerous articles, her picture gracing the cover of magazines on newsstand racks across the country. But despite the almost universal accord lavished upon her in article after article, what prompted nearly all the public attention and response was that in many of the early pictures and drawings of her she was wearing sleeveless outfits, her bare arms exposed to the gaze of all. Most notably, or infamously, depending upon your viewpoint, was the reaction to the image of her that appeared on the February 25, 2009 cover of *People*, her bare right arm relaxed in her lap, her left arm casually leaning atop a sofa cushion, and her body framing the less than provocative title of the article, "Our Life in the White House."

By the time *People Magazine* hit the newsstand, the hue and cry over her going sleeveless was already in full crescendo mode. When she was photographed earlier at her husband's address to Congress wearing a *Narcisco Rodriguez* sleeveless dress, the event sparked into full flame the cinders of controversy already smoldering from the iconic visual rendering of her and her husband on the July 21, 2008 cover of *The New Yorker*. In that earlier portrayal, Michelle was dressed in military fatigues, her likeness cast as a mix between a gun-totting Patty Hearst and a young be-afro'd Angela Davis. Barack was in turban and robes fist bumping his wife. This portrayal had come dangerously close to feeding the irrational frenzy of Obama haters into a call for action, this despite the erstwhile efforts of the cover artist and editor of *The New Yorker*, Barry Blitt and David Remnick, to dampen down the hyper-ventilating rhetoric with their claims of satiric intent.

As to the hullabaloo over her sleeveless outfits, much of it was framed in Emily Post terms as a breach of social etiquette, reminding Michelle that as first lady she must adhere to the protocols her new station in life demand of her. "Someone should tell Michelle to mix up her wardrobe and cover up from time to time," Sandra McElwaine (quoted in Dowd, 2009) commanded, conveniently eliding the history of first ladies being photographed at official events. As Bonnie Fuller (2009), reminds us, "America's most fashionable previous First Lady, Jacqueline Kennedy, practically made sleeveless looks her uniform, whether they were dresses or two piece shirt and skirt ensembles." There was also the two-for-the-price-of-one catty comment by the *New York Times'* David Brooks (cited in Dowd, 2009), who opined, "sometimes I think half the reason Obama ran for president is so Michelle would have a platform to show off her biceps." Brooks not only drains the legitimacy from Obama's election by turning him into a sleazy run-way promoter of his wife's physique, but shamelessly turns her into an object to be gazed at, appropriated and used as others pleased, her arms a synecdoche for her body.

So what is going on here? One might understand these comments if they were directed at Michelle because she is a woman. But does it matter that she is not only a woman, but also a Black woman? Is it, as Dr. Cooper reminded us years ago, that women of color must deal not only with the 'woman" question but with the "race" question as well? If so, then what do Michelle's fashion choices have to do with race? Is this yet another instance of what Black women who are working to do well "have to contend with that many of our racial counterparts rarely do?" (Goff, 2009).

I ask these questions about Michelle Obama as the pretext to my discussion of women of color in higher education. My contention is that the response to Michelle Obama's arms is a response to her as a Black woman and is different only because it takes place in the political arena rather than in the hallowed "ivy-covered" halls of America's institutions of higher education. And no different from the response to smart, politically savvy women of color who are in leadership positions in whatever setting they find themselves.

As a social psychologist, I understand that the various responses to her sleeveless outfits have less to do with her fashion choices than with how people view themselves in relation to her. According to Roseman (1979), emotion theory proposes that the way a person reacts to another has much to do with how they relate past, present, and future events to their own goals and strivings. While most Americans do not grow up wanting to be first lady, or first man (however much the belief that anyone can be president forms a recurring theme in our shared communal upbringing), the belief is still a powerful determinant of the way Michelle Obama is perceived as First lady.

The theoretical argument is that she has something others want and desire, but to the extent that those desires are culturally shaped and historically bound, to have a Black woman as First Lady does not harmonize with the overdetermined set of images most Americans have of what the person who occupies that "office" should look like. As a consequence, she, as the occupant, is seen not as deserving her position but as someone *occupying* it, as in *taking-it-over*, as the image of her as a revolutionary in the 2008 *The New Yorker* cover suggests. Hence her deservingness as First Lady is called into question, the focus on her sleeveless and toned arms masquerading the real issue, which is, as a Black woman, she is perceived as *out of place*. Her alleged fashion *faux pas'* are emphasized while the positives involved in her personal story are subsumed into the ad hominem criticisms directed at her. Lost in the shuffle is the fact that she is a highly educated and accomplished person.

Her story is instructive for women of color in higher education. Our deservingness whether to be tenured faculty or senior academic administrators, is often met with the kinds of distracting responses directed at Michelle Obama. In the same way that the issue for her is not her toned arms but the color of her skin, we who are similarly hued find our deservingness for the positions we hold, and aspire to, questioned and challenged by those who perceive us as out of place. These masking responses take various forms, but many will sound familiar. Is our research *worthy* enough, which translated usually means, Are we only doing "race" related research? Are we sufficiently *transparent, collaborative*, and *inclusive* enough, which generally means Have we ceded authority to those who for one reason or other covet our *places*? Their challenges to our level of accomplishment make it difficult for us to navigate through the tenure and promotion process, regardless of how deserving we may be.

There is a conviction among most people of color that we cannot be merely good, but must be far better than anyone else holding similar positions or doing similar work. This belief is both gendered and racial. As a woman of color, I know that having to work twice as hard for half the recognition can have an impact upon one's professional self-concept, to say nothing about our sense of self-worth, especially when what we accomplish is not adequately rewarded or acknowledged. Studies show that women of color in higher education are often the lowest paid among the faculty, often receive less positive evaluations than others, are less likely to have a mentor, and are less likely to receive tenure. And if they do, they are less likely to reach the rank of full professor.

Moreover, those who have the potential to advance are often steered into administrative positions like diversity officers or student affairs administrators too early in their careers, making it even harder to attain the level of full professor. According to a recent study conducted by the American Council of Education (King & Gomez, 2008), only three percent of all senior administrators and chief academic officers in higher education are women of color, a number that dramatically decreases when nonacademic senior administrators are eliminated from the total.

As disheartening as these figures are, the miniscule percentage of women of color in senior academic positions is directly correlated to the small number who hold the rank of full professor. Since the path to an executive or senior-level administrative position is often from the rank of full professor, the low number of women of color at that level has negative implications for those aspiring to reach senior administrative positions.

The reasons for this condition are many, not the least of which is that women of color are usually the last to be considered for senior academic positions. When the provost at my institution announced he was stepping down and the search began to recruit internally for an interim replacement, I had a conversation with one of my colleagues about the position, who mentioned as possible candidates the names of other deans, but not mine. When I stated that I was interested in the position, I was met with a surprised, "I never thought about you, I didn't think you would be interested." I remember thinking at the time, "Why would I not be interested?" Did he truly believe I would not be interested, or was it that I would not be considered if I were? Was he projecting his views onto others who like him were unable to see beyond my gender and race and imagine me in the position?

When I reflected on this later, I thought of what Frederick Douglass said in his famous and enduring "What to the Negro is the Fourth of July" speech, delivered to a White audience on July 5, 1852, in a country still almost ten years away from the titanic struggle that would be waged not to free the slaves but to preserve the union. In his speech that day, one that deserves broad reading today, he said,

> For the present, it is enough to affirm the equal manhood of the Negro race. It is astonishing that, while we are ploughing, planting, and reaping, using all kinds of mechanical tools...that, while we are reading, writing, ciphering, acting as clerks, merchants and secretaries, having among us lawyers, doctors, ministers, poets, authors, editors, orators and teachers; that while we are engaged in all manner of enterprises..., we are called upon to prove that we are men! (quoted in Miller & Biral, 1997)

Douglass's words continue to resonate today not only down the corridors of academia but in every small town and large city neighborhood in our country. His challenge to his audience is to rethink who is deserving of the two mainstay values upon which our country was founded: "liberty and equality" (Miller & Biral, 1997). In terms of emotion theory, because Blacks had little to offer and nothing to give except their bodily labor, there was little for Whites to covet, and therefore even less to relate to in the shaping of their goals and desires. Douglass's call to his White audience that day was to make visible the invisible. It is a call many of us continue to have to make today. When my colleague and I were discussing the interim provost position, his failure to consider me could be construed as an inability to *see* me, conditioned as he was by the long historical legacy of invisibility, which cloaks and inhibits our access to opportunities that he and others never have to think about.

Sojourner Truth once stated, "That man over there says that women need to be helped into carriages, and lifted over ditches, and to have the best places everywhere. Nobody ever helps me into carriages, or over mud-puddles, or gives me any best place! And ain't I a woman?" Like her contemporary, Fredrick Douglass, Sojourner Truth was demanding that she and other Black women be made visible, so that they could take their place in society. Her demand like Douglass's is for both liberty and equality.

Liberty as Participation and Inclusion

Douglass's and Truth's words are powerful reminders that the promises inscribed in the Declaration of Independence were yet to be fulfilled for people like them, denied as they were the full benefits of "life, liberty, and the pursuit of happiness." In both speeches, the two are not so much questioning the place of Black women and men in American society, as they are demanding a repositioning of the *place* they have been afforded. They both ask, How can one deserving of liberty and equality attain those values unless one is visibly recognized as having the right to do so.

My argument in this paper has been that *place* for women of color is therefore both a physical and mental site and is synonymous with the amount of liberty one has in order to actively participate in all aspects of life and work. In higher education, examples abound where the actions of others impede liberty by cordoning off the *places* one is permitted to go. The denial of tenure when one's scholarship is equal to or exceeds that of others is an impediment to liberty. The assumption that women of color are not qualified to hold senior-level administrative positions is an impediment to liberty. Not given the opportunity to participate as a full and equal member of one's academic community is an impediment to liberty. "There are words like Liberty That almost make me cry If you had known what I know You would know why," Langston Hughes writes in his poem "Words Like Freedom," expressing what we all know and understand about the elusive connection between liberty, place, and deservingness.

Women of color are still striving to attain liberty within the academy, despite the swelling numbers receiving Ph.D., MBA, M.D., and law degrees. I am hopeful that when our numbers of full professors and senior leaders within higher education and other professions begin to mirror our impressive graduation rates, that *deservingness* will be recognized and *liberty* achieved. I am hopeful but not confident.

Women of Color as Change Agents

In this section, I will focus on the perception of me as a change agent, a label fraught with potential dangers. I became Dean of the College of Education and Social Services at the University of

Vermont in 2005. During the airport interview for the position, I was informed of various problems facing the College, not the least of which was a long-standing budgetary deficit, which I, as the successful candidate, would be expected to address and fix. Moreover, after an intensive review of the College documents and conversations with people in the College, I was able to identify additional problems, all of which were viewed within a context of doability.

During the on-campus interview, I shared with the faculty and staff what I had identified as the issues facing the College, and the word quickly spread that I was a "change agent." To be called a change agent is flattering, but to be lulled into believing only the positives of that label is to ignore its less than salutary underside. Once others invest you with this belief, you are charged with carrying out what you propose. And by taking on the responsibility, you also risk receiving the blame if change does not come in the timely manner others might expect. This is the rub in the ointment. When is change meant to occur, and how? How does one communicate to a diverse group of faculty and staff, all of whom have personal timetables for change to happen, that change requires more than the stroke of a pen or the issuing of command decisions. That might work in the military but not in academia.

For women of color, the rules of the game have additional twists. They might be told, as I was, to lead efforts to bring about change within a college or the university but not be advised or warned about the obstacles standing in the way to leading a successful effort. And the stakes increase if change requires not only the moving around of a few offices or minor personnel changes but also a change in the cultural climate of the unit. The question always becomes: how does one communicate that changes will be made to those who have an investment in keeping things the same, particularly those who have grown comfortable with the status quo? How does one communicate to them and others that change is needed if the college is to maintain its viability within the University and secure its growth in the future?

Theoretically, change becomes acceptable to a faculty if they can operationally define and determine what constitutes change. Change becomes desirable if the faculty is in control or plays the dominant role in the process of change. These *axioms* are consistent with emotion theory research, where issues of transparency, collaboration, and inclusiveness turn upon the extent to which someone other than you determines the process and implements the change. In short, change becomes possible if someone other than you decides what it should be. So, if confronted with this dilemma, how do you as a "change agent" overcome this cycle of control and dominance, particularly when autonomy has been established as the accepted norm, and power has been placed in the hands of the few? As my mom would say in her succinctly idiomatic way of getting to the truth of the matter, "Hard ain't easy."

Experiences from the Field

When I arrived at the University of Vermont as dean, I discovered that the deficit was considerably larger than indicated by the financials I reviewed prior to accepting the position. I also learned that the deficit, located in one department, resulted in part from a limited understanding of budgets and belief in the central administration's willingness to cover or forgive all departmental deficits. The question for me was, do I allow the deficit to continue unchecked, or do I develop a strategy to address it? The former was clearly not an option being that I had been hired to address the deficit; the latter became imperative because the faculty in other departments were looking to me to stop the drain on their resources from the fiscal mismanagement of one department.

Furthermore, I was not naive to think that if allowed to continue, the deficit would not leach into perceptions about my deservingness to be the dean, or affix itself to questions about my effectiveness as a leader. So, because I had a mandate, and because it was the right thing to do, I moved forward to address the deficit. At the same time, to impede negative perceptions about my leadership, I decided that the process must become public knowledge across the University.

Once the University community and others became aware of the deficit, two responses resulted. On the inside, questions were immediately raised by faculty about my knowledge of budgets and ability to manage. On the outside, the Board of Trustees was fully in support of my efforts and was unquestioning of my ability to bring about fiscal responsibility to the College. I attribute these unlike responses to differences in authority and proximity to the actions taken. On the one hand, the Board of Trustees had actual power and control but was only indirectly affected by the actions taken to resolve the deficit. On the other hand, the faculty has perceived power and control within their particular academic units, but unlike the members of the Board, several in the program were directly affected by my actions. The outlying nature of the Board allowed for a more objective response, whereas the proximal nature of the affected faculty prompted some to launch ad hominem attacks upon me, some quite raw and highly inappropriate.

As a woman of color, my experience at the University of Vermont to address the fiscal deficit is an instance of the pattern of behavior to which I have referred above, where the need to control and dominate is expressly manifested by a pattern of questioning about my knowledge, transparency, level of collaboration, and inclusiveness. All of this made my decision to go public even more compelling. Interestingly, although I received counsel by many not to make the deficit public, not one person of color, male or female, when told of the situation, suggested I remain silent. In fact, to a person, they stated, "If you do not go public, you will be blamed for creating the deficit," each understanding intuitively the thorny situation before me.

The 2009 academic year was a challenge for most of us in higher education, with the trickling down of the global financial crisis having a profound impact on the health of University budgets. Across the nation, colleges and universities were instituting staff and program cuts and/or hiring freezes. In the College of Education and Social Services at UVM, we returned over $60,000 to the central budget in 2008-2009 and were asked to prepare and implement a plan that would return 4.75% of our annual budget, plus an additional 4.50% penalty for not reaching our enrollment target of 13:1.

I openly and aggressively challenged the penalty and successfully argued that it be removed. Citing convincing evidence at odds with the University's enrollment target numbers, I was praised for standing up for and representing the College and applauded for my efforts by faculty and staff during a meeting attended by the President, Vice President for Finance and Administration, and Associate Provost. That I should work so diligently on their behalf was expected, and I was applauded when my actions benefited them. Conversely, the same expectation was neither recognized nor applauded when the personnel decisions I made negatively affected them or their friends. I do not mean to imply that my faculty and staff can only think parochially, but the insularity of the culture within academic units limits one's ability to be the change agent that is wanted and expected. Yet, when it becomes necessary to make decisions, the process and result can be met with a narrowness of self-interested response.

In order to keep faculty and staff informed during the financial crisis, I met with each department several times, met with all staff, and held four college-wide meetings between December 2008 and March 2009. At each of the meetings, I outlined the financial situation at UVM and repeatedly stated that the college would feel pain through layoffs. I also indicated what I would return to the central budget so as to minimize human capital loss. In addition, I stated that each academic department would need to contribute to the College's 4.75% return to the central budget. Each department chair was asked to meet with his or her faculty to determine how they might meet their financial responsibility. Department chairs submitted their plan to me, and I made the final decision as to what would be returned to the budget.

I share this information because despite all the step-by-step efforts I made to keep my faculty and staff informed of the process leading to the budgetary decisions I had to make, soon after making them I received a letter signed by a small group of faculty, critical of my decisions. In it they said, "We are mindful of the need for transparency" and "we are confident that through renewed communication and collaborative efforts we can [improve] transparency."

The letter I received is further evidence of the argument I am making in this paper, that under the guise of well-intended and proffered guidance, the use of the words "transparency" and "collaboration" are code words for control and dominance. In this case, the message contained in the letter I received was that although I could do the work necessary to make the layoff decisions, I had no authority to decide who received a layoff notice. That power rested with the letter writers, their request for collaboration and transparency thinly disguised moves to control the process. Faculty, many of whom were liberal-minded and committed to the idea of social justice, challenged my authority to make and implement decisions that were not only within my power, but necessary in carrying out my fiduciary responsibilities for the college.

This response did not at all come as a surprise. As argued above in the distinction I made about the power differences between the Board of Trustees and the faculty, as long as my decisions did not infringe upon specific faculty and their programs, I could do as I pleased. But when personally affected, they responded with what I would characterize as an inversion of David Elkind's notion of personal fable, resituated as an adult model of behavior to explain why they responded the way they did. According to Elkind, personal fable is a form of egocentrism and a mental construction—not a social reality—that occurs when people believe that the experiences and/or feelings of others are unique and will not happen to them. So, similar to adolescents constructing the belief that they will live forever, those touched by my decisions stood in disbelief when they found they were directly affected.

What I had done, of course, was cross a line that they themselves had drawn. By venturing into their domains, my actions were tantamount to an invasion. As a consequence, not only was I aggressively denounced in public documents and conversations, but my authority and commitment to the programs and people in the College were challenged and undermined. This occurred even though I had sought multiple public opportunities to work with faculty and staff and share what I knew and what I was doing on their behalf. In short, despite my efforts for transparency, collaboration, and inclusiveness, all three were found wanting.

Why? Am I not perceived as qualified for the position? Am I not deserving of the role of dean? No one in the University would answer no to these questions. But liberty and justice have different connotations for women of color in the academy. In the same way that our legal codes in discrimination law make a distinction between "disparate treatment" and "disparate impact", one specific to an individual, the other generalized to groups, the impact of differential treatment is not always readily apparent to others, nor evident to those whose behaviors contribute to it. My point here is not to argue the complex legal distinctions between "treatment" and "impact" but to identify and conceptualize a pattern of response that finds wide expression throughout the academy. My "treatment" may or may not have been disparate, but its generalized "impact" cautions many women of color seeking advancement within the academy to consider only "race-based" positions, such as affirmative action or EEO officers. To step outside that well-defined channel often results in the cautionary tale I weave here from my experiences, where issues of place, belongingness, deservingness, and liberty are problematized within the politics of race and gender.

Negotiating One's Place Within the Academy

In the previous sections, I discussed the challenges that women of color in leadership roles often confront. I focused on identifying the problem and discussing the "place" of women in academia. I have presented patterns of behavior that can often be stressful for women of color. That said, however, the opportunities for women of color to become university or college presidents, provosts, vice presidents, and faculty is steadily increasing, as is evident from the numbers who now hold such positions across the country. And while the number deserving of such positions continues to outpace those who secure them, we who have succeeded have an opportunity to help those behind us in the queue to confront and navigate their way around the obstacles that may stand in their way.

As a first premise, I will assert what I have found to be the baseline necessity to success in leadership environments: the ability to *reflect*—to think about what has been, what is, and what should be (Schön, 1983). A second premise is that effective leaders understand and appreciate both uncertainty and instability. It follows then that once a comprehensive view of the environment is gained, one must devise *methods* to respond effectively. The standard approach to dealing with uncertainty and instability is to listen, ask the right questions, and be prepared to act. I would add one more item to the list, and that is to be *intentional*, which is to know what you want and to be determined to accomplish it. No easy task in environments which are unstable and uncertain.

What follows is a plan of action that aims to achieve intentionality. It incorporates ideas from my experience as well as ideas proposed by others (Kotter, 2007; Reardon, 2007). While not always specific to women of color, it includes the three processes critical to the success of any plan: *knowledge generation, reflection,* and *input.*

Knowledge generation: Since the outcome of any action is change, the problems associated with any decision you make must first be clearly identified and operationally defined. Is the problem urgent? This question needs to be answered with specific and compelling data, and if you decide after doing the necessary research that it is urgent, then the sense of urgency can be conveyed with certainty and confidence.

Reflection: Why is the change necessary once the urgency is understood? Sometimes even the need for urgent change does not always translate to change "now." Before making any decisions, the actions you propose must be reviewed within several contexts, including your vision for the College or department.

Input: Critical to the first two stages is the need for input. Communication can never be underestimated. Be prepared to look for ways not only to communicate your vision but also to seek from and share information with those in your unit. To this end, build a team of supporters—I convened a "kitchen cabinet-like" group of three people, whom I came to rely on for their input, both pro and con, and who then became my "voice" when I needed to be heard. Change will be slower than necessary if support for change is not apparent. Opposition to you as a leader and what you hope to accomplish may still remain, but if you "speak" with many voices echoing your support, then opposition will decline.

The Path to Senior Leadership Roles

There are many paths to senior leadership in higher education. The one with which I am most familiar is the academic path. I, therefore, begin with the role of assistant professor.

Identify a Mentor: One of the more critical decisions one can make early in their academic and professional career is to identify a mentor. No one enters higher education with a how-to-book. Women of color, however, are the least likely to have a colleague as a mentor. A mentor can shepherd you through the university or college, introduce you to potential colleagues at other universities, and provide critical feedback during the research and writing phases.

A mentor will often serve as a co-author or provide access to others for or with whom you might write a book review, chapter, or invited article. This is one way to identify one or more co-authors. I focus on the mentor or co-author topic because women of color often write by themselves. This is neither required nor expected in most fields. Identifying a writing partner early during one's career increases the probability that you will have a significant body of work for annual reviews, promotion from assistant to associate professor with tenure, and promotion to full professor later. Annual reviews are often neglected in favor of preparation for promotion and tenure. Annual reviews are important. They are used to determine year-to-year or post three-year contract renewals as well as salary increases.

It was during my postdoctoral fellowships years at Yale University that I met those who would become my close colleagues and friends. They have served as a source of support and as a sounding board for critical academic and administrative decisions I have made over the years. They have also provided me with publishing and conference presentation opportunities. More importantly, I have amassed a cohort of key people who know me both professionally and personally and can therefore serve as references for me. The relationships that I have made are some of the more important aspects of my career.

Learn to Say No: A women of color is the go-to person when a space on a committee becomes vacant. Be selective and strategic about the committees you ultimately choose. You will need to do some service work so do not say "no" to every committee request you receive; otherwise, you will not be seen as a team player. Your mentor can help you learn how to be strategic in the committees you select. I recommend that you grow your visibility outside the college by agreeing to serve on a senior-level search committee. Within the department, you might agree to sit on the curriculum review committee.

The second element of saying "no" has to do with the amount of time you give to students. Students want and deserve time with their professors. This does not mean that you should maintain an open door-policy. If you do, your research and teaching will suffer. Be mindful, however, that you will be viewed as less accessible even when you are as available to students as your colleagues.

As a new Assistant Professor of Psychology at Brown University and the only female tenure-track member of the department faculty (There was no woman with tenure in the department when I was hired), the task of developing the undergraduate concentration was given to me. This was a major undertaking and meant that I was the primary contact for all undergraduates in my department. Although I gained some valuable administrative experiences, I did not have the time that the others in the department had to devote to research. Fortunately, I was still able to amass a body of work. This, however, can be very difficult to do when engaged in administrative work early in one's career.

Do Your Homework: Always be prepared! Know both sides of an issue before making a decision. Collect the data necessary to inform your decision. Do not let your emotions, devoid of fact, rule the day. I was able to successfully argue against the financial penalty the College received as a response to the University's economic woes by providing data to support the argument I mounted.

If It Smells Like a Rat It Is a Rat: Trust your judgment, and instincts, but make sure you ascertain that a pattern of behavior exists before stating that it does. If an inappropriate comment makes you feel uncomfortable or is aimed directly at you, excuse yourself from the meeting, then immediately write down what was said or done, by whom, and when. Do not, I repeat, do not, blame yourself for another's inappropriateness.

If you choose to share your "suspicions" about the behavior of someone towards you or in your presence, be prepared to defend your experiences or have them validated. Both responses might come as a surprise. It is not unusual for those who identify with the person engaging in the inappropriate behavior to minimize or justify the behavior, or to suggest that you are overreacting to what they see as inappropriate, but "innocent" behavior. Also be aware that you might get labeled as a "troublemaker" for doing the right and safe thing—reporting the inappropriate behavior. My advice is to be prepared by documenting your experiences as they occur.

Participate in Professional Development Opportunities: Conferences, leadership programs, and other professional development programs often provide you with the opportunity to develop your skills in particular areas. In addition, participation provides you with another cohort of colleagues and mentors. It is often through professional development programs that opportunities for advancement become known.

Do Not Be Flattered When Asked to Assume an Administrative Position: Before you jump at an opportunity offered to you to assume an administrative position, think carefully about it by including it in your list of career goals. If your goal is to become a full professor, then getting involved in nonacademic administrative positions might lessen your chances of doing so in the future. If you want to become a dean or provost, doing so from a nonacademic position and a rank lower than professor means that this will probably not happen. Diversity positions are often slated for a person of color. If you want to be a diversity officer and spend most of your career working primarily on diversity issues, then this is the right position for you. However, before you take such a role, check to see to whom the diversity person reports. This is critical for positioning yourself in ways that make your contributions valuable to the institution.

Appearances Matter: The way you dress matters. While you do not have to wear the latest designer clothing, you need to make sure that you present yourself well in all aspects. Students, colleagues, and administrators notice. Rarely will you see a woman of color in a senior-level position who neglects her physical appearance. Also, the way you present yourself gives others some idea about your level of confidence and ability to "command" attention, garner support, and get results. I am often asked whether or not wearing "ethnic'"clothing is an impediment to climbing the senior administrative ladder or being heard in the academy. One thing for sure is that you are not invisible when you are the only one in the room or in your academic unit who wears what some might consider ethnic clothing. The question I would ask is what is the nature of your visibility? Are you visible solely because of the type of clothing you wear and not because of the quality of your research and teaching?

If a woman of color has a solid academic and/or administrative record, then what is worn might be of less importance than what she knows and how she presents what she knows. If your teaching and research is less than stellar, then I suggest that you be careful and not allow yourself to be known to others only because you wear ethnic garb. We are immediately visible when we walk in a room because of our color and/or ethnic identification; we can choose to let people remain focused on the physical components, or we can force them to focus on our intellect.

I do not profess to be an expert on the effect of ethnic dress in the academy. My observation is only that women of color who are in the professoriate role are more able to wear ethnic dress without a great deal of negative attention or consequences for their career than women of color who are high-level senior administrators. In all my years in higher education I have yet to meet a woman of color who is a President, Provost, or academic dean at a predominantly white or research institution who wears ethnic clothing on a daily basis.

Find a Balance: Senior administrative jobs like academic ones are not 9 to 5 positions. They are not even weekday only. They can be all consuming. As women of color in senior-level positions, we feel the pressure of having to work harder and longer more acutely than others might. We can also have the added pressures associated with being a significant member of a family unit. We therefore have to learn to work smarter, not longer. Finding and supporting the right team is critical to working smarter. Do not rush this process. A team of people who are smart, self-disciplined, responsible, and committed is critical for effective and successful leadership. Once you have your team, trust them to do the work, get out of their way, and hold them accountable.

Know The Finances: If you are in a position with substantial budgetary oversight, do not leave the management and understanding of the finances to others. If something is amiss financially, you will be blamed. So know what you are being asked to sign, know how to read and interpret budgets, and learn all that you can about finance and administration. If you review the list of failed presidencies or senior leaders in the academy, a common component emerges: money. They used university funds to purchase personal items or mismanaged how others used funds. My advice to you is simple: do not touch the money, especially to purchase personal items. Make sure there are checks and balances in place when you must spend money on travel or for other university purposes.

The list of suggestions for a successful career as a senior administrator or to be tapped as someone who could rise through the ranks in higher education is not exhaustive. Some of the suggestions I listed are basic leadership information; others are what I think are necessary to navigate in higher education. Women of color are often the visible minority in the room. The best advice I ever received was from my mother. She said, "People will always focus on what you look like; let them start there if they want, but whatever you do, don't let them stop there."

I have worked in higher education for over 20 years. I have experienced its joys and disappointments. I have had to stand tall against adversity and adversaries. I have also had many moments of great satisfaction. I realize that I love what I do. As one of my mentors said when talking about her own experience, "I have the best job in the world." This is true for me as well. Never once have I questioned my decision to become an academic or senior administrator. Over the years I have learned how to successfully navigate through the ivy vines and locate that rose. My experiences, while unique to me, are not unlike those of many other women of color. We are becoming more visible. We are taking on more leadership roles. We are succeeding in academia. We are successfully plucking the thorns off the rose, one thorn at a time.

References

Crisp, R. J., & Turner, R. N. (2007). *Essential social psychology*. London: Sage.

Dovidio, J. F., & Gaertner, S.L. (2005). Color blind or just plain blind? The pernicious nature of contemporary racism. *The NonProfit Quarterly* (Winter), pp. 1-11.

Dowd, M. (March 7, 2009). Should Michelle Cover Up? *The New York Times*. Retrieved from http://www.nytimes.com

Fuller, B. (March 2, 2009). Michelle Obama's sleevegate: Why can't America handle her bare arms? *The Huffington Post*. Retrieved from http://www.huffingtonpost.com

Gaertner, S. L., & Dovidio, J.F. (1986). The aversive form of racism. In: J.F. Dovidio & S.L. Gaertner (Eds.), *Prejudice, discrimination and racism: Theory and research*. Orlando, FL: Academic Press, pp. 61-89.

Goff, K. (March 11, 2009). Michelle Obama: Wonder Woman. *The Huffington Post*. Retrieved from http://www.huffingtonpost.com

King, J. E., & Gomez, G. (2008). *On the pathway to the presidency: Characteristics of higher education's senior leadership*. *American Council on Education*, Publication #311685. Washington, DC: American Council on Education.

Kotter, J. P. (2007). When a new manager takes charge. *Harvard Business Review: On the tests of a leader.* Boston, MA: Harvard Business School Press, pp. 165-183.

Lang, P. J. (1984). Cognition in emotion: concept and action. In Izard, C. E., Kagan, J., & Zajonc, R.B. (eds.), *Emotions, cognition, and behavior.* Cambridge, MA: Cambridge University Press.

Lemert, C., & Bhan, E. (1998). *The voice of Anna Julia Cooper: Including a voice from the south and other important essays, papers, letters* (edited volume). Oxford: Rowman & Littlefield Publishers, Inc.

Miller, F., and Biral, R. (1997). What to a Black person is affirmative action? *American Behavioral Scientist, 41*(2), 272-279.

Reardon, K. (2007). *Courage as a skill. Harvard Business Review: On the tests of a leader.* Boston, MA: Harvard Business School Press, pp. 23-38.

Roseman, I. (1979). *Cognitive aspects of emotion and emotional behavior.* Paper presented at the meetings of the American Psychological Association, New York, NY.

Schön, R. (1983). *The reflective practitioner: How professionals think in action.* New York: Basic Books.

Walking on a Trampoline:
The Role of Complexity, Change, and Execution in Leading a School of Education

Duquesne University

Introduction

In many ways, leading a School of Education at a research-intensive university is like "walking on a trampoline." You seek and crave, stability while simultaneously preparing for the unexpected bounces, tensions, natural, and unsettling results of seeking to attain greater heights with each jump. In their explanation of "complexity theory," Pascale et al. (2000) suggest that they regard the journey as analogous to walking on a trampoline with each step altering the whole topography in unpredictable ways: "What was 'up' at the start may be somewhat 'down' farther along the route, and the ascent may become steeper as the destination draws near" (pp.105-106)

At a time of increasing reliance on the dean's leadership in an atmosphere where the minutest changes can have similar unanticipated and profound consequences, "walking on a trampoline" aptly captures my own experiences leading the School of Education at Duquesne University.

Driven by academic discipline from below and constrained by budgetary concerns from above, college deans straddle a jittery enterprise whose members at once cling to tradition and toy with the notion of breaking out of the mold.... A desire for normalcy drives an administrative expectation that these deans be change agents bent on improving the institution (Allen-Meares, 1997; Wisniewski, 1998 cited in Wolverton et al, 2001, p. 1). Indeed, as I reflect on the unpredictable topography I've encountered during my four-year tenure, I realize that much of the knowledge on which I've staked my most important decisions resided at a tacit and somewhat instinctual level, one that I would find particularly difficult to describe, especially in a chapter. Still, I appreciate this opportunity to reflect on my practice, an activity I strongly advocated in the many graduate courses I've taught over my 32 years in public and higher education. Indeed, in that context, I've often argued that reflection was the "sine qua non" of quality administration and pedagogy. Thus as a practicing administrator, it seemed to me that reflection on my leadership was especially apropos at a time Schools of Education were being subjected to intense scrutiny and even more intense criticism.

I undertook to begin that reflection by deconstructing my practice in an attempt to determine how closely it mirrored my leadership philosophy. I examine this connection by focusing on three theories that have recently influenced my thinking on the practice of leadership. Fullan (2008) quotes the biologist David Sloan Wilson's definition of a theory as "merely a way of organizing ideas that seems to make sense of the world" (2007, p. 16 cited in Fullan, 2008). In short, according to Fullan, the best theories are at their core solidly grounded in action (p. 1). Moreover, good theories are critical because they provide a "handle" on the underlying reason (really the underlying thinking) behind actions and their consequences. In the absence of a good theory, an individual is left with nothing more than the acquisition of techniques—simply surface manifestations of the underlying rationale. Thus, techniques can be borrowed or even stolen but a philosophy cannot (Fullan, 2008, p.16).

For me, this chapter represents the revisiting of a reflective journey that began the first year of my deanship. That year, I was invited to present a paper on my first year as dean at a session on leadership held at the University Council on Educational Administration Convention (2006) in San Antonio. This chapter continues a reflection that began that first year and continues as I conclude my fourth year. This chapter is intended to explore through that reflection the interrelated nature of my philosophy and practice of leadership. For me, one's leadership and the philosophy/(ies) that inform it should result in a practice that is grounded in reflection. Mintzberg best captures this idea, noting ,"Learning is not doing; it is reflecting on doing" (p. 228 cited in Fullan, 2008, p. 5). Moreover, he states that "managing may be instinctive but it has to be learned too, not just by doing it but by being able to gain conceptual insight while doing it" (p. 200 cited in Fullan, 2008, p. 5).

In their study of the leadership dimensions of Education Deans Wepner, D'Onofrio and Wilhite (2008) adopted a conceptual framework grounded in the psychology of the self-concept and the evolution of a professional identity that depended on the differentiation and integration of the intellectual, emotional, social and moral attributes of leadership in their approach to solving leadership problems (p. 156). These researchers believed that "the skills, attitudes, and dispositions that education deans have reflected their professional self-concept and professional identity for serving in such a role" (p. 154). Moreover, they conclude that effectiveness in the deanship is a combination of the person and the institutional culture. Thus, education deans must, on a daily basis, determine ways to balance individual, institutional, community and societal needs by reflecting on the ways in which they solve problems according to their personal as well as institutional histories (p. 166).

The chapter begins with an introduction to my institution and a summary of my professional preparation. From there it moves to the conceptual framework I have used to organize my discussion of the three perspectives on leadership that have influenced my practice. I conclude the chapter with the question that will guide my ongoing interrogation of my leadership philosophy and the administrative practices connected with it. Let's begin with an introduction to my institution—Duquesne University of the Holy Spirit.

Duquesne University of the Holy Spirit

Duquesne University of the Holy Spirit is a private Catholic institution founded over a Pittsburgh bakery by members of the Congregation of the Holy Spirit to educate immigrant and orphaned children during the latter part of the 19th century. The Holy Ghost Fathers, or Spiritans, as they call themselves, built the institution's identity around a mission of serving God through serving students. They actualized that mission by their commitment to excellence in liberal and professional education linked intentionally with a profound concern for moral and spiritual values. Now numbering 10,000 students in 10 Schools, Duquesne University maintains an ecumenical atmosphere open to diversity and dedicated to providing service to the Church, the community, the nation, and the world. Thus, all Duquesne students complete service-learning projects through a core curriculum that directly involves them with marginalized and diverse populations in Pittsburgh and the surrounding areas. For Duquesne students, social justice means feeding the homeless, providing clothing for the needy, participating in campaigns aimed at drawing attention to breast cancer and disability awareness and at eradicating all forms of discrimination.

This commitment to social justice is exemplified by the Holy Ghost Fathers who maintain international ministries in Latin America, the Caribbean, and Africa. They reside on Duquesne's campus, providing leadership in student and academic affairs as tenured faculty members, distinguished professors and chairs, university administrators, and individual priests serving a variety of student populations on campus and in greater Pittsburgh.

The School of Education, one of the first Schools established on the Duquesne campus, has existed for 77 years and occupies a beautiful, recently renovated building on campus. It serves 1,200 students and boasts a faculty of 54 across three academic departments: the Department of Instruction and Leadership in Education; the Department of Counseling, Psychology, & Special Education; and the Department of Educational Foundations & Leadership.

Professional Background

Before coming to Duquesne, I had spent most of my professional life in preparation for teaching and, eventually, a career in higher education administration. I completed an undergraduate degree at Howard University, graduating Phi Beta Kappa and second in my class with a major in history and a double minor in Education and English. I pursued a master's degree in the Education of the Deaf at the University of Tennessee (Knoxville), one of the nation's premier institutions in Deaf Education. I taught at Gallaudet University's Model Secondary School for the Deaf and also at the Tennessee School for the Deaf, later serving as its middle and high school principal.

At 28, I obtained my doctorate in Educational Administration and Supervision from the University of Tennessee, at that time one of the nation's strongest administration preparation programs. Two years later I returned to that institution as an assistant professor, becoming a tenured, associate professor and then full professor. Eventually, I was asked to chair two academic departments (the Department of Counseling, Deafness and Human Services and the Department of Educational Leadership and Policy Studies). After a 26-year career at the University of Tennessee as a faculty member and administrator, I became the Dean of the School of Education at Duquesne in July 2005. Despite my preparation in educational administration, I engaged in no formal study for the position.

In his study of the academic deanship, Krahenbuhl (2004) notes that "there are no formal professional programs for those seeking positions of academic leadership. There are programs that study academic leadership as an area of inquiry, but most such programs reside in colleges of education, where they attract few enrollees in the form of faculty from other disciplines intending to become deans" (p. 1).

Traditionally, the trajectory for an academic deanship begins with an appointment to a tenure-track faculty position, with movement by the individual from assistant to full professor in a timely fashion. "Most deans are individuals who are called upon to provide leadership as unit heads, directors, or department chairs. Success in such roles often results in these individuals considering positions with a greater scope of responsibility" (p. 2).

Thus, if one wanted to examine my deanship as a case study, focusing on managerial aspects such as my relationships with faculty, staff, and students and the impact of my leadership on these populations, then data would need to be collected from a variety of sources on campus (e.g., staff and students in the School of Education, my dean colleagues on campus, the provost and president of the institution), as well as identified, off-campus, professional stakeholders at the local, state, and national levels in education, politics, and in the private sector, with whom I interact on behalf of the School. Moreover, one would need to examine print materials (e.g., letters, school documents generated since my arrival, Executive Committee minutes, etc.) as well as conduct scheduled and unscheduled observations of me in a variety of venues (e.g., School faculty meetings, parent meetings, student meetings, community and civic meetings, and various state education meetings).

In short, you would need to compare the data drawn from these and other contexts with my analysis to formulate a more complete instrumental case study of the fit between the leadership philosophy I set forth in this chapter and my practice as dean. Therefore, I want to acknowledge the absence in this chapter of other perspectives on my leadership.

According to Wepner et al. (2008), "The exclusive reliance on self-reports of deans is a limitation. Self-perceptions are clearly not always accurate, and it is certainly possible that the deans in this study exhibit leadership behavior that is not consistent with their responses" (p. 164).

I intend to "frame" the discussion by engaging in the reflective process I identified earlier. I'm interested in examining some of the leadership theories that have impacted my thinking about my practice. Using this framework forces me to examine the link between my philosophy and the outcomes I seek. Forging this link is critical to the change process I am leading in the School of Education. Indeed, Fullan (2003) suggests that if leaders in education are to effect not only change but also reform, they must "find ways to reintroduce motivation or moral purpose into the enterprise" (p. 11). To illustrate, he cites the work of Parker Palmer and his colleagues, who call for a reawakening of teachers' moral purposes through a reflective process grounded in the following questions:

- Why did I become a teacher in the first place?
- What do I stand for as a teacher?
- What are the gifts I bring to my work?
- What do I want my legacy to be?
- What can I do to "keep track of myself"—to remember my own heart? (Levsey with Palmer, 1999, p. 16 cited in Fullan, 2004, p. 11).

These questions resonate with my reflective process on my leadership philosophy and the tasks I set for myself during the first year of my deanship. In brief, I became a dean because I wanted to establish a premier school of education at the graduate and undergraduate levels that prepared educational leaders who "made a difference" in the lives of children and youth. For me, this is the goal and legacy I hope to leave at Duquesne University. To this process I bring strong interpersonal skills, experience in secondary and postsecondary teaching and administration, and a commitment to achieving synergy between my philosophy and my administrative practice. My efforts to achieve this synergy have been influenced recently by the perspectives on leadership I describe within the following conceptual framework.

Conceptual Framework

I have chosen the conceptual framework developed by Bossidy and Charan (2002) because of its focus on a tacit though little discussed goal in organizations, execution, or getting things done. Like other administrators, deans are expected "to execute." However, I would argue, that few educational administration programs deliberately or intentionally pay sufficient attention to this aspect of leadership. Nor does "execution," this essential ingredient in leadership studies and strategic planning, receive the attention it deserves in the professional literature on educational administration. Consider, for example, how often administrators convene faculty meetings, carefully craft agendas around particular goals or outcomes, and, still in the end, fail to determine how to execute these same goals and outcomes.

When discussing execution in business organizations, Bossidy and Charan (2002) define it as "the gap nobody knows; the gap between what a company's leaders want to achieve and the ability of their organization to achieve it" (p. 19). Moreover, they define execution as:

> a systematic process of rigorous discussion involving assumptions about the organization's environment, assessment of the organization's capabilities, linking strategy to operations and the people who are going to implement the strategy, synchronizing these individuals and their various disciplines, and, finally linking rewards to outcomes. It also involves developing mechanisms within the organization for changing assumptions as the environment changes and upgrading the company's capabilities to meet the challenges associated with an ambitious initiative or strategy. (p. 22)

In short, "in its most fundamental sense, execution is a systematic way of exposing reality and acting on it" (p. 22).

Further, Bossidy and Charan (2002) suggest that execution must be embedded in the culture of an organization so that it is identifiable in the reward systems and in the norms of behavior that everyone practices. To that end, execution involves three core processes by the leader: "picking other leaders, setting the strategic direction, and conducting operations" (p. 24). These actions are the substance of execution and cannot be delegated by the leader, regardless of the size of the organization.

As I stated previously, I chose "execution" as my own frame because it is a basic principle often ignored by educational administrators. A leader's philosophy governs or should govern his/her behaviors. Bossidy and Charon (2002) note that this constitutes the first building block of leadership.

Building Block One: The Leader's Philosophy and Essential Behaviors

Wolverton et al. (2001) quote research which suggests that at one time or another, deans in U.S. colleges have been expected to be "all things to all people," faculty leader, scholar, student adviser and disciplinarian, admissions officer, bookkeeper, personnel manager fundraiser—deans have done it all (Thiessen & Howey, 1998; Tucker & Bryan, 1988 as cited in Wolverton et al. 2001, p. 12).

Thus, as a university's demands increase, deans are compelled to maintain credibility in the eyes of faculty who deny any assertion of that authority (M. Wolverton et al., 1999 as cited in Wolverton et al., 2001), even as they balance the demands of multiple internal (i.e. provosts and presidents) and external constituencies (e.g. parents, alumni, field-based partners in school systems and other professional contexts, and external donors, both private and governmental).

In order to execute you must (a) know your people and your business, (b) insist on realism, (c) set clear goals and priorities, (d) reward the doers, (e) expand people's capabilities, and (f) know yourself.

In the list of these characteristics, I found "knowing oneself" most closely aligned with the questions around moral purpose posed by Palmer et al. As I stated earlier, much of my leadership philosophy operates at a tacit, and in some ways instinctual, level, a level tied to my belief systems and to Palmer's insistence on identifying "what one stands for." Not surprisingly, then, the first Building Block discussed by Bossidy and Charan (2002) addresses the crucial connection that must exist between the leader's philosophy and the behaviors he/she exhibits. Using this foundation, I turn to a description of three perspectives on leadership behavior: (a) leadership for change, (b) adaptive leadership, and (c) level 5 leadership. Recently, I've considered each of these perspectives in seeking to learn how closely my leadership philosophy aligns with my administrative decisionmaking and actions.

Leadership for Change

My preparation in educational administration occurred during the 1970s, a time when theoretical debates centered on whether effective leaders were "born or made." Arguments for or against these positions were often advanced in business and management theories grounded primarily though not exclusively in positions that supported the dichotomy between management skills and leadership dispositions. This differentiation is one that Fullan (2001) termed *artificial*. Instead, his work on leadership for change suggests that leadership and management overlap and that both are needed qualities. Further, Fullan (2001) only supports the differentiation that "leadership is needed for problems that do not have easy answers...problems of the day are complex, rife with paradoxes and dilemmas...for which there are no once and for all answers" (p. 2). This view dovetails with Freire's (1970) concept of "praxis," which he defines as the inseparability of theory and practice. From my perspective, the inseparability of theory and practice has meant that I've never been overly concerned with differentiating my management style from my leadership philosophy, preferring instead to view them, like the Roman god Janus, as "two sides of the same administrative coin." Moreover, I have been and remain deeply committed to the concept of dispositional knowledge in administration. In spite of arguments against the importance of dispositional knowledge in the preparation of preservice teachers, I am convinced that teachers who clearly link their practice to an identified "moral purpose" are essential if we are to achieve the educational reform we seek. Similarly, for educational administrators, whether they operate in K-12 settings or higher education, having a clear sense of moral purpose intentionally linked to the execution of systemic reform efforts is critical.

Adaptive Leadership

Pascale (1997) has noted that an entity qualifies as a complex adaptive system when it meets four tests. First, it must be comprised of many agents acting in parallel; it is not hierarchically controlled. Second, it continuously shuffles these building blocks and generates multiple levels of organization and structure. Third, it exhibits entropy and winding down over time unless replenished with energy. In this sense, complex adaptive systems are vulnerable to death. Fourth (a distinguishing characteristic) all complex adaptive systems exhibit a capacity for pattern recognition and employ this to anticipate the future and to learn to recognize the anticipation of seasonal change" (p. 84).

In discussing adaptive leadership, Pascale et al. (2000) begins by citing the observations of Ronald Heifetz, Director of the Leadership Education Project at Harvard University's John F. Kennedy School of Government. Heifetz notes that leadership is frequently equated with authority, which is misleading. He observes that a great many people in authority do not provide leadership, whereas others with little formal authority have changed the world through extraordinary examples of informal leadership (e.g., Jesus, Gandi, Nelson Mandela and Susan B. Anthony).

Fullan (2001) also offers Heifetz's (1994) statement about the selection of leaders when a crisis exists:

in a crisis…we call for someone with answers, decision, strength, and a map of the future, someone who knows where we ought to be going—in short someone who can make hard problems simple…Instead of looking for saviors, we should be calling for leadership that will challenge us to face problems for which there are no simple, painless solutions…problems that require us to learn new ways (p. 3).

For Heifetz, the essence of leadership is not mobilizing people to solve problems for which the answers are already known but rather the art of helping them confront problems that have not been successfully addressed (Fullan, 2001, p. 5). Thus, Heifetz makes a distinction between "technical (i.e. operational) leadership and adaptive leadership" (Heifetz as cited in Pascale et al., 2000, p. 37). Technical leadership involves the exercise of authority and represents an entirely appropriate response in conditions of relative stability and what Pascale et al. term "equilibrium." Adaptive leadership, on the other hand, "makes happen what isn't going to happen otherwise. As such, it is a surefire recipe to disturb the equilibrium in an organization" (Pascale et al., 2000, p. 39). Often educational institutions face both operational and adaptive challenges simultaneously. The point is that overtime (and even concurrently), organizations need evolution and revolution (Pascale et al., 2000, p. 38). Yet, unlike the "white horse" leader who is expected to "fix the problems" and "provide decisive directions," Heifetz suggests that adaptive leaders proceed more slowly, not moving on an issue too rapidly nor reaching for a "quick fix." Instead, such leaders (1) communicate the urgency of the adaptive challenge, (2) establish a broad understanding of the circumstances creating the problem, to clarify why traditional solutions won't work, and (3) holding the stress in play until guerilla leaders come forward with solutions (Pascale et al., 2000, p. 40).

As a result, their style creates tension and anxiety.: tension because people are expecting and even looking for authority as bulwark against the anxiety associated with uncertainty and risk, anxiety because this kind of leadership disturbs the inertia in ways that people may find uncomfortable or even vigorously question and resist. History provides examples of this kind of resistance (i.e., Winston Churchill's warnings about Hitler prior to World War II).

Heifetz also suggests that this discomfort and risk may lead followers to turn to authority as a bulwark, a tact that must be vigorously resisted by adaptive leaders. "Instead, they must (1) hold the collective feet to the fire, (2) regulate distress such that the system is drawn out of its comfort zone (yet contain stress so it does not become dysfunctional), and (3) manage avoidance mechanisms that inevitably surface (such as scapegoating, looking to authority for the answer and so forth)" (Heifetz as cited in Pascale et al. (2000, p. 40). Thus, the concept of adaptive leadership is necessary when an organization is challenged to do what it has never done before. This is certainly true with respect to the utility and existence of Schools of Education, questioned as they are in both professional and public arenas. Moreover, it represents a particularly daunting challenge for deans, because traditionally the academy has adroitly and vigorously resisted any change it views as threatening its historic prerogatives.

I found the discussion of adaptive leadership particularly useful as I thought about the faculty's efforts to develop an identity statement for the School of Education at Duquesne University during the initial year of my deanship. Although a mission statement and connected faculty commitment statements existed for the School, I asked the faculty to develop an identity statement that captured who they were as a School of Education, rather than individual departments or the degree programs within them. I made external consultant assistance available to the faculty and essentially "left them alone" to grapple with the task. I did so believing that vision could not be a "top-down" enterprise but rather must arise from and be owned by those who would be expected to implement it. While I arrived with a vision for the School, I shared and linked my vision to the identity the faculty developed and owned.

Level 5 Leadership

Collins et al. (2001) suggest that transforming an organization from good to great is actually a "Black Box" enterprise of "buildup followed by breakthrough." In their five-year study of the histories of 28 successful and unsuccessful companies, they identified three broad stages of transformation related to breakthrough: (a) disciplined people, (b) disciplined thought, and (c) disciplined action. Within each of these broad stages are two key concepts, encompassed by a "wrap around" concept termed "the flywheel" which "captures the gestalt of the entire process of going from good to great" (p.12). The authors begin their discussion by describing the leadership philosophy that produced "great companies." They termed it *Level 5 Leadership* and provided several characteristics. As a preface to this description they noted:

> We were surprised, shocked really, to discover the type of leadership required for turning a good company into a great one. Compared to high-profile leaders with big personalities who make headlines and become celebrities, the good-to-great leaders seem to have come from Mars. (p. 12)

These leaders are self-effacing, quiet, reserved, a paradoxical blend of personal humility and professional will. By way of illustration, these leaders

a) Create superb results and a clear catalyst in the transition from good to great by demonstrating a compelling modesty and are never boastful, shunning public adulation.

b) Demonstrate an unwavering resolve to do whatever must be done to produce the best long-term results, no matter how difficult, by acting with quiet, calm determination; relying principally on inspired standards, not inspiring charisma, to motivate.

c) Set the standard of building an enduring company and will settle for nothing less; by channeling ambition into the company, not the self; thereby setting up successors for even greater success in the next generation.

d) Look in the mirror, not out the window, to apportion responsibility for poor results. Never blame other people, external factors or bad luck. By looking out the window, not in the mirror, to apportion credit for the success of the company–to other people, external factors, and good luck. (Collins, J., 2001, p. 36)

In reflecting on this definition of the Level 5 leader, I was struck by its consonance with Krahenbuhl's (2004) description of the effective dean:

Deans lead their organizations...Each decision made by a dean slightly reshapes a college and serves either to improve or degrade its competitive advantage...A college will be dynamic, if, in part, the dean creates an environment where the people who make up the college—its faculty, students, staff, alumni, and friends—are empowered to imagine the possibilities...This means looking ahead and being optimistic, expecting that the future will be better because of ideas that emerge to be pursued. This means that the dean wants a proactive organization, aggressively shaping the future (pp. 3-4).

Moreover, Level 5 Leadership, adaptive leadership and leadership for change suggest the need for a philosophy that "makes happen what wouldn't happen otherwise" (Pascale et al, 2000, p. 38). Bossidy and Charan (2002) capture this dynamic well in describing their second building block: Creating the Framework for Cultural Change.

Building Block Two: Creating the Framework for Cultural Change

Bossidy and Charan (2002) introduce this building block by asserting that most efforts at cultural change fail because they are not intentionally linked to improving the organization's outcomes:

The ideas and tools of cultural change are fuzzy and disconnected from the strategic and operational realities. To change a...culture, you need a set of processes...social operating mechanisms—that will change the beliefs and behavior of people in ways that are directly linked to bottom-line results (p. 85).

Although the academy rarely frames its outcomes in terms of the bottom-line, more and more successful leadership on university campuses is being measured by the results it produces. Krahenbuhl (2004) also speaks of the need for deans to lead in a manner that produces positive results for their Schools or Colleges.

> Colleges, like corporations operate in a competitive world, and colleges exist today in a time of great change...If a college is well-led it will become stronger, improving its position on the campus and among those institutions with which it most directly competes. If a college is ineffectively led, it will suffer in the campus competition for support and will be viewed less favorably in external comparisons. (p. 4)

Michael Fullan (2001) describes change as a double-edged sword, with positive and negative aspects. He provides an overview of the terms that people generate associated with change (i.e., excitement, danger, exhilaration, loss, improvements, and anxiety) and notes that because change arouses strong emotions, leadership is the key. Neither superhuman leaders, (who cannot be emulated) nor charismatic leaders (who inadvertently often do more harm than good through their episodic improvements), but leaders with the ability to focus on a small number of core aspects by "developing a new mind-set about the leader's responsibility to himself or herself and to those with whom he/she works" (p. 2). In his conceptual diagram, Fullan (2001) suggests that in addition to possessing enthusiasm, energy, and hope, leaders who would effect organizational change must:

> a) possess moral purpose-acting with the intention of making a positive difference in the lives of employees, stakeholders, and society as a whole;
> b) understand the change process which is the ability to comprehend and apply novel ways of thinking about and implementing the change process within the organization;
> c) recognize the critical necessity of building relationships with diverse people and groups;

d) possess the ability to turn information into knowledge that is created and shared across the organization;

e) engage in coherence building, that is, making clear that change is complex causing a disequilibrium in the organization that will result in the perennial pursuit of coherence (pp. 4-6)

With this philosophy, the leader can build the external and internal commitment from the members, resulting in "more good things happening and fewer bad things happening" (p. 4). What makes this model so powerful is its insistence that the leader understand the change process not as a linear or even hierarchical endeavor but as an interpersonal enterprise grounded in a strong moral purpose, which Fullan defines as "acting with the intention of making a positive difference in the lives of employees, customers, and society as a whole" (p. 3). Changing an environment for the best also requires the leader to be a student of complexity theory.

Complexity Theory and Leadership

Pascale et al. (2000) suggest four bedrock principles that are applicable to the living system of an organization:

• Equilibrium is a precursor to death. When a living system (i.e., an organization) is in a state of equilibrium, it is less responsive to changes occurring around it. This places the system at maximum risk. Indeed, "prolonged equilibrium dulls an organism's senses and saps its ability to arouse itself appropriately in the face of danger" (p. 21).

• In the face of threat, or when galvanized by a compelling opportunity, living things move toward the edge of chaos. This condition evokes higher levels of mutation and experimentation, and fresh solutions are more likely to be found.

• When this excitation occurs, the components of living systems self-organize, and new forms emerge from the turmoil.

• Living systems cannot be directed along a linear path. There are unforeseen consequences that are inevitable. The challenge [for the leader] is to disturb them in a manner that approximates the desired outcome (p. 6).

In describing how Steve Miller "disturbed" the complex system at Shell Oil, Pascale (1998) notes that Miller called for a different definition of vision and change, one in which the leaders provide the vision and are the context setters. However, in his vision, solution to the thousands of strategic challenges encountered every day, have to be found by the people closest to the action. "Once the people at the grassroots realize they own the problem, they also discover that they can help create and own the answers, and they get after it very quickly, very aggressively, and very creatively, with a lot more ideas...than could ever have been prescribed from headquarters" (Miller cited in Pascale, 1998, p. 93). Thus, Pascale concludes that when strategic work is accomplished through a design that allows for emergence, that work never assumes that a particular input will produce a particular output. Thus, complexity science is not built on the assumption that one can proactively control what will happen. Rather it emphasizes nimble reactions and understanding and coping with the world as it unfolds unexpectedly.

Consequently, if one views leadership as analogous to "walking on a trampoline," one does not engage in a leadership philosophy of social engineering, with all variables carefully controlled through the use of SWOT (strengths, weaknesses, opportunities, and threats) reports or through a top-down approach to managing people and resources.

When I interviewed at Duquesne, both the search committee and faculty used the phrase "at a crossroads posed to move with the 'right' leadership" to describe the School of Education. The excitement connected with the possibility of change was clearly articulated in more than one meeting, along with a desire for the incoming dean to provide the "vision" that would drive the change. Yet humans are both attracted and repulsed by the process of change. With feet firmly planted in both the future and the past, they "tend to regard as chaotic that which they cannot control" (p. 6).

An adaptive leader can assist individuals to view chaos as the "sweet spot," a condition rather than a location, a permeable, intermediate state through which order and disorder flow, not a finite line of demarcation (p. 61).

Reflecting on complexity theory reminds me that "walking on a trampoline" means that one has to go down to go up, particularly if the goal is to reach the higher fitness peak. In such an atmosphere, new ambitions and possibilities take form, not engineering, predictable or unilateral approaches to organizational change. Nor does the leader engage in practices intended to provide the veneer of participation to engender buy-in (p. 13). In short, the leader must bring the organization to the "edge of chaos," a fertile domain for revitalization, a precondition for transformation to take place (p. 66). This process depends on having the right people in the right place, the third building block of execution.

Building Block Three: The Job No Leader Should Delegate—Having the Right People in the Right Place

Collins et al. (2001) suggest that good-to-great leaders "first got the right people on the bus, the wrong people off the bus, and the right people in the right seats—and then they figured out where to drive it" (p. 13). Similarly, Fullan (2001) views developing relationships as the "remarkable convergence" within the organization that is essential to the coherence-making, knowledge-creation, and commitment on which change depends (p. 5). Pascale et al (2000) also speak of adaptive leadership that "surfs the edge of chaos" by recognizing that living systems cannot be directed along a predetermined path, but, by respect for and alliance with the intelligence and capabilities residing within the organization (p. 154).

Kouzes and Posner (1998) provide a compelling argument for "encouraging the heart" as a process leaders might use to attract and retain the "right people." Indeed, Kouzes and Posner observe that leaders create relationships based on caring. As a relationship, leadership requires a connection between leaders and their constituents over "matters of the heart." It is personal and it is interpersonal (xiii).

Exemplary leadership that moves an organization from "good to great" cultivates relationships, acts with humility and will, and "encourages the heart." Such leaders:
- Model the way
- Inspire a shared vision
- Challenge the process
- Enable others to act (p. xiii).

In short, they don't delegate the job of getting the right people in their organization or the job of encouraging those who are already there.

This involves moving to a relationship-first rather than a product-first formula of leadership. Social interactions invite a kind of learning about context that helps in learning the "rules." In other words, acquiring operational knowledge required to succeed in one's professional role is accompanied by problems and dilemmas that "go against the grain" and require substantive discourse among professional colleagues so that novel problems that test the boundaries of the rules can be solved" (Wepner et al., 2008, p. 155). Thus, "interpersonal competence evolves from learning about the traditions, norms, and expectations of the professional culture within which one works. Technical competence evolves from mastering the technical core of professional skills required of one's role" (p. 155). Before adopting any theory, however, Fullan (2008) provides one overriding caution: the world has become too complex for any theory to have certainty. Thus, there can never be a blueprint or silver bullet (p. 8). Thus, Fullan suggests the use of a "good theory," because theories never assume absolute certainty, and they are humble in the face of the future. Moreover, he continues, good leaders are thoughtful managers who use their theory of action to govern what they do while being open to new data that direct further action (p. 8).

With this introduction, Fullan (2008), who has studied organizational change for more than thirty years, offers six secrets of change which bear further examination. The brief overview of these secrets below is offered verbatim:

- Love your employees. Build the organization by focusing on employees, enabling them to learn continuously and find meaning in their work and in their relationship with coworkers and to the company as a whole.
- Connect peers with purpose. This comes from leaders who embed strategies that foster continuous and purposeful peer interaction. The job of leaders is to provide good direction while pursuing its implementation through purposeful peer interaction and learning in relation to results.
- Capacity building prevails. This "secret" centers on leaders investing in the development of individual and collaborative efficacy of a whole group or system to accomplish significant improvements.

- Learning is work. Fullan suggests that there is far too much going to workshops, taking short courses, and the like, and far too little learning while doing the work. Learning external to the job can represent a useful input, but if it is not in balance and in concert with learning in the setting in which one works, the learning will end up being superficial.
- Transparency rules. Fullan describes transparency as a clear and continuous display of results, as well as clear and continuous access to practice (what is being done to get results). He asserts that when transparency is consistently evident, it creates an aura of "positive pressure"— pressure that is experienced as fair and reasonable, that is actionable in that it points to solutions, and that ultimately is inescapable.
- Systems learn. Two dominant change forces are unleashed and constantly cultivated knowledge and commitment. "Individuals learn new things all the time, and their sense of meaning and their motivation are continually stimulated and deepened" (Fullan, 2008, p. 13-14).

As I conclude my fourth year as Dean, it means continuing to reflect on the nature of my leadership philosophy and the extent to which that philosophy is evidenced in my administrative practice. And, perhaps most pointedly, it means examining my own leadership philosophy, including the tensions and challenges in relation to the question posed by Goffee and Jones (2000, cited in Fullan, 2001), "Why should anyone be led by you?" (p.55)

References

Bossidy, C., & Charan, L. (2002). *Execution: The discipline of getting things done.* New York: Crown Business.

Collins, J. (2001). *Good to great: Why some companies make the leap...and others don't.* New York: HarperCollins.

Denzin, N. K., & Lincoln, Y. S. (Eds.). (2005). *The Sage handbook of qualitative research.* (4th ed.). Thousand Oaks, CA: Sage.

Freire, P. (1970). *Pedagogy of the oppressed* (M. B. Ramos, Trans.). New York: Seabury (Original manuscript published 1968).

Fullan, M. (2001). *Leading in a culture of change*. San Francisco: Jossey-Bass.

Fullan, M. (2004). *Change forces with a vengeance*. London: Falmer Press.

Fullan, M. (2008). *The six secrets of change: what the best leaders do to help their organizations survive and thrive*. San Francisco: Jossey-Bass.

Jackson, J. F. L. (2004). Toward a business model of executive behavior: An exploration of the workdays of four college of education deans at large research universities. *The Review of Higher Education, 27*(3), 409-427.

Kouzes, J. M., & Posner, B. Z. (2003). *Encouraging the heart*. San Francisco: Jossey-Bass.

Krahenbuhl, G. S. (2004). *Building the academic deanship: Strategies for success*. Westport, CT: American Council of Education/Praeger.

Pascale, R. T., Milleman, M., & Gioja, L. (2000). *Surfing the edge of chaos*. New York: Three Rivers Press.

Wepner, S. B., D'Onofrio, A., & Wilhite, S. C. (2008). The leadership dimensions of education deans. *Journal of Teacher Education, 59*, 153-155.

Wolverton, M., Gmelch, W. H., Montez, J., & Nies, C. T. (2001). *The changing nature of the academic deanship*. ASHE-ERIC Higher Education Report, 28(1).

Cross-Cultural Mentoring Relationships:
A Recipe for Success

Wanda Heading-Grant and Judith A. Aiken
University of Vermont

There are two ways of spreading light—
to be the candle or the mirror that reflects it.
    —Edith Wharton

Mentoring in higher education institutions is neither new nor uncommon. Interest in faculty mentoring has grown significantly in the past decade because many new faculty arrive on campus inexperienced and unprepared for the cultural and organizational realities they face (Boice, 1997; Mertz, 2001; Moody, 2004; Turner, 2002). The transition to the role of a successful faculty member can involve considerable stress and struggle (Petrie & Wohlgemuth, 1994). Junior faculty members typically come to their new positions with much experience in academic settings, but the experience is usually centered on extensive coursework and research in their chosen discipline, rather than on the challenges of being a faculty member that adds teaching, service, and scholarship to the agenda (Sullivan-Catlin & Lemel 2001). Thus, the importance of a mentor to help new faculty by providing knowledge, affirmation, and a model for how one should work in the profession is an important area of inquiry.

Given how institutions of higher education work extremely hard to recruit and retain quality faculty, especially faculty of color, it is imperative that higher education administrators ensure their success. Yet, faculty of color represent only a small percentage of professors at both two-year and four-year institutions, often earning lower salaries and fewer benefits than many other faculty (Trower & Chait, 2006). For these reasons, the development of formalized structured faculty mentoring programs is an important means for colleges and universities to retain faculty. (Alleman, Cochran, Doverspike, & Newman, 1984; Blackburn, Chapman, & Cameron, 1981; Boice, 1997).

Mentoring is viewed as a way to retain more faculty of color by helping them overcome unique obstacles in the workplace during this critical stage in their career (Boreen & Niday, 2003; Moody, 2004; Ragins, 1997; Turner, 2002). An underlying assumption in these mentoring relationships is that, if new faculty of color were sponsored and guided by tenured faculty members, their chances of attaining tenure would be greatly enhanced. A number of writers have also pointed out that mentoring helps to advance many goals of the institution, in particular those related to diversity (Boice, 1997; Burke, McKeen, & McKenna, 1993; Gayle & Cullan, 1995; Luna & Cullen, 1995; Ragins, 1997; Smith & Markham, 2004). Not only does mentoring give the mentor an opportunity to contribute to someone else's success, such relationships can also result in new forms of collegial partnerships leading to enhanced opportunities to learn and grow as a faculty member on a number of levels. A mentor who engages with diverse faculty members has the chance to learn about other cultures, issues, and become more self-aware of his or her professional beliefs, values, and styles. Thus, mentoring people of color has the potential to contribute to changes that help to dismantle barriers toward tenure, advancement, and empowerment.

Cross-Cultural Mentoring Relationships

As stated above, mentoring has long been identified as an important factor in the career success of faculty but may be even more critical to the career success of faculty of color (Morrison, White, & Van Velsor, 1987). Research suggests that racial issues have been increasingly important in the role of mentoring. Due to the disproportionate number of tenured white men and women compared with tenured ALANA (African, Latino, Asian, Native American) faculty, mentors and mentees often differ in race, ethnicity, and cultural background, leading to distinct and important differences in mentoring processes and outcomes (Ensher & Murphy, 1997; Ragins, 1997; Tillman, 1998).

Cross-race mentoring raises special issues that are absent in the typical white male-to-male relationships, especially when the mentoring relationship is between white male mentors and female mentees of color (Ragins, 1997). Because many mentoring models are based on the dominant group, white males, these models cannot be generalized to other groups. Subsequent theory that has attempted to differentiate the effects of race has been largely ignored (Ragins, 1997). Thus, although there has been much progress in the research on mentoring in the last ten years, there still remains a gap in the literature regarding cross-cultural mentoring, especially from the mentor's point of view.

The concept of mentoring is not new, but over the years the trend has moved from informal mentoring to a formal structure. Traditionally, white senior men have been mentors for the newcomers in their profession, who were usually white males as well (Chao, Walz, & Gardner, 1992; Ragins, 1997). Now with the increase of both women and racial minorities in the workforce, the art of mentoring requires more effort and broader involvement (Ensher & Murphy, 1997; Healey & Welchert, 1990; Peterson & Hart-Wasekeesikaw, 1992; Ragins, 1997).

The basic distinctions between formal and informal mentorship relationships lie in the formation of the mentor/mentee relationships (Chao et al., 1992). Informal mentorship has been defined as a spontaneous relationship between different institutional members, which occurs without external involvement from the organization (Chao et al., 1992). However, research shows that informal mentoring is less likely to happen with faculty of color, especially at predominantly white institutions (Redmond, 1990). Formal mentoring relationships, however, are typically managed and supported by the organization and usually consists of a coordinator, a facilitated pairing process, established goals, and a time frame (Bryson, 2001; Chao et al., 1992; Noe, 1988; Zey, 1984). Formal mentoring programs tend to provide for mentoring opportunities for all faculty, but especially those from marginalized groups (Moody, 2004).

Mentor and Mentoring

The term *mentor* has been subject to many interpretations. Some scholars trace the origins of mentorship back to Greek mythology and Homer's epic, *The Odyssey* when Ulysses chose his wise and trusted friend, Mentor, to guard and guide his son, Telemakhos. However, it was not until the 1970s that mentoring started showing up in the professional literature where varied interpretations and different emphases in definitions of a mentor or a mentoring relationship appear. Bova and Philips (1981) discuss various roles that the mentor may serve but state that most definitions point to someone who plays a supportive role and nurtures the newcomer and is able to guide the protégé in professional development.

Other writers describe mentors as role models, advisers, and partners, and use the term *mentor* interchangeably with words such as coach, advisor, role model, and sponsor (Anderson & Shannon, 1995; Boice, 1997; Bova & Philips, 1984). Some theorists take a more formal view and say that a mentor is someone who serves as a guide and oversees the career development of another person, through teaching, counseling, promoting, and sponsoring all of which is done formally within an organization (Anderson & Shannon, 1995; Daloz, 1983; Zey, 1984). Defining who and what a mentor is in our society is not an easy task, but almost all descriptions view a mentor as someone who is willing to invest oneself in the mentee's success and is more likely than not to have knowledge or expertise that helps to nurture the talent and ability of the mentee. There also appears to be consistency around how mentors transition and guide mentees at critical and noncritical points in their career toward success.

Definitions of mentoring relationships include many applications and contradictions, but most often, they seem to depict various kinds of relationships between a junior and senior colleague (Kram, 1985; Moore & Salimbene, 1981). Merriam (1988) describes mentoring as a powerful emotional interaction between an older and younger person, a relationship in which the older member is trusted, loving, and experienced in the guidance of the younger. Smith, Smith and Markham (2000) note, "mentoring is an intense interpersonal exchange between a senior experienced colleague and a less experienced junior colleague" (p. 251). Alleman and his colleagues (1984) support these findings and see mentoring as a relationship where a person of higher ranking teaches, guides, and develops a novice in an organization, aligning several different functions to the relationship such as counseling, protecting, befriending and giving of information. What is also clear in the literature is that the relationship aspects of mentors and mentees need to be constructed upon such vital factors as trust, mutual respect, commitment, communication, and friendship, and these factors become most important in the mentorship relationship (Moody, 2004; Stanley & Lincoln, 2005).

Research Context and Methodology

This study focused on the experiences of faculty as mentors and the role that diversified mentoring relationships played in their professional lives at a university that, to protect their privacy, we have given the fictitious name Northeastern Mountain University. A better understanding of the impact of these diversified relationships on the mentees also surfaced in the study. The participants were white faculty mentors in cross-racial mentoring relationships. The study was qualitative in nature in that data was gathered through semistructured interviews and focus group discussions. The study focused on several key questions: (a) How are the words *mentor* and *mentoring* defined by the mentors in the study? (b) How do the mentor's definitions of mentor and mentoring compare with the descriptions of themselves as mentors? (c) What were the advantages and challenges experienced by the mentors as a result of participating in a formal mentoring relationship? (d) What kinds of changes did the mentors experience in their professional career and university community as a result of participating in a formal mentoring relationship? and (e) What kind of impact did the racial identity of the mentees have on the mentoring relationships?

To gather perspectives of the mentors, a process of deep self-exploration of the intricate relationships they experienced with their mentees was the focus of the inquiry (Maxwell, 1996). The research also evolved from a more constructivist research perspective in which "reality is socially constructed, complex and ever changing" (Glesne & Peshkin, 1992, p. 6). Qualitative approaches also provided a framework in which participants are able to express their understanding in their terms (Glesne, 1999; Patton, 1990). Given that this study was aimed at gathering an understanding of how the mentors made sense of their mentorship experiences, a qualitative design seemed most appropriate (Maxwell, 1996).

Participants in the study were tenured full and associate professors at Northeastern Mountain University, a medium-size, land-grant higher education institution in the Northeast. Northeastern Mountain University is viewed as a research and teaching institution comprised of eight academic colleges. It has an undergraduate and graduate population of approximately 10,000 students. It has approximately 1,100 full and part-time faculty. Eighty-nine of the 1,100 faculty members are identified as faculty of color. The University has a history steeped in progressive work by the students, faculty and staff promoting diversity. This institution was chosen in particular for its efforts to develop diversity initiatives to hire more multicultural faculty and attempting to involve senior faculty in the effort.

At the time of this study, there were 12 white faculty members who were mentoring junior faculty of color. Of the 12 mentees, four were men and eight were women. All 12 of the white faculty mentors participating in cross-racial mentoring relationships were invited to participate in this study. Nine agreed to be a part of the study. Once a mentor expressed interest and gave permission to participate, he or she was contacted through a letter and telephone calls to schedule interviews. Seven of the partnerships involved white male or female mentors and women of color as mentees. Generally the participants ranged in age from 35 to 64 and collectively spanned from 10 to 35 years of experience at Northeastern Mountain University.

Data was primarily collected from mentor participants through responses to interviews and focus group discussions. Merriam (1988) states in qualitative research that some, and occasionally all, of the data are collected through interviews. A standardized open-ended interview guide consisting of questions carefully worded allowed the participants flexibility in their responses. Nine interviews were conducted over a period of two months and ranged from 50 minutes to 120 minutes. Interviews were taped, and a professional transcriber was used to transcribe the interviews verbatim. Field notes were maintained and organized into information categories that included all recordings of ideas, observations, mental associations, and reflections that impacted the study. The data was analyzed using major themes that emerged from the interviews. Member checking was utilized to verify that the data was appropriately interpreted and reported with satisfactory protection of identity (Gall, Borg, & Gill, 1996; Glesne, 1998; Lincoln & Guba, 1985). At the conclusions of the mentor interviews, two focus-group meetings were held with the mentees, all represented as faculty of color, to explore their experiences and seek ideas to better improve the mentoring program.

The data was collected and analyzed simultaneously to help shape the study through a process of content analysis for themes. An inductive analysis of the data was performed, while looking for common themes and pattern, which emerged from the interviews, rather than identified a priori (Patton, 1990). The content analysis followed Patton's (1990) and Miles and Huberman's

(1984) general procedures of data organization, coding, categorizing, display and presentation, and conclusion determining and verification.

A number of emergent themes help frame the discussion of findings that are tied to the primary research questions. The focus of this study was to explore mentors' perceptions of their experiences as faculty mentors in a formalized structured faculty mentoring program and to learn what role it played in their professional lives as senior faculty. A secondary goal was to learn more about the impact of cross-cultural mentoring on junior faculty of color and ways to improve the mentoring program (Frierson, 1998).

Mentor and Mentoring as Defined by the Mentors

Although none of the participants had any formal experiences with serving as a mentor, many of them talked about mentors and mentoring using similar definitions and descriptions as found in the literature. Some participants used the words *advisor, counselor, teacher, supporter, coach, motivator, role model,* and *helper* to encompass the definitions of mentor. Some viewed the role of the mentor as one who provided direction to the novice. One participant described a mentor as "someone who teaches and models behavior" or as "someone who's keeping an eye out for that person's career development." One respondent sees the mentor as someone who "clearly can evaluate what and where a person is in their career development," including their limitations and being "able to tell them the bad as well as the good."

There was general consistency about the mentor's role in promoting the mentee's career, using such phrases as "having the know-with-all to survive" and "Why reinvent the wheel when there is someone who already has the instructions?" A few participants expressed that their "seasoned experience should count for something" and believed that career advancement needed to be planned out, particularly for women and people of color. They saw their roles as helping outline plans with their mentee. In the words of one mentor:

> My mentee and I have put together a tentative plan for what she needs to do and by when. I think time lines are good and it helps to focus you and she needs to be focused or at least get her priorities together....Because I know how the tenure system works here, I encouraged

my mentee to check items off of a list she developed from
a source that gives ideas about how to obtain tenure.
Several mentors shared how *patience, loyalty, honesty, commitment,* and *knowledge* are what distinguish an effective mentor
from an ineffective mentor. The importance of helping the mentee meant "molding oneself to the needs of the mentee" and providing the "emotional and personal guidance" the mentee needs,
but in an honest and patient way.

When asked about mentoring and what it meant, the mentors gave varied definitions, but there was a consistent focus on
serving as a *supporter* and *role model,* and on *giving direction.*
Getting the participants to define the word meant first hearing
how they felt. Such responses as "It's great," "It's just a rewarding and enjoyable thing to do," or that "It feels good when people
you work with have success and you somehow played a part in
it" often arose. A few of the mentors, however, were able to give
more concrete definitions, describing it an action-oriented process where you must move someone from one point to the next
in his or her career path. In the words of one participant, "Mentoring relationships are always changing. There are a series of
emotions, steps and activities that's going on at the same time."
In other words, some recognized that there is a set of functions
that must take place before one is considered to be mentoring.
In general, most mentors defined these functions as it related to
the actual duties and activities in which they engaged with their
mentees.

The mentors had no problem sharing their definitions of the
concepts *mentor* and *mentoring*, but they had difficulty describing themselves and their *roles* as mentors. What appeared were
a number of diverse views as to whether or not they fit the descriptions they provided. Although all of the mentors agreed that
they tried to fit the definitions they gave of mentor, some felt
they had "come up short in carrying out their mentoring duties."
As one participant expressed:

I know I should have done better by my mentee. I was
just stuck on how to approach her after not hearing from
her for some time. I also had some of my own issues regarding departmental politics, but that is not an excuse.
The last time I offered advice it was several months ago.
I feel bad.

Some felt they could have been better role models and could have talked more about such things as teaching style and approach with their mentees but felt 'it was a delicate issue to bring up." One mentor expressed that he knew his mentee was having difficulties but did not quite know how to bring it up, and this made him question his role as mentor even more. For some, being a mentor was a way of giving back. As one participant stated,

> I don't need an appreciation dinner to be a mentor. Mentoring comes with the job. At least I think so. Wouldn't you do it? I know you would be a mentor. This kind of stuff is important and women and people of color have to give back and this is my way of doing so. I'll find the time to be available. I strongly disagree with anyone who says that to mentor is a problem.

As the mentors described themselves, some appeared embarrassed by the positive and supporting words they used in their definitions. Others may or may not have been able to articulate their interactions with their mentees, or were just modest about their efforts. Modesty and humility appeared to have played a part in their thinking about their own roles as mentors. Some also felt an alternative term may better fit the activities or interactions some mentors were engaging in with their mentees, but did not suggest any.

They also appeared to be somewhat uncomfortable when asked to define their objectives for mentoring another faculty member. Many of the responses centered on improving or increasing their interaction with their mentee. One mentor shared that he wanted to build his relationship to the point that if the mentee left the institution, they could continue to work together. Others indicated that they wanted tenure for their mentees and wanted them to be content at the university. One mentor stated clearly that her "ultimate goal was to get more tenured women and people of color on campus." Many of the mentors indicated that they would like to have more contact. Laced in some comments was a sense that they were seeking more guidance from the university in terms of expectations and objectives, especially about issues of diversity and gender. This help was not always present.

Understanding Challenges, Opportunities and Contribution

A number of studies cite a variety of challenges and advantages to mentoring and unique circumstances mentors face (Anderson & Shannon, 1988; Noe, 1988, Ragins, 1997). More importantly, cross-race mentorships create even more challenges. The mentors faced a number of challenges which they often described as related to cross-cultural communication and working across different disciplines and areas of scholarly interest. Because of teaching and other faculty duties, mentors reported not having enough time to meet with their mentees and only being able to "grab quick moments to talk." They also found that too often their mentees were "stretched rather thin" and were being asked by department chairs and other administrators to take on more service and program-related duties, thus leaving them struggling to find time with their mentor. One participant noted that she tried to protect her mentee from numerous requests to participate in college and university activities, but often felt that this created conflict or tension between her and the mentee.

In talking about their challenges as mentors, the importance of effective communication often came up as vital to building trusting, supportive relationships. However, several respondents in the study talked about some difficulty they experienced in communicating with their mentee. As one stated, "she (the mentee) would not make eye contact with me and always said everything was fine." Not being sure how to interpret this communication often led to misunderstandings or incorrect interpretations of behavior. The literature is replete with the importance of communication style and its relationship to race and ethnicity (Sue & Sue, 1990). Others shared how they felt constrained to present constructive feedback and were fearful of how their mentee might respond given differences in personality, experiences, gender, and racial backgrounds. One example was related to the area of communication. The participant mentor expressed concern that the communication style of her mentee had the potential to be "off-putting" or a "turn-off" to others with whom they needed to work. In the words of the mentor,

I'm concerned about how to tell my mentee that her style of communication has been a turn-off to others without offending her. Regardless of race or gender, my mentee is a little abrupt and independent and she does not have to be that way.

Cross-cultural communication issues became evident in some other comments by mentors who shared that they did not know how to bring up matters related to race. Most chose to avoid the conversations entirely. Comments such as "I don't think I am prepared to talk about race" or "We just don't discuss race" revealed some of these tensions. Communication style can impact face-to-face encounters, especially when the mentoring style of the mentor does not necessarily match the communication style of culturally different mentees (Kram, 1983). Several respondents shared that they would value some professional guidance in terms of cross-cultural communication.

A final challenge the mentors faced was how they understood diversity and their awareness of issues of racial bias and equity. For some, it raised some tensions and feelings that were impacting the mentoring relationship. However, some mentors believed that one's racial identity or gender did not necessarily impact the mentor–mentee relationship and felt that the challenges were more about meeting institutional norms and expectations for success. Statements and questions such as "I think junior faculty of color and white junior faculty have experiences that are much more alike than unalike" or "I don't believe it is about race; it is about, Can you do the job?" framed such ideas. However, others were adamant that to be a good mentor, one must "be aware that people are treated differently because of the color of their skin." Others felt that unjust treatment of women and faculty of color at the university was evident and that the mentor was in a unique position to help combat such unfair treatment, but wasn't always sure how to convey this. In general, there seemed to be concerns that when involved in more diversified mentoring relationships, the knowledge, skills, and empathy needed for effective communication were lacking.

Yet many participants also found advantages to mentoring across cultural differences such as meeting and making new friends across the university through introductions by their mentees. Others talked about how they became interested in new fields of inquiry, drawing from their mentee's field of work. Connecting with other mentors and sharing experiences also opened new channels of communication for senior faculty. In addition to new friendships and contacts, all mentors talked about a sense of "personal satisfaction" and a feeling of "giving back" to the university in some way. One mentor in particular noted that he felt that by mentoring a person of color, he was helping "to promote diversity" at the university. In addition, mentors also mentioned enjoying such rewards as, meeting people outside their departments, reading new research conducted by their mentee, and for a few, gaining new cultural insights. Two male mentors expressed that their interaction with their female mentee opened their eyes to inequities that women sometime face. Previously they believed that in some cases women contributed to the unfair treatment they experience because of their own paranoia, resulting in a self-fulfilling situation.

The mentors shared that they had gotten involved with the mentoring because of a personal invitation, earlier role model, or need to give back to their profession. Most of the mentors did not believe that their involvement in the mentoring program had any significant impact on their own careers or involvement in other activities at the university. They spoke about changes in their mentees, but few changes in themselves. Although the literature indicates that mentoring may result in skill enhancement, leadership opportunities, rejuvenation, and/or a sense of service for mentors, the participants expressed modest outcomes related to these areas. None of the mentors interviewed in the study saw their involvement as a stepping-stone for something bigger. The mentors mostly spoke of gains only for the institution or the junior faculty member. As one mentor stated,

> There is no money or incentive to do this kind of work. I'm not saying that there should be money because you don't want anybody trying to be a mentor just for the cash. This requires committed individuals, but it doesn't enhance my career in any way or at least I don't see where it has advanced me.

Another talked about the fact that mentoring did not necessarily impact his professional career, but could see ways it can enhance the university in general, especially with recruitment and retention of diverse faculty. One participant stated,

> This was a good idea. Many other institutions have mentoring programs and it can be an important recruitment tool. It may help a person of color in his or her decision. It is useful to the University in many ways.

It was assumed by the mentors that a mentoring program for junior faculty would only enhance Northeastern Mountain University's reputation for caring and being an institution committed to diversity. However, according to the mentors, no new research or articles emerged as a result of any of the relationships. Some shared that the fact that their mentees were in different areas of study that did not allow for much collaboration across disciplines.

However, once the question was asked, all were all in agreement that their participation could be viewed as a contribution to the diversity efforts. Comments such as, "Yes, my work contributes to promoting racial, and gender diversity" or "My mentoring role is a contribution to the university's 'diversity objectives" demonstrated this belief. Several of the mentors acknowledged that this was community service to the university and a way of getting involved, but participation did not seem to rank in the same way as other university activities. One mentor expressed, "It doesn't count. You know it doesn't really count very much as professional activity for me, because it's not that kind of professional reward, but just gratifying." In summary, while the mentors did not always make a natural connection between their mentor role and service to the university, they all agreed that there was no professional gain for their careers, only personal satisfaction as mentors.

Racial Dynamics

One of the main themes of this chapter pertains to the racial dynamic associated with cross-racial mentoring relationships. The findings concur with the literature regarding cross-racial mentoring and the issues that can arise (Alleman et al., 1984; Noe, 1988; Ragins, 1997; Smith et al., 2000). The mentors were somewhat divided in their knowledge of issues related to the different dynamics of race. Some mentors, particularly two of the women, appeared well informed regarding racism, discrimination and oppression. They knew how to try to get out in front of problems associated with racial identities. Others struggled with knowing what to do in certain situations. Some claim never to have experienced issues related to race, and others did not even believe that race was a factor for them or their mentee. Some mentors were not resigned to settle for this behavior, but they recognized the challenges before them. One mentor believed that if the number of women and people of color increased on campus, this would be "a way of combating some of the issues that come out of bias thinking and behaving."

Some of the male mentors took racism for granted by not reflecting on it and recognizing that this may have had an impact on their protégé. The literature notes the importance of recognizing cultural aspects of a mentee and all the issues that arise as a result of pairing two people from different backgrounds (Lee & Richardson, 1990; Ragins, 1997; Sue & Sue, 1990), but for many of our mentors, it had no impact. Mentors felt a need for support in addressing the challenges that come with diversity and cross-racial mentoring. Ways to provide mentors with strategies and techniques that are consistent with the life experiences and career goals, as well as the cultural values of mentees surfaced as important areas of concern.

Research has pointed out the challenges invloved in cross-cultural mentoring relationships (Chin, Lott, Rice, & Sanchez-Hucles, 2007; Peterson & Wasekeesikaw, 1994; Tillman, 1998, Turner, 2002). In conversation with several mentees, it became clear that they valued the opportunity provided by the formal mentoring program and felt that without it, they would be excluded from these important networks. However, the need to connect with senior and successful faculty of color as mentors remained an issue for our mentees. The advice and support they received related to career advancement, the tenure process, and teaching were discussed as positive outcomes of the cross-cultural mentoring experience. However, several indicated the need for a "safe haven" in the environment of higher education and did not feel that their mentor always provided that safe space. Several talked about communication issues and challenges of being understood, which they felt were determined by their gender and race at times. As one mentee expressed,

> It would be great if there were more insight to where I was coming from as a person of color and as a woman. The task of explaining my concerns and challenges is always risky because I may be seen as not able to cut the mustard rather than there being systemic issues.

One participant indicated that she worried about making mistakes and did not always feel supported in her research and approach to teaching. She wasn't sure her mentor really "got what it means to be a faculty of color in an all-white classroom of college students" or to be the only faculty of color in her department. She struggled to find support for her scholarship and teaching both in her department and in her mentoring relationship. As she stated,

Yes, being the only one is isolating. This is why these conversations are so rewarding because I know or at least think everyone here gets it. The feeling of being labeled not authentic regardless of the never-ending list of achievements on my CV is frustrating. In my teaching, white male students in particular can challenge you and then you have to defend your course delivery approach. Or you are always finding a way to announce where your degrees as though you need to be authenticated.

Another participant was surprised by what she felt was a total lack of support from her white female mentor at times, although she thought their gender connection would enhance the mentoring relationship. As pointed out by Montero-Sieburth (cited in Turner, 2002), "being female does not necessarily guarantee the sympathy of mainstream women toward them nor does it offer entry into mainstream academic domains" (p. 81). However several mentees expressed feeling much more comfortable talking about their efforts to balance family and work related responsibilities with women mentors.

Almost all of the mentees expressed concern that, even through the mentoring process, they did not feel that they received clear and consistent information regarding the reappointment and tenure process. This, too, is consistent with some research that points to how detrimental the lack of clear criteria and expectations is, especially for women and faculty of color (Perna, 2001).

Improving Mentor Training and Cross-Cultural Mentoring Programs

Northeastern Mountain University's faculty mentoring program appears to be well received by the mentors in the study. All of the mentors felt that this initiative was one of the better ideas coming out of the institution. Some of the mentors got involved because of personal concerns, interest, and a desire to give something back by guiding junior professionals. All of the mentors wanted to continue their roles with their current mentee and would gladly do it again. However, many mentors acknowledged that they could use some more help at certain times. As one mentor stated:

> I don't want to seem like I don't know what I'm doing, but my mentee doesn't really talk to me or at least not as often as I would like. I really believe it is because of his cultural background and maybe he should have been reassigned to someone else a long time ago for his sake.

As stated above, it was interesting that none of the participants had any formal experience with being a mentor, yet all of the mentors were committed to their roles, in spite of the challenges and lack of understanding at times about what their roles expected of them and the way to handle challenging situations, particularly those involving racial dynamics.

It is clear from this study that any mentoring program has to make sure it provides all the elements for a successful relationship and help the mentors see their roles as serious contributions so that they may act more accountable to the program and the mentees. There remains a strong need for academe to attract more racial/ethnic diversity to the profession. Racial minorities can offer a dimension and a viewpoint that act as a counterbalance to information being provided by the dominant culture in society (Sue & Sue, 1990). As colleges and universities create and maintain programs that promote the retention and success of faculty of color, the use of assigned faculty mentoring programs may be an initiative that has promise beyond any informal practices within or between departments. Thus, we close this chapter with a number of implications for the training of mentors with respect to cross-cultural mentoring programs in higher education and the development of improved cross-cultural mentoring relationships in support of faculty and women of color.

The mentoring literature suggests that little effective training is done with mentors to provide them with appropriate skills and knowledge with which to mentor (Gibb & Meggenson, 1993; Kram, 1983). Garvey (1995) suggests that mentors have three developmental needs: training in mentoring, opportunity to discuss mentoring with fellow mentors, and access to material on mentoring. A lack of development in these areas may explain some of the differing opinion about mentoring as a developmental tool within the workplace (Garvey, 1995). Certain information is provided to the mentors as a way of enhancing their skills, but not on a sufficiently regular basis. Training should focus on introducing issues relevant to the target population and general mentoring issues.

> The goal of the training is to equip the mentors to be flexible about their expectations of the protégés, and to learn how to assess and respond to the needs of their protégé, rather than imposing personal expectations on the protégés. (Single & Muller, 1999, p. 11)

The multicultural realities in higher education call for mentors who can effectively address the challenges that can come with diversity. Cross-racial mentoring is a fact of life for most junior faculty of color, given the current racial makeup of higher education. In order to engage effectively in diversified mentoring, it would be important to examine the effect of an institutionally designed, ongoing professional development process focused on cultural competence. The focus of this process should be the development and upgrading of skills to impact the professional lives of protégés from a variety of cultural backgrounds (Lee & Richardson, 1990; Ragins, 1997; Sue & Sue 1990). The ultimate training goal is to have a culturally skilled mentor who uses strategies and techniques that are consistent with the life experiences and cultural values of mentees.

One of the emerging thoughts in the literature on cross-racial mentoring is that one must become more fully aware of one's own heritage as well as possible biases or lack of information that may interfere with helping others (Lee & Richardson, 1990; Sue & Sue, 1990; Ragins, 1997). At the risk of scaring away mentors and mentees of color, cultural information must be presented as part of the training curriculum, yet not in a way that forces it to stand out as burdensome or additional work. When institutions present initiatives, efforts and trainings related to diversity in a format that makes it appear as an-add on rather than a part of its composition, then those within the institution will see it as something extra and may expect more benefits for their participation or, may not take it as seriously as other institutional objectives.

Another important focus of mentor training must be on skills development. How does one actually mentor someone from another culture? What cultural dynamics can affect communication and interpersonal relationship? What approaches are more effective with different populations of our society? In summary, providing skills training centered on how to integrate cultural dynamics into the act of mentoring is critical. This approach may provide valuable insight into developing successful cross-racial mentoring relationships.

From the perspectives of the mentees, it is important for mentors to understand the racial, gender, cultural, and ethnic differences they bring to the mentoring relationships (Stanley and Lincoln, 2005). Additionally, it is important to match mentees with mentors who understand the challenges female faculty face as they try to balance professional and personal responsibilities. The female mentees felt more comfortable sharing personal challenges and asking for help from a female mentor. We also suggest that support for their research could be enhanced if mentors were more familiar with the research topics of their mentees or could direct them to other faculty who shared similar interests. For some, it may mean support for what has been thought of as "non-mainstreamed forms of research" (Stanley and Lincoln, 2005). Additionally, providing mentees with clear and consistent information regarding the criteria for reappointment and promotion remains a critical needs in cross-cultural mentoring programs.

A final recommendation is the formation of developmental alliances or networks among faculty of color within and without the institution. Such networks can also provide mentoring and opportunities for feedback and collaborative research experiences. Additionally, such networks should foster feelings of connection to faculty of color at other institutions and create new venues for the assessment and evaluation of cross-cultural mentoring programs. Both mentors and the diverse faculty they support will grow in cultural understanding through such diversified mentoring partnerships. Through these relationships, institutions of higher education will be enriched by efforts to retain diverse faculty and the contributions of their teaching, research, and service.

References

Alleman, E., Cochran, J., Dover Spike, J., & Newman, I. (1984). Enriching mentor relationships. *Personnel and Guidance Journal, 62*(6), 329-332. .

Anderson, E. M., & Shannon, A. L. (1995). Toward a conceptualization in mentoring. In T. Kerry & A. S. Mayes (Eds.), *Issues in Mentoring* (pp. 25-34). London: Routledge.

Blackburn, R. T., Chapman, D. W., & Cameron, S. W. (1981). Cloning in academe: Mentorship and academic careers. *Research in Higher Education, 15,* 315-327.

Boice, R. (1997). What discourages research-practitioners in faculty development? *Higher Education: Handbook of Theory and Research, 12,* 371-434.

Boreen, J., & Niday, D. (2003). *Mentoring across boundaries.* Portland, MA: Stenhouse.

Bova, B. M., & Philips, R. R. (1984). Mentoring as a learning experience for adults. *Journal of Teacher Education, 35*(3), 16-20.

Bryson, J. (2001). *Effective mentoring manual.* Upper River Saddle, NJ: Pearson Education.

Burke, R., McKeen, C., & McKenna, C. (1993). Correlates of mentoring in organizations: The mentor's perspective. *Psychological Reports, 72,* 883-896.

Chao, G.T., Waltz, P.M., & Gardner, P.D. (1992). Formal and informal mentorships: A comparison on mentoring functions and contrast with nonmentored counterparts. *Personnel Psychology, 45,* 619-636.

Chin, J. L., Lott, B., Rice, J. K., & Sanchez-Hucles, J. (2007). *Women and leadership: Transforming visions and diverse voices.* Malden, MA: Blackwell.

Daloz, L. (1983). Mentors: Teachers who make a difference. *Change, 15*(6), 24-27.

Ensher, E. A. &, Murphy, S. E. (1997). Effects of race, gender, perceived similarity and contact on mentor relationships. *Journal of Vocational Behavior, 50,* 460-481.

Frierson, H. T., Jr. (Ed.). (1998). *Diversity in higher education: Examining protégé-mentor experiences.* Stamford, CT: JAI Press.

Garvey, B. (1995). Healthy signs for mentoring. *Education and Training, 37*(5), 12-19.

Gall, M. D., Borg, W. R., & Gall, J. P. (1996). *Educational research: An introduction.* White Plains, NY: Longman.

Gibb, S., & Meggenson, D. (1993). Inside corporate mentoring schemes: A new agenda of concerns. *Personnel Review 22*(1), 40-54.

Glesne, C. (1999). *Becoming qualitative researchers: An introduction* (2nd ed.). New York: Longman.

Glesne, C., & Peshkin, A. (1992). *Becoming qualitative researchers: An introduction.* White Plains, NY: Longman.

Healy, C., & Welchert, A. (1990). Mentoring relations: A definition to advance research and practice. *Educational Researcher, 19*(9), 1-21.

Kram, K. E. (1983). Phrases of mentor relationship. *Academy of Management Journal, 26*(4), 608-625.

Kram, K. E. (1985). *Mentoring at work: Developmental relationships in organizational life.* Grenview, IL: Scott Foreman.

Lee C. C., & Richardson, B. L. (1990). Multicultural issues in counseling: New approaches to diversity. Alexandria, VA: American Association for Counseling and Development.

Lincoln, Y. S., & Guba, E. G. (1985). Naturalistic inquiry. Newbury Park, CA: Sage.

Luna, G., & Cullen, D. L. (1995). Empowering the faculty: Mentoring redirected and renewed. *ASHE-ERIC Higher Education Report, 3,* 37-45.

Maxwell, J. (1996). *Qualitative research design*. Thousand Oaks, CA: Sage.

Merriam, S. B. (1988). *Case study research on education: A qualitative approach*. San Francisco: Jossey-Bass.

Mertz, N. (2001). *Unraveling the definitional threads: Mentoring and academe*. Paper presented at the annual meeting of the American Educational Research Association, Seattle, WA.

Miles, M. M. & Huberman, A. M. (1984). *Qualitative data analysis: A sourcebook of new methods*. Newbury Park, CA: Sage.

Moody, J. (2004). *Good practices for campuses in recruiting minority faculty*. Boston, MA: New England Board of Higher Education.

Moore, K. M., & Salimbene, A. M. (1981). The dynamics of the mentor-protege relationship in developing women as academic leaders. *Journal of Educational Equity and Leadership, 2*, 51-64.

Morrison, A. M., White, R.P., & Van Velsor, E. (1987). *Breaking the glass ceiling*. Reading, MA: Addison-Wesley.

Noe, R. A. (1988). An investigation of the determinants of successful assigned mentoring relationships. *Personnel Psychology, 41*, 457-479.

Patton, M. Q. (1990). Qualitative Evaluation and Research Methods (2nd ed.). Newbury Park: CA: Sage.

Perna, L. (2001). Sex and race differences in faculty tenure and promotion. *Research in Higher Education, 42*(5). 541-567.

Peterson, B., & Hart-Wasekeesikaw, F. (1994). Mentoring women in higher education: Lessons from the elders. *College Teaching, 42*(2), 72-77.

Petrie, T. A., & Wohlgemuth, E.A. (1994). In hopes of promoting cohesion among academics: New and established. *Counseling Psychologist, 22*, 466-473.

Ragins, B. R. (1997). Diversified mentoring relationship in organizations: A power perspective. *Academy of Management Review, 22*, 482-521.

Redmond, S. P. (1990). Mentoring and Cultural Diversity in Academic Settings. *American Behavioral Scientist, 34*(2), 188-200.

Single, P. B., & Muller, C. B. (1999). *Electronic mentoring: Issues to advance research and practice.* A paper presented at the annual meeting of the Intern Mentoring Association, Atlanta, Georgia.

Smith, J., Smith, W. J., & Markham, S. E. (2000). Diversity issues in mentoring academic faculty. *Journal of Career Development, 26*(4), 251-262.

Stanley, C., & Lincoln, Y. S. (2005). Cross-race faculty mentoring. *Change, 37*(2), 44-53.

Sue, D. W., & Sue, D. (1990). *Counseling the culturally different: Theory & Practice* (2nd ed.). New York: Wiley.

Sullivan-Catlin, H., & Lemel, R. (2001). The mentoring experience: Reflections on a university mentoring program. *The Journal of Faculty Development, 18*(2), 65-72.

Tillman, L. C. (1998). The mentoring of African-American faculty: Scaling the tenure mountain. *Diversity in Higher Education, 2,* (141-155). Greenwich, CT: JAI Press Inc.

Trower, C. A., & Chait, R. P. (2006). Harvard Magazine. Retrieved from http://www.harvrd-magazine.com/print/03028.html.

Turner, C. S. V. (2002). *Diversifying the faculty: A guidebook for search committees.* Association of American Colleges and Universities. Washington, DC.

Zey, M. G. (1984). *The mentor connection.* Homewood, IL: Dow Jones-Irwin.

African American Women Administrators in Academe:
Transgressing Multiple Marginality

Fred A. Bonner II, *Texas A&M University*
Pamela C. Smith, *University of Texas, San Antonio*
Aretha F. Marbley, *Texas Tech University*
La Vonne I. Neal, *University of Colorado at Colorado Springs*
Lora Battle Bailey, *Brenau University*

Women of color within academia face myriad challenges associated with establishing a sense of identity and confronting issues of marginality. Of particular importance for these women is their noted struggle to combat *behavioral conformity*. With the incessant pull of the academic culture to not only frame but also to dictate cultural, behavioral, and professional norms, these women often find themselves caught in an ongoing cycle of trying to establish some sense of agency in an enclave that devalues their very existence.

Thus, this chapter focuses on strategies that African American women in academe, who are leaders in both academic and student affairs administration use to transgress multiple marginalities and subsequently to find their sense of self-definition in majority (i.e., predominantly White) contexts. As a theoretical framework, we find it imperative that we address the unique experiences these women have with interlocking systems of oppression (Hill-Collins, 1991; Howard-Hamilton, 2003).

We also recognize the importance of utilizing frameworks, like Black and multiracial feminism, that underscore multiple, intersecting, and interlocking inequalities, and also reveal the resolve and strength of African American women and their individual and collective abilities to deal competently with oftentimes oppressive realities. Specifically, this chapter will focus on African American women administrators and the formidable challenges and the milestones associated with (a) identity and self-definition, (b) marginalization and oppression, and (c) social and professional integration. The use of narrative vignettes will provide "voice" to the experiences of three African American women administrators—two deans in colleges of education and one associate professor who served as a Dean of Students at a vocational and technical college.

This chapter falls in line with the unique perspective the editors of this volume are conveying by weaving themes highlighting social justice, leadership and the experiences among women of color in academe. Ultimately, we seek to tell the stories of how these women, these current and former higher education administrators, deftly navigate the series of negotiations that are required for them to be successful in the academy.

Identity and Self-Definition

Any discourse of identity and self-identity for women administrators of color must begin with a conversation of multiple identities, oppressions, and marginalities and should be framed in the principles of Black feminism, womanism, and multiracial feminism. Multiracial feminism stresses the importance of examining the role identity of men and women within a framework that addresses multiple racial groups, feminist perspectives and systems of domination (Oyewumi, 1999; Zinn & Dill, 1996). These theories also view race, rather than culture, as a power system that interacts with other structured inequalities to shape genders.

Black feminism, the more radical and revolutionary theory, emerged as a direct response to the societal oppression of Black women and also as a counterpoint to the racism found to exist within frameworks that espoused White middle class ideologies and values as normative. Like multiracial feminism, Black feminism and womanism attacks the multiple oppressions of racism, sexism, and poverty emphasized within the structure of sexist and racist power systems (Collins, 2000; Hamer & Neville, 1998; Mori, 1999; Riggs, 1994; Taylor, 1998; Walker, 1983).

These theoretical approaches frame the conversations related to the impact of sociocultural contexts on the identity and perspectives of African American women. Each approach emerges from the unique history, experiences of gender and racial discrimination, and stereotyping that occurs within the context of patriarchal and masculinized institutions. A good starting point to contextualize these theoretical approaches is the historical stance and relevance of Sojourner Truth's (1972) message. Truth, a Black abolitionist womanist, stated in an 1853 speech:

That man over there says a woman needs to be helped into carriages and lifted over ditches and to have the best places everywhere. Nobody ever helped me into carriages or over mud puddles or gives me best place...And ain't I a woman? Look at me! Look at my arm! I have plowed and planted and gathered into barns and no man could head me . . . And ain't I a woman? I could work as much and eat as much as a man—when I could get it—and bear the lash as well, and ain't I a woman? I have borne 13 children and seen most all sold into slavery and when I cried out a mother's grief none but Jesus heard me . . . and ain't I a woman? That little man in black there say a woman can't have as much rights as a man cause Christ wasn't a woman. Where did your Christ come from? From God and a woman! Man had nothing to do with him! If the first woman God ever made was strong enough to turn the world upside down, all alone, together women ought to be able to turn it rightside up again.

Most of the extant literature on women administrators in higher education is anecdotal, rather than empirical, and sandwiched somewhere between the feminist research on White women and the ethnic and racial research on men of color. Nonetheless, the literature suggests that African American women struggle with their multiple identities in the broader society ,as well as in their roles as higher education administrators—a struggle that often leads to inequities and a lack of parity compared with their male and White female counterparts.

Academe is particularly challenging for African American women, as they face misperceptions and distortion of their identity and role within their respective institutions. That is to say, women administrators of color face pre-existing societal stereotypes, biases, and discrimination that negatively impact their progress and their image as leaders in the male-dominated, patriarchal, sexist, and racist structure of academe (Task Force on Women in Academe, 2000). In spite of impeccable credentials, African American women are constantly having to prove their academic qualification and having their research and achievements minimized, all of which adversely impacts their identity. In essence, the higher education terrain respresents a social microcosm of the stereotypes and discrimination against women viewed in larger society (Eagly & Karau, 2002; Krefting, 2003).

Divide-and-conquer tactics have often been implemented to undermine the competence and minimize the power of African American women administrators. This includes discourse that attempts to define, dissect, and decontextualize their interlocking identities. In other words, for African American women administrators to be successful, they often feel the need to denounce one or more vital parts of their identity (e.g., choosing to align ideologically and philosophically with African American men or White women). And for those who do manage to successfully move up the administrative ladder, the less support they have, the more vulnerable they become, and the more they are expected to function like White men.

Consequently, African American women administrators are not allowed to define their leadership roles in ways that celebrate the way gender, race, culture, and class interconnect to shape their identities. So instead of embracing their multidimensional identities and using it as strength, for African American women, these multiple social identities and realities turn quickly into multiple marginalities that become barriers in their work and shape and that limit their opportunities. African American women administrators who embrace their multiple identities force the academy to consider change; however, problems ensue due to the longstanding history of academe being change averse. According to Turner (2002), the identities of women's of color are defined in a discriminative manner that is "defined out" rather than "defined in," meaning that institutions sometimes use identity as a means to negate recommendations or circumvent opportunities for advancement for African American women—a practice that is at best unfair and at worst detrimental (Ottinger & Sikula, 1993; Rusher, 1996).

As authors of this chapter we are suggesting that rather than silencing the voices of women of color by attempting to erase their identities, their identities should be embraced and viewed as complementary to the higher education context (Marbley, 2007; Singh, Robinson, & Williams-Green, 1995; Wildman & Davis, 1995). In the spirit of multiracial and Black feminism and womanism, womanist leadership skills that are identified by Walker (1983) as "outrageous, audacious, willful, serious, responsible, grown-up, and the like" should be respected as unique and valuable assets that these women bring to the higher education context.

Marginalization and Oppression

In Robinson and Kenninton's (2002) article entitled "Holding Up Half the Sky: Women and Psychological Resistance," they state, "Both a healthy psychological resistance and a womanist model are congruent with healthy self-definition, empowerment, and relatedness" (p. 167). These authors are speaking to the necessary ingredients in the elixir designed to quell the infirmities that often plague women of color who traverse the terrain within predominantly White settings, particularly the inclusion of a womanist model that is reflective of the gendered experiences among women of color in patriarchal society. For women of color, finding viable strategies to resist marginalization and oppression are critical. According to Lorde (1984),

> the need and desire to nurture each other is not pathological but redemptive, and it is within that knowledge that our real power is rediscovered. It is this real connection which is so feared by a patriarchal world. Only within a patriarchal structure is maternity the only social power open to women. (p. 4)

As a first step, it will be important to understand just from whence these marginalities and oppressive structures originated, how they are experienced, and what proper processes, policies, and procedures can be enacted to lessen the severity that they enact on African American women.

For women in general and African American women in particular, "When the contemporary feminist movement began, it helped many women to see that the sacrificial model was really designed by patriarchal men to keep women subordinated" (hooks, 2001, p. 39). Although the implementation of the sacrificial model that hooks alludes to, a model predicated on women repressing their own needs for the needs of others (i.e., husbands, children, family), impacted both White and women of color communities, several added dimensions and situational nuances made for a different engagement with this model for African American women. According to Patricia Hill Collins (1991), to fully understand how African American women—more pointedly Black women—experience themselves in the constellation of American society, it is important to consider the way the confluence of self-definition, self-valuation, and female-centered analyses impacts their relative status. Hence, the feminist movement as it was enacted, with its roots in the White female tradition, fell short of providing an inclusive framework upon which African American women could append their struggles. While White women grappled with marginality based on their gender status, African American women were forced to tackle a hydra that presented several heads: gender, race, and socioeconomic status. To reify this point, Collins states that "Black women should be among the first to realize that minimizing one form of oppression, while essential, may still leave them oppressed in other equally dehumanizing ways" (p. 471).

Although African American women experience marginalization and oppression in diverse venues such as corporate America and higher education, the attendant impact on their well-being is still quite similar. In speaking to the multiple forms of domination and oppression that exist for women of color who engage with various institutional structures, Patton (2004) says,

> Often it is the current U.S. hegemonic order that insists on the either/or belief—you are either oppressed because you are a woman or because you are an ethnic minority. Interlocking systems of domination take into account the interdependent nature of oppression through a both/and or dialectical perspective—you are a woman or because you are an ethnic minority. Interlocking systems of domination take into account the interdependent nature of oppression through a both/and or dialectical perspective— you are a women and an ethnic minority and a lesbian who may be oppressed. (p. 189)

To reify this statement, Harley (2007), in her article "Maids of Academe: African American Women Faculty at Predominantly White Institutions" reports that African American women, at Predominantly White Institutions (PWIs) are plagued by "a form of race fatigue—the syndrome of being over extended, undervalued, unappreciated, and just knowing that because you are the 'negro in residence' that you will be asked to serve and represent the 'color factor' in yet another capacity" (p. 21).

Thus, for the African American woman administrator in higher education, finding affirming ways to recognize but to not be concomitantly crippled by racist and sexist institutional structures is essential. Key researchers (Bell-Scott & Johnson-Bailey, 1998; Hughes & Howard-Hamilton, 2003; Patton, 2004; Watt, 2004) have suggested strategies such as the development of sister circles, sharing of counterstories and use of spirituality as a form of transgression for African American women to affirm and build supportive structures for their psychological well-being. These strategies underscore the need for African American women to develop "home grown" and authentic strategies of affirmation and resistance that are not part and parcel to the very systems that created them (Bell, 1992; Burke, Cropper, & Harrison, 2000; Harley, 2007; hooks, 1990; Lorde, 1984; Patton, 2004; Robinson & Kennington, 2002).

From a process, procedures, and policy-making standpoint, divining a framework that is inclusive of the unique struggles of African American women administrators and their experiences with marginalization and oppression must be inclusive of the struggles these women face at the intersections of multiple and interlocking identities, which is what the previous section and this chapter attempt to underscore. Processes and procedures need to begin from an epistemological perspective that maintains the integrity of African American women and their ways of knowing. The use of conventional frameworks as a means of tapping into the engagements that African American women have had with institutional racism and sexism will continue to lead to a dilemma that Patton (2004) articulates in her research; namely reprivileging hegemony because "I am trapped by a discursive cycle that makes it difficult to de-center the status of the privileged class" (p. 189).

Hence, some set of understandings or bracketing of commonly held views regarding processes and procedures that are grounded in traditional and hegemonic discourses and that devalue the experiences of African American women administrators should be developed. Although specific recommendations will be offered in the conclusion section of this chapter for those who desire a more structured approach at combating problems associated with marginalization and oppression, an ever-present focus should be on the way multiple oppressions and marginalization is nuanced for this group. From a policy-making perspective, it will be important to create in some venues, and highlight in others, an awareness among the higher education community that African American women administrators experience interlocking systems of domination at the microlevel that in turn generate problematic outcomes for them at the macrolevel (Patton, 2004).

Social and Professional Integration

African American women have always lived in two worlds, faced with the everyday task of balancing mainstream reality and Black cultural reality (Alexander-Snow, 1999). More than two decades ago, Boykin (1981) noted in his research the myriad psychological realities existing among college student populations within PWIs. To cope with these circumstances, African American women administrators must balance their realities—the reality of being caught in two worlds. Within this liminal space that these women occupy, they often find it difficult to fully integrate into the social and professional culture of the PWI. To be successful in academe, these women are fully aware of the importance of establishing productive social and professionals relationships with their colleagues. However, many women experience a "chilly climate" that is at best indifferent and at worst hostile to the cultural nuances they bring to the higher education setting (Turner & Myers, 2000; Smith, 1997). The social structure in higher education, with its adherence to priority membership bestowed upon members of "the club," often require women of color to make certain sacrifices in order to "fit in." All too often these sacrifices require African American women to alter or truncate their unique ethnic, cultural, and gendered identities.

For African American women, recognizing the existence of two worlds within higher education contexts is not a novel discovery. Yet research has documented that their perspectives regarding their "dual existence," an existence that is often associated with marginality, oppression, and inequality remains just that—their perspectives. Singh et al. (1995) reported that African American women held significantly different views on collegiality within their institutions compared with their White counterparts and compared with their African American male peers within their respective institutions. According to Singh et al., women were less satisfied with the organizational culture of their institutions and had lower levels of "faith in their institutions' leadership" (p. 406).

Various standards, often covert or "hidden" from nonmajority communities, are maintained by institutions; thus, memberships to exclusive clubs in which key decisions are made are often limited. Prime examples of these exclusionary processes are operationalized in the concept of *social closure*. Social closure refers to processes in which members of high-status groups do not permit members of low-status groups to fully participate in organizations (Halaby 1979; Tomaskovic-Devey 1993). James (2000) argues that these social closure practices "represent exclusionary activities at the group level" (p. 494). He also adds that these exclusionary practices are meant to exclude those who are considered part of the "out-group" (James 2000). Research has documented that African Americans often experience the negative repercussions of social closure practices. For many African American women administrators in higher education, they face these social closure practices on a regular basis, because they are often relegated to low-status memberships. Consequently, these experiences manifest in the failure to gain access to collegial relationships that are career enhancing, and in the lack of access to important organizational networks (Cianni & Romberger, 1995; Dreher & Cox, 1996; Ibarra, 1995; James, 2000; Thomas, 1990).

In order to combat the potential negative effects of social closure practices, African American women in academe often have to resort to tactics that enable cultural congruity. The theory of cultural congruity has primarily been researched among undergraduate college student populations; however, it is important to note that this theory focuses on the congruence found to exist or not exist among students' values and the values of their respective institutions (Constantine & Watt, 2002; Gloria & Robinson Kurpius 1996). Notwithstanding the application of this theory to undergraduate populations, African American women in academe can also be viewed from this theoretical perspective. For example, the university environment not only affects students' attitudes and their perceived fit within the campus context, but the campus environment also impacts African American women who struggle to find congruence with these contexts.

Additionally, research has underscored findings revealing that when prolonged divergence between individual and institutional values exists, the resultant effect is typically heightened levels of undue stress (Contantine & Watt, 2002; Feagin, Vera, & Imani, 1996; Lang & Ford, 1992). For African American women, particularly those who are in administrative capacities, it is essential that they find viable agents, as well as mechanisms that will assist them to integrate into the campus culture on both social and professional levels. As a result, women of color may need to seek out alliances with nonminorities in order to get their foot in the door to achieve some form of recognition.

In an effort to address a number of the problems associated with African American women in higher education administration, it will be critical for institutions to recognize that differences do exist. The quest for diversity and inclusion must not sidestep key cultural differences and nuances that African American women experience on campus; additionally, cultural perspectives and differential engagements with the higher education environment should inform decisionmaking (Smith, 1997; Strange & Banning, 2001). Foster (1989) postulates that critical leadership is defined as an analysis of organizational occurrences combined with a commitment for change, critical reflection and reevaluation (Jean-Marie and Normoer 2006). African American female administrators, equipped with knowledge of their personal struggles with social and professional integration, must take hold of this concept of critical leadership in order to promote change in university environments.

Narratives: African American Women Administrators Speak

The following narratives are offered to reify the topics previously discussed in this article and to provide a degree of authenticity to the claims made about the experiences of African American women administrators in academe. Each woman was asked to respond "in her own way" and provide insight on what she thought were salient experiences regarding her current or past tenure as a female administrator in predominantly White higher education contexts.

Narrative One: Dr. Aretha Marbley, Professor of Counselor Education at Texas Tech University and Former Dean of Students at Revell Vocational College.

I completed a three-year tenure as a student affairs administrator in a vocational/academic educational school back in the 1980s in a tumultuous era when female administrators and administrators of color were few and not well respected. Due to the advent of computers and rapid growth of technology that spurred such an immediate need for employees with computer and technological skills, vocational technology schools and programs sprouted up in inner city communities all over the country.

Shortly after I was hired as an academic counselor, these schools were swiftly gaining a reputation as being exploitative to people of color, specifically poor people. Barely a couple of years past completing my masters' program in career counseling, I was hired as an academic counselor and was quickly promoted up the chain to Director of Student Services and in less than a year, I was promoted to Dean of Student Services. Looking back, I now know that my promotion had more to do with the large number of students of color being recruited than with my vast experience and knowledge of higher education administration.

As a young (early 30ish) whippersnapper armed with a couple of master's degrees and a little over 10 years experience in social services firmly tucked under my belt, I was confident, and just ambitiously naïve enough to believe that I could do anything. My previous work experience included a couple of lower-level pseudo-administrative-type positions such as *coordinator of* and *assistant to* type jobs. I remember being so excited about receiving this promotion, knowing that it would provide me with the opportunity to do some much needed systemic changes. I believed that the students entering the program, regardless of their academic backgrounds, social realities, and socioeconomics, could benefit from the education and training they would receive at my institution.

Identity and Self-definition

Conceptually, because of my academic training, I thought of myself as a counselor. My counselor identity had been nailed to me as my *public display* identity; however, my core identities as an African American and woman were tucked away in my personal closet. These tucked away identities became estranged from my professional life from the day I entered a predominantly White college to pursue my undergraduate degree. Ironically, the student body at my institution was roughly 90% inner-city African American and Hispanic/Latino students, yet the owners and senior-level administrators were all White/European American men.

There were two African American women (Director of Education and Director of Financial Aid) and one African American man (Director of Recruitment) who were in administrative positions parallel to mine. In essence, there was no room, nor tolerance for discourse on or expression of our gender or ethnicity within the context of our administrative roles in the organization. Yet, for us women folk there were major inequities, starting with inequities among our salaries—White men were at the top and African American women administrators at the bottom of the pay scale. In reality, there was an unspoken understanding that male administrators (regardless of parallel positions) were in charge and the female administrators were responsible for the outcomes. Thus, my role had been clearly defined before I entered the position as Dean of Students.

As an African American woman, I, like my other female counterparts, took my lot in stride and never thought about carving out my identity in this racist, patriarchal system. In fact, I felt privileged to have a job with such an impressive, powerful title, one that satisfied my ambition and afforded me the opportunity to help my people, even though my salary was far from what I would consider to be rewarding.

Like so many professional African American women in my generation, I defined my identity within the framework of race-uplifting, which emanated from the Black Socialist movement of the '60s, '70s, and '80s. That is, Black women were told by Black men that sacrificing their gender identity was necessary for the benefit of the Black race. In essence, they were told that their liberation as women was less important than the liberation of Black men (Stone, 1979)

Marginalization and Oppression

Looking back, I accepted the oppression and marginalization of African American women and Black folks as a reality of the time I lived in. Thus, the discrimination and marginalization that I experienced in my administrative role, though unfair and blatantly discriminative, was expected. The other African American women and I discussed how unfair it was, but we did not know how to eliminate these racist and sexist practices.

Social and Professional Integration

My social and professional integration experiences were almost exclusively experienced with African American female administrators—although I did have one African American male administrator who I viewed as an ally. I vividly remember a couple of holiday/Christmas parties that senior-level administrators hosted for us as a token of thanks for the fine work that we had done. Everything, the mood, food, music, and tone was steeped in White culture. The gathering would either be on college grounds after classes had ended or at some nice neighborhood restaurant across the street. Yet all of us Black administrators (men and women), especially the men, smiled politely and pretended that the social event was the best thing since apple pie. And at the same time, we all knew we would not be invited to the real parties where the big decisions were being made. The social gatherings at the Palmer House (Downtown Chicago) or some other upscale establishment were where the real (i.e., White) administrators would gather together. We also knew there were occasional golfing, river boating, and out-of-town business and professional development meetings that we were not being invited to. As a consequence of not being invited to those events, social integration for us came from the ones we created among ourselves.

Narrative Two: *Dr. La Vonne I. Neal, Dean of the College of Education at the University of Colorado at Colorado Springs.*

Currently, I am dean of a College of Education, but my leadership experiences include three careers. Listed chronologically they are:(1) 13 years' experience as U.S. Army Intelligence Officer managing battlefield intelligence operations, (2) 12 years' experience managing production operations in the corporate sector, and (3) 9 years' experience in higher education administration). All my leadership experiences (e.g., battlefield intelligence, production operations, higher education administration) have been in predominantly White settings with predominately White male colleagues and predominately White male senior administrators.

My Leadership Philosophy

My legs of leadership are spirituality and vision. The word *leg* has many definitions, but I am referring to leg as an extension of a branched object. My leadership has many extensions that support and guide me. As a visionary leader, I understand the "process of vision." As noted by Dr. Myles Munroe, an educator, "Sight is a function of the eyes, while vision is a function of the heart." I am of the opinion that vision—that which we long to do or accomplish, that to which our heart is inclined—should fuel our sight. Where there is no vision or longing of the heart, people perish. The eyes function, but we have no clear direction as to where we are headed.

Spirituality is not simply an intellectual pursuit, Mahatma Gandhi (a spiritual leader who fought for social justice) once said, "God must rule the heart and transform it." Spirituality transcends humanity in that it relies on a power greater than intellect to transform the heart. Spirituality, a leg of my leadership, is that which gives me focus and keeps me focused. It grounds me and causes me to be sensitive to the needs of those around me. As a leader, I am attuned to the needs of those I lead.

My Leadership Style

As a transformational leader, I encourage faculty and staff to help each other and the College of Education. To that end, I lead by example as an administrative and academic leader. Additionally, as a reflective leader and data-driven decision maker, I engage in ongoing, systematic, coordinated planning to position the College of Education in the front ranks of our peers nationally and globally. Moreover, I foster dynamic engagement of all constituencies who can be helpful in strengthening the unit. I use my insider perspectives on what it means to be a member of a traditionally underrepresented group in a position of leadership in academe to help my faculty see themselves as cultural and complex beings who as teachers, have an academic, and social/personal responsibility to their students.

Maintaining Identity Through "Sister and Brother Circles"

I am the first and unfortunately the only African American academic dean at my university. My academic dean colleagues are supportive, but they do not always recognize the crippling obstacles of institutional racism and sexism and their privileges. I maintain my identity as an African American and woman of color by developing "sister and brother circles," (Patton, 2004; Watt, 2004) in communities and organizations beyond my work environment. For example, my current "sister and brother circle" includes four academic deans who are African American and are from universities with diverse missions (e.g., two public regional comprehensive universities—one private, urban, liberal arts college and one historically Black college). We are the support entourage that is not always present at our respective universities. Even though we are full-time administrators, we are active researchers contributing to the leadership discourse. We began our journeys as academic deans during the same year and through our research studies have chronicled our experiences as administrators who are African American. We refer to ourselves as the "Five Heartbeats" who help one another maintain the rhythm of who we are. We have presented two research papers, "The First 100 Days of Leadership: Reflections of New African American Deans," and "Navigating in the Eye of the Storm: Three-Year Reflections of New African American Deans," at the American Educational Research Association (AERA) and the American Association of Colleges for Teacher Education (AACTE) conferences.

Our research focused on our reflections of our first one hundred days, as well as our three–year academic leadership experience and the way we have remained connected to who we are (African Americans) with what we do. We reflected on remaining obstacles and best practices that contributed to successes in dealing with faculty/staff, fundraising, and internal administrative politics. Through our lens, we presented models of leadership that demonstrate blueprints for the way we have survived being a dean while maintaining our African American identity.

Narrative Three: *Dr. Lora Bailey, Dean of the School of Education, Brenau University*

As an African American female in academia, I identify myself foremost as teacher/mentor, researcher, scholar, and, most importantly, a Christian, mother and wife. Navigating the academy while simultaneously attending to all aspects of my identity is akin to many African American female experiences. Nonetheless, such attempts have both complicated and strengthened my efforts to break the glass ceiling that exists in academia for Black women. Adding to this complexity has been my attempt to move forward in leadership roles while situated within the deep South, in states like Alabama, South Carolina, and Georgia, where African Americans continue to be marginalized and where their voices are often silenced.

Tribulations and Inherent Complexities

Before becoming a dean, I served as program chair for early childhood programs at two doctoral/research intensive universities for a total of four years. As an administrator within each College of Education, common themes emerged. Common to each experience were resistance to my authority and ensuing resentment, often presented by White women. White men, on the other hand, seemed to more readily accept my leadership role. They lauded my ability to develop strategic plans to strengthen the institutions, and were often among those who urged me to seek the positions. This phenomenon is somewhat common throughout our society—the idea that White men can afford to elevate Black women while diminishing their counterparts, Black men. Despite the fact that it is within my very fiber to take seriously all tasks before me and to overachieve, even if overachieving means working three times harder than my peers, White women attempted to rally together to present complications, even when my hard work elevated their causes, whether within an academic or social capacity. Nevertheless, I soared past their attempts at sabotage, because of my academic, professional and intellectual prowess.

Scholarship in the Life of an African American Female Administrator

My accomplishments as researcher and scholar made me a role model for others within my field. My research in early childhood education has focused on investigating and uncovering practices that impact outcomes in mathematics for minority children who have been traditionally underrepresented in mathematics classrooms. My success at garnering grant funding to support my research agenda, and my professional writing skills that enabled me to publish a plethora of research and practitioner-based articles to disseminate the results served to elevate my stature as a leader within my field of early childhood education making it possible for those seeking leadership for their colleges to consider me as a viable candidate, despite inherent biases that some faculty within the segregated south might harbor.

Mentor-Teacher-Administrator

As a mentor and teacher, my research plays a pivotal role in informing my practice and guiding those who face difficulties similar to my own in their attempts to navigate the academy. I have interwoven ideals of social justice and equal access to high-quality instruction throughout my instructional and service related activities. In that vein, I have developed an identity that reflects a zeal for building collaborative relationships with doctoral students, preservice teachers and families with children from diverse backgrounds. This level of advocacy is germane to who I am—one who understands the complexities of serving in many capacities as an African American female while simultaneously attaining the goal of breaking the glass ceiling that exists within academia for African American women.

Grounded by Spirituality and Family

As a Christian, I rely on my God and Christian-like beliefs to guide my decisions in all facets of my life and in my quest to engage in social justice activities. As a mother and wife, I apply what I know about teaching and learning to my children and family. I purposefully interweave my Christian beliefs to guide my practices as wife to sustain my marriage. As a mother, I am forever cognizant of the way my children's interactions with their parents and teachers impact their self-confidence and ability to thrive in school settings. My husband understands the many struggles I face in my capacity as an African American administrator in the South and at every opportunity seek to support me. At the end of the day, my identity remains multifaceted, and it is my intent to devote an equal amount of time to each characteristic so that I feel complete as an African American female administrator.

Recommendations and Conclusion

The narratives offered in this chapter provide an intimate view of the way African American women administrators in academe navigate moments of marginalization and personal and professional stress through the use of affirming support structures and strategies. Notwithstanding the challenges they face regarding identity development, marginalization, and social and professional integration, these women are able to transgress oppressive frameworks and identify support mechanisms that assist them in maintaining their standards of professionalism. As Dr. Aretha Marbley shares, African American women must often create opportunities for professional and social integration for themselves. Or, as Dr. Neal states in her narrative, it is the critical balancing act that must be modeled and operationalized into a blueprint that provides clear insight for other African American women who seek similar administrative experience. Yet it is Dr. Bailey's narrative that is resolute in its tone regarding the importance of spirituality and the accumulation of spiritual capital that too provides the necessary support that these women need to be successful.

Their narratives show a track record of success in multiple arenas, yet, as African American administrators, they rely heavily on their spirituality to shape their vision, purpose, and personal missions and to choreograph their interlocking identities into a oneness that makes them strong. In essence, spirituality provided them with the foundation and strength to navigate and in many cases transcend the struggles of being Black women administrators in academe. It is from that strong belief in God that they are able to look both within and outside of themselves for validation and strength—to rely on those traditional African American indigenous networks, such as family, church, and friends.

In many ways, this chapter can best be described as portraiture, "a work incorporating two statements, one by the portrait artist about perception, style and skill and another by the portrait subject on his or her place in the world" (http://www. artspan.com/portraiture). This chapter presents a framework for understanding the critical intersection of gender, race, and professional identity. Concomitantly, this chapter utilizes the personal narrative approach to allow three successful and accomplished African American women, who are leaders in higher education, to speak about the tools they use to transgress and resist hegemonic frameworks to ensure that their "voices" and emic perspectives do not fall on deaf ears.

In conclusion, we offer up the following recommendations in an effort to frame policy, structure processes, and create institutional environments that are affirming and supportive of African American women administrators in academe, particularly for those women who embrace administration as their life's calling.

1. Institutions should establish alternative mentoring programs. The goal of these alternative mentoring programs would be to educate those with seniority on the cultural and professional differences that exist among African American women administrators.

2. Senior-level administrators should take a more active role in highlighting the unique identities among cohorts

of African American women. Their differences should not be viewed as deficits but rather used in an effort to not only retain these women but also to help them become successful.

3. Women administrators of color must take the initiative to integrate key leadership skills and strengths that emanate from their multiple and interlocking identities; these skills and strengths should be integrated into a framework that builds on their experiences as administrators in higher education.

4. Institutions should provide support for African American women administrators to attend key conferences and to be engaged in critical professional networking opportunities that affirm their experiences in academe. Noteworthy are the organizations and networks that affirm the multiple and interlocking identities that these women embody—namely, organizations that speak to their identities as woman, woman of color, woman administrator of color, and woman administrator of color in a predominantly White institution.

5. Institutions should use the extant research (Hughes & Howard-Hamilton, 2003; Bell-Scott & Johnson-Bailey, 1998; Lorde, 1984; Patton, 2004; Robinson & Kennington, 2002; Watt, 2004) which provides key insight on ways to improve conditions for African American women administrators in higher education. Topics ranging from cross-cultural mentoring to spirituality as a form of resistance are key areas of focus that should be explored in terms of their relevance to the administrative experiences among this cohort.

References

Alexander-Snow, M. (1999). Two African American women graduates of historically White boarding schools and their social integration at a traditionally white university. *The Journal of Negro Education, 68*(1), 106-119.

Bell, D. A. (1992). *Faces at the bottom of the well*. New York: Basic Books

Bell-Scott, P., & Johnson-Bailey, J. (1998). *Flat-footed truths: Telling black women's lives*. New York: Henry Holt.

Boykin, A. W. (1981). The triple quandary and the schooling of African American children. In U. Niesser (Ed.), *The school achievement of minority children* (pp.57-92). Hillendale, NJ: Erlbaum.

Burke, B., Cropper, A., & Harrison, P. (2000). Real or imagined—Black women's experiences in the academy. *Community, Work, and Family, 3*(3), 297-310.

Cianni, M., & Romberger, B. (1995). Perceived racial, ethnic, and gender differences in access to developmental experiences. *Group Organization Management, 20*(4), 440-459.

Collins, P. H. (2000). Gender, Black feminism, and Black political economy. *The Annals of the American Academy of Political and Social Sciences, 568,* 41-53.

Constantine, M. G., & Watt, S. K. (2002). Cultural congruity, womanist identity attitudes, and life satisfaction among African American college women attending historically black and predominantly white institutions. *Journal of College Student Development, 43, 2,* 184-194.

Dreher, G. F., & Cox, T. H. (1996). Race, gender, and opportunity: A study of compensation attainment and the establishment of mentoring relationships. *Journal of Applied Psychology, 81*(3), 297-308.

Eagly, Q. H., & Karau, S. J. (2002) Role congruity theory of prejudice toward female leaders. *Psychological Review, 109,* 573-598.

Feagin, J. R., Vera, H., & Imani, N. (1996). *The agony of education: Black students at White colleges and universities*. New York: Routledge.

Foster, W. (1989). Toward a critical practice of leadership. In J. Smyth (Ed.), *Critical perspectives on educational leadership* (pp. 39-62). New York: Falmer.

Gloria, A. M., & Robinson Kurpius, S. E. (1996). The validation of the cultural congruity scale and the university environment scale with Chicano/a students. *Hispanic Journal of Behavioral Science, 18,* 533-550.

Halaby, C. N. (1979). Sexual inequality in the workplace: An employer-specific analysis of pay differences. *Social Science Research. 8*(1), 79-104.

Hamer, J., & Neville, H. (1998). Revolutionary Black feminism: Toward a theory of unity and liberation. *Black Scholar, 28,* 22-29.

Harley, D. A. (2007). Maids of academe: African American women faculty at predominantly White institutions. *Journal of African American Studies, 12,* 19-36.

Hill-Collins, P. (1991). *Black feminist thought: Knowledge, consciousness, and the politics of empowerment.* New York: Routledge.

hooks, b. (2001). *Salvation: Black people and love.* New York: Harper Collins.

hooks, b. (1994). *Teaching to transgress: Education as a practice of freedom.* New York: Routledge.

hooks, b., & West, C. (1991). *Black women intellectuals. In breaking bread: Insurgent Black intellectual life.* Boston: South End Press.

Howard-Hamilton, M. F. (2003). Theoretical frames for African American women. *New Directions for Student Services, 104,* 19-27.

Howard-Vital, M. R. (1989). African-American women in higher education: Struggling to gain identity. *Journal of Black Studies, 20*(2), 180-191.

Hughes, R. L., & Howard-Hamilton, M. F. (2003). Insights: Emphasizing issues that affect African American women. *New Directions for Student Services, 104,* 95-104.

Ibarra, H. (1995). Race, opportunity, and diversity of social circles in managerial networks. *Academy of Management Journal, 38*(3), 673-703.

James, E. H. (2000). Race-related differences in promotions and support: underlying effects of human and social capital. *Organization Science, 11,* 493-508.

Jean-Marie, G., & Normore, A. H. (2006). A repository of hope for social justice: Black women leaders at historically Black colleges and universities. *International Electronic Journal for Leadership in Learning, 10*(20). Retrieved March 19, 2009 from: http://www.acs.ucalgary.ca/~iejll/

Kettle, J. (1996). Good practices, bad attitudes: An examination of the factors influencing women's academic career. In L. Morley & V. Walsh (Eds), *Breaking barriers: Women in higher education* (pp. 53-66). London: Taylor & Francis.

Krefting, L. A. (2003). Intertwined discourses of merit and gender: Evidence from academic employment in the USA. *Gender Work and Organization, 10,* 260.

Lange, M., & Ford, C. A. (Eds.). (1992). *Strategies for retaining minority students in higher education.* Springfield, IL: Charles C. Thomas.

Leithwood, K., Jantzi, D., & Steinbach, R. (1999). *Changing leadership for changing times.* New York: Open University Press.

Lorde, A. (1984). The master's tools will never dismantle the master's house. In A. Lorde (Ed.), *Sister Outsider* (pp. 110-113). Berkeley, CA: Crossing Press.

Marbley, A. F. (2007, Winter). Finding my voice: An African-American female professor at a predominantly White university. *Advancing Women in Leadership* (online). http://www.advancingwomen.com/awl/winter2007/finding_my_voice.htm

Mori, A. (1999). *Toni Morrison and Womanist discourse.* New York: Peter Lang.

Ottinger, C., & Sikula, R. (1993). Women in higher education: Where do we stand? *Research Briefs, 4*(2), 9-10.

Oyewumi, O. (1999). Multiculturalism or multibodism: On the impossible intersections of race and gender in the American White feminist and Black nationalist discourses. *Western Journal of Black Studies, 2*(3), 182-189.

Patton, T. O. (2004). Reflections of a Black woman professor: Racism and sexism in academia. *The Howard Journal of Communications, 15,* 185-200.

Riesman, D. (1982). The personal side of the presidency. *AGB Reports, 24*(6), 35-39.

Riggs, M. (1994). *Awake, arise, & act: A womanist call for Black liberation.* Cleveland, OH: Pilgrim Press.

Robinson, T. L., & Kennington, P. A. D. (2002). Holding up half the sky: Women and psychological resistance. *Journal of Humanistic Counseling, Education and Development, 41,* 164-177.

Rusher, A. W. (1996). *African American women administrators.* New York: University Press of America.

Singh, K., Robinson, A., & Williams-Green, J. (1995). Differences in perceptions of African American women and men faculty and administrators. *Journal of Negro Education, 64*(4), 401-408.

Smith, D. & Associates (1997). *Diversity works: The emerging picture of how students benefit.* Washington, DC: Association of American Colleges and Universities.

Stone, P. T. (1979). Feminist consciousness and Black women. In J. Freeman (Ed.), *A feminist perspective* (2nd ed., pp. 575-588). Palo Alto, CA: Mayfield.

Strange, C. C., & Banning, J. H. (2001). *Educating by design: Creating campus learning environments that work.* San Francisco: Jossey-Bass.

Task Force for Women in Academe (2000). *Women in academe: Two steps forward, one step back. Washington*, DC: American Psychological Association.

Taylor, U. Y. (1998). Making waves: The theory and practice of Black feminism. *Black Scholar, 28,* 18-29.

Thomas, D. A. (1990). The impact of race on managers' experience of developmental relationships (mentoring and sponsorship): An intra-organizational study. *Journal of Organizational Behavior, 2,* 479-492.

Tomaskovic-Devey, D. (1993). The gender and race composition of jobs and the male/female, white/black pay gaps. *Social Forces, 72,* 45-76.

Truth, S. (1972). Black women speak of womanhood. In G. Lerner (Ed.), *Black women in White America: A documentary history*. New York: Vintage Books.

Turner, C. V. S. (2002). Women of color in academe: Living with multiple marginality. *Journal of Higher Education, 73,* 74-93.

Turner, C. V. S., & Myers, S. L. (2000). *Faculty of color in academe: Bittersweet success.* Boston: Allyn & Bacon.

Vargas, L. (Ed.). (2004). *Women faculty of color in the White classroom*. New York: Peter Lang.

Walker, A. (1983). *In search of my mother's garden: Womanist poetry*. New York: Harcourt Brace Jovanovich.

Watt, S. K. (2004). Come to the river: Using spirituality to cope, rest and develop identity. In M. F. Howard-Hamilton (Ed.), *Meeting the needs of African American women* (pp. 29-40). San Francisco: Jossey-Bass.

Wildman, S., & Davis, A. D. (1995). Language and silence: Making systems of privilege visible, *Santa Clara Law Review, 35,* 881-906.

Zinn, M. B., & Dill, B. T. (1996). Theorizing difference from multiracial feminism. *Feminist Studies, 22,* 321-331.

Part II

The Faculty

The Humanities

The Social Sciences

Education

Gender Intersectionality:
Unfinished Business of Justice Advocacy

Marsha J. Tyson Darling
Adelphi University

Intersectional Analysis and Equality

In recent decades, a growing number of progressive educators and human rights advocates have expressed concerns and advanced efforts to create learning initiatives that reinvigorate the ongoing work directed at safeguarding domestic civil liberties, and advancing global human rights for women and girls who live multiple and intersecting identities that serve to marginalize them and render them unable to exercise rights and privileges. In this century, one of the most important pedagogical challenges we will face as educators will be helping students interpret how the production of knowledge and its applications socially construct human identity. In our world, gender is never apart from other intersecting identities, and hence it is naïve at best, and obscuring at worst to present gender as if it stands apart from the meanings and consequences of national identity, skin color, ethnicity (including religion), socioeconomic class, ability/disability, sexual orientation, age, and caste.

Against a backdrop of decades-old social justice advocacy on behalf of racial equality and social justice, intersectional analysis, an analytical tool has derived from attempts by primarily women of color theorists, writers, and social justice activists to explain the consequences of multiple and intersecting discriminations for the lived experiences of millions of women and girls of color. In this vein, Intersectionality emerged in the twentieth century as the analytical centerpiece of much of the early scholarship, pedagogy and grassroots advocacy on behalf of women of color. In the United States, it has been Black women writers, public speakers, scholars, grassroots activists and artists, who have used their respective mediums to denote Black women's historical experiences of multiple and intersecting racial, gender, sexual and class identities and the discrimination, marginalization and subjugation that has been directed at Black women because of those socially constructed identities (Brewer, 1993, 2002; Christian, 1997; Collins, 1990, 1998; Crenshaw, 1991; Davis, 1971, 1981, 1989; hooks, 1984; Hull, Scott & Smith 1982; McIntosh 1997).

Black women theorists, writers, artists and activists were first to render a previously White gender analysis far more complex, as their work demonstrated that the Black women's relationship with intersecting identities, discrimination and subsequent marginalization, was unique, while also intertwined with the historical experiences of the discrimination and marginalization of Black men. Hence, an intersectional analysis that examines the lived experiences and consequences of the intersection of skin color and race, gender, and class is integral to most work on Black women's plight, even if explicit references to intersectional analysis and intersectionality are not present. In this way, the earlier context-specific contributions that analyzed Black women's intersecting and compounding discriminations were a precursor to the later theoretical explanations of the consequence of multiple and intersecting identities and discriminations. Furthermore, in this manner, a theoretical analysis that has proven to be an accurate, explanatory and effective vehicle for addressing remedial social policy changes has followed, not preceded, an assessment of the lived experiences of marginalized women.

Intersectional analysis is an essential paradigm, theoretical in its reach and applicability, and particularly useful for understanding, analysis and advocacy. It is also compelling as a tool for creating social policy and institutional change that really addresses the unfinished business of gender equality for all, not just some women and girls in the 21st century. An essential tool in our repertoire of pedagogical resources, an intersectional analysis offers an assessment of the ways in which multiple identities, most often socially constructed by others who exercise greater privilege and hence social control, intersect to create compounding discriminations that marginalize millions of women and girls. Intersectional analysis is a resourceful paradigm in our work as educators who are intent on teaching content rich in relevancy to this and future generations, who are beneficiaries of the Civil Rights Movement's rapid, broad and monumental social changes.

Intersectional analysis is a tool that is important to us as educators, as we assess teaching pedagogy and strategies that explore the multiple identities and discriminations that a diverse range of women and girls experience. As we examine the impact that socially constructed identities—largely beyond the control of most women and girls—exerts on women's access to the exercise of rights, entitlements, and opportunities, we come to understand that much of women's marginalization is not in women's control. Furthermore, teaching about the ways women's identities are socially constructed by those who exercise greater privileges, rights and opportunities affords educators an opportunity to help students examine women's multiple and intersecting lived identities from social justice and social development perspectives. In this way, intersectionality facilitates an exploration of the connection between pedagogy and the acquisition of knowledge and skills that enable citizen advocacy based on valuing justice and acting to achieve social equality.

Intersectionality and Human Rights in the Era of Globalization

Intersectionality is an effective analytical tool for addressing the complex diversity of women's experiences. Intersectionality is also an analytical tool for strengthening teaching pedagogy, social justice advocacy, and creating multimedia resources for teaching about the complex ways in which the lived experiences of multiple and intersecting discriminations directly contribute to the unique ways in which women experience oppression. On the other hand, Intersectionality is also useful for identifying the ways in which some women experience multiple and intersecting privileges, rights and opportunities, thereby advancing their social standing, status, and contributions to social development. This is critically important as we assess the importance of gender equality work at the local, state, national and international levels. There are profound differences in the multiple identities that intersect with a woman's gender, and therefore there is diversity in women's experiences in terms of our interest in furthering gender equality work. Hence, there is the unfinished business of global gender equality work—namely the process of rethinking the challenges connected with understanding the unique burdens marginalized women confront in the context of progressive efforts to further gender equality for marginalized women and girls.

One of the main weaknesses in teaching about the world's women, and in promoting gender equality work, has been the inability to address the consequences of diversity in women's identities. Differences in color, class, religion, race, ethnicity, age, ability, caste, sexuality, and geographical locations that create barriers to the exercise of rights have caused less privileged women to experience even more marginalization. This fact has not escaped the many whose advocacy focuses on promoting anti-discrimination standards, policies, and actions, including those who work to advance legal standards for women's human rights that have been established by the United Nations Charter and the Universal Declaration of Human Rights.

Women's rights advocates have made important inroads into making gender-specific abuses more visible and hence more likely remedied. Racial/ethnic justice advocates have made important advances into raising the bar for the exercise of civil and human rights. However, the difficulty of clearly understanding and intervening in the abuses of women and girls who experience multiple and layered identities, and intersecting and compounding discriminations, remains a persistent challenge to social justice and women rights advocates and concerned educators everywhere.

Here, I am referring to the multiple and compounding discriminations millions of women and girls experience based on skin color, caste, descent, accent and language, age, religion, disability, immigration status, refugee status, trafficked and migrant status, sexual orientation, and national or ethnic origin. This suggests the importance and timeliness of our focus on learning and teaching about intersectionality. What is intersectional discrimination? What does it look like, particularly in light of our concerns to advance conceptual frameworks that render women's marginalization more visible? How does an intersectional approach help us to create and sustain interventions and remedies that work to respect, protect, fulfill and develop women? What are some examples of the multilayered and intersecting identities that cause women to be marginalized and discriminated against? Further, what should we do to integrate marginalized women's issues, their problems, and, where accessible, their self-defined agendas into our teaching pedagogy, social justice advocacy, and human rights and development work?

Intersectional methodology is a relatively new language designed primarily to conceptualize and render as visible the long-standing, real-world, multiple discriminations lived by millions of the world's women and girls. Intersectional analysis is a theoretical approach that conceptually represents the racial, ethnic, economic, sexual, cultural, and gender dimensions of multiple and compounding forms of discriminations against women and girls. As such, Intersectionality starts with the recognition that women live multiple, even-layered identities that derive from social relationships lived within patriarchies that are racialized, as well as gendered, thereby producing social relations with men and women of far more socially dominant groups.

As a concept, Intersectionality is a tool that helps us visualize how the convergence of multiple discriminations in women's lives takes place. Multiple discriminations produce marginalization for millions of women and also reinforce and maintain marginalization as inevitable. The Disempowering of women's multiple identities is the consequence of social rejection and exclusion by dominant social groups. Racial and ethnic discrimination do not affect women and men in the same way. The racial discrimination that women experience may remain unnamed unless the differences between the way women and men experience racial discrimination in their public and private lives is recognized.

Second, certain forms of racial discrimination are directed toward women because of their gender. Consider the gender and ethnic based violations of women in Bosnia, Burundi, Rwanda, and more recently, the Congo, in which women's enslavement, sexual abuse and rape took place while in detention or under attack during armed conflict. Also, consider how little we know about ethnic and gender violence against Palestinian girls and women under Israeli occupation or American occupation of Iraq. Furthermore, stereotypes about women as evil seductresses; beliefs about women as property, particularly as extensions of male honor; beliefs about women's genital uncleanliness; and women's alleged unrestrained sexuality often have been used as a rationale for sexual assault and rape and for female genital mutilation. Also, sexualizing women in racist and overtly misogynist ways fairly well assures that some members of dominant groups will target women, who are marginalized by discrimination and negative stigma, for sexual assault. It also means that often violence against marginalized women by marginalized men is dismissed or excused away, and the woman who is violated is blamed in some way for "causing" or "deserving" the violence.

Sometimes ethnic and gender-based sexual assault takes place while women are in detention in the criminal justice system. For instance, women of color are the fastest-growing prisoner population in the United States. Sexual assaults that target racialized women in U.S. prisons are largely invisible. In addition, consider the race-based sexual assault of migrant, trafficked, refugee, and undocumented women while they are detained in a state's immigration system. In many countries, sexual violation against women while they are in state's immigration custody are largely invisible. Female workers are often abused by their employers in the formal sector. Female domestic workers, particularly those required to live with their employers while employed abroad, also face abuse from their employers and sometimes have their wages withheld. Female migrants and workers often experience mistreatment, abuse, assault and deprivations at the hands of private parties. For example, female Filipino foreign domestic workers in Hong Kong are particularly vulnerable to abusive employers, as Hong Kong law requires their departure within two weeks after the expiration of their employment contracts.

It is also important to note that many women marginalized by discriminatory actions against them will be unable to secure redress, for they lack access to effective complaint mechanisms because of gender and racial bias in the legal system and pervasive discrimination against women in the private sphere. We might aptly refer to this interlocking web of discriminations and diminishing or nonexisting recourses as compounding discriminations. As many women's rights advocates now argue, women's multiple, varied and layered identities require us to understand that what works to advance some women's access to opportunities and the exercise of human rights will not necessarily work for more marginalized women. In terms of gender equality mainstreaming, this means that what empowers relatively socially privileged women will not work to empower deeply marginalized and socially excluded women and girls.

Socially constructed identities intersect in a woman or girl's lived experiences. Marginalizing identities are assigned low status by many members of socially dominant groups who discriminate against whoever occupies such identities. To visualize this, let us say that discrimination travels along differing and intersecting roads where power relationships are acted out on the meanings accorded to gender, color, ethnicity, descent and ancestry, class, sexual orientation, religion, language, migrant, refugee and trafficked status, and physical ability. The greater the number of discriminations practiced against a woman, the greater is her marginalization and oppression. In terms of trends emerging in globalization, we know that patriarchy and subordination based on color, descent, ethnicity and cultural and religious differences create and sustain marginalizing categories for women and girls. Intersectional analysis unmasks the invisibility by which the perpetrators of discriminations commit harmful, marginalizing, and even violent actions toward females marked for discrimination.

In this way, intersectional analysis prompts us to look for the constructed identities that allow members of socially dominant groups to publicly and privately discriminate against vulnerable women. In many instances, because past discriminations and physical subordinations have already established the economic, political, social and cultural distances, marginalized women have been pushed from the exercise of civil and human rights. Without meaningful intervention, intersecting discriminations compound, as socially derived subordination is transmitted intergenerationally and may even appear to "naturally" be the choice of marginalized women and girls (Amott & Matthaei, 1996; Lorde, 1984).

Imagine representing a state and its institutions, agents and cultures as lodged within a large circle. Imagine that those standing at the center of the large circle receive privileges by having access to economic opportunities and the exercise of political protections and legal immunities. Further, consider that the center of the circle is where one's quality of life is relatively unfettered by debilitating discriminations. The discriminations that have forced many women to the margins have been established over time, so that accumulating disadvantages and negative stigma have become institutionalized and structural, as the state has often been complicit in constructing the multiple discriminations. Unfortunately, the marginalization and subordination in these instances now has the force of intergenerational momentum behind it, so that one easily assumes that some women are naturally poor because they are inferior and inferior because they are poor (Charlton, 1989; Mohanty, 1997; Mies & Shiva, 1997).

This oppression is also systematic because without significant and purposeful reform, the victims of multiple discriminations (marginalized women and girls) cannot readily escape the poverty that discriminations impose or the racialized stigma that follows them. Marginalized women and girls sometimes even blame themselves and other victims of discrimination for their own marginalization. Regrettably, this situation of "blaming the victim" illustrates the way marginalization and oppression are compounded and are systemic and systematic. Such pervasive marginalization seriously retards the social development of marginalized women and girls, as often the oppressions are internalized. Subjugated women are often so mentally colonized by their oppressed circumstances that they are unable to deconstruct and properly denote the causes of their oppressions, thereby naturalizing their marginalization.

The real key to understanding the foundation on which multiple discriminations are erected is to assess the impact of differences in opportunities and access to rights. Over time, many of those in socially dominant groups act to discriminate against marginalized women and men, thereby establishing privilege for themselves and those in the dominant group who do not necessarily themselves act to exclude or marginalize. Such "derivative privilege" is evident everywhere in our observations about visible entitlements for some who have derived from longstanding discriminations against victimized and marginalized groups, as well as marginalized women and girls. Importantly, those who receive "derivative privilege" in socially dominant groups have the option fo expressly deploring racial/ethnic or caste-based cultural stigma and the subordination and victimization it occasions for marginalized women and girls. In recent decades, increased references to the marginalizing impact of White privilege now accompany longstanding concerns about the subjugating effects of male privilege, and class and settler status/colonial privileges on marginalized social groups, especially women and girls.

For instance, racial and cultural discrimination against European Roma and South Asian Indian Dalit women are accompanied by deep economic disempowerment and economic discriminations leading to marginalization. In this way, over many generations, social inequalities have become entrenched as dominant groups have expended considerable effort to justify their exploitation and exclusion of Roma and Dalit. Such effort fuses racial, caste, and cultural discriminations with economic marginalization and allegations of the alleged inferiority of those being exploited. Though all women have been subordinated, indigenous women, women of color, disabled women, migrant, displaced, trafficked and refugee women, lesbians, bisexuals and transgender women have been pushed farthest from the exercise of rights, privileges and immunities.

Lesbians are often marginalized in the mainstream societies in which they live, and if they are women of color, racialized women or minority women, they often experience negative stereotyping and exclusion from their ethnic communities as well as marginalization from socially dominant groups. Racialized women who are lesbian, bisexual or transgender often face exclusion and racism from social justice movements that promote gay, lesbian, bisexual and transgender rights. These layered identities and intersecting discriminations cannot be understood and effectively negotiated solely by examining broad racial and gender categories. Failing keep sexuality related issues in our view would further render these forms of discriminations against women invisible, while at the same time empowering the perpetrators of abuse to practice discriminatory behaviors including violence and other human rights violations. Furthermore, failing to deal with the real world intersections that order women's identities weakens the work of social justice advocates and strengthens homophobic, gender, and racial/ethnic subjugations and subordination (Silvera, 1991).

Members of socially dominant groups—males, Whites, heterosexuals, physically more-able and affluent individuals—might not themselves practice discrimination against marginalized people in order to derive access to opportunities, but their access to opportunities has been made easier because of a legacy of discrimination that has stymied access to opportunities and rights for marginalized others. If the prevailing conceptual framework were used to examine rights and deprivations, if we view gender discrimination and racial discrimination as mutually exclusive problems, then other forms of intersectional discrimination escape scrutiny, and hence intervention. Consider the trafficking of girls and women. The factors that contribute to trafficking are often viewed too narrowly, namely, only within the context of gender discrimination. Girls and women enter trafficking networks because of the racial and social stratification and discrimination that marginalizes them, renders them far more vulnerable and likely targets for the racial, sexual and descent-based discriminatory treatment operating in trafficking networks.

Consider also the racial, ethnic and gender dimensions of the longstanding problem of coerced or nonconsensual sterilization of women belonging to certain racial or ethnic groups. An intersectional analysis keeps our attention on the ramifications of compounding discriminations imbedded in social policies, namely the intersection of economic, racial, ethnic, geopolitical location (neocolonial status), and gender. The social result of the compounding discriminations just mentioned is the denial of reproductive justice for indigenous and marginalized women. Further, the involuntary surgical sterilization of American Indian, Puerto Rican, Black American, Peruvian, and Roma women and girls and the surgical sterilizations of Vietnamese and Indian women have targeted marginalized poor women under the widely held guise that their fertility is out of control and contributes to an impending population explosion (Incite, 2006).

By way of illustrating the distance between marginalization for some women and privileges for others, in contrast to poor women's lack of reproductive autonomy, it is important to note that during the same decades in which an alarm about the "excess fertility" of women of color has been sounded, pro-natal financial incentives and rewards and unregulated fertility-enhancing biotech protocols have been offered to middle class White women in global North countries. The consequence of this disparity is that much of international aid and global state-sponsored social policy has focused on assigning blame for global "overpopulation" to the "excess fertility" of poor women of color, particularly in the global South, while explicitly encouraging population increase and "excess fertility" of White women in the global North. Of course, this is an example of the multiple, intersecting and compounding discriminations embedded in the gender inequality that characterizes population policy globally. These policies increase White birth rates and strengthen reproductive autonomy for White women while laying the blame for global overpopulation concerns squarely on the backs of poor women of color. In this manner, austere policies directed at controlling women stereotyped as promiscuous, lazy, and uninterested in upward social mobility deprive marginalized women of reproductive justice (Darling, 1999, 2001; Hartmann, 1995).

Intersectional discrimination is also class or economic based. Consider the impact of cuts in government spending on basic social services that fall disproportionately on women living in poor households who remain responsible for their usual family responsibilities while having to compensate to fulfill those services now removed by economic restructuring. In such situations, global South Structural Adjustment Programs (SAPs) and policies and welfare reform policies in the U.S. exert a heavy burden on already poor women who now strain to meet their families needs in a social context in which they are already denied economic access and opportunities. It is important to assess the degree to which poor women are blamed for their poverty, even though state assistance is minimal or non-existent (Fuentes & Ehrenreich, 1989; Kirk & Okazawa-Rey, 2007; Lindsay, 1980; Raj, 2002).

Because equality discourse often separates the designation of racism from sexism and other forms of discrimination, a binary divide sometimes follows in which the adverse experiences of women who confront racism, caste and descent based discriminations and other discriminatory intolerances like xenophobia, homophobia and discrimination against the disabled are unaccounted for in much of what is recommended as solutions. Note that when our interventions are not informed by an accurate measurement of interrelated and intersecting discriminations, remedies may be inadequate and ineffective. As leaders and educators who value equality as a social justice ideal, and as advocates for women's rights, we must challenge the received paradigm whereby only some women deserve access to the exercise of human and civil rights. Essentially, that means breaking with and transcending the patriarchal standard of using privilege as a tool to advance oppositional constructions of women's identity and privileges (Back & Solomos, 2000; Butler & Walter, 1991; Johnson, 2004; Omolade, 1994; Schulz & Mullings, 2006; Wing, 1997).

Conclusion

In closing, with the goal of strengthening pedagogy, learning and social justice engagement, this essay has reflected on challenges embedded in understanding, teaching and applying intersectionality theory. Women's civil rights and human rights, and gender equality are at the center of meaningful social development efforts toward an inclusive human rights agenda in the 21st century. However, women's experiences of gender inequality vary. A "gender remedy" that obscures the intersection of gender with race, ethnicity, class, caste, sexual orientation, sexuality, religion, age, ability and nationality will fail to mitigate the obstacles to equality and human rights for many women and girls.

Social justice engagement calls upon us to interrogate the limiting paradigm that we have inherited from a dualistic and oppositional valuing system that accords some women (mostly White) privileges and rights while denying most other women the same privileges and rights. Arguably, if we are to secure a lasting commitment to justice, equality, and peace, we must grapple with and challenge one of globalization's main tenets, namely, that some woman's privileges are accrued and held in place by other woman's subordination and marginalization. This amounts to saying that today one of our challenges as educators must be to render the complexities of intersecting discriminations plain enough to see and act upon. The consequence of such clarity is that marginalized women will be the subject of our talk about effecting positive social change, and active participants in the actions to which we commit ourselves in future directions within the women's movement, and in the fora in which we teach and learn.

Questions abound as we consider the challenges related to transforming teaching pedagogy and deepening public awareness of how to integrate Intersectionality into the way we think and act in relation to the complexities embedded in understanding inclusive gender equality. How will the global women's movement pursue the goal of inclusive gender equality and the exercise of human rights for all women? In this context, will women privileged by other women's exploitation and marginalization resist advocating for the rights of marginalized women? Will ideological constructions obstruct rather than facilitate? How do we invent new meanings that serve the well-being of all, not just some women and girls, in the context of globalization?

We will need deep analysis and some soul searching about practical and structural change and transformation regarding the gap between privilege for some women and girls and deprivation for other women and girls. This is an important threshold point for 21st century social development, namely, enriching teaching pedagogy, furthering commitments to global scale broad-based participatory democracy, and institutionalizing the egalitarian goals of the women's movement, including disseminating the use of an Intersectional analytical framework to facilitate an understanding of the complexities and diversities of women's' experiences globally. As we go about learning, leading and teaching, Intersectionality must accompany our concern to advance an inclusive gender equality that builds on the hard won and often yet fragile 20th century human rights gains for women; this is the unfinished business of the social justice advocacy.

This essay is derived from a plenary presentation, "Human Rights for All: Understanding and Applying 'Intersectionality' to Confront Globalization," presented at the Association for Women's Rights in Development (AWID) 9th International Forum, October 5, 2002; I thank the editor for inviting this longer version of my comments.

References

Amott, T., & Matthaei, J. (Eds.) (1996). *Race, gender and multicultural economic history of women in the U.S.* Cambridge, MA: South End Press.

Back, L., & Solomos, J. (Eds.) (2000). *Theories of race and racism: A reader.* New York: Routledge, 2000.

Brewer, R. M., Conrad, C. A., & King, M. C. (2002). The complexities and potential of theorizing gender, caste, race, and class. *Feminist Economics, 8*(2), 3-18.

Brewer, R. M. (1993). Theorizing race, class and gender: The new scholarship on black feminist intellectuals and Black women's labor. In S. M. James & A.P A. Busia. (Eds.). *Theorizing Black feminisms: The visionary pragmatism of Black women* (pp. 13-30). New York: Routledge Press.

Butler, J. E., & Walter, J. C. (Eds.) (1991). *Transforming the curriculum: Ethnic studies and women's studies.* Albany: State University of New York Press.

Charlton, S. M., et al. (1989). Women, the state, and development. In S. Ellen, M. Charlton, J. Everett, K. Staudt (Eds.), *Women, the state, and development*. Albany: State University of New York Press.

Christian, B. (1997). The race for theory. In S. Kemp & J. Squires (Eds.) *Feminisms*. New York: Oxford University Press.

Collins, P. H. (1990). Black feminist thought: Knowledge, consciousness, and the politics of empowerment. New York: Routledge Press.

Collins, P. H. (1998). It's all in the family: Intersections of gender, race, and nation. *Hypatia, 13*(3), 62.

Crenshaw, K. (1991). Mapping the margins: Intersectionality, identity politics, and violence against women of color. *Stanford Law Review, 43*(6), 1241-1299.

Darling, M. J. T. (2001). Gendered globalization, state interests, women of color and marginalized Women. *International Feminist Art Journal*, 8, 65-73.

Darling, M. J. T. (1999). The state: Friend or foe? Distributive justice issues and African-American Women. In J. Silliman & Y. King (Eds.), *Dangerous intersections: Feminist perspectives on population, environment, and development*. Cambridge, MA: South End Press.

Davis, A. Y. (1971). Reflections on the Black woman's role in the community of slaves. *Black Scholar 3*, 2-15.

Davis, A. Y. (1989). *Women, culture, and politics*. New York: Random House.

Davis, A.Y. (1981). *Women, race, and class*. New York: Random House.

Fuentes, A., & Ehrenreich, B. (Eds.) (1989). *Women in the global factory*. Cambridge, MA: South End Press.

Hartmann, B. (1995). *Reproductive rights and wrongs: The global politics of population control*. Cambridge, MA: South End Press.

hooks, b. (1984). *Feminist theory: From margin to center.* Cambridge, MA: South End Press.

Hull, G. T., Scott, P .B., & Smith, B. (Eds.) (1982) *But some of us are brave: All the women are White, all the Blacks are men.* Westbury, NY: Feminist Press.

Incite! Women of Color Against Violence. (Eds.) (2006). *Color of violence: The INCITE! anthology.* Cambridge, MA: South End Press.

Johnson, P. C. (2004). Inner Lives: Voices of African American women in prison. New York: New York University Press.

Kirk, G., & Okazawa-Rey, M. (Eds.) (2007). *Women's lives: Multicultural perspectives.* McGraw-Hill.

Lindsay, B. (Ed.). (1980). Perspectives of third world women: An introduction, and third world women and social reality: A conclusion. In *Comparative perspectives of Third World Women: The impact of race, sex, and class.* (pp. 1-22 and 297-310). New York: Praeger.

McIntosh, M. (1997). Queer theory and the war of the sexes. In S. Kemp & J. Squires. (Eds.). *Feminisms.* (pp. 364-367). New York: Oxford University Press.

Lorde, A. (1984). Age, race, class, and sex: Women redefining difference. In *Sister outsider: Essays and speeches.* The Crossing Press.

Mies, M., & Shiva, V. (1997). Ecofeminism. In S. Kemp & J. Squires, (Eds.) *Feminisms.* (pp. 497-502). New York: Oxford University Press.

Mohanty, C. (1997). Under Western eyes: Feminist scholarship and colonial discourses. In S. Kemp & J. Squires. (Eds.) *Feminisms* (pp. 91-95). *New York:* Oxford University Press.

Omolade, B. (1994). *The rising song of African American women* pp.129-136). New York: Routledge.

Raj, R. (Ed.). (2002). *Women at the intersection: Indivisible rights, identities and oppressions.* (pp. 83-118). New Brunswick, NJ: Rutgers University Center for Women's Global Leadership.

Schulz, A. J., & Mullings, L. (Eds.) (2006). *Gender, race, class, and health: Intersectional approaches.* Jossey-Bass.

Silvera, M. (Ed.) (1991). *Piece of my heart: A lesbian of colour anthology.* Toronto: Sister Vision, Black Women and Women of Colour Press.

United Nations Office of the High Commissioner for Human Rights. (2001). *Gender dimensions of racial discrimination: report based on the meeting and the background paper for the expert meeting on gender and racial discrimination, convened by the United Nations division for the advancement of women, in Zagreb, Croatia, November 21-24, 2000.* Geneva, Switzerland: United Nations.

Wing, A. K. (Ed.) (1997). *Critical race feminism: A reader.* New York: New York University Press.

African American Women Artists as Leaders:

The Visual Crusade for Social Justice

Amy Helene Kirschke
University of North Carolina, Wilmington

W. E. B. Du Bois, the towering intellectual leader of African Americans in the early 20th century, used art, drawings, cartoons, and photography to elucidate the most important issues of the day. Du Bois served as the founding editor of *The Crisis*, the first significant national African American magazine. *The Crisis* was an organ of the National Association for the Advancement of Colored People (NAACP) and an integral part of the struggle to combat American racism. Du Bois, who helped found the NAACP, came to New York in the summer of 1910 to take the position of director of publicity and research for the organization and to assume the role of editor of the journal, which debuted in November later that year. Du Bois would remain in this position until Summer 1934.

From his first days as editor, Du Bois employed women illustrators to help express the most serious issues of the day. Under his direction, women artists played a prominent leadership role in the magazine's efforts to bring about social justice for African Americans. This role was enhanced by Du Bois's trusted colleague and contributing writer and eventual associate editor, Jessie Fauset. Among his other contributions, in March 1912, the Philadelphia-born novelist Fauset (a Cornell graduate, elected to Phi Beta Kappa) started writing the "What to Read" section of *The Crisis*. Fauset helped run the magazine when Du Bois fell ill from kidney stones in Summer 1916. Fauset also edited Du Bois's *The Brownies' Book,* which was created for African American children, and, of course, also appealed to *The Crisis*'s female readership.

Du Bois had some previous experience in publishing as an editor for the journals *Moon* and *Horizon* between 1906 and 1910. But this endeavor would be different. Du Bois intended to make *The Crisis* the principal crusading voice for civil rights on a national scale. Created at the height of the Jim Crow era, the magazine would speak to Black Americans who had been disenfranchised and were struggling to improve their marginalized status. Southern Blacks were still largely relegated to agricultural and service positions, with limited educational opportunities. Black Americans lived in a land plagued by White terror, with lynchings still common in the South, and racial discrimination the pattern throughout the United States. As editor of *The Crisis* magazine, Du Bois would attempt to address many concerns, using the magazine as a means of racial uplift—celebrating the joys and hopes of African American culture and life —and as a tool to address the injustices and sorrows of persistent discrimination and racial terror(especially lynching), experienced by Black Americans. The written word was not sufficient—visual imagery was central to bringing the message home to readers and emphasizing the importance of the cause.

Du Bois placed political cartoons, drawings, photographs and prints on the cover and through the pages of *The Crisis*. But they were different from images of African Americans in other magazines. Du Bois's images were from a Black perspective, almost entirely created by Black artists who were connected to the importance of the causes addressed in the journal. The art was dignified, respectful and exuded race-pride. The more tragic images were direct and graphic in their ability to express the violence that African Americans faced in daily life. Not only were women artists employed, but women were also often depicted on the pages of *The Crisis* to express emotion, sorrow, and the suffering experienced by the Black race. Du Bois was always interested in issues of African American identity, but how would visuals aid in the development of a stronger Black identity? And how could visuals in *The Crisis* help define a collective memory for his Black readership, a memory that Du Bois believed had been seized and largely shaped by a White dominated culture? Visuals, with or without text, might aid in the establishment of a greater African American identity, a collective identity that had been denied them by the ravages of slavery and the dashed hopes of Reconstruction.

Du Bois, a lifelong proponent of social justice, including issues particularly important to women, not only utilized women artists and writers regularly, but also worked closely with associate editor and collaborator Jessie Fauset to make sure that women's issues were properly represented on the pages of *The*

Crisis magazine. Some of Du Bois's most important illustrators were African American women. Never before had African American women been employed in the visual arts in such a politically meaningful and visible way. Women artists, including Vivien Schuyler, Laura Wheeler Waring, Joyce Carrington and Celeste Smith, regularly contributed to the magazine.

Du Bois was a strong advocate of women's rights, including economic rights, the right to vote, and reproductive rights, which he called the "right of motherhood at her own discretion." Du Bois's commitment to women went beyond that of solely African American women; as a strong advocate of the Pan-African movement, he saw the strength in all women of African descent. This commitment to women of color can be seen in Du Bois's writings separate from *The Crisis* magazine. In *Blackwater*, published in 1920, he wrote of the oppression of women in Western societies: "Our women in black had freedom thrust contemptuously upon them...we have still our poverty and degradation, our lewdness and our cruel toil; but we have, too, a vast group of women of Negro blood who for strength of character, cleanness of soul, and unselfish devotion of purpose, is today easily the peer of any group of women in the civilized world" (p. 185). His writings and the art he included on the pages of *The Crisis* spoke to the hard work of women of African descent and their importance in the community. Du Bois, a man known for his appreciation of beautiful women, which is carefully documented in David Levering Lewis's two volume biography, noted, "I honor the women of my race. Their beauty—their dark and mysterious beauty of midnight eyes, crumpled hair, and soft, full-features...No other women on earth could have emerged from the hell of force and temptation which once engulfed and still surrounds Black women in America with half the modesty and womanliness that they retain" (p. 185). Du Bois hoped to bring tribute to women of African origin, women he believed the White world enjoyed insulting and ridiculing, women who suffered in silence.

Much of Du Bois's work addressed the need to reclaim a lost history. Thus, he dealt directly with issues of identity and memory. Du Bois realized that visuals could greatly aid him in the development of his audience and in better expressing the political and social issues of the day. He used original artwork, cartoons, drawings, and photography to support editorials and essays on the questions of his day: lynching, war, education, women and children, labor, racism and prejudice, and a new relationship with Africa. He used the covers of *The Crisis* to entice readers to open the magazine and explore the contents. Visuals could tell a more poignant story to his audience.

In 1903, Du Bois stated that the Negro race (like all races) "is going to be saved by its exceptional men. . . . Can the masses of the Negro people be in any way more quickly raised than by the effort and example of this aristocracy of talent and character? Was there ever a nation on God's fair earth civilized from the bottom upward? Never; is it, ever was and ever will be from the top downward that culture filters." Du Bois believed that only the best and brightest of the race, which he referred to as the "Talented Tenth," could and should lead the race into the twentieth century, and that part of their duty was to propagate high culture. Art in *The Crisis* was a part of that process, part of the expression of the "Talented Tenth," serving to educate from the top down.

Du Bois's goal of helping his community remember its past took place in a social environment that was hostile to that project. As Mitch Kachun has noted, "During the generation after the 1870s, Black Americans concerned with the race's historical memory grew increasingly frustrated by their inability to alter White America's racial ideology or Whites' refusal to acknowledge the Black presence in the nation's history and culture." Yet Du Bois knew that keeping memory of the past (including that of the Civil War) alive within the Black community and among progressive Whites was a primary tool in the fight against racism and oppression. Du Bois did not want the pain of the past to overshadow hope for the future; he wanted the lessons of the past to be applied to the harsh realities of the present. *The Crisis* was the primary tool for such an endeavor.

Women as Leaders and Illustrators: The Art of Social Justice

The 1924 cover of the issue dedicated to the memory of lynching victims was done by Laura Wheeler and entitled "Lest We Forget" (see Figure 1). The title flanks either side of the illustration, and the lettering is meant to resemble woodblock letters in the arts and crafts style. The illustration is framed in a simple black outline and contains the image of Abraham Lincoln in silhouette, shown deep in thought. Lincoln faces several Klansmen, including a crowned Ku Klux Klan (KKK) member whose skeleton hands reach from his long white robe. This Klansman holds a scepter in his left hand, and a small figure of a lynched Black man dangles from his right hand. A woman in a black robe bends in half, overcome with grief, at the feet of Lincoln, her hands covering her face. It is the woman who is used by Wheeler to express the full sorrow of the lynching.

Figure 1 – *The Crisis* February 1924

Du Bois was concerned about the plight of the women artists who worked at the journal. He knew that their opportunities for training and patrons were even scarcer than those of their male counterparts. Most American artists who hoped for proper training during this time went to Paris to study. This was difficult for a woman to engineer. They had few opportunities to exhibit their work, and receive payment for their art. He cited sculptor Meta Warrick Fuller as an example of an artist who had recently created a beautiful piece of work for the betterment of the Black race, even though she was not paid for her work. With little opportunity for training and sales, the plight of the African American female artist was a lonely one. Those who were fortunate enough to study abroad also faced discrimination. When Meta Fuller went to study in Paris, she was denied access to a women's youth hostel due to her race. Artists like Fuller who ultimately combined career with motherhood (she had three children) found that society did not support a woman with a career and family. Finding buyer for her work was a constant struggle. Working in a small space with marble dust and poor ventilation, her health suffered. Initially, Fuller resisted advice from Du Bois to create works about her own race; she found it too limiting. Ultimately she turned to her race and womanhood as a primary inspiration for her career.

Other sculptors faced similar challenges. Sculptor May Howard Jackson did not receive adequate compensation for her portrait busts. Artists like the sculptor Elizabeth Prophet, whom Du Bois spotlighted in *The Crisis* December 1929 issue, had sacrificed their wealth and health to create Black art for a Black audience. While studying in Paris, Prophet was so poor, frail, and hungry that it compromised her ability to sculpt. Prophet struggled with a lack of support from her family. Her parents wanted her to marry and have children.

The desire to connect Africa to America can be seen in Laura Wheeler's "Africa in America" of June 1924 (see Figure 2). She uses a torso in the Amarna style of the Eighteenth Dynasty of traditional Egyptian art as the prototype for her shapely figure, a sculpture often identified as Nefertiti. In the Amarna-style sculptures of Nefertiti, the sculpted fabric clings to the queen's body, revealing her pubic triangle. In her characteristic black-and-white style, with only a few details of the human form, Wheeler creates a voluptuous woman, clad with a sheer garment that reveals all the lines of her body as if she were nude, adorned with jewelry, including wrist and armbands, earrings, necklaces, and a ceremonial headpiece. The numerous bracelets are not typically Egyptian, nor is her necklace, which is not the usual broad collar piece. Wheeler combines different elements of African art and is not true to one style. The woman carries a covered urn on her shoulder. Behind her is a map of the Atlantic ocean with a ship crossing in full sail, a symbol of the Middle Passage and the long and harrowing journey from Africa to slavery in the Americas. The figure is strong and erect, proud and lovely. She is a symbol of Africans brought to America against their will who still retain their African heritage.

Figure 2 – *The Crisis* June 1924

Wheeler's cover connected to a long article in which Du Bois discussed the opportunities available to Black Americans who wanted to migrate to Africa. He noted that *The Crisis* periodically received requests from readers who sought advice concerning such migration. Here Du Bois recognized the hardships connected to emigration. He discouraged his readers from emigrating, including those who hoped for work, since Africa had an abundance of skilled and unskilled laborers. "There is a magnificent chance for pioneers but the point is, pioneering is a far different thing from going to work in a fully developed land" (*The Crisis,* June 1924, p. 58), he wrote. Liberia needed professionals—physicians, dentists, and nurses. The "spiritual harvest of practical missionary work would in the end be far greater than we can now dream" (*The Crisis,* June 1924, p. 58). Du Bois also noted how polite the "natives" were to each other, both young and old. "I have often thought, when I see the awkward and ignorant missionaries sometimes sent to teach the heathen, that it would be an excellent thing if a few natives could be sent here to teach manners to Black and White" (*The Crisis,* June 1924, p. 58)

As a statement about racism, Du Bois included James Weldon Johnson's "To America" in November 1917. The poem was accompanied by a drawing by Laura Wheeler of six youthful figures in classical chitons or togas around a statue. These figures were typically used to symbolize White European high culture, but these figures are Black (see Figure 3). Johnson's poem is superimposed on the image:

> How would you have us, as we are
> Or sinking 'neath the load we bear
> Our eyes fixed forward on a star
> Or gazing empty at despair?
>
> Rising or falling? Men or things?
> With dragging pace or footsteps fleet?
> Strong willing sinew in your wings?
> Or tightening chains about your feet?

The Artists

Little is known about the artists who illustrated for *The Crisis*, although a few women artists, life and body of art are well documented. Waring, born Laura Wheeler in Hartford, Connecticut, was Du Bois's most frequently featured woman artist

Figure 3 – *The Crisis* November 1917

on the pages of *The Crisis*. The daughter and granddaughter of ministers, Waring recalled that even as a young child she delighted in visiting the art galleries of Hartford, not only for the joy of an outing but also because she loved the paintings, the colors, and the beauty of the galleries. She always loved to paint and draw, and her parents often joined their children in these activities. Both her parents, especially her mother, had some artistic talent. Waring was dedicated to becoming the best artist she could possibly be and pursued that dream tenaciously. She received teacher training at the Cheyney Training School for Teachers at the State Normal School in Cheyney, Pennsylvania. When the family fell on hard times, Laura took responsibility for the younger children. She needed to work, and this took away from her chance to paint. She managed to spend summers studying "the teaching of drawing" at Harvard and Columbia, among other places.

In 1924, Waring made her second of three trips to Europe and went to France to study painting with Boutet de Monvel and Prinet at the well-respected *Academie de la Grand Chaumiere* in Paris. Waring called this the "only period of uninterrupted life as an artist with an environment and associates that were a constant stimulus and inspiration" (Waring, Nov. 12, 1928). She kept in contact with Du Bois while studying in Europe. She wrote a letter to him indicating her dissatisfaction with the low pay and sometimes the lack of pay for the illustrations she provided from Paris. She noted the cost of postage and paper and expressed her discomfort about telling Du Bois this information (Waring, Oct. 1, 1923). Clearly *The Crisis* was working on a tight budget. She even met Du Bois for dinner once when he visited Paris. Upon her return home, she studied under Henry McCarty at the Pennsylvania Academy of Fine Arts. After six months of studying at the academy, Waring won a Cresson Traveling Scholarship, which allowed her to spend three months in Paris to "study in the great galleries of Europe."

In 1927, at the urging of friends, she entered her work in a contest sponsored by the Harmon Foundation and listed Henry O. Tanner as a reference on her application. The Harmon Foundation was established in 1922 by a White businessman to recognize achievements by African Americans. The foundation was the first of its kind to offer juried exhibitions of African American art. She won a first-place Harmon Foundation medal and a prize award of $400 that year, followed by a bronze medal from the Harmon Foundation in 1930. Waring wrote to a supporter that this was the busiest time of her life. For six months, she studied and worked on her art at the Pennsylvania Academy of Fine Arts, usually seven days a week.

Waring was interested in furthering the chances of other artists to receive support and patronage from organizations such as the Harmon Foundation. She wrote to William E. Harmon in January 1928 to express her deep gratitude for the chance she had been given by the foundation. She emphasized the important impact these awards had on artists and explained that she was writing him "only to testify that these results were real." She explained to Harmon that she had spent so much time teaching to support herself that she had little opportunity to devote to her art. But the Harmon Foundation award had given her "this stamp of approval on my work. I have the assurance to decide to give up nearly all of my teaching next year and devote the major part of my time to painting" (Waring, Jan. 26, 1928). Waring reassured Harmon that she planned to make a record of "interesting characters of the American Negro in paint" (Waring, Jan. 26, 1928) and that she had been invited to bring the exhibit to Paris when it was finished. She hoped to use the exhibit to "create more interest in inter-racial identity" (Waring, Jan. 26, 1928). Waring's work was exhibited in such notable locations as the New York Water Color Club, the Corcoran Gallery of Art in Washington, the Chicago Art Institute, the Pennsylvania Academy of Fine Arts, and numerous private venues.

Waring faced the same problems that all African American artists encountered in the United States during this decades—that of finding funding and patronage to support her training and work. In a reference letter for a Guggenheim Fellowship, supporter Dr. George Haynes wrote that Waring had "become more enthusiastic about the idea of devoting more time and attention to the searching out and portrayal of Negro types" after winning the Harmon Gold Award. Haynes explained to the committee that Waring's main handicap was the fact that she had to spend most of her time teaching. "I believe a year or two with freedom to travel and see various Negro types, with time to devote her undivided time and energy to painting them, would give outlet to her ambition in this direction and doubtless result in some permanent contribution to the Fine Arts" (Haynes, 1928).

Waring's portraits of women or children and drawings of African life appeared frequently on the pages of *The Crisis* during Du Bois's years as editor. Some of the art in *The Crisis* stood alone; Waring's art usually illustrated a particular essay or poem. Her work accompanied the writings of Georgia Douglas Johnson, James Weldon Johnson, and Jessie Fauset, among others. Waring did not create political cartoons for the journal.

Painter Vivian Schuyler Key was another female artist who did work for Du Bois. She was born in Hempstead, Long Island, in 1905 and graduated high school in 1923 with honors, as one of two Black graduates. She attended Pratt Institute for art training at the considerable sacrifice of her family. Key recalled her three years at the Pratt Institute, where she commuted from Hempstead to Brooklyn every morning:

> They were very difficult years, years which I will never forget. I was the only colored person and the poorest one in my class. I was too conscious of my poor clothes and empty pocketbook. I had to forego many lunches for a brush or tube of paint. I was very retiring and very lonely. I loved the work however and did well in my classes, so I never once thought of quitting. I was encouraged by most of my instructors to keep going. (Hanes, 1928)

Evenings after school were spent doing her homework by oil lamp, drawing and painting at the big dining-room table. Vivian spent so many sleepless nights working in the cold house that she contracted a series of colds and a severe case of bronchitis from which she never fully recovered. Schuyler married her husband, William Key, in 1929. She had little opportunity to paint, although she did design textiles and painted china gifts to sell. Her husband provided her little support for her career; this fact and her duties as a mother made her efforts to paint even more of a challenge.

Schuyler contributed several drawings and covers for *The Crisis* and won the Amy Spingarn Art Award. The Amy Spingarn Art Award was established in 1921 by the Spingarn family and awarded through *The Crisis* magazine to an artist of "Negro descent, in order to encourage their aptitude for artistic expression" (Heyd, 1999, p. 7). Schuyler also exhibited with the Harmon Foundation. Du Bois saw her work after being introduced to her by musician Minnie Brown and artist Aaron Douglas.

Key hoped to exhibit at the International House annual exhibition in 1930 and thus applied for a Harmon Award for distinguished achievement, hoping it might improve her chances (Key, 1930). She noted in her International House application letter that she might not appear to be distinguished but that she was capable of doing something "very great." Her need to make a living, her modest upbringing, and the limits in her training had hampered her efforts, but she was determined to continue. She faced discrimination against her gender and lamented that it was her "misfortune to be born a girl, a thing which I have regretted even though I have recently married" (Key, 1930). Her greatest desire was to please her hardworking mother and to become a success in her mother's eyes. While Key was never famous, she was a respected artist among the small circle of illustrators working for *The Crisis*.

Women as Subjects: Expressing the Need for Change

The artists of *The Crisis* used the image of women to express some of the more difficult issues of the day and the extreme emotions associated with those issues. A January 1911 cartoon called "The National Pastime" by John Henry Adams is particularly moving. It features a grieving Black woman, her head down on the desk, holding a newspaper, with the headlines, "Negro Lynched: Brute Struck White Man, Made Confession" and "American People Love Justice and Fair Play" (see Figure 4). Her hair is wrapped in a kerchief or mantle, making her more vulnerable, even tying her to the image of Mary, mother of Jesus. Within the cartoon, positioned next to the woman is the framed portrait of a respectable Black man dressed in a coat and tie as the image of an upstanding and fine citizen. The caption below reads, "Seventy-five per cent of Negroes Lynched have not even been accused of rape." This was a reference to the research of Ida B. Wells, who had made it her life's work to prove that in fact, lynchers rarely accused their victims of rape, even though rape and alleged violence against women were the primary excuses for a lynching. Booker T. Washington also often cited this in his attacks on lynching. Wells demanded in 1892 that the White press stop printing the lie that Negro men rape White women (Wells, 1892). Wells noted that innocent people were often marked for lynching because they were related to another lynching victim or solely because of their race.

Some political cartoons also encouraged readers to seek out higher education in order to escape menial positions. The September 1913 issue features a cartoon by Lorenzo Harris showing a young Black woman working in a kitchen, her arm grabbed firmly and forcefully by a White employer wearing a suit and bow

Figure 4 – *The Crisis* January 1911

tie and sporting a goatee (see Figure 5). Here Harris employs the visual vocabulary of the Southern figure that was often utilized by Black illustrators; he has "Confederate" attributes, including a goatee, handlebar mustache, long jacket, and soft bow tie, symbols of a Southern "gentleman." He holds the woman prisoner across a kitchen table, a fierce look on his face, the knuckle of his left hand grounding his power, pushing into the table. The text reads, "The New Education in the South: Domestic Science for Colored Girls Only." The implications are obvious—the South wanted to confine Black women to roles of domestic servitude. If the South had its way, that would be their future, the only education worth pursuing. The reader was clearly supposed to find inspiration to escape such a fate by pursuing education. The woman in the drawing is fearful; the readers of *The Crisis* were reminded of the difficult positions African American women had to face in such domestic service.

The Crisis often featured special issues dedicated to education and noted the important roles African American women played in the Black community, as teachers. One of the more noteworthy education covers featured a composition by Charles C. Dawson (see Figure 6). It shows two figures. One is young Black man wear-

Figure 5 – *The Crisis* September 1913

THE NEW EDUCATION IN THE SOUTH: "DOMESTIC SCIENCE FOR COLORED GIRLS ONLY."

Figure 6 – *The Crisis* August 1927

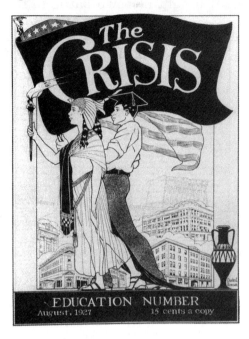

ing a mortar board and carrying the banner of *The Crisis* with an American flag partially exposed behind it. In front of him is a young woman in Egyptian dress with the nemes headdress, holding a torch. She ties the student to the past of African history and culture via Egypt and leads him to the future. A traditional classical vase flanks the right side of the page. Several buildings, institutions of higher education and financial institutions, make up the background of the piece. Here the artist is saying that African American young people needed to be grounded in their cultural roots as well as formal education.

Crisis artists often emphasized the important role of motherhood, and the strength of Black women. The idea of the mother as a protector is particularly poignant in John Henry Adams's cartoon, "Woman to the Rescue!" in the May 1916 issue (see Figure 7). A woman raises a large club while her two young children, a boy and girl, cling to her long skirts. The club, labeled "Federal Constitution," is swinging at horrible birds that swoop down to attack her and her children. She attempts to beat off the advances of "Jim Crow Law," "Segregation," "Grand-Father Clause," "Seduction," and "Mob." A Black man in a traditional Southern suit and top hat runs away. His caption reads,

> I don't believe in agitating and fighting. My policy is to pursue the line of least resistance. To h— with Citizenship Rights. I want money. I think the White folk will let me stay on my land as long as I stay in my place . . . (Shades of Wilmington, N.C.).[1] The good Whites ain't responsible for bad administration of the law and lynching and peonage, let me think awhile, er—.

The Black woman battles the forces of evil alone, with no support from the Black male. She will fight her own battle to the end.

Lynching remained a constant topic on the pages of the magazine. The February 1923 issue of *The Crisis* included a special section entitled "The Shame of America." It listed state-by-state lynching statistics for 1922, as well as statistics about the means of violent death for African Americans other than lynching (burn-

Figure 7 – *The Crisis* May 1916

WOMAN TO THE RESCUE!

[1] "Wilmington, N.C." refers to the overthrow of an elected black government and to the brutal attack on black business owners in Wilmington, North Carolina, in 1898.

Figure 8 – *The Crisis* February 1923

ings, beatings, shootings, torture, drownings) complete with graphic photographs of several lynchings. These were placed next to a cartoon with a moving image of the crucifixion (see Figure 8). It features a Black Christ figure with "American Negro" written inside the halo over his head. Skeletons are piled up at his feet with the words "Crucified, Murdered, Lynched," next to them. A woman covers her face in sorrow and horror like Mary, mother of Jesus, but this time she is "A Black Mother," as the words on the side of her apron inform us. The Christian iconography was familiar and recognizable, reinterpreted to connect lynching to the death of Christ and the actions of "Christians." This imagery worked on many levels. It connected the crime of lynching to a central truth of Christianity, merging African American identity and religiosity together. It also painfully underlined the horror of lynching to sympathetic White Christians, again affirming the power of imagery over simple text. The issue included a full-page statement in support of the Dyer Anti-Lynching Bill.

Aaron Douglas was one of Du Bois's favorite artists. Douglas often used women to express the sorrows and strengths of the Black community. Douglas's life-long connection with Du Bois would greatly influence his art, including his images of women. Douglas provided the September 1927 cover, "The Burden of Black Womanhood," which is the ideal image of the African American woman in charge (see Figure 9). This composition includes the figure of a woman in a long, Egyptian-influenced garment. We see a side view of her hips and a silhouette of the front of her body. She holds up a round shape, "The World." She looks up, with face in profile and slit eyes that resemble African masks of the Ivory Coast, a style frequently employed by

Douglas. Her lined hair recalls the headdress of the nemes. She has been called an "Afro-Deco Caryatid"—a new variation on the ancient figure of a woman serving as an architectural support, utilized in classical Greek architecture. (This term was coined by Dr. Richard Powell of Duke University.) A cityscape is included below, resembling art deco drawings of skyscrapers, with the billowing smoke of industry behind it. One simple cabin, perhaps representing her humble beginnings, is on the far right. On the left, we see three pyramids and a palm tree, perhaps indicating her origins. Papyrus blossoms in outline, with a deco handling, are scattered in the composition. The woman bears the burdens of the world; the image appealed directly to the female audience of *The Crisis*.

Figure 9 – *The Crisis* September 1927

Social realist, cubist-inspired, art deco and modernist art appeared on the pages of *The Crisis* magazine. The artists of *The Crisis* were not merely illustrators; many were fully engaged in modernist movements. The artists, under the direction of Du Bois, openly dealt with the issues of racism, education, labor, war, and women's issues, with rich visuals to elucidate the magazine's political agenda.

Through the art and written word in *The Crisis,* Du Bois hammered home to his readers the need for a strong sense of identity and the need to record history accurately, to take the power of history-telling away from the White majority. Unless history was told accurately, the mistakes of the past would be repeated. As Du Bois said, "One is astonished in the study of history at the recurrence of the idea that evil must be forgotten, distorted, skimmed over. . . . The difficulty of course, with this philosophy is that history loses its value as an incentive and example; it paints perfect men and noble nations, but it does not tell the truth." (1935, p. 722)

The artists of *The Crisis* undertook the telling of truth under the direction and inspiration of Du Bois, joining readers through common hope and common sorrow in a collective African American identity and creating their own authentic historical memory. It was a singular and important achievement, a tribute to what David Levering Lewis has called an "avatar of the race." As Du Bois put it 1921, "We Americans have settled the race problem and will not have our settlement tampered with. The truth of Art tampers. That is its mission" (1921).

Women played a vital part in this process of truth telling, of expressing the need for social justice. As artists and as subjects on the pages of *The Crisis,* women artists played a strong leadership role in defining the direction and presentation of *Crisis* magazine.

References

Du Bois, W.E.B., (1935). *Black reconstruction: An essay toward a history of the part which Black folk played in the attempt to reconstruct democracy in America, 1860-1880*. New York: Harcourt Brace & Co..

Du Bois, W. E. B (1921, February 23) "The Shadow," *New Republic.*

Du Bois, W. E. B. (1997). *The Souls of Black Folk.* Boston: Bedford Books.

Du Bois, W. E. B. (1975). "The Damnation of women," *Darkwater: Voice from within the veil.* Millwood, NY: Kraus-Thompson.

Haynes, G. E. (1928, November 12). Support letter for Laura Wheeler Waring for a Guggenheim Fellowship, Harmon Foundation Papers, Box 43.

Heyd, M. (1999). *Mutual reflections: Jews and Black in American art.* New Brunswick: Rutgers.

Kachun, M. (1998). Before the eyes of all nations: African American identity and historical memory at the Centennial Exposition of 1876. *Pennsylvania History 65*(3), 321-322.

Key, V. S. (1930). Biographical statement. Harmon Foundation Papers, Box 48.

The Crisis. (1917, November). 13.

The Crisis. (1923, February). The Shame of America. 168-169

The Crisis. On migrating to Africa. (June, 1924). 58

Waldrep, C. (1892). The War of Words: The controversy over the Definition of lynching, 1899-1940. In I. B. Wells (Ed.), *Southern horrors: Lynch law in all its phases* (pp. 75-100). New York: New York Age Print.

Waring, L. (1928, November 12). Artist's statement for a Guggenheim Fellowship, , Harmon Foundation Papers, Box 45.

Waring, L. (1923, October 1). Letter to Du Bois, , W. E. B. Du Bois Papers, Library of Congress.

Waring, L. (1928, January 26). Letter to William E. Harmon. Harmon Foundation Papers, Box 45.

Resistance and Affirmation:
Teaching Spanish in the U.S. Academy

Yolanda Flores
University of Vermont

Spanish in the United States

"Estamos Open" read a hastily made cardboard advertisement outside a furniture store on Thanksgiving Day this past November 2008 in my native hometown of Bakersfield, California. This bilingual announcement signaled more than just a cute linguistic phrase aimed at luring potential shoppers on a quintessential national holiday; it signaled the merging of cultures. On the one hand, the announcement suggested the recognition of the national holiday (Otherwise, there is no need to advertise that, contrary to most commercial establishments, the furniture store is open). On the other hand, the recognition of the holiday does not prevent this establishment from remaining open, even if it is a national day of rest.

In varying degrees according to the geographical location in which the reader may find her/himself, the evidence of the omnipresence of the Spanish language is everywhere: in the names of cities, the automated ATM and telephone options "Para español, oprima el número dos," the radio and tv airways, in the bits of conversations we overhear on the street, etc. Still, few outside of academic circles know that the United States is the fifth largest Spanish-speaking country in the world. And whether we trace the origins of this linguistic presence to the Spanish explorers who arrived in Florida in the sixteenth century, the Spanish-American War (1846-1848), the first massive flight of Mexicans to United States during the Mexican Revolution of 1910, or the more recent wave of immigrants from Latin America in the 1980s, the fact remains the same: Spanish is the second language in the United States.

Education for members of historically racialized communities in the United States has always been a vehicle for achieving empowerment. Knowledge is power. Education is necessary for critiquing hierarchical, hegemonic constructions of knowledge.

Civil-rights-educated academics of color have intuitively known that the production and dissemination of knowledge are political acts intimately linked with the advancement of equity and social justice. For example, research centered on studying the differences between white faculty and faculty of color has concluded that faculty of color are 63 percent more likely than are white faculty to pursue a position in the academy because they draw a connection between the professoriate and the ability to affect change; that is, they use their talents for the cause of social change (A. L. Antonio). While cognizant of the limitations of grouping all faculty members of color into one single monolithic category, one that would carry the indirect, false implication that all faculty of color share a common identity politics, one inspired by a commitment to social change, I admit that for me, the pursue of higher education has always been liked with an underlying search for equity and social justice.

I am a Chicana of working-class background born in California's San Joaquin Valley, the state's central agricultural heartland, the birthplace of the farm workers union, and the rural segment of activism that composed the Chicano Civil Rights Movement of the late 1960s and 1970s. These are personal, cultural, and historical markers that have propelled my desire to pursue higher education and become a university professor. To this date, I continue to use my status as a professor to work in research, pedagogies, and service projects that advance social justice. Moreover, my field of choice for graduate studies was a personal political response to California's passing an amendment pushed by conservatives to dictate English as the only language in which to conduct all state affairs: Proposition 63, 1986. This amendment to California's State Constitution, Article III, Section 6 reads:

> English is the official language of California. The Legislature shall enforce this section by appropriate legislation and officials of the State of California shall take all steps necessary to insure that the role of English as the common language of the state of California is preserved and enhanced. The legislature shall make no law which diminishes or ignores the role of English as the common language of the state of California." (Charles V. Dale and Mark Gurevitz).

As an undergraduate student at UC Berkeley, I completed a double major in History and Spanish. Until 1986, the year prior to my completing of my undergraduate degree and the year Proposition 63 was approved, I had planned to pursue graduate studies in history, not Spanish. The passage of Proposition 63 changed that original intention for me. As a student of history, I knew that Spanish, not English, was the first European language spoken in the United States. In addition, I knew that Spanish, not English, was the dominant language of the most vulnerable segments of the Mexican American community, the agricultural workers and other recent immigrants who did not master the English language well enough to navigate the legal, social, and political spheres necessary to participate in a civic, public life; in other words, to become fully recognized, protected, and responsible citizens. Prior to the 1960s, it was not uncommon to be a second, or third generation Mexican American and still have limited schooling or, by the standards of this country, to be considered largely illiterate. Drawing from personal experience and anecdotes that I will place in dialogue with recent research on this topic, my purpose in this essay is to shed light on the miniscule presence of faculty of color, more specifically of U.S. born Mexican-Americans or Chicanos/as and other U.S. born Latinos/as, teaching Spanish in the American academy.

The paucity of minority faculty members teaching Spanish in higher education might potentially have adverse consequences. One of them is the negative response of Spanish language purists "authorities" to a minority student population whose "home" language is both English and Spanish; their cultural identity is precisely the mixture of two or more languages and cultures. A second potentially negative effect is the extreme isolation and lack of a community of support to the lone faculty of color engaged in pedagogical practices that challenge academic practices of internal colonialism, imperialism, and racism.

Without this segment of minority faculty in academia constantly intervening to challenge the hegemonic, invariably hierarchical constructions and dissemination of knowledge, the entire higher education enterprise runs the risk of becoming a powerful tool to maintain an unequal, unfair, and unbalanced social status quo—in and outside of the academy.

I distinguish between U.S. Latinos/as and those born in Latin American and Spain because U.S. born-Latinos have a different experiential affiliation with the Spanish language, one that often carries layers of sentiments of resistance, affirmation, and anti-imperialism based on the way U.S. Latinos have been historically racialized in this country. In the United States, the history of racialization that Chicanos and other U.S.-born Latinos/as have undergone has always been more complex than just physical traits—language itself has become a prominent feature in the construction of U.S. Latinos/as' "otherness" and status as second-class citizens. I wish to focus on language, on Spanish, because it is an aspect often neglected in academic discussions that promote the advancement of social justice. Furthermore, for the civil-rights'-inspired, politically-aware U.S. Latina/o scholar, teaching Spanish language and cultures is a fruitful and important site for the contestation of hierarchical, imperialistic, and colonizing constructions and presentations of knowledge. Thus, in this essay, one of my goals is to suggest that in order to advance a more comprehensive social justice agenda, one that begins in the academy but whose ramifications might go beyond the cloisters of university campuses, there needs to be a stronger effort to attract and retain U.S.-born Latinos and other faculty of color to teach the "other" language of the United States—Spanish.

Chicanos as People of Color in the Academy

Unlike African Americans who can trace and cherish a long list of postgraduate-educated writers, scholars, and leaders who obtained national recognition as early as the 19th century; this is not the case for Chicanos or Mexican Americans—the oldest group of Spanish-speaking Latinos in the United States. It was only after the political activism of the Chicano civil rights movement that the doors of higher education were opened to large numbers of Mexican-Americans. As a matter of fact, Tomás Rivera's autobiographical ...Y no se lo tragó la tierra, the novel literary scholars consider to be the first to begin the Chicano literary canon, was only published in 1975. Although Tomás Rivera had earned a Ph.D. in Spanish literature and was, at the time of the publication of his novel, a Spanish literature university professor, he wrote ...Y no se lo tragó la tierra in a Chicano variation of Texan Spanish.

To depict the lives and struggles of the 1950s Texan, Mexican American farm workers on their annual, seasonal migrations to the Midwest, Rivera believed he had to write his novel in the language that reflected the reality of the community he depicted in it. As is the case with Tomás Rivera, the first wave of Chicano literary scholars to enter the academy and obtain national recognition received their Ph.D. training in Spanish, not English departments. For example, María Herrera-Sobek, Diana Tey Rebolledo, Juan Bruce Novoa, and Norma Alarcón are members of this first generation of Chicano literary scholars who were trained in Spanish Ph.D. programs. These pioneering Chicano literary scholars believe in the importance of the Spanish language as a form of cultural and professional resistance to the dominant English language and a strategy of cultural affirmation, particularly given that the academy at that time had largely ignored the historical presence and contributions of the Chicano/a population in the United States.

In her 1987 classic theoretical text, *Borderlands / La Frontera, The New Mestiza,* Gloria Anzaldúa predicted, "By the end of this century, English, and not Spanish, will be the mother tongue of most Chicanos and Latinos" (Anzaldúa, 1987). Given the rise of Spanish as the second national language that I discussed at the beginning of this essay, Gloria Anzaldúa's prediction might seem completely off the mark. And yet, it is not, in particular as it reflects the number of U.S. born Chicanos and U.S. Latinos in higher education. While studies indicate that the number of Hispanis/Latinos who earned Ph.D.s is slightly higher in the foreign languages than in English, my experience contradicts this data (Stewart, 2006).

In the five years I spent as an undergraduate student, my year at the University of Chicago earning my first M.A. in Spanish Literature, and my six years earning a second M.A. and a Ph.D. at Cornell University, not once did I have a Chicano or U.S.-Latino-born professor or any other type American minority professor in any discipline, not even in Spanish! During my year at the University of Chicago, I met a classmate of Puerto Rican extraction who was born in the mainland. She is the only other fellow U. S.-born Latina who had also earned her Ph.D. in Spanish literature during my entire seven years of postgraduate education.

During my six years at Cornell, I met Puerto Rican graduate students born and raised on the island. Puerto Ricans, regardless of whether they were born, in the island or the mainland, are U.S. citizens, and hence, are a large constituency of the U.S. Latino/a population, However, Puerto Ricans born on the island, especially those upper-middle class who are able to gain admission to Ivy League institutions, are culturally Caribbean or Latin American and often do not share with Chicanos and Puerto Ricans born on the mainland the history and political consciousness of being a racialized minority in the United States. During my academic training at Cornell, I met four Chicanas earning their Ph.D. in English (Only three completed the program) and one in history. In 1995, the year I completed my Ph.D., I became the first Chicano/a to earn a Ph.D. in Cornell's Department of Romance Studies.

Fourteen years have passed since completing my doctorate studies; I still remain the only Chicana to have earned a Ph.D. from this department. At Cornell, Anzaldúa's prediction, that by the end of the twentieth century English and not Spanish would be the language of the Chicano/Latino population, did, indeed, reflect the reality of the few Chicanas/os completing Ph.D. degrees at this Ivy League institution. All four Chicanas in the English Department at Cornell were raised in an English, monolingual environment; the little Spanish these women spoke they learned in college. While generational longevity may account for this shift in favor of the English language, the origins of this trend, it seems to me, are multilayered, involving but not limited to class origins, levels of cultural assimilation, and the presence or lack of an identity inspired by the ideals of contestation and resistance to the dominant culture.

While this anecdotal evidence might lead one to believe that Chicano and other U.S.-Latino literatures are incorporated into the American literary cannon because they are taught in English and under the auspices of English departments, this is not the case in some institutions. When Chicano literature began to be incorporated into academic literature programs, Spanish programs were much more receptive than English departments to hiring faculty members to teach this field. In some ways, this made a lot of sense. On the one hand, most of the Chicano and other U.S.-Latino literature produced in this country prior to 1950 are written in Spanish. It is worthy, for instance, to remember that Rivera's canonical Chicano text ...*Y no se lo trago la tierra*, was written in 1970 in Spanish.

However, since the 1980s, the largest component of literature written in the United States by Chicanos and other U.S.-Latino/a group is written almost entirely in English, with a few words of Spanish sprinkled on the text. Even if these works contain words in Spanish, Chicano, and other U.S.-Latino/literatures belong to the American literary cannon and should be taught in English departments, just as Asian American literature is. For example at Cornell and Chapman University (a private, liberal arts college in Southern California, where I secured my first tenure-track position), I taught U.S.-Latino/a literature for the English departments of these institutions, even though I had earned my Ph.D. in Romance Studies. At my present institution, I teach U.S.-Latina/o literature under the rubric of world literature, the same category under which Russian literature in translation is taught.In contrast, Asian American literature is taught under the auspice of the English Department and, hence, is unquestionably part of the American literary cannon. U.S.-Latino literature is still not, even if it is written and taught in English.

Hispanics/Latinos –People of color?: Teaching Spanish in the U.S. Academy

Once I began my professional career as a university professor in Spanish, I continued to witness the paucity of Chicanos and other racialized U.S. Latino/as entering the profession. In the fourteen years since completing my doctoral degree, I have served in five search committees aiming to recruit a Spanish professor. Each time more than 250 applications have been reviewed each time by the search committee. Of a roughly estimated 1,250 applications that I have examined in the last fourteen years, I recall encountering no more than four or five candidates who could potentially be Chicanos or other type of Latinos born in the United States. In each of these five searches, no U.S born Latino/a was hired to fulfill the open position: What explains, then, the higher number of Hispanics/Latinos earning doctoral degrees in the foreign languages that I cited earlier in this essay?

One major aspect that illuminates this apparent contradiction lies in way university administrations conflate individuals with a Spanish surname with the designation of Hispanic or Latino. These terms are generally used interchangeably. Hispanic refers to Hispania, to Spain. It includes all people with Spanish last names, whether they speak Spanish or not, whether they are white, brown, or black. The term Latino/a is generally used to refer to individuals of Latin American origin or descent. As author Cherrie Moraga notes, "Latinos in the United States do not represent a homogenous group. Some of us are native born, whose ancestors precede not only the arrival of the Anglo-American but also of the Spaniard...U.S.-Latinos represent the whole spectrum of color, class, and political position" (Moraga, 1993). Moraga is defining U.S.-Latinos based on a shared life experience in the United States—those born in other countries but who immigrated to this country as children, and, thus, have experience their life as U.S. Latinos (not as native citizens of Argentine or Mexico).

In order to increase the number of "minority" faculty member and, hence, create the false image of a diverse professoriate, university administrations often do not distinguish between U.S.-Latinos and citizens of Chile or Spain, for example, who pursue graduate studies in this country and, upon completion of their Ph.D. programs, decide to pursue a university teaching and research career in the United States. Most university administrations are only too eager to easily fulfill their "diversity" slogan, and because the ethnicity of an individual born and raised in Peru or Spain is Latino or Hispanic, there is no attempt to search for a U.S.-Latino candidate. There are great differences between a Mexican American and a Mexican national who came to this country to pursue graduate work and who decided to stay in this country after the completion of her graduate program. Because of common life experience as an historically racialized minority of this country, Mexican-Americans will align with other U.S. racialized groups—with other people of color.

Spanish and Latin Americans who immigrate to this country as adults do not share with U.S. Latinos a history of belonging to a U.S. racialized minority. They do not see themselves as people of color, and they lack the political consciousness that comes with a personal history of a racialized experience in the United States. Most often these Latin American and Spanish individuals who immigrate to this country to pursue graduate school are from the elite, educated, upper, -middle-class. European and Latin American elites are the dominant cultural, political, economic, and social groups; they are not the marginalized, colored, and disenfranchised segments of their countries of origin. Because the legacies of colonialism and racism have served the advancement of these elites in their mother countries, these individuals, transplanted to a North American context, lack the political consciousness and the desire to effect social change and seek social justice in all aspects that permeate their professional life—teaching, research, and service. Rather, these elites tend to fit rather well with the status quo.

Perhaps this explains why American universities favor, in their hiring practices and in their graduate program admissions process, foreign-born over U.S. born Latinos/as. Similarly, this trend extends to the preference of Africans and Asians over African Americans and Asian Americans. The foreign born are perceived as more docile and less likely to use their professional status to further an agenda of social justice—one that has ramifications beyond the immediate academic context.

Yet another level of difference between a U. S. Latino and a Spanish or Latin American individual who pursues a doctorate degree to become a Spanish professor in the United States is the particular association U.S. Latinos have with the Spanish language. Unlike the Latin American or Spanish person who grows up speaking the dominant language of their country (Spanish), this is not the case for U.S.-born Latinos. For the latter group, if Spanish is spoken at all at home, it is more than likely some variation of Spanglish. Chicana cultural theorist Gloria Anzaldua writes in *La Frontera / Borderlands*,

> For a people who are neither Spanish nor live in a country in which Spanish is the first language; for a people who live in a country in which English is the reining tongue but who are not Anglo; for a people who cannot entirely identify with either Standard (formal, Castilian) Spanish nor standard English, what recourse is left to them but to create their own language? A language they can connect their identity to, one capable of communicating the realities and values true to themselves—a language with terms that are neither espanol ni ingles, but both. We speak a patois, a forked tongue, a variation of two languages. (Anzaldúa, 1987)

For politically aware U.S. Latinos, some variation of Spanglish is not only the language that is true to their life experience and identity but is also a form of cultural resistance to both—standard Spanish and English.

Yet within the academy, forms of Spanish that do not fit the standard model are shunned upon and seen as deficient. The U.S.-Latino individual who enters a graduate program to study Spanish must surmount the sentiment that her/his version of Spanish is inadequate and must learn to master formal, academic Spanish. A U.S.-Latino—a person of color—teaching in an environment in which Peninsular Spanish (from Spain) or from Latin America dominates is, unfortunately, frequently viewed as suspect, as less than those native speakers of a "purer" Spanish.Hierarchies of power are enacted through language and they color, if not define, everyday interactions in all aspects of life, personal/professional and public/private.

Still, it seems to me that, albeit difficult, a U.S.-Latino/person of color teaching in Spanish program, even if just at the undergraduate level, can exert leadership in ways others cannot. On the one hand, the U.S.-Latino faculty member can challenge notions of purity and hierarchies of power manifested in ways that include academic curriculum and that would otherwise most likely go unexamined and unquestioned. On the other hand, a U.S.-Latino faculty member's experience in life, culture, language, and academia is much closer to those of the undergraduate population of U.S. Latinos at that institution. At the graduate level of study, particularly at the most prestigious universities, most graduate students and faculty members identified by the university administration as Hispanic/Latino are individuals who immigrate to the U.S. in their adult life. In contrast, the undergraduate student population of Latinos in most American universities are primarily those who were born here and those who immigrated to this country as children. Hence, for these undergraduates, a U.S. Latino professor represents a role model, someone who has surmounted the obstacles they are experiencing and who by her/his mere presence in the academy, is a testimony to what they can achieve.

This significance becomes even greater when one recalls the linguistic ambiguity that U.S. Latinos have in relationship to standard, academic Spanish language. Furthermore, U.S. Latino faculty members are much less likely to espouse lower expectations and stereotypical assumptions than other foreign native speakers of Spanish might in regard to U.S. Latino students. Sadly, more times than I wish, I have witnessed or overheard comments by fellow departmental colleagues at various institutions and settings in which they refer to U.S. Latino students as "lazy," and "substandard." Unfortunately, many of the same stereotypical assumptions that European American, mainstream academia has held of students of color in general are applied to the U.S. Latino students but, in this case, by "Hispanic/Latino" faculty members.

Although university administrations in their hiring and admissions committees continue to conflate individuals with a Spanish surname under the label "Hispanic/Latino" in order to increase their numbers of "diversity" faculty and graduate students, no serious attempt is done to recruit U.S. Latinos—racialized U.S. minorities. Unfortunately, even the otherwise progressive commission, "Affirmative Action Activism," of the Modern Language Association of America, the professional organization of all modern languages taught in the United States, fails to make this distinction and, to examine this predicament in a more nuanced, critical manner (Rodríguez, 2007). In reports by this commission, previously known as the Commission of Faculty of Color, there is no discussion on the status of U.S. Latino professor in Spanish programs.

It is assumed that Chicano/Latino scholars teach in English not Spanish departments. And if U.S. Latino literature is taught in a Spanish program, it must be taught by someone who is not a native of this country. In my current department, for example, there are six faculty members with Spanish surnames and four European Americans who are tenured or on tenure-track lines, teaching for the Spanish program. On the surface, these numbers give the appearance of a diverse program—there are even more Hispanic/Latinos than White Americans. Yet I am the only person of color teaching in the Spanish program and, to make matters worse, in the department of Romance Languages (including French and Italian).

In the fourteen years of my teaching career at the university level (four years in a private college in Southern California and the last ten at the public university of the New England state in which I now reside), I have encountered, and in some instances taught undergraduates of many Latino ethnic extractions—Colombians, Argentineans, Puerto Ricans, Cubans, Honduran, Mexican, Salvadorians—but who share the commonality of a life experience in the United States as a racialized minority group. Setting modesty and the false sense of self-importance aside, there is no doubt that these students have found in me a role model. A perception that is based on the way these students relate to me not just because of the subject matter than I may be teaching (a U.S. Latino literature course, readings and discussions on Spanglish in Spanish language courses, etc.) but also by the way I teach and relate the material I am teaching to their experience in everyday life.

With gratitude and humbleness, I still recall the eyes of my Chicano students, beaming with pride while they were taking my classes in Southern California. Sadly, just as I was the first Chicano/a to earn a Ph.D. in the Department of Romance Languages at Cornell, I was the first U.S. Latina to be hired for a tenure-track position at Chapman University and the University of Vermont, not just in a Spanish program, but in all of the academic programs of the Colleges of Arts and Sciences of both universities. In 2003, I became the first U.S. Latina to have earned tenure at my current university. To this date, I am still the only tenured U.S. Latina faculty member.

In the Spring of 2009, I co-organized a lecture by Gloria Cuadraz, the Chicana feminist sociologist featured in the documentary "Shattering the Silences," which deals with the challenges faculty of color face at predominantly white institutions. I had met Gloria more than two decades ago, when she was a graduate student, and I an undergraduate, at UC Berkeley. We were both enrolled in a class entitled "Empowering Ethnic Minority Women." From the discussions we had in this course, a group of students from this class organized the first Women of Color conference at UC Berkeley, a tradition that still goes on. During Gloria's recent visit to my institution, I shared with her the significant impact meeting her and the other Chicana/Latina, and women of color graduate students had on me, especially because I was just an undergraduate student at the time.

As I stated earlier in this essay, because I did not have a single faculty of color in two undergraduate disciplines—history and Spanish—it was Gloria and the other graduate students in this course who planted in me the seed of the possibility that I may someday pursue a Ph.D. program, become a university professor, use my knowledge and skills to promote the democratization of higher education, and, thus, through my professional training and expertise, continue advocating for equity and social justice. Prior to my coming in contact with this group of women of color graduate students, I had never imagined a future career as a university professor. Whether I planned it this way or not, there is no doubt in my mind that I serve as a role model to other U.S. Latino students and other students of color.

La profesora de color: Leadership beyond the classroom

The production and dissemination of knowledge has always been and continues to be a crucial site for questioning old paradigms of power and for disrupting stereotypical, incomplete representations of knowledge. As I stated at the beginning of this essay, the desire to effect social change is a strong incentive for many faculty of color to join the university's professorial ranks. Once in this position, one can exert leadership in ways that transcend the classroom setting and a publication profile. One has the opportunity to covert the seemingly trivial expectation of "service" to the university into a subversive, political act. For example, the power that comes from this form of leadership was clearly exemplified by the visit of human rights activist and co-founder of the United Farm Workers of America, Dolores Huerta.

To celebrate the fifth anniversary of the Latino/a Heritage Month celebrations that I founded at my university in the Fall of 2006, I organized the historic visit of Mrs. Huerta to my university and to the state of Vermont. During the fundraising campaign I launched to secure funds to bring Mrs. Huerta to campus, I was shocked to discover the number of educated professors who did not know of Mrs. Huerta's forty-plus years of human rights activism and her important place in U.S. labor history. I was even more dismayed to learn that feminist faculty members who had built their academic careers as "experts" of U.S. women of color did not know the one U.S. Latina named by Ms Magazine and the feminist foundation as one of the most influential women of the twentieth century. Mrs. Huerta's activism, a lifespan that includes fighting for the rights of women, labor, immigrants, and gays and lesbians.

The chapel where Mrs. Huerta delivered her lecture was filled to its maximum capacity by students, faculty, members of the local community, and other activists who drove from surrounding communities to campus to hear Mrs. Huerta's speech on community activism. Mrs. Huerta's lecture discussed the many social, political, economic, and environmental areas in great need of more active citizenship. She drew comparison between the first group of individuals—mostly poor, Chicanos, Mexicans, Afro-Puertoricans, Filipinos, and even African Americans (most of whom had little formal schooling)—who began organizing to form the United Farm Workers Union, with the hundreds of poor, undocumented Mexican and Central American workers who are keeping the state's dairy industry alive. Being undocumented, this group of workers was one of the most vulnerable segment of the population in Vermont. As it was for those pioneer founders of the UFW, the language in which they conducted their first organizational meetings was some form of Spanish, as is the language of the Latino dairy workers in Vermont.

Over forty years before a charismatic, biracial presidential candidate popularized the slogan, "Yes, we can," there was a Dolores Huerta who, called for the farm workers in Central California to unionize under the slogan, "Sí, se puede." It is these words that guided these individuals, who by mainstream standards are marginalized, uneducated, and powerless, to make history by achieving the first labor contract for agricultural workers. It is these words that inspired millions of new voters to engage in the 2008 presidential political process. It is these words that university administrators should uphold in maximizing their efforts to recruiting and retaining faculty of color. "Sí, se puede" are inspirational words learned in my childhood that have carried me through the challenges and possibilities of being a Chicana, a U.S. Latina in positions of leadership.

References

Alonso, C. J. (2007). Spanish: The foreign national language. *Profession,* 218-228.

Anzaldúa, G. (1987). *Borderlands / La Frontera, the new Mestiza.* San Francisco: Aute Lute.

Antonio, A. L. *Faculty of color and scholarship transformed: New arguments for diversifying faculty.* Retrieved from www.diversityweb.org/digest/W99/diversifying.html

Dale, C. V., & Gurevitz, M. (Oct. 17, 1995). *Legal analysis of proposals to make English the official language of the United States.* Washington, DC: Congressional Research Service.

Moraga, C. (1993) "For an art of resistance." Latinas in the arts. *Crossroads* 2-5.

Rivera, T. (1975). *...Y no se lo tragó la tierra: And the Earth Did Not Devour Him.* Houston, TX: Arte Público Press.

Rodríguez, J. M. (2007) The affirmative activism project. *Profession,* 156-167.

Stewart, D. (2006). Report of the survey of earned doctorates. *ADE Bulleting, 145,* 73-80.

Disappearing Acts:
Black Face and the Tyranny of Intellectual Imperialism

Melba Joyce Boyd
Wayne State University

At the tender age of 21, you can't anticipate what evil will feel like, and I suppose the allusive manner my parents employed to forewarn their children about racism and sexism was also insufficient, either by description or as philosophical armor. My first encounter with racism occurred in the first grade classroom. No doubt, when this teacher first arrived as a young woman at Boynton Elementary School in Detroit, her students were offspring of aspiring, white, working class families. But as economic seasons shifted, an influx of blacks from the South poured into the city, seeking better jobs and educational opportunities for their children; hence, the demography of the neighborhood was transformed by Ford Motor Company to accommodate housing demands and de facto segregation of black workers and their families. My teacher must have been incredibly unhappy, feeling trapped in a classroom filled with little brown children.

Otherwise, our community was almost idyllic: neat, modest cottages; two-car garages; plush, green lawns; and playgrounds equipped with baseball diamonds, swings and sandboxes. But racial vestiges of Southern culture migrated north as well, so when I arrived in the first grade already able to read, the teacher resented my precociousness. She rebuked and scolded me in front of my classmates whenever I raised my hand. It was not until my father came to class to speak to her about my "C" in reading that I was no longer the primary recipient of her wrath. I overheard my parents talking about the conference (although I was not invited into the discussion, as we were taught to always respect teachers and elders). There was no harsh name-calling, and my father did not take pride in "setting her straight," but he was forthright about the deficiencies of her teaching techniques. But I'm sure she was surprised that he was college-educated and spoke perfect English. My grandmother was also a teacher. To

my secret satisfaction, there was an uncanny resemblance between my teacher and the wicked witch in *The Wizard of Oz*.

This memory re-emerges from time to time, especially when I
must engage unsubstantiated critiques of my work or engage in
defense of assistant professors and graduate students for whom
I feel responsible. Cleverly constructed dismissals cast without
collegial consideration sting as deeply as my first grade teacher's
tongue lashings for helping a struggling classmate sound out a
word. I came to understand that I am one of those "uppity Negroes," who doesn't know her place. But since I come from a long
line of "uppity Negroes," for me it was a badge of courage, which
was sorely needed when I became an adult and entered graduate
school, immediately after receiving my bachelor's degree.

Although I cannot comprehensively represent all of the highs,
lows, heartbreaks and satisfactions in my relationship with the
academy, I will try to illuminate experiences refracted though
the lens of memory and with some poetic consistency. Through
a prism of subjective–objectivity, I hope to share some of my insight with persons in similar circumstances, especially those
seeking a progressive, academic life. I think of my experiences
in academia as a relationship, rather than as a career, because
what began as an objective, matter-of-fact-decision to become
a professor, became an intense interaction that not only challenged my intellectual acumen and creative fortitude but also
tested my personal resilience and dogged-determination. Even
more so, my survival in the academy required a sense of humor
as well as sound, practical common sense.

Surviving the Academy

Although I was a good student in high school (at least most of
the time), I did not find my intellectual identity until I entered
Western Michigan University (WMU) in 1967, after graduation
from high school, the autumn following the 1967 Detroit Race
Riot. I was immediately enthralled by the Socratic structure for
discourse and the acceptance of creative expression in my analytical essays. Even more so, I loved the intensity of the cerebral
atmosphere. Because it was the 1960s, the political climate influenced textbook lists of progressive professors, contextualized our
dormitory debates, and infused my perception of the university
as a vessel for change, as we challenged the curriculum, protest-

ed the Vietnam War, and participated in strikes and demonstra-
tions to implement curricular change.

Western Michigan University was the site of the first chapter of Students for a Democratic Society (SDS) and the Black
Student Movement (BAM) on Michigan university campuses.
Many contemporary views have mocked, minimized, and trivialized the significance of the 1960s, but appreciating this historical context is essential to understanding the underpinnings that
girded my survival in the academy. A purpose emerged that was
larger than my initial motivation to pursue a successful career.
At home, neighborhoods were terrorized by the police, and while
Detroit was suffering from domestic unrest, letters posted from
Vietnam haunted my thoughts about my brothers, who were in
peril in an unjust war. The centrifugal force of the times redefined my life. In the pursuit of peace and justice, like many of
my fellow students, I was on a mission to transform American
society.

In 1972, I entered graduate school with the deliberate intention to pursue the study of African American literature through
directed studies or papers written in Modern or American Literature courses. I elected to pursue scholarly activities that were
not visible on my transcript. To a large extent, this maneuver
allowed me to achieve my agenda while securing my passport
to teach on the college level, as I conspired with "Others" in the
construction of a Black Studies curriculum. I was "passing," con-
spiring to alter the sacred canon with black literature that the
gatekeepers had managed to banish to the margins of the library. Hence, my survival in the academy as graduate student,
professor, and administrator has largely been variations of a disappearing act.

In 1972, my candidacy to achieve a MA in English was resented and actively resisted by the department chair, who, unbeknownst to me, openly stated at a university-wide, administrative meeting in 1968 that he would never approve a Black
American Literature course for the English curriculum. Despite
the chair's protestations, the course was admitted by his administrative superiors. But when I arrived in his undergraduate/
graduate course in American literature, he soon realized that I
did not aspire to imitate him or to reiterate the narrative of the
white literary masters. My cover was blown, and I became the
target of his acrimony. From his perspective, I was trespassing,

contaminating the sanctity of the academy with blackness. He tried to make me *really* disappear, to drop his course and the graduate program. He employed intellectual harassment, ostracism, and outright rejection of my work. Despite my appreciation of various literary styles of dead white authors, on every essay I submitted he filled the margins with vertical streams of question marks, cascading down the paper until they reached the last page and the same damning sentence: "This is not writing befitting of a graduate student." When I visited him in his office, he sat behind his desk, with tight lips grinning like a Cheshire cat, refusing to explain, advise or engage me in conversation.

One day, a young, white student stopped me before entering the classroom to express his anger and support for me. He said he was opposed to the way the chair dismissed any of my comments during class discussions and that he and his compatriots were ready to launch a public protest against this abuse. His expression of concern and activism was encouraging, but I wanted to protect him. So I told him I appreciated his interest in my plight but assured him that I would deal with it. Ironically, the chair had inadvertently triggered a radical response. His wickedness was not going unnoticed, as other students sighed at his sarcasm, and many refrained from discussion after his brutal responses to my comments.

I took a less confrontational strategy, albeit a failed one. I appealed to the university's ombudsman, who offered me tea and cookies as he assured me that I must be mistaken because the chair was a member of the local NAACP chapter. This information only served to intensify my consternation about the "esteemed" chair's diabolical nature, as well as the viability of the local chapter of this civil rights organization. The subversive intentions of the chair to flunk me out of the graduate program and the power he held as a gatekeeper could not be circumvented by appealing within the institution or to his better conscience. Concurrently, I had another professor read my essays before I turned them in for grading. I had taken Prof. Stallman for two courses as an undergraduate. He was a hard grader but was generally respected for his brilliance and his fairness. When I returned with another C-, he told me, "I don't know what to say, except there is nothing wrong with this essay. Although these readings did not change the recurring "C-" grade, it did assure me that it was not my writing skills that were deficient.

I did not realize that I had physically internalized this turmoil until my menstrual cycle went haywire. My gynecologist's first question was about stress. I told him an abbreviated story about my academic plight. Dr. Hill gave me some advice that I've used since that day, words that echoed my father's sage: "I know school is important, but nothing is more important than your health." Calmness came over me as I walked toward my dormitory in the valley. "Fuck it," I told myself, "This man was not going to make me sick."

The only black person in or near the English Department was Hazel Carlos, who had been employed to teach Black American literature to undergraduates. After another professor suggested I publish an essay that I had written for his Modern Fiction class, "The Element of Blindness in Chester Himes' *Blind Man with a Pistol*," Hazel forwarded it to her cousin, an editor at *Ebony Magazine*, who then handed it to Hoyt Fuller, who just happened to be compiling a special issue on Himes for *Black World* (formerly *Negro Digest*). Before the end of the semester, I received a letter of acceptance for the essay, which made it impossible for the chair to fail me. I also submitted this piece for my Master's essay. If there is such a thing as divine order, it was working for me in that instance.

But the extent of the chair's skullduggery was revealed the next semester when I elected to take courses from professors I thought I could trust. Unbeknownst to me, one of them had been corrupted. The professor who had encouraged me to publish my essay on Chester Himes had also given me A's on two of three essays in his course, so when I received a "B" for my final grade, I was shocked. When I went to his office to discuss the grade, he handed me my third essay marked with a "C," which lowered my final grade. His comments on my paper were as allusive as the question marks from the chair. He moved nervously about the room, stacking papers and shelving books to avoid eye contact.

In the previous semester, he praised my comments in class and encouraged my participation, but now he was evasive, and at one point even insulting during a discussion about *A Walk on the Wild Side,* which startled the dozen or so graduate students in the seminar. The room grew quiet, and an uncomfortable silence disrupted our collegial mood. But I had matured since last semester, and without hesitation, I repudiated his derisive tone and hostility with a quick retort that disarmed and embarrassed him. After that unfortunate incident, he was never rude to me again. However, on those rare occasions when our glances connected, I glimpsed genuine remorse. But I, in turn, felt only pity.

On the one hand I was thankful for his suggestion to publish my essay, which also helped to circumvent the chair's devious scheme. But, on the other hand, this professor had acquiesced to departmental politics and lowered my final grade, which advanced the plot to undermine my academic standing. Hence, I never received a grade higher than a "B" from him, and the reasons were further crystallized during a conference with Prof. Stallman. That same semester, I took a Victorian Literature course and an independent study in Black Poetry from Professor Stallman. About midterm, he revealed a telephone conversation he had with the graduate advisor, who informed him that if I did not receive an "A" in at least one of the courses I was taking that semester, I would flunk out. He told the advisor that he was sure that I would, who then retorted, how can you be sure? Stallman replied, because I'm the professor. After telling me this, he said, I'm sharing this with you because I know you are capable of earning that "A."

In the first case, Prof. Stallman was well aware of my skills and talent, but even more so, I think because Prof. Stallman was an ex-beat poet and a free thinker, he was to some extent an outsider, and he could sympathize with my plight. He recognized that these men were trying to stack the deck against me, and he refused to go along, not just to protect me, but because it was the honorable thing to do.

When it was time for me to schedule my oral examination, the graduate advisor told me to select two professors for my review panel, but the third party had to be a departmental administrator, either him, the chair or the undergraduate advisor. I did not know the current undergraduate advisor but the two culprits were not possible considerations. It was the beginning of the end of my last semester, and a polite tone was the only courtesy I accorded him with my response: "Definitely not the chair, and definitely not you." He then tried to get me to do my master's thesis on Milton's *Lycidas*. I promptly reminded him about university regulations, whereby the candidate decides the topic, which I announced would be "Pan-Africanism in the Imagery of Black American Poetry."

A guerilla insurgent knows that once your cover has been blown, it is time to counterattack, retreat, or seek harbor in safe havens, and I dealt in all three strategies. However, I refused to assume whiteface, to disguise my true face—to lose face, to mask the features of intellectual articulations for the sake of acceptance—or to surrender without honor. I knew I had to stand up for myself, but it was also important to have allies. In addition to the insight my allies provided about my work, their professional integrity helped me to maintain balance and to not lose sight of what is most important—my health and intellectual freedom. So when I entered a doctoral program at the University of Michigan four years later, I was firmly equipped with an understanding of my talents as well as of the strategies and nuances of social injustice in the academy.

During the interim years (1972-76), I taught English, Black Studies and Women's Studies at the community college in Detroit, and sometimes as an adjunct lecturer at Wayne State University. But most importantly, I became Dudley Randall's protégé. As his assistant editor at Broadside Press, my editorial and poetry skills flourished under his influence and guidance. However, the most tumultuous event in my life occurred a few months after returning to Detroit. My two older brothers, who survived the Vietnam War, were assassinated by police on February 23, 1973. Their efforts to rid the black community of heroin drug trafficking resulted in direct conflict with police corruption. This is a story that cannot be adequately addressed in this literary context but I mention it because their deaths became the subtext that girded and intensified my commitment to the social justice movement.

Doctoral Studies at the University of Michigan

The University of Michigan is an intellectual tradition in my family, encompassing three generations of alumni that matriculated in a range of disciplines and levels of degrees in English, Education, Mathematics, Engineering and even Actuarial Science. On various occasions when I was a child, I visited the campus with relatives who were doing research in the libraries or seeking advanced remedies at the university hospital. The eternal green ivy covering aging brick buildings, the subtle hills and valleys, and the leisurely saunter of students criss-crossing exquisitely manicured lawns enchanted me. As a child, I envisioned myself as a student there someday. Perhaps it was the impressive high ceilings of the library and the intellectual energy pondering a rapidly changing American consciousness. Or perhaps it was the ancient burial grounds deep beneath the campus lawn and Native American ancestors signaling my spirit.

At the same time, I entered into a marriage, which except for an amazing sojourn we took to East Africa, digressed into unanticipated traditional sabotage that was at cross-purposes with my emergence as an intellectual and a poet. My domestic disappointment and the subliminal enchantment of the campus may have subconsciously influenced my decision to attend the University of Michigan (U of M), but the more practical and immediate motivation was to secure a terminal degree in the face of growing hostility about affirmative action in national politics and the dismantling of Black Studies Programs at universities across the country. Tenure denials, reductions in financial assistance, and the abandonment of the antipoverty programs in urban centers indicated that the political winds were shifting to the right and that it was time to make a move before the doors were shut. Moreover, the polity of U of M was still associated with radical thought and movements of the 1960s and 70s, and my mentor, poet Dudley Randall (class of 1951, M.A., Library Science), encouraged me to go because at that time, Detroit native and poet Robert Hayden (class of 1946, M.F.A. English) was a Professor of English there.

The university felt familiar, and the intellectual climate I encountered in 1976 was receptive and stimulating. After my devastating experience at WMU, at U of M I felt like I had died and gone to heaven. In almost every respect, I felt like I belonged there, until I stepped outside the Department of English and tried to take a course in filmmaking offered by the Department of Art. The interdisciplinary subject of my dissertation included an analysis of the interconnections between film and literature based on psycholinguistics, visual perception and verbal processes. When my advisor, Prof. Alexander, contacted this particular professor about a directed study in filmmaking related to my dissertation topic, he was receptive, even enthusiastic. But when I appeared at his office for a scheduled appointment, a shocked expression flung his eyes and mouth wide open. As my grandmother later explained, I was a horse of a different color.

While he stumbled over a few irrelevant excuses about why he could not agree to an independent study with me, a young, Latino undergraduate seated in a nearby corner with his head bowed, which also conferred a disturbing setting. I suppose, from the professor's point of view, "colored people" were coming out of the woodwork. I stood there staring at the professor, thinking, "Ain't this a trip," when in a flash of frenzy the professor shouted, "I can't help you!" He then turned to the distraught young man for support, "Can I?" Without looking up, the student shook his head in negative affirmation.

This was one of the most cowardly acts I have ever witnessed in higher education and it was the only prejudice I experienced at the University of Michigan. But at the same time, it was consistent with the intermittent prejudice I encountered far too often. When we spoke on the telephone, this professor assumed that I was white. He was also impressed that I was a student of Rudolph Arnheim, a distinguished professor of film theory in the Department of Art History. But judging from the condition of that Latino brother, whatever that professor was teaching, I did not want any part of it.

These racialized experiences as a graduate student prepared me for the long haul in the academy, because it forced me to recognize that abstract forces we had identified in our potent language, on placards, and in dialogues at political meetings were concrete realities with personal consequences. In academia, we were contradicted and threatened, not physically, like the National Guard armed with tear gas, dogs and rifles in the "Spring of '68," or by corrupt police officers protecting drug dealers, but intellectually and systematically, as we encountered the arrogance of cultural imperialism and the power accorded them through institutional status. These gatekeepers engaged in conspiracies and covert actions to block the issuance of degrees, vote down hires of minorities and women, and stop tenure and promotions—all attempts to make us disappear.

Becoming a Professor at the University of Iowa

As time passed, I graduated and successfully trespassed into the academy, as a professor. But there are many sides to the paradox of racialized identities in America. At the invitation of Prof. Darwin T. Turner, the preeminent scholar of Black American literature and the director of the Afroamerican Studies Program, I accepted a visiting appointment at the University of Iowa. I first met Prof. Turner at Western Michigan University when he gave a lecture on Black Theatre and was a professor at the University of Michigan. My visitation resulted in a tenure-track position, teaching American literature and writing, but there was considerable resistance to my appointment to teach writing. After Black American literature was admitted into the curriculum, it was effectively marginalized; however, it was problematic for me to cross the color line into the center of the discipline, to be regarded as an artisan of the language.

As a poet, this resistance posed another barrier, another veil to make me disappear. The black face segregation of my art justified their denial of my creative skills and affirmed their cultural supremacy. But in response, I engaged an unanticipated disappearing act. I went to Germany, where my poetry was translated into a foreign language and was celebrated by white people whiter than them. My writing was appreciated for its cultural specificity, unique lexicons, and aesthetic configurations. This demonstrated that the world is larger than the United States and that one should not write for acceptance but rather for honest interactions with audiences.

Germany was not a place that surfaced in my daily thoughts as a consideration for future paths. But as the universe reveals its own mysteries, I investigated the possibility when a fellow Detroiter suggested I teach in Bremen as a Fulbright professor. After leaving John and Maya's father in Detroit, the children and I lived in Germany for the 1983-4 academic year. I put the children in a German kindergarten, and they were speaking fluent German in less than four months. Our reconstituted family became a strong triumvirate, strengthened by international travel and a shared advocacy for each other's talents.

My Fulbright year in Germany occurred during a critical moment in history in a special place on the planet, and my invitation came from persons intricately and passionately committed to the peace movement in that country. Likewise, my political history in the United States interfaced with theirs, and was grounded in similar philosophical principles that I found in the forefront of progressive intellectual thought in Germany. What became imminently clear in this context was the consciousness that characterized "1968" traversed continents and transcended cultures.

Conversely, on the frontline of the Cold War during the 1980s, African American culture became a major influence on Germans seeking to construct an alternative vision for themselves and their cultural identity. This quest led them to American minority cultures and the realization that conventional American practices contradicted its democratic ideal, and that the imperialist activities of the United States as a world power were not sincere or honest enough to reconfigure German political or institutional structures in a manner that would sufficiently eradicate the ravages of fascism.

More often than not, in comparative studies, African American culture is considered vis-á-vis the imperialist perspective or within the African diaspora context. Both of these considerations often ignore the unique aspects that constitute African American culture and circumstances and thereby belittle its value in the evolving global consciousness. As a distinct force, African American culture is axiomatic to New World thought and diametrically opposed to the repressive designs of the New World Order, which was attractive to German audiences. Historically, African American artists and scholars found Europe to be a more receptive space for them and their aesthetic aspirations. Indeed, W.E.B. Du Bois studied in Berlin at Humboldt University in the 1890s, and even before Du Bois's personal contact with German culture, we find the literary and spiritual influence Goethe had on Frances Harper in her 1871 poem "Let the Light Enter" (*The Dying Words of Goethe*), as well as the personal, philosophical and political engagements between Ottilie Assing and Frederick Douglass for nearly thirty years (*Love Across Color Lines: Ottilie Assing and Frederick Douglass* by Maria Diedrich, 1999).

Needless to say, I was lionized in West Germany. When I spoke, people listened. Ironically, the color of my skin in this context was regarded as affirmation of a cultural experience that was respected, while my talents were appreciated. I was invited to lecture and read poetry throughout West Germany, and my poetry was subsequently translated into German (*Song for Maya / Lied fur Maya,* 1989). This reception was such an extreme contrast to my stature in the English Department at the University of Iowa, that when I returned, I felt even more like a misfit. Even the liberal members of the department seemed out of touch with serious, global conflicts being discussed by European intellectuals—issues about world repression and the threat of nuclear destruction.

At the same time, the German experience reiterated my earliest academic values and commitments, which emerged at Western Michigan University and reinvigorated my purpose to expand the cultural dimensions of the literary landscape with Chicano and Native American writers, which was immediately challenged by many of my colleagues, who did not understand why I cared about these "Others." The inability of so many academics to perceive anything beyond or besides a discourse with mainstream culture enforces intellectual imperialism and contradicts the principles of academic freedom.

But I persisted. At that time, I had already published three books of poetry (one in Germany), but the powers-that-be insisted that I needed to prove myself as a literary scholar. In fact, someone suggested I write on T. S. Elliot, as if there needed to be another book on *The Wasteland*. It felt like déjà vu at WMU. I assured them that was not going to happen. Instead, I began writing a bio-critical study on Frances E. W. Harper, a nineteenth century poet, who was an abolitionist, a feminist, and an educator. Initially, this decision to write a comprehensive study of this neglected nineteenth century poet seemed to satisfy their demand for me to become a literary critic, but the venture was further inspired by the discovery of copies of four of her rare books of poetry in the University of Iowa Library, which felt like destiny.

Over time, my adversaries were not always white males. Ironically, there was an attempted hijacking of my project on Frances Harper by a black woman, whose appointment and early tenure in the English Department was championed by the African American Studies (AAS) Program. I enjoyed a joint appointment with the AAS Program, and for the most part, this small cadre of scholars (black and white) shared the same purpose and similar academic goals. We assumed early tenure for a new faculty member would bring stability to our ranks and strengthen the academic environment for the rest of the assistant professors, who were overworked and underappreciated as we served on multiple departmental, university and graduate student committees. To our surprise, our new colleague was intellectually arrogant and an alcoholic, psychological mess. Prof. "Sister Girl" provoked disruptive and even confrontational encounters with black faculty and graduate students alike.

In my case, she maneuvered a prominent historian from her *alma mater* to pressure me into sharing my work on Harper with her. Because of his stature in the field, Prof. "Brother Man" was contracted as an outside reviewer for the AAS Program, and in this capacity he asked to see my current research. I sent him an essay about a John Sayles's film, "But Not the Blackness of Space: *Brother from Another Planet,*" and a chapter of my work-in-progress on Harper. He declined comment on the film essay because he said he didn't know anything about that subject. And although he also didn't know anything about literary criticism or poetics, he stated, "If you do not consult with Prof. ["Sister Girl"], when your book on Harper comes out, it will be met with hostility by Prof. ["Ivy League"] and the rest of the black literary community." I was shocked and appalled by his gall. When I showed the letter to one of my senior colleagues, Peter Nazareth, he assured me that Prof. "Brother Man" had no right to even request to see my work.

Nothing became of the incident, and when *Discarded Legacy: Politics and Poetics in the Life of Frances E. W. Harper, 1825-1911* came out, it was widely acclaimed, was not received with hostility from Prof. ["Ivy League], and was impaled by only one negative review. Although Prof. "Sister Girl" identified herself as a Black studies and feminist scholar, she ascribed to the hierarchical design of intellectual tyranny in order to position herself above the rest of us and to advance her precious career. She referred to me as "an activist," a term meant to diminish my scholarship. This insinuation was far more injurious than any of the other "insults" I had endured; she was a black face in a white mask. Prof. "Sister Girl," who actually resembled my cousin in Selma, Alabama, proceeded to discredit my work in order to become the "only one."

After all of the aforementioned blockades and barriers constructed by white, male gatekeepers, the wrath of cultural imperialism assumed an even more insidious form, as her grinning "blackface" spouted the dialectical advantages of whiteface paradigms and cultural values. Many "race traitors" occupy professional positions and postures to accommodate institutional tyranny. These persons engage (actually aspire), for acceptance, until their intellectual guise antagonizes their identity and they are transformed by a much more dangerous disappearing act—a cognizant, schizophrenic fissure envelopes them and estranges them from other African Americans as well as their previous self. Much like the tyranny I experienced as a graduate student at Western Michigan University, Prof. "Sister Girl" engaged in skullduggery behind closed doors to undermine my prospects for tenure. Because she was tenured, and was black and female, she would be viewed by the English faculty as the "in-house" authority on black women's literature. I didn't want to stick around for that lynching party. In lieu of the situation, I took an associate professor position at Ohio State University. It was an exit strategy, another disappearing act that delivered me from academic doom and got me out of Iowa City, where there was not a single jazz club. Besides, Columbus, Ohio was closer to my family and friends in Detroit.

Black-Maled at Ohio State

I was recruited by Manning Marable, who was the chair of the Black Studies Department at OSU at the time. I met Manning years ago at a poetry reading I gave at UC Berkeley, after I published my first book, *Cat Eyes and Dead Wood* (1978), and I thought this retreat to the largest Black Studies Department in country would be secure and exciting. However, the divisiveness and acrimony among the faculty paralleled the petty scrimmages I witnessed in the English Department at the University of Iowa. Most of the men were male chauvinists, and viewed my joint appointment in Women's Studies with disdain and suspicion. Enter the third cast of characters—black men who try to "black-male" the race by promoting their own identity politics. They denounced emerging literature and scholarship by and about black women and attempted to counteract and sabotage all of Manning Marable's progressive, curricular decisions with their macho *bodaciousness*.

During a faculty search, one of the committee members became incensed when I defended Alice Walker's critical view of female circumcision in Africa. After the meeting, Prof. "Idi Imin" followed me to my office to reiterate his position by telling me, "In my African country a woman is not considered clean until she has been circumcised." My impassioned reply was, "Well, I come from a black country called 'Detroit,' and we don't believe in that shit."

Circling: Returning Home

I was recruited by my alma mater the following year to become director of the African American Studies Program at the University of Michigan, Flint campus. That same year, I was tenured. I had returned to the University of Michigan for safe haven and permanence in the academy. Although more stories followed in subsequent years, especially when I became the chair of the Department of Africana Studies at Wayne State University. But those episodes are too raw to be resurrected for this essay, and they have less to do with racism and sexism than with injured and confused humanity that did not survive intact on the battlefields of academia.

I now view these incidents as reckonings with my own naiveté about black unity and false sisterhood. Selfish ambition can transform character as people acquire or assume damaging complexes, an unfortunate feature of the American, competitive profile. A similar internalization of mainstream values is sometimes reflected in white women, who position themselves above people of color in an effort to access race privilege as consorts of white male authority.

I was never alone. Despite some nerve-racking scenarios, I was hired, published, tenured, granted academic and artistic awards and invited to present my scholarship and poetry around the world. The resilience that supported me in this grueling climb through the academic stratosphere is embedded in my work. I never stopped writing, and I never stopped advocating the mission to free the academy of undemocratic practices. An even more important survival aspect was the love and emotional stability my children brought to my life.

Being a mother fortified me with boundless joy and a more important duty than professional acceptance or success. As early as their appearance in my womb, the children invigorated my life. I wrote my dissertation when I was pregnant with John, racing to completion before his due date, and I completed my second book of poetry, *Song for Maya*, while carrying my daughter. John graduated with a degree in Mechanical Engineering from the University of Michigan, while Maya accomplished a B.F.A. degree with honors from Moore College of Art and Design in Philadelphia. Now, John assists me with his video technical skills, and

Maya illustrates my poetry with the same creative enthusiasm she conveyed when she drew images between the stanzas of a poem inscribed with her name.

My final point is that the contradictions of consciousness are not necessarily packaged by genotype. The oft-quoted adage, "You can't judge a book by its cover," is appropriate and its meaning intensified by my identity as an author, scholar, educator and mother. Within the various ironies of this intellectual demography, over time, or in sync with it, hundreds of scholars and writers, like and unlike me, who teach and write about African American literature all over the planet in a myriad of dialects, have effectively altered the fabric of world literature and the nature of the academy.

After thirteen books, countless essays, numerous awards, honors, and grants, I was designated Distinguished Professor by the Board of Governors of Wayne State University on November 30, 2005. Needless to say, because of decades of struggle with academia, I was startled when the president of the university, Irvin Reed, nominated me for this distinction. But my thoughts on the matter, after considering what has transpired in this long standing relationship with the academy, is that I finally got what Aretha Franklin advocated in song in 1966, before I graduated high school: "R-E-S-P-E-C-T."

Ungrateful and Un-American:
The Silencing of Asian Sisters

Kathleen Ja Sook Bergquist
University of Nevada, Las Vegas

The Andrews Sisters, the Holocaust, World War II, and Bob Hope were among suggested topics given to my daughter's fifth grade class for a research project on the 1940s. As I scanned the assignment I turned the page over certain I would find mention of Jim Crow laws; the Japanese internment; the contributions of the highly decorated Tuskegee Airmen and the segregated Nisei 442nd Infantry and 100th Infantry Battalions who fought for a country that would question their loyalty and rights as U.S. citizens; or the Japanese American No-No Boys who resisted pressure to prove they were American-enough (Moye, 2002; Park, 2008; Yenne, 2007). Determined not to let a teachable moment pass, we—or perhaps I—had a discussion about the absence of non-majority narratives in the school curriculum. I sent my daughter to school the next day with a carefully worded note meant to educate rather than berate:

> Wouldn't it be nice if my daughter could see herself, as an Asian American, reflected in her curriculum? It is important that we teach our children U.S. history that includes the contributions and experiences of all groups.

Certain that her teacher would be appreciative of having the oversight brought to his attention, I was unprepared for his absolute disregard and dismissive pronouncement that Brittany should go to another class if she wants to learn "such things." I was completely nonplussed.

Silence and invisibility are themes that pervade feminist discourse and writings of people of color in the United States (Dun, 2003). As a woman and a person of color, I join Patricia Hill Collin's (1990) resistance to an additive analysis of oppression. The situation of my learned silence and the inability to be seen, except as an imagined "other," stems not from any one experience, or even the sum of my experiences as a socialized member of the "weaker sex," or as a positive minority, or even as a "rescued" child. Rather, as Kawahara, Esnil, and Hsu (2007) concluded in their study of Asian American women leaders, "it is impossible to examine one identity dimension at a time (e.g., race) separate from other dimensions (e.g., gender)" (p. 311). Indeed, it is not the categories with which I identify that render me mute or imperceptible; rather it is the "matrix of oppression" that circumscribes and defines ways in which I may be seen or heard. Within that matrix, gender and race not only intersect but enmesh and are recreated into stereotypical proscriptions—which for Asian women get reconstituted as Yen Le Espirtu describes as the orientalized back-walking "China doll" or "geisha," the dangerously exotic "Dragon Lady," or the more recent caricature of the asexual math-whiz "foreign student."

My inability to respond to my daughter's fifth grade teacher and his entrenched position as a White male actually provided a teachable moment—not for him or my daughter as I had hoped, but for me. The familiar feelings of inauthenticity and ungratefulness were immobilizing. I considered if; it was reasonable to expect a fifth grade social science teacher to address the breadth of U.S. history; if I was being inauthentic in my representation as an Asian American, having been raised in a white family; and whether my expectation that the teacher would be receptive derived from a misplaced sense of entitlement as a middle-class, educated pseudowhite woman.

Despite—or perhaps because of—my tenuous relationship to or understanding of my Korean heritage I have always been aware that being an Asian American and/or female has shaped my interactions with others. As most women can attest to, I have felt infantilized, if not non-existent, when waitstaff have turned to male companions for my order. Men have had conversations in business settings with my chest or legs rather than engage with me as a peer. Moreover, as an Asian American woman I have stood in line for service, in white suburban or rural communities, and more than once been overlooked. In such incidences I have purposely sought eye contact to communicate my desire to be served. Do they really not see me? Or are they afraid of imagined communication barriers? Perhaps they hope I will go away if I am ignored long enough? I have been chased down the street or stopped by U.S. military men who tell me I look like their girlfriend in Korea or the Philippines, or wish to practice their Korean with me. I have been stopped in an Irish pub and asked "How do you like it in this country?" and accosted outside a movie theatre after seeing *Seven Years in Tibet* by a woman demanding that I speak for Asian Americans regarding the Chinese treatment of Tibet.

I have been told by white Americans that I am not really Korean (an honorary white), reminded by Koreans that I am not really Korean (banana or Twinkie), and I have been told by African American colleagues that Asians do not experience discrimination or racism —or if they do—it cannot be comparable to that of black Americans. I have been told by "well meaning" people how fortunate I am to have been rescued from an orphanage and afforded an opportunity to pursue the American Dream, rather than being (as Koreans call orphans) "dust of the street" (Clement, 1998).

The lesson I learned from my daughter's social science teacher that day is how profoundly I had internalized the interrelated messages that I should be *grateful* for the opportunity to be American, to have been delivered from certain poverty, and to have been picked by my adoptive family (especially as a girl). Being adopted I lack *authenticity* and am in a questionable position to advocate or speak for representation or social justice for "my people," and have no real claim to being Korean, Asian American, or American/white.

However, my battle to be heard and seen has not derived from a personal need to "find my voice" or a need for self-validation, but from something much larger. As Kawahara et al. (2007) learned from the Asian American women they interviewed, leadership requires giving a voice to something you are passionate about and creating a vision that will inspire others. Pei-te Lien (2001) chronicled Asian Pacific American (APA) women's political activity from the mid-1800s (e.g. Filipinas in Hawai'i and Chinese garment workers in San Francisco striking for livable wages and shorter hours); to student-led demands in the mid-1960s for Asian studies curricula which spawned the early Asian American movement; to current organizations that address the sociopolitical and legal interests of APA women such as the National Asian Pacific Women's Forum (NAPAWF), Center for Asian American Women, Organization of Pan Asian American Women, Organization of Chinese American Women, Asian American Women's Safety Net, and Asian Women's Shelter (AWS).

Despite their activism, APA women have largely been viewed as Pie-te Lien (2001) describes, "compliant and nonresistant," leading to the question, "Where are all the Asian American sisters?" Esther Ngan-Ling Chow (1992) concludes that Asian American (AA) women face "specifically inherent" barriers to political activism (p. 100). She identifies two categories of barriers, internal and external, under which she details three subcategories. Internal barriers are those which she considers to be unique to Asian American women within their own communities and families, while external barriers are those that exist "primarily in American society at large" (p. 100).

Internal barriers include psychological constraints, cultural restrictions, and patriarchy and structural impediments. Psychological constraints are two-fold: (1) the tension between ethnic identity and gender identity and (2) navigating racialized stereotypes. Asian American women have been notably absent, or arguably excluded, from the feminist movement (Dun, 2003; Kawahara et al., 2007). Some found themselves in the untenable position of having to choose to identify as either a feminist or an Asian American, while others simply experienced their ethnic and/or racial identity as more salient in their advocacy work. Additionally, Chow explains that Asian Americans are at risk for internalizing categories of oppression as the "subservient, obedient, passive, hard working, and exotic" and then are further susceptible to becoming "victims of the stereotypes imposed by others" (p. 101). Cultural restrictions reflect tensions between generalized expectations, values, and mores that Asian communities bring with them when they emigrate to the United States juxtapositioned against "American" cultural norms that include: (1) obedience vs. independence, (2) collective (or familial) vs. individual interest, (3) fatalism vs. change, and (4) self control vs. self-expression or spontaneity (p. 101). Accordingly, Chow posits that given the identified cultural characteristics, those who are less acculturated are more likely to avoid rather than engage in political activism. Similarly, the traditional patriarchal structure of Asian families often limits women's ability to participate due to perceived role conflicts.

Restrictive U.S. immigration policies—the product of anti-Asian sentiment—such as the Naturalization Act of 1870, Chinese Exclusion Act of 1882, andExclusion Act of 1924, have resulted in the relative absence of women in early immigration from

Asia. Chow argues that "the community still bears the long-term effect of cultural, socioeconomic, and political exploitation and oppression" (p. 103). As targets of race and economically-based exclusionary and discriminatory policies and practices, Asian American women found that the decidedly white middle-class agenda of the feminist movement was insensitive and unreceptive to their interests and concerns.

While Chow's work provides a starting point to understand the limited participation of Asian American women in leadership roles in general, and feminist work more specifically, it seems to be grounded in static notions of identity. "Asian American" women in the 21st century are not a monolithic group but rather include shifting, dynamic, and complex identities incorporating recent immigrants as well as fourth generation Americans; multiracial and multiethnic families; adoptees from Korea, China, Cambodia, Philippines, Vietnam, India, Thailand; small-business owners; those who are college-educated and labor in the agricultural, service, and garment industries; wives of U.S. military men; and, the most invisible, women and girls trafficked into the United States. As Chow points out, Asian American women's participation and leadership has tended to focus more broadly on social justice issues, and "many tend to place a higher priority on eradicating racism than sexism" (p. 104). Thus, gaining a more nuanced understanding of Asian American women's participation in social justice work requires an examination of lived experiences that push the boundaries of "Asian America."

As a transracial, transcultural, transnational, international, intercountry adoptee from Korea, I have been largely left to my own devices to figure out what it means to be Asian American. My Americanness is immersed and inseparable from my status as an orphan and the humanitarian responses of my adoptive family and the U.S. government. I was able to fast-track through the immigration and naturalization process, predicated on the Korean government's willingness to pass title and relinquish my citizenship and rights to claim parentage in Korea. I was "reborn" in Hawai'i at the age of 20 months and favored with U.S. citizenship in Minnesota when I was five years old. As a child, my Asianness felt like an ill-fitting coat that I could not take off. I would sometimes forget I was wearing it and look around in wonder when kids made fun of it. Without a family or community to reflect my experience, I looked to others to shape and define what it is to be Asian in America, realizing that many were as uncomfortable with my ill-fitting coat as I was. Thus, themes of gratitude and authenticity, or lack thereof, have pervaded and fomented the passion Kawahara et al. (2007) speak of to engage in social justice and critical race discourse.

Such a Lucky Girl

While attending a gathering of *East of California*, a caucus of Asian American studies programs situated largely in the Midwest and East Coast, an attendee from the University of Hawai'i shared a story about a non-Asian colleague who had adopted a son from Cambodia and was struggling with normal parenting challenges, which included finicky eating habits (Lee, 2003). Her colleague's husband was exasperated by their son's "ungratefulness" because, as he concluded, "if he were in Cambodia he'd be eating dirt." Transracial adoptees receive implicit, if not explicit, messages that they should be grateful. As a researcher and adoptee, I have encountered numerous narratives of adoptees who expressed an inordinate need to prove that they "beat the odds" as an expression of gratitude to, or in some cases in spite of, their adoptive parents and birth parents and the rejection of a nation and culture that could not or would not accommodate them.

Elizabeth Kim (2000) recalls in her autobiography an urgent need to please her adoptive parents at a young age, fully cognizant that she had been "rescued" from an orphanage. Similarly, while interviewing adult adoptees for my master's thesis, I met a man who was about 40 years old, who spoke earnestly with a faint trace of a Korean accent hidden behind his words. His story has haunted me over the years. During the course of our conversation, he described a sense of gratitude toward his adoptive parents who were willing to take him in as a preteen, an age at which most would consider him unadoptable. He also carried with him an obligation to fully embrace the opportunities afforded him in the United States that his birth mother, despite loving him, was unable to provide raising a mixed-race child in Korea as a single parent. This included, in his mind, completely recreating himself to include losing his native language.

The fear of appearing ungrateful silences adoptees in their own families, as well as in other aspects of their lives. Adoption from Korea began in earnest in 1954 by Harry Holt, and to date there have been over 160,000 children who have been placed with families in the United States, Canada, Western Europe, and Australia (Freundlich & Lieberthal, 2000; South Korean Ministry of Health and Welfare, 2007). First-generation Korean adoptees have come of age and have organized around their common experiences but also have become active in shaping public policy and perception regarding adoption in their adoptive countries and in Korea. As they have increasingly raised their voices, often challenging the institutionalization of international adoption, adoption agencies, adoptive parents, and the media have dismissed them as being "angry" and thus ungrateful. Jane Jeong Trenka (2006), a Korean adoptee activist living in Korea, responds to the categorization of an angry adoptee:

> I believe that for the adoptive parents who do so, it makes them feel better about their own choices, to minimize and exempt my voice from the list of those they should take the time to listen to, so that they only perceive reassurance and praise for doing a kind thing by adopting.

Themes of gratitude are not unique to international adoptees but are shared by Asian Americans and presumably other immigrants as well. The proscription often directed to those assumed to be nonnative is "if you don't like it here, you can go back from where you came." This has been internalized in Asian American families as silence and hard work with an awareness that as a "perpetual foreigner" there is extraordinary pressure to justify one's presence in the United States (Takaki, 1998; Wu, 2002).

The expectation of gratitude is particularly salient for Asian American women who are not only positioned as a positive or model minority but have been deemed more palatable than Asian males in the American imagination. Orientalized and exoticized, Asian women are re-imagined through racist and misogynistic fantasies. In a complaint filed with University of Pennsylvania's grievance commission challenging a denial of tenure, Rosalie Tung alleged race, sex, and national-origin discrimination when the chairman of her department "embarked on a ferocious campaign to destroy and defame" her after she rejected his sexual advances (Cho, 1997, p. 167). Despite a finding that Professor Tung had been discriminated against, the provost did not act. A colleague explained to a local newspaper that Professor Tung was perceived as least likely to "kick over the tenure-review apple cart" because she was "elegant, timid, and not one of those loud-mouthed women on campus" (p. 168).

Silenced also within their own homes, Chow (1992) points to structural barriers constructed through Confucian patriarchy that devalue and subjugate, and create role stress for women who seek to engage in political activism. However, role conflict and patriarchal proscriptions do not derive exclusively from traditional Asian familial and societal structures. That is, Asian girls in the United States also receive Easy Bake ovens and baby dolls that serve to define their role within the home, and they quickly learn that being "ladylike" entails self-control and putting others' needs first. In her cartoon, "Angry Little Asian Girl," Lela Lee, a 1996 University of California Berkeley graduate, captures the frustration of young Asian American women who have been silenced on multiple levels (PBS, 2004). In an interview, Lee explained, "You didn't get angry in our house. If you got angry you were a bad child" (read "ungrateful"). Lee unabashedly confronts racialized constructions of language and perpetual foreigner stereotypes:

> In one early cartoon, an adult tells Kim that she speaks "good English." Kim can't hold back: "I was born here, you stupid dip s*?%@! Don't you know anything about immigration? Read some history books, you stupid ignoramus!" (PBS, 2004)

The popularity of Lee's work illustrates the emergence of a younger generation of women who are increasingly resisting being silenced; however, the anime-like cartoon format risks trivialization as being "adorable" and "cute."

Within my own family I felt, and still feel, an intense need to ensure that my adoptive parents know that I am not "ungrateful." That is, while I have never felt indebted to my parents for "saving" or "rescuing" me, I consider it a priority to let them know I appreciate their love and support. In doing so, I can remember as a child self-censoring anything that might be construed as being ungrateful and thus question their role as "real" parents. I also share Professor Tung's experience that others' ascribed expectations of me include avoiding confrontation, which has undoubtedly been self-fulfilling (Cho, 1997). Perhaps, as Chow (1992) suggests, I have become a victim of internalized stereotypes. I have learned that it is easier to put my head down and simply work harder—which I have professionally reframed as staying out of the political fray. At the same time, I lack a sense of authenticity and am fearful lest anyone find out that I am not really Asian.

You're not "really" . . .

Korean and other adoptee communities from Asia exist in what Tobias Hübinette (2004) describes as a "third-space." They are-hybridized and in-between. Earlier characterizations have positioned adoptees lingering at the margins or in the shadows of their birth and adoptive cultures. However, a third-space conceptualization seeks to empower and create room for self-definition. Despite resistance to limiting and bifurcated either/or, ascribed constructions of identity, adoptees are still left with navigating others', as well as their own, racialized notions of ethnicity, place, and nationhood.

Becoming Asian has been a process. The yellow hue to my skin, and eyes that disappear when I smile, unquestionably mark me as Asian or "Oriental," not quite American enough. Demands to know if I am Chinese or Japanese and ching-chong Chinaman taunts from my childhood have been replaced with veiled compliments about my flawless English and knowing smiles when strangers learn that I am a professor . . . *of course, Asians are such hard workers*. . . the unspoken comparison hangs in the air. At the same time, Koreans are often confused, amused, and offended by my inability to respond to simple social cues and speak Korean, and by my apparent rejection of Korean culture. Korean ethnic churches in the United States serve as refuges for the cultural and social lives of their members, and many churches have incorporated outreach to Korean adoptees as part of their mission (Chang, 2006; see, e.g., Korean Church of Champaign-Urbana). Consequently, I have been invited to numerous Catholic, Baptist, and Presbyterian churches where I first learned to appreciate the warmth, generosity, and passionate faith of "my people."

However, it was within these congregations that I also became aware that I was the "outsider within" (Trenka, Oparah, & Shin, 2006). Among other Koreans, I felt both inauthentic and oddly reassured, as though I was encountering a song or movie that I had long forgotten. I would fumble through the service, watching those around me to know when to stand and when to pray, the Korean words one-dimensional and lifeless to my eyes. Occasionally I, and the inevitable non-Korean spouses, were given head phones with whispered translations which marked us as outsiders. Some, I was told, thought that I was second-generation Korean and that I refused to learn Korean, which generated disapproval. That experience was pivotal for me; instead of feeling self-conscious and inauthentic, I realized that by embracing my not-knowing, I could push boundaries and either would be forgiven for my ignorance or free to not "hear" my detractors.

Breaking the silence

I would like to think, on my better days, that my voice is in chorus with the likes of my Asian "sisters"—Jessica Hagedorn, Maxine Kingston Hong, Angela Oh, and Yen Le Espiritu—who refuse to be silenced or trivialized as a "positive minority." Inescapably, internalized narratives of ingratitude and inauthenticity have at times been paralyzing and seemingly insurmountable. Coming out of the shadows of ascribed identities that limit and essentialize has led me to find my place in a third space that frees me from the borderlands and has shaped the way that I think about and engage in social justice work and critical race discourse (Anzaldua, 1999). That is, my experiences have framed for me the need to push the boundaries of "Asian America," to reject additive constructions of oppression, and to embrace not-knowing.

In 2004, Asians numbered approximately 13.5 million, or 4.7 percent of the U.S. population (U.S. Census). Asians are defined for purposes of the Census as "people having origins in any of the original peoples of the Far East, Southeast Asia, or the Indian subcontinent" (p. 1). Despite the pan-ethnic designation of Asian American, nationalistic, linguistic, and ethnic identities have deep historical roots that reach back to "different shores." As early as the mid-1800s immigrants, from diverse national, political, historical, economic, and social backdrops have ventured across the Pacific seeking, among other things, economic opportunity; education; to join families; to form families; and escape from persecution, war, and poverty (Takaki, 1998).

The "Asian American" community represents a heterogeneous grouping of people who struggle with an overly-broad racialized identity that has little salience in their daily lives. The racial categorization cannot account for the myriad of ethnic, cultural, religious, national, and generational perspectives that make "pan-ethnic coalitions among Asian Pacific Americans, often difficult to construct, [and] . . . short lived" (Nakanishi & Lai, 2003, p. 9). Omi and Winant (1994) explain that such racial categories are a part of a "*system* of racial meanings and stereotypes" that serve to maintain social order, rather than to instill a collective conscience based on empowerment and coalition building (p. 7). Junn and Masuoka (2008) questioned whether group-based political behavior in Asian America even exists, noting that distinctive national origin groups may be favored over pan-ethnic identity. They sought to determine if group consciousness has political consequences for Asian Americans, discovering what they term a "latent solidarity," which can be triggered by an event or issue. Their findings are contrasted with solidarity among African Americans, which is predicated more on a shared historical experience and "over-determinacy of race on individual life chances" (p. 736).

Identity politics create chasms, not just between groups, but also within groups. Tribal responses to ethnic and political differences or interests benefit few, serve to keep communities isolated, and maintain the status quo. I learned first-hand in my work in the Asian community in central Virginia that my very presence, as a pseudo-Asian/Korean/English-only/adopted/divorced/30-something/single mom who was oblivious to convention and Asian male privilege, not only pushed, but perforated boundaries or "borders" that circumscribe racialized constructions of identity. In 2001, while presenting findings of a study that sought to understand racial and ethnic identity development in Korean adoptees, I was among a handful of scholars who included adoptees within Asian American Studies. Notably, within the past couple of years adoption researchers have organized a transnational adoption caucus within Asian American Studies (AAAS, 2007). Similarly, the increased inclusion of feminist and queer studies within Asian American Studies demarcates a movement toward greater inclusion and a renegotiation, or perhaps a reclaiming, of our pan-ethnic identity—at least within a scholarly context.

Although my parents were raised in small Midwestern towns, I spent my formative years in Chennai (then Madras), India and Kent, England where my father served in global missions through the American Lutheran Church. Our home often served as a layover and meeting place for fellow ex-pats, as well as my father's colleagues and students from all over the world including Germany, Brazil, South Africa, Hong Kong, Hungary, Korea, and of course England and India. My worldview and global perspective was shaped by those whose lives were serving others, including my father's colleague, fellow clergy, and friend, Desmond Tutu. Thus, during my early years, I did not experience being Asian as constructed and formed through American sociopolitical forces, yet I was aware of white privilege and the displacement and subjugation of indigenous persons in the wake of colonialism. At a very young age, I realized that I did not represent the oppressor or the oppressed, allowing me to move freely around, between, and within "borders" without detection.

My initiation to the politics of identity in the United States came my freshman year in college when I was engulfed in whiteness, endless snow drifts, lutefisk (a Scandinavian dish of white fish prepared with lye), and towering blondes. Searching for kindred spirits with a passion for social justice, human rights, and the shared experience of being a person of color on a predominantly white, small liberal arts campus, I found myself at a "minority" student organization meeting. As the only non-black student, it was clear that I did not fit within what Juan Perea (1997) calls the "black/white binary paradigm of race." Moreover, it was also apparent in this context that "minority" was a proxy for "black." Similarly, Frank Wu (1995) observed that constitutionally "majority" has been synonymous with "white" and "minority" has been used interchangeably with "black."

Once again I was constructed as invisible and rendered irrelevant, neither truly oppressed nor a minority. I found that the most compelling lessons about identity politics came not from scholarly journals or critical race theorists but from young people whose lives were acted upon by a construction of race that polarized and whose minds were imprinted with us/them ideologies, relegating the "other" only in comparison to degrees of "whiteness" or privilege. Unindoctrinated into political correctness, young people demanded that I identify myself, seeking to place me on the "color line" (White, 1925). Was I white, black, or "mixed"? They were unable to conceive of "whites" as the target of persecution, enslavement, and extinction when challenged to consider the experiences of Jews in Hitler's Germany, or to conceive that debt bondage provides the U.S. with a steady stream of free labor from impoverished communities across the globe in what is considered modern-day slavery (U.S. Department of State, 2008). However, young people were easily able to add up their multiple identities and oppressions that made them winners in the "Oppression Olympics," such as black, poor, born into a legacy of enslavement and Jim Crow laws (Hill Collins, 1990). Audre Lorde (1983) debunks the notions of hierarchical or additive oppressions/identities in her seminal work:

> From my membership in all of these groups I have learned that oppression and the intolerance of difference come in all shapes and sexes and colors and sexualities; and that among those of us who share the goals of liberation and a workable future for our children, there can be no hierarchies of oppression. (pp. 306-307)

Frank Wu (2002) further challenges a binary construction of race that positions Asian Americans as exemplars, models of success and hard work to which other racial minorities are to aspire. The positive stereotype not only misrepresents economic and social realities, it also has serious implications with regard to access to social services, healthcare, education, and employment. A 2005 report compiled by Asian American LEAD (Leadership, Empowerment, and Development), Hmong, and Laotian Americans at "half that of whites and below that of African Americans, Latinos, and American Indians," with 12.5 percent of Asian Americans living in poverty, and one in five Asian immigrants not completing high school (p. 1).

> Thinking Asian Americans have succeeded, government officials have sometimes denied funding for social service programs designed to help Asian Americans learn English and find employment. Failing to realize that there are poor Asian families, college administrators have sometimes excluded Asian American students from Educational Opportunity Programs (EOP), which are intended for all students from low-income families (Takaki, 1998, p. 478)

The model minority myth reinforces a racial hierarchy and undermines the ability of communities to form meaningful collaborations to begin to unravel the matrix. I look for the connections within the matrix that inextricably entwine us, recognizing that we are all oppressed and oppressive.

Beverly Eckert, whose husband died in tower two of the World Trade Center on 9/11, and who was herself recently killed in a tragic plane crash, was described as a "reluctant advocate and activist" for a special independent commission to investigate the attacks (Munoz, Owens, & Pazniokas, 2009). In a 2004 National Public Radio interview, she described how she "commandeered" a conference room after being bounced around from one congressional office to another, forcing lawmakers to come to her. She confided, "Sometimes it's advantageous if you don't know how the game is played" (Siegel, 2004).

Not-knowing is a reframe of the burden of inauthenticity. That is, rather than experiencing myself, and allowing others to define me, as not being sufficiently Korean/Asian/American/ white or otherwise fragmented, I have found power in embracing my complex and multifaceted identity that is irreducible. Not-knowing allows me to traverse and transcend identities that would limit and essentialize me. In my community-based work, not-knowing allows those I encounter to be the experts of their experiences and allows me to accept people as I find them. Not-knowing is not about ignorance. It's not about challenging social convention, rather, it's about moving forward and shedding the weight of ascribed identities. That is, as a pseudo-Asian/Korean/English-only/adopted/divorced/remarried/40-something/halmoni, not-knowing gives me the freedom to address culturally sensitive issues such as human trafficking in Asian ethnic communities, to challenge the compartmentalization of Asian versus Asian American studies, to teach beyond the black/white paradigm with authority, and to take a leadership role in social justice work and critical race discourse.

Conclusion

Although I responded to the teacher's admonitions in self-fulfilling stereotypical silence—my silence, and the silence of my Asian American sisters, should not be interpreted as complacency, apathy, or acquiescence. Rather, as Duncan (2003) argues, silence can be a means of resistance, or perhaps a prelude to action. Within a westernized construction of resistance, "speech" is construed as being integral to empowerment and activism. Although Asian American women have been positioned as perpetual foreigners and subjected to both dominant Judeo-Christian and traditional Eastern patriarchal productions of family and gender roles, women have fashioned forms of resistance and leadership in their homes and communities that are both quiet and fierce. Lisa Lowe (1996) points to the daily acts of resistance of Chinese women in America, while Ji-Yeon Yuh considers the sisterhood of Korean wives of U.S. military men who have created an "imagined community" as a way of "claiming the Korean identity that both Koreans and Americans would deny them" (Hune & Nomura, 2003, p. 231). Asian women's agency and leadership may not be performed in ways that conform to masculine or Western formations, but it is in the silence between and behind words that we find our voice.

Reference

Anzaldua, G. E. (1999). *Borderlands / la frontera: The new mestiza*. San Francisco: Aunt Lute Books.

Asian American LEAD (AALEAD). (2005). *Invisible Americans: The hidden plight of Asian Americans in poverty*. Silver Spring, MD: Office of Minority Health Resource Center.

Association of Asian American Studies (AAAS). (2007). *Crosstown connections: Asian American urbanism and multiracial encounters. Program for the Annual Meeting*, April 4-7, 2007. Retrieved from http://aaastudies.org/programMarch1.pdf

Bergquist, K. J. S. (2001). *Expanding the boundaries of Asian American studies: Racial and ethnic identity development in Korean adoptees*. Paper presented at the 18th Annual Meeting of the Association for Asian American Studies, Toronto, Canada.

Chang, C. T. (2006). *Korean ethnic church growth phenomenon in the United States*. Paper presented at the American Academy of Religion in Claremont, CA, March 12, 2006. Retrieved from www.duke.edu/~myhan/kaf0603.pdf

Chinen, J. N. (1997). Sewing resistance into the grain: Hawai'i's garment workers at work and at Home. *Race, Gender & Class, 4*(3), 165-179.

Cho, S. K. (1997). APA women and racialized sexual harassment. In E.H. Kim and L.V. Villanueva (Eds.) *Making more waves: New writing by Asian American women*. Boston: Beacon Press.

Chow, E. N. (1992). The feminist movement: Where are all the Asian American women? *U.S.-Japan Women's Journal, English Supplement, 2*, 96-111.

Clement, T. P. (1998). *The unforgotten war: Dust of the streets*. Bloomfield, IN: Truepeny.

Collins, P. H. (1990). *Black feminist thought: Knowledge, consciousness, and the politics of empowerment*. Boston: Unwin Hyman.

Dun, P. (Ed.). (2003). *Tell this silence: Asian American women writers and the politics of speech*. Iowa City: University of Iowa Press.

Espiritu, Y. L. (2007). *Asian American women and men: Labor, laws and love*. Lanham, MD: Rowman & Littlefield.

Freundlich, M., & Lieberthal, J. K. (2000). *The gathering of the first generation of adult Korean adoptees: Adoptees' perceptions of international adoption*. Evan B. Donaldson Adoption Institute. Retrieved on February 21, 2009 at http://www.adoptioninstitute.org/proed/korfindings.html

Hübinette, T. (2004). The adopted Koreans and an identity in the Third Space. *Adoption & Fostering, 28*(1), 16-24.

Junn, J., & Masuoka, N. (2008). Asian American identity: Shared racial status and political context. *Perspectives on Politics, 6*(4), 729-740.

Kawahara, D. M., Esnil, E. M., & Hsu, J. (2007). Asian American women leaders: The intersection of race, gender, and leadership. In J. L. Chin, J. K. Rice, & B. E. Lott (Eds.), *Women and leadership: Transforming visions and diverse voices*. Hoboken, NJ: Wiley.

Kim, E. (2000). *Ten thousand sorrows: The extraordinary journey of a Korean War orphan*. New York: Doubleday.

Korean Church of Champaign-Urbana. (2003). *Love Korean Adoptees (LKA)*. Retrieved on Februrary 21, 2009 at http://www.kc-cu.org/lovekoreanadoptees/

Lee, S. S. (2003). Building Asian American and ethnic studies in the Midwest: Challenges, growth prospects, and new opportunities in the Heartland. *Asian-American Village*. Retrieved on January 31, 2009 at http://www.imdiversity.com/Villages/Asian/education_academia_study/lee_aas_midwest.asp

Lien, P. T. (2001). *The making of Asian America through political participation*. Philadelphia: Temple University Press.

Lorde, A. (1983). There is no hierarchy of oppressions. In *Homophobia and education*. New York: Council on Interracial Books for Children.

Lowe, L. (1996). *Immigrant acts: On Asian American cultural politics*. Durham, NC: Duke University Press.

Moye, J. T. (2003). The Tuskegee Airmen oral history project and oral history in the National Park Service. *The Journal of American History, 89*(2), 580-587.

Munoz, H., Owens, D., & Pazniokas, M. (2009, February 13). Stamford widow of 9/11 victim dies in plane Crash. *Hartford Courant*.

Nakanishi, D. T. T., & Lai, J. S. (2003). *Asian American politics: Law, participation, and policy*. Lanham, MD: Rowman & Littlefield.

Omi, M., & Winant, H. (Eds.) (1994). *Racial formation in the United States: From the 1960s to the 1990s* (2nd ed.). New York: Routledge.

Park, Y. (2008). Facilitating injustice: Tracing the role of social workers in the World War II internment of Japanese Americans. *Social Service Review, 82*(3), 447-483.

Perea, J. (1997). The black/white binary paradigm of race: The "normal science" of American racial thought. *California Law Review, 85*, 1213-1258.

Public Broadcasting Station (PBS). (2004). *Searching for Asian American*–Episode 3. Retrieved from http://www.pbs.org/

Siegel, R. (2004). Families see hope in Sept. 11 panel reforms. National Public Radio (July 22, 2004). Retrieved from http://www.npr.org

South Korean Ministry of Health and Welfare (2007). *Statistics from the Ministry of Health and Welfare.* Seoul: Ministry of Health and Welfare.

Takaki, R. (1998). *Strangers from a different shore: A history of Asian Americans.* New York: Back Bay Books.

Trenka, J. J. (2006). *Picking teams. Twice the rice: Open mind. Insert perspective.* Retrieved February 21, 2009 at http://twicetherice.wordpress.com/2006/08/21/picking-teams/

Trenka, J. J., Oparah, J. C., & Shin, S.Y. (2006). *Outsiders within: Writing on transracial adoption.* Cambridge, MA: South End Press.

U.S. Census. (2004). *The American community—Asians: 2004.* Washington DC: U.S. Department of Commerce.

U.S. Department of State. (2008). *Trafficking in persons report.* Office to Monitor and Combat Trafficking in Persons.

White, W. F. (1924). Color lines. *Survey Graphic, 6*(6).

Wu, F. (1995). Neither black nor white: Asian Americans and affirmative action, *Boston College Third World Law Journal, 15*, 225-284.

Wu, F. (2002). *Yellow: Race in America beyond black and white.* New York: Basic Books.

Yenne, B. (2007). *Rising sons: The Japanese-American GIs who fought for the United States in World War II.* New York: St. Martin's Press.

Yuh, J. Y. (2003). Imagined community: Sisterhood and resistance among Korean military brides in American, 1950-1996. In S. Hune & G. M. Nomura (Eds.), *Asian/Pacific Islander American women: An historical anthology* (pp. 221-236). New York: New York University Press.

From "Shattering the Silences" to the Politics of Purpose:
Reflections on the Culture of the Academy

Gloria Holguín Cuádraz
Arizona State University

I like to believe that I arrived at Arizona State University's West campus as an enthusiastic and committed assistant professor. I was full of energy and anticipation; now, with the experience of fourteen years of earned hindsight, I realize I seriously underestimated what it would mean in everyday life to negotiate the culture of the academy—a culture fraught with an ethos of individualism, deceit, and hypocrisy. In 1994, I joined a Department of American Studies comprised of scholars trained in history, English, sociology, anthropology, and Spanish and American studies, and a College of Arts and Sciences whose mission emphasized interdisciplinary scholarship and teaching. With a doctorate in sociology from the University of California at Berkeley, I was drawn to the stated commitment to interdisciplinary research and teaching and to working with students transferring from the community colleges to our upper-division campus.

I had been at my job for approximately one year when I received a call from the director and producer of the film that would eventually be titled "Shattering the Silences: Minorities Break into the Ivory Tower," who asked to meet with me and discuss my research and my own journey into higher education (Pellett & Nelson, 1996). In the film, my story is presented in the context of my rural, working-class background, along with my status as a first-generation college student who earned scholarships to continue her education. During the filming, I am captured at campus-wide meetings to illustrate the special demands that faculty of color face in assisting the campus to achieve ethnic representation; I am shown teaching in and outside the classroom, with stories from students I was mentoring. In the evening I can be seen showing students around campus, welcoming them and connecting them with financial aid counselors. Then, making the personal political, I am depicted as a woman in her late thirties, deliberating on whether to pursue tenure or start a family, while enjoying the company of Chicana/Latina friends and colleagues who share similar cultural backgrounds and tensions in their own journeys in academia. The message of the film as a whole was to signal the presence of faculty of color in the academy and to show the influence we are having with the questions and foci we bring to our respective research fields and our teaching at universities and colleges across the United States.

Creation of the ASU West Campus

When I interviewed for an assistant professorship in the Department of American Studies (AMS) in 1993, I was attracted to the campus for three reasons. First, its upper-division structure meant I would be teaching and working with students transferring from community colleges, many of whom were first-generation college students. Second, the research-based mission and 2/2 teaching load (two courses each fall and spring semester) would enable me to continue my scholarly work. Third, the emphasis on interdisciplinary research and teaching within the department and the college promised to be provocative and innovative.

The development of my new academic home dates back to as early as 1963 (A review of ASU West's historical development, 2004). The impetus to establish a branch campus of Arizona State University was to provide the growing and expanding citizenry in western Maricopa County with an accessible baccalaureate-granting institution. After several tentative launches, a proposal to establish an upper-division and primarily nonresidential branch campus eventually gained financing and approval in 1984 from the governor, Arizona Board of Regents and Arizona State Legislature (S.B. 1245). The authors of the campus's first strategic planning document envisioned creating an academic atmosphere that focused on "building research-based, professional and traditional academic programs that share a liberal arts foundation and an interdisciplinary emphasis" (A review of ASU West's historical development, 2004).

Months after I arrived in 1994 with a freshly minted Ph.D. in hand, the Arizona Board of Regents (ABOR) announced that they wanted to eliminate tenure for all university faculty. After considerable internal organization on the part of the faculty and respective academic senates, a compromise was reached. The

compromise was a posttenure review system that required tenured faculty to be reviewed annually, but on the basis of three
years' worth of evidence in research, teaching, and service. A faculty member who received the score of "1" on a scale of 1-3 in a
review in any of the three areas of research, teaching or service
was to be put on a one-year contract to improve his or her record.
If no satisfactory improvements were seen, he or she was to be
terminated. After the political storms had quieted, little did I
know that this would be a howling harbinger of changes yet to
come.

Disciplinary Antagonisms in an Interdisciplinary College

My main priorities as a junior faculty member were to teach,
mentor, and move my research to publication. So it is difficult
even now to articulate the precise process of how a series of institutional tensions unfolded into what they did, but they snow-
balled nonetheless. I remember going to my mailbox on a Monday afternoon at the end of a full day of meetings and teaching to
find a lengthy memo announcing the splitting of the Department
of American Studies. Without any discussion having taken place
among the group as a whole (fourteen faculty and two lecturers),
the document was signed off by our dean of six weeks, newly
hired through an external national search. The English faculty
and the one Spanish faculty member had apparently cut a deal
to separate from the American studies and history faculty and
establish their own department. They did not want to be ruled
by the "hegemonic historians," hence their desire to secede. The
defection was led by our newly appointed chair, who had reluctantly agreed to serve in the position, exclaiming at the time she
was nominated that she didn't "have one administrative cell in
her body."

My own views on why I became an academic left me confused
by the chair's reluctance to take on a leadership role within the
university. From my perspective, it was an opportunity to lead,
guide, mentor, and build one's academic program. I did not understand the disdain faculty had for work unrelated to their own
research. After all, I pursued higher education because I wanted
the responsibilities that came with it, and, however clichéd as
it may sound, I had a desire to "make a difference." I had yet to
learn to differentiate between work done for one's own research

record and work done on behalf of the university, because, for me, they were one and the same.

The dynamics immediately following the announcement became, at best, hideous. I vividly remember the meeting convened to discuss the split, where I witnessed faculty members screaming at each other, a few even going so far as to threaten each other physically. The fact that certain individuals had met with the new dean behind the backs of their colleagues insulted my senior colleagues to no end. Inevitably, tensions rose so high that colleagues avoided going to the bathroom lest they encounter members of the other party in an enclosed space. The status of my new departmental home rested in the hands of an inexperienced dean who had been blindsided. Disruption devastated the academic environment, which up until that point had provided a decent enough stability for a junior faculty member. Although I would not characterize the pre-existing state of social relations as ideal, I believed that the skills I had earned in working within predominantly white and elitist environments allowed me to negotiate my position carefully within the changing landscape of institutional politics. Part of what allowed me to manage such tensions was the development of a broad range of relationships with colleagues, many of them faculty of color, from throughout the college.

During the first decade, there were enough of us to form our own community, which we did partly out of affinity and partly out of a need to provide for each other what was missing from our respective departments: competent leadership, mentoring, and guidance to successfully meet the requirements for promotion and tenure. In the absence of these crucial qualities, several of us organized a manuscript-writing group to mentor ourselves through the tenure-track process. Meanwhile, the hiring of a Latina in a key administrative position whose job responsibilities included supporting the recruitment and retention of a diverse faculty, helped to provide accountability and consistency to our process. After she left—having been recruited to accept a presidency at another university—I realized that having a supportive administrator in a position of authority played an important role in shaping the overall campus climate.

For four academic years, we (faculty in the former AMS) existed in an awkward stasis with two cochairs overseeing the separate units. To describe the serial set of "chairs" and the un-

predictable and discriminatory dynamics of hostility that en-
sued does not do justice to the daily, grinding, micro-aggressions
(Solorzano, 1998) that so aptly describe my routine during those
years. Moreover, neither of the divided units managed to do anything with their programs other than to subsist. In 2003, with a
new dean in place, we were forcibly reconstituted into one unit
and renamed the Department of Language, Cultures, and History. In 2004, when our department had an external chair search,
we hired a target-of-opportunity candidate, a classification used
by the university to pursue highly qualified and accomplished
individuals in a particular field, thereby pre-empting the standard job announcement and targeting these individuals for hire.
Under this new leadership, I experienced a brief respite from the
incessant chaos, during which I launched a new research project
and applied for external and internal grants.

I have at times wondered how the interdisciplinary structure of the West campus may have created many of the problems
of cohesion and collegiality with which we continually wrestled.
Despite the articulated interdisciplinary mission of my department, disciplinary degree programs were allowed to continue as
discrete programs (e.g., American Studies housed degree programs in history, Spanish, English, and American studies), which
inadvertently led to tensions between degree programs and to
the undermining of the interdisciplinary mission of the department. As my former English and History colleagues were fond of
saying, "all we can offer are degrees in 'English-light' or 'history-
light,'" none of which rendered our graduates competitive for top
graduate programs in these fields. The model assumes that interdisciplinarity would either magically appear or, as has most
often been the case, would rely on individual scholars to claim
that they are teaching and dispensing knowledge in an interdisciplinary manner. As a consequence, the existing infrastructure
never invited a collaborative interdisciplinary praxis. With limited resources, options to co-teach or rotate pedagogical models
in a multi- and cross-disciplinary exchange were abandoned in
an attempt to fulfill the more standard curriculum associated
with traditional degree programs.

Another layer of complexity in the social dynamics at work
was the ratio of assistant professors to full professors. At West,
assistant professors comprised over 60% of the faculty. Thus junior faculty members were largely responsible for the task of

building a campus as they simultaneously built their publication records, all without the experience, insights, and mentoring that in an ideal setting, senior faculty would presumably be responsible for. This approach had its drawbacks. In a 2007 internal document, a full professor noted that, since the 1987 plan, "From a population of over one-hundred tenured faculty appointed or promoted to Associate Professor, only *seven* individuals advanced as internal promotions to full professor" (Mc-Govern, 2007, p. 17) (my emphasis). Full professors who could serve as models of productivity were too few to make a difference in the culture at large. Further lacking was a disciplinary pool of senior colleagues from which junior faculty could call upon.

Over the years, I have come to appreciate fiscal realities and limitations on academic visions. I also appreciate the fiscal limitations that lead to placing numerous disciplinary programs under a departmental umbrella. These budgetary limitations were manifested in the dearth of national chair searches. Lacking the money for external chair searches, we often ended up putting faculty members into decision-making positions who were not only averse to serving in those capacities, but frankly, were outright incompetent. Some were even destructive.

Building Ethnic Studies

Out of a partial discontent with the lack of a race-centered approach in the curriculum of American studies, racial and ethnic studies faculty rallied to develop a way to develop the teaching and thinking about race and ethnicity for our students. The dean at the time (1998-99) was sensitive to our concerns and appointed a faculty advisory board to put together a plan that allowed us to establish the need for a baccalaureate degree program in ethnic studies. Within the first year of planning, we succeeded in establishing an ethnic studies minor and certificate program, garnered support from a highly interdisciplinary and diverse group of faculty within the college, and began the process of building a community among undergraduates. A key feature of the program was an internship that offered students the opportunity to develop their skills by requiring first-hand experiences in the field and that allowed them to get a feel for where they might work in the future.

The provision of a small personnel and operations budget to pay a stipend for a director and a part-time staff member allowed the program to grow. For the first couple of years of the program's existence, the program became a popular base in which students could participate in academic and student life. An Ethnic Studies Annual Lecture series was created to spotlight the program as we set about to build a strong foundation. Organizationally, we were considered a distributive program, one that sat outside the traditional departmental structures, incorporating faculty from across the various programs. Faculty members involved with the program were, in effect, helping to build a program, in addition to fulfilling the duties and responsibilities in their departmental homes. There was an intellectual and steadfast commitment to build the program, and despite the "double duty" for faculty, the spirit and camaraderie of the group (with already unusually high and demanding service loads commensurate with being at a new campus) was such that we went out of our way to build and diversify the curricular offerings within the College of Arts and Sciences.

Two different directors oversaw the program in its first year-and-a-half. In the summer of 2000, following the granting of my tenure, I was asked by the new dean to serve as the director of the program. I was also given the charge to develop a proposal to create a bachelor of arts in ethnic studies. The degree would be the first of its kind in Arizona, as both the University of Arizona and Arizona State University had programs designed around individual racial/ethnic groups but none conceptually tied together. Northern Arizona University was thinking along the same lines, with a minor in ethnic studies underway as well.

With a written mandate from the dean, I launched into facilitating the process to write the proposal. Every faculty member did a share: some researched counterpart programs, and others wrote a justification for the program, while others collected data. Within a six-month period, we had the proposal ready to submit. At our annual event, with our provost and other administrators in attendance, my opening remarks included my proud announcement that we were ready to submit our proposal to the Arizona Board of Regents for approval. Students, of course, were pleased to hear the news. I had no idea that my public announcement did not sit well with the campus leadership.

It was not long before I received requests from the upper administration to write a concept paper before submitting the actual proposal. Suddenly there were new rules, and it appeared that the administration was attempting to stall our efforts to become a degree program. So we went back to the drawing board and drafted yet another document. The summer went by with no response from the administration.

I will never forget that on September 11, 2001, my program coordinator tracked me down to inform me that the vice-provosts and the new interim dean (the dean who had mandated me to create Ethnic Studies had been forced to resign) were looking for me and demanded my presence at a meeting that afternoon. I felt like I was being called into the principal's office. Two vice-provosts and my dean sat around the table; their first comments conveyed that they and the provost had been shocked to learn on the evening of our Ethnic Studies Annual Lecture that we were planning to become a degree program. They described the provost's reaction as "her jaw having dropped" when she heard my announcement. "How did you get the idea that you had *permission* to go to the regents to apply for a new degree program?" one of them asked. By this time, all my socialization came into focus as I calmly responded, "The dean gave me the mandate when he asked me to serve." For a split second I sensed their disbelief as their eyes narrowed, and they collectively inhaled. I proceeded to explain, "I have the mandate in writing if you'd care to look at it." With this added piece of information, obviously new to them, they backed off and said that they and the provost, as the executive team, had no knowledge of this mandate and that they had their concerns about whether this proposal could go forward.

I knew by the time I walked out of the meeting that we wouldn't obtain their permission. I have been around higher education long enough to know that when the administration wants something to happen, it can happen overnight. When the administration does not, they engage in a wait-and-see game, relying on the intricacies of the bureaucratic infrastructure to defeat and cripple even the most noble of efforts. I left the meeting with the promise to provide them with a copy of the letter, which I did, and the agreement that one of them would provide feedback to our proposal. Indeed, the feedback arrived within a month: a three-page memo outlining the reasons we couldn't go forward, including "requests for additional data," such that our efforts were brought to a halt.

Often the processes by which faculty-led changes occur can appear bureaucratically possible. What all the forms, steps, and levels of approval don't reveal is how contingent the ability to pursue development of a given academic degree program is on the particular inclinations or goals of a given administrator. Politically, establishing a degree program in ethnic studies was threatening to the already existing degree programs, some of which had been largely unsuccessful in attracting students to their major. As a faculty, however, we were not dissuaded by the challenges. Instead, we agreed to hold steadfast until a time when they were willing to grant us permission to go forward. In the meantime, we concentrated our efforts on building our numbers, visibility, and service to students.

Restructuring Arizona's Higher Education: Diverting the Demographics

To begin this part of the story requires returning to the year 2004, a week after classes ended, approximately the third week of May. Indicative of the state of our institutional communication, I opened the Sunday paper to discover the headline: "University aims for 2-tier system" (Slivka, 2004, p. A22-A23). The announcement that our campus was going to be "spun off" by the Arizona State University System (AUS), be renamed Central Arizona University, lose our research mission, and become a second-tier university whose primary purpose was to offer undergraduate teaching, hit me like a ton of bricks. Part of the rationale presented in this article was that Arizona was expecting a surge of Latino students, which by my knowledge of higher education history meant that they were planning to "divert" Latino students to the second tier (Brint and Karabel, 1989, pp. 128-131; Arizona Board of Regents, 2004).

That very Monday a campus emergency meeting was held with the vice-provost and two members of the board of regents. The entire campus showed up and expressed outrage. Apparently, this was news to the university administration and the board of regents, who had somehow gleaned the impression that we would welcome such a move. There was no transparency at the campus administrative level, as our own lame-duck provost was almost as surprised by the announcement as we were, having heard herself only two days before the announcement that this was to be publicized. Furthermore, this spin-off was blatantly contrary to the "One University, Many Places" visionary document that ASU President Michael Crow had presented just one week earlier, situating ASU West as entrenched in ASU's research mission.

To save our campus's research mission, I believed that I had no choice but to throw my every energy into a series of campus- and community-wide meetings that were organized against the spin-off. For a year, I was among a core group of faculty who worked tirelessly and took action to a) hire lawyers; b) generate research, data, and presentations to counter the proposal; c) meet and work with different community interest groups; d) participate in official state-wide university stakeholder groups; and e) meet with student organizations and leaders. By the year's end, we produced a document that outlined a new vision for a learner-centered metropolitan university (Arizona State University West, 2004). Although our challenge was ultimately successful, within a year following the decision to keep us within the system, the university decommissioned our campus's separate accreditation, and we lost our legislative budgetary allocation, the latter raided by an increasingly centralized administration governing from the Tempe campus.

Little did we know that this foreshadowed even more negative decisions. In 2007, we lost control of our curriculum (having gone from a consultative relationship with Tempe to having to obtain their authorization), the New College of Interdisciplinary Arts and Sciences was restructured into divisions and lost its departments and Chairs, and our research child care center was closed, much to the dismay of campus and community members who used the subsidized center. In 2008, our campus lost two of its four colleges (School of Global Management and Leadership and the College of Human Services) and all remaining research centers. And in 2009, our campus lost its only doctoral degree (Wright, 2009, p. Z18).

Departmental Demise and the Derailing of Dissent

Thanksgiving week of 2007, my colleague, who for six years had served as chair of one of the interdisciplinary departments and was a founding member of Ethnic Studies, came into my office to reveal that the new dean/vice-provost announced that effective January 1, 2008, the seven departments in New College would be reorganized into three divisions. The seven chairs would be replaced with three division heads, and "this was not open for negotiation." Whether this transpired out of backroom discussions between a few disgruntled faculty and associate deans or on orders from the central administration at the Tempe campus remains a mystery. Although ABOR approval was required for the dismantling of departments, the decision was presented as a *fait accompli*, and the dean made it very clear that no dissension was to be tolerated. Rumors circulated that she threatened the chairs when she heard that a rebellion might be afoot, and a climate of fear and demoralized resignation prevailed. In the process, chairs were put on paid leave for the spring semester, their classes cancelled, while faculty were assured that despite the new structure, their former departments' promotion and tenure criteria would be honored, and degree programs would remain intact.

The lack of transparency and broad-based faculty input extended into the next set of iterations of power, whereby one chair was retained as division director, an associate dean assumed an additional role as director of a division, and one faculty member involved in the restructuring assumed a directorship with the promise to expedite his promotion to full professor.

For me, this meant that I had gone from initially joining a department of American Studies to finding myself a member of a divided and strangely renamed Department of Language, Cultures, and History (with my third leg in the distributive program of Ethnic Studies) to being herded into a now reconstituted division with four former departments and the program of Ethnic Studies, unilaterally named the Division of Humanities, Arts, and Cultural Studies. In place of the only chair of color within New College, we were suddenly informed that our new director would be the only associate professor empowered in this now *all white-male* leadership structure. Among the four "new" white male directors were two former New College deans who had been previously removed from their positions as deans. Indeed, I escaped losing my administrative position in this gleaning, as I had resigned from my six-year position as director of Ethnic Studies at the end of the 2007-8 academic year. As Ethnic Studies director, I had worked with all of the chairs and directors for over five years. With an apparent lack of concern for competency, merit, and diversity, the administration removed three white women and two men of color from their leadership positions.

Three weeks into the new regime, the associate-professor "director" resigned his position, having discovered that he was not up to the challenge of leadership, but he was asked to stay on by the dean/vice-provost for the rest of the semester. By the end of the semester, it was announced that the inaugural associate-professor director and the associate director (one of the former deans) would both be stepping down at the end of the semester, a semester in which they failed to call even one division meeting. Dissension reached unprecedented heights. In this semester, two tenure-track positions were given (without searches) to two white male faculty members' white wives, teaching loads were arbitrarily lowered for select faculty, raises to salary baselines and monies to select faculty were distributed without transparency (and without actual offer letters from competing universities), and at least one tenure-track hire was made without any faculty consultation. Also, midstream in this semester, faculty lost control of (a) having consultation and input in what courses they were assigned to teach, (b) the times of their courses, and (c) the size of their classes. In fact, efforts were made to prevent faculty from seeing their fall schedules. The other associate dean, an African American full professor who herself had gone through three different administrative assignments during her three-year assignment to our campus, now was asked to clean up the mess left by the "acting" director and associate director, thus becoming interim director.

Losing Ground: The Exodus of Faculty of Color

When I arrived in 1994, ASU prided itself on having the largest percentage of Latina/o faculty at a four-year public university in the United States. ASU West was especially diverse. Between 1994 and 2008, however, I witnessed a systemic failure on the part of the institution to retain faculty of color. This history could fill the pages of one chapter. I can, with utmost certainty testify that the reasons my former colleagues left do not support the popular institutional argument that faculty leave for "better opportunities." Rather, their reasons were very much tied to the issues and conditions documented in this essay. I cannot emphasize enough how important it is for institutions to understand that the decisions they make, especially whom they hire or appoint as chairs, directly influence the extent to which faculty, especially faculty of color, will thrive, fail, or succeed.

I cannot begin to capture the dynamics involved in my colleagues' respective departures. At least two of my colleagues have been or are in the process of documenting their trials and tribulations at our campus (Elenes, 2008; Tellez, forthcoming). Of the four American Indian tenure-track or lecturer faculty, each was fired, denied tenure, or pushed out. I also know that despite years of search committees to identify and successfully recruit five African American tenure-track faculty, as of 2009, none remain (with the exception of one colleague who was not hired through traditional search processes). Again, despite having recruited some very successful Latina/o faculty who came to ASU West interested in working in the Southwest and with our largely first-generation students, since 1994 we have lost eight Latina/o faculty.

Even though each loss has its particular circumstances, each person experienced the following conditions: (a) chairs who were incompetent, abusive of the position once empowered, or both; (b) an unstable college environment with perpetual administrative turnovers; (c) the failure to be mentored; (d) noncollegial departmental meetings in which a hostile culture was allowed to persist over time; (e) constantly shifting expectations with respect to promotion and tenure; (f) administrative application of criteria that were inconsistent and arbitrary; (g) an environment of favors for select individuals in administrative promotion and tenure, spousal hirings, and other critical decisions; and (h) an unequal and inordinate service burden for faculty of color with no honoring or reward system in place for that service. Finally, any increase in representation of faculty of color required advocacy on the part of faculty of color, and often on the part of the community, for promotions or positions of influence to be realized.

A Culture of Shifting Expectations

Change has been the only constant at ASU West. Promotion and tenure criteria went from the expectation that a balanced record of integrated and interdisciplinary research, teaching, and service would be valued to a shift in which research and grantsmanship formed the primary basis for promotion and tenure. The number of external letters of recommendation required for promotion and tenure went from a minimum of three to five up to ten. Criteria for external letters went from a requirement that they be written by experts in one's field to a requirement that they come from experts at Research 1 Universities. At the departmental level, we operated for more than fourteen years under informal promotion and tenure criteria that were revisited on a nearly annual basis. The last iteration of the standards included "more stringent" research criteria and approval.

However, with less than one year of approval, the new director is now discussing the distinct possibility of overriding the documents into one new combined document. Thus a newly hired tenure-track person could have had five different sets of criteria before coming up for tenure. Teaching loads went from four courses to five courses per academic year, but only for faculty at the West campus (with arbitrary exceptions here and there). West went from having an independent curricular process to a Tempe-centric process, from serving solely upper-division students to functioning as a four-year university, from having our own accreditation with the NCA (Northern Central Association) to having one central accreditation. We went from chairs being the sole evaluators for faculty annual reviews to having to face a personnel committee, with no elections by the faculty to either decide the structure or elect the members of the committee.

When I arrived, the campus's legislative mission of interdisciplinarity was taken seriously, and we were required to document the extent to which we met this criterion in our research, teaching, and service. This emphasis disappeared and was replaced by an emphasis on one's disciplinary field. When we were helping to build the institution, service was highly valued and played a significant role in one's annual review and promotion. Now, junior faculty are protected from service, having been strongly advised that it is devalued, while an entire cohort of associate professors remain handicapped because of their previous attention to serving and building the institution. Yet, no respite or strategic plan is in place to provide this cohort with the resources or support to assist in their advancement.

There was also the issue of our "belonging" to the ASU system. First we were a separate campus with our own mission, then we were possibly not a part of ASU, then we were a part of ASU but not with a research mission, then we were a part of ASU, but we had a differentiated mission that had to be explicitly addressed in any programs we put forward. Today, we have been colonized such that we are a part of ASU (The administration removed the campus's ASU West sign, and we were forbidden to refer to ourselves as ASU West). Recently we were proposed for closure,

putatively because of the state's budgetary crisis. Progressing toward this status, however, we were to consider ourselves as one
of four campuses of ASU, but we were to have a higher teaching
load, fewer resources, and no doctoral programs (although we
could propagate unique master's programs), and we could belong
to graduate clusters of faculty to serve on doctoral committees
(with Tempe's approval of our CVs).

Despite the inequitable conditions, we were all still subject
to the new centralized committee of twenty-four full professors
who were to evaluate our files for promotion and tenure. With
every new administrator, there was a new mission to be written,
a new vision to be crafted. No one served long enough to have an
historical appreciation for the institution, much less be in a future position to implement anything. Even as I wrote this essay
in the spring semester of 2009, we learned from a press release
that a plan to strip the West campus of all its master's degree
programs was to be effective immediately, a plan that was re-
tracted a week later, largely due to "outrage from the West valley
legislators, citizenry, and businesses (Wright, 2009, p. Z18).

I distinctly remember being given the charge, while serving
as director of Ethnic Studies, to obtain at least $10,000 in exter-
nal research funding for my program. The dean was given a goal
for the college to acquire $10 million. I remember a young junior
Filipina faculty member coming to my office, distressed over how
and where she was going to build a record in her second year so
that her midcareer record would not be jeopardized for failing
to have obtained external monies. She said to me, "I'm working
on my book; I thought that was what I was supposed to be doing." My junior colleague's angst can best be summarized by a
senior colleague who noted in an internal document responding
to the departmental demise, "Even a mature organization with
well-entrenched bureaucratic structures would be left reeling
by such systemic upheavals" (McGovern, 2007, p. 18). In fact,
there has never been a stable period of significant length in
which to thrive. It has been a serial culture of macro and microaggressions (Solorzano, 1998; Solorzano & Yosso, 2001).

Since my fortuitous arrival at ASU West, I have endured the
Arizona Board of Regent's attempt to end tenure; a covert and
strategically successful division of my department which lasted
several years; a subsequent reconvening of the same department
under a new name; an attempted spin-off of our campus; the

dismembering of our original legislative mission; a succession of eight provosts (three interim), eight deans (four interim), eight chairs (leading one department, a split department, a reconvened department with a new name, to an abolished department); and now, within a period of a year-and-a-half, a succession of three directors. For my loyalties, I face a compression to my salary (I sit on mid-year probationary reviews for junior faculty who earn more than I do), and in my first meeting with my new director, I was informed of preliminary plans to reorganize the "small" academic degree programs within our division (Ethnic Studies, Women's Studies, and American Studies) into one degree program.

Thus, the six-year effort to create an ethnic studies program which we hoped would eventually become a department is now at risk of being morphed into yet another configuration. Only now, no resources are committed to the program, no state funds or operating funds accompany the effort, and all that remains are those of us affiliated and loyal to the program's existence. The once organic energy we had as a set of interdisciplinary colleagues interested in working together to offer a vibrant and intellectual space for our students and for each other is, for the most part, gone. Junior faculty who once contributed to the program have either left, been denied tenure, or directed their energy to obtaining tenure amid ever-changing criteria. Those of us who founded the program suffer from what I call PTSD—*perennial* traumatic stress syndrome—recognizing that the instability, the constantly changing rules, and a demoralized and disaffected faculty are not the ingredients or conditions from which to build an academic degree program, much less successful careers. Our energies have dissipated into the in-between spaces carved out by an adminstration seemingly incapable of effectively leading, managing, and implementing a vision.

Conclusion

Does this mean I would discourage students from pursuing scholarly careers or warn freshly minted doctoral students to stay away from new campuses or nontraditional campuses? Moreover, why did I stay? As a student of higher education, I know all too well that the problems and issues I have captured in these pages, while they may be specific to having joined a new campus with an interdisciplinary mission, reflect broader structural and cultural issues endemic, (albeit in varying degrees), to academic life. I would caution the young scholar to think carefully about the type of institution she or he wants to commit to when first pursuing the job market. Be clear on whether you expect to dedicate more time to your research than to teaching and the kinds of resources you will need to establish yourself as a scholar (Along those lines, make sure you have your teaching load included in your contract letter). Inform yourself about the history of the departments and colleges you are prospectively joining. Has there been a high turnover? If so, why? How do faculty members talk about the culture of their campuses and departmental homes? What kind of social support and engagement do colleagues appear to have with one another, and how important is it for you to be connected socially versus working in isolation? Moreover, think about the population of students you will be likely to serve at the institution of your choice. Do you want to work with first-generation college students, students who have full lives and work in addition to their university commitments, or teach privileged students from elite backgrounds?

So why did I stay? My reasons are largely personal. My family of origin and the subsequent two generations of family are just a four-hour drive from my Phoenix home. My partner's children live in this state. And, in the end, the desert environment is home. Be what it may, I insist on working at a public university whose purpose it is to educate and maintain access to higher education for Arizona's diverse population. Arizona State University, for all its strengths and weaknesses, personifies that mission.

To build on President Obama's principle of the "audacity of hope," I tend to understand the competing forces in terms of having an "audacity of purpose." I am honored to have a profession that allows me to maintain meaning and purpose in the work I do. Three principles guide me: (a) stay in touch with students; (b) maintain friendships with colleagues; and (c) establish and nurture ties in the broader community. A mentor at UC Berkeley once advised me to be sure to stay in touch with students of many years past. "Students will keep you honest," he said. Indeed, the relationships I forged with students, especially those I individually mentored and assisted with their applications to graduate and professional programs throughout my years at the West campus, have been priceless. In these students I rest my hope and dreams for a more just and democratic society, trusting that they will "pass it forward" in one form or another in their respective paths. The second principle involves the friendships I have enjoyed with colleagues and staff across campus and across the profession. They helped make life tolerable, kept it "fun" even under the most ludicrous of circumstances, and challenged me intellectually. Even though I have had to say goodbye more times than I would have desired, as I said to my campus colleagues during our struggles against restructuring, "in the end, what we'll remember is how we treated each other and the sense of community that came out of this." Third, but not least, is to keep ties and establish relationships in the community.

In 2005, I began a research project interviewing families and former workers who had lived in the labor camps established by Goodyear Farms, a subsidiary of the iconic Goodyear Tire & Rubber Corporation. The partnership I developed with community members from the Litchfield Park Historical Society re-energized and strengthened my purpose as a scholar. Before I knew it, we had collected more than 50 videotaped oral histories for the "Mexican Americans of Litchfield Park Oral History Project," produced a film (*Voices from the Camps of Litchfield Park*), and organized a photo exhibit showcased at the West campus (Cuádraz, 2006). My relationships in the community have grounded me and reminded me of the reasons I pursued a scholarly life in the first place, and the importance of staying strong for the goal of greater social justice. If I have any pearls of wisdom to share from my fifteen-year career as a Chicana scholar, they reside in this paragraph.

References

Abnone, M. (2004, April 23). Arizona State U. plans for 61% more students. *The Chronicle of Higher Education*, A28.

Arizona Board of Regents. (2004). *Redesigning Arizona's university system*. Phoenix, AZ: Arizona Board of Regents.

Arizona State University (2009). *ASU History.* Retrieved from Arizona State University Web site: http://www.asu.edu/about/history/.

Arizona State University West. (2004). *A learner-centered public metropolitan research university: An alternative vision for Arizona State University West.* Phoenix, AZ: Arizona Board of Regents.

Arizona State University West (2004). *A review of ASU West's historical development.* Phoenix, AZ: Arizona State University West Library.

Brint, S., & Karabel, J. (1989). *The diverted dream: Community colleges and the promise of educational opportunity in America, 1900-1985.* New York: Oxford University Press.

Cuádraz, G. H. (Producer). (2006). *Voices from the camps of Litchfield Park* [motion picture]. Arizona State University: Arizona Board of Regents.

Elenes, C. A. (2008). Continuity and change in women's studies programs: One step forward, two steps backward. In A. Ginsberg (Ed.), *The evolution of American women's studies: Reflections on triumphs, controversies and change* (pp. 165-182). New York, NY: Palgrave Macmillan.

McGovern, T. (2007). *Academic pluralism, faculty development, and interdisciplinary curricula: continuing the narrative for the new college of interdisciplinary arts and sciences.* Unpublished manuscript.

Pellett, G. (Producer) & Nelson, S. (Director). (1996). Shattering the silences: Minorities break into the ivory tower [motion picture]. United States: Gail Pellett Productions.

Slivka, J. (2004, May 23). University aims for 2-tier system. *The Arizona Republic*, A1; A22-A23.

Solorzano, D. (1998). Critical race theory, race and gender: Microaggressions and the experience of Chicana and Chicano scholars. *Qualitative Studies in Education 11*(1), 121-136.

Solorzano, D., & Yosso, T. (2001). Counterstory telling: Chicana and Chicano graduate school experiences. *Qualitative Studies in Education 14*(4), 471-495.

Tellez, M. (2009). "And now, I'm a mom": Voice and experience as a transformative institutional practice in the academy. In S. Fryberg & E. Martinez (Eds.), *Engaging our faculties: Junior faculty of color speak back to the academy.* Manuscript submitted for publication.

Wright, L. (2009, February 21). Crow, West side tangle: ASU chief harbinger of doom. *The Arizona Republic*, Z18 weekend.

Leadership With Grace

Nakeina E. Douglas & Susan T. Gooden
Virginia Commonwealth University

Introduction

A remarkable lady of incredible talent and vision, Dr. Grace Edmondson Harris has a unique experience with Virginia Commonwealth University (VCU). A native of rural Halifax County in southern Virginia, she was denied admission to graduate study at VCU (then Richmond Professional Institute), a large public university in Richmond, Virginia. Ironically, later in 1967, Dr. Harris became the first African American female faculty member in the School of Social Work at VCU and ascended the ranks to become Dean of the School of Social Work, Provost, and Acting President prior to her retirement in 1999. Although Dr. Harris has strong ties to the African American community, to situate her contributions to VCU solely in terms of a "segregation to integration" narrative misses the mark. It fails to capture her success in leading the School of Social Work and her clear vision in her capacity as provost and in developing VCU's First Strategic Plan. She continues to share her leadership talents through the Grace E. Harris Leadership Institute, which was established at VCU in her honor upon her retirement. Most recently, in 2008, an academic building on VCU's campus was named "Grace E. Harris Hall." Through a series of interviews with Dr. Harris, as well as with current and former administrators and faculty at VCU, we offer a description and analysis of Dr. Harris' leadership style spanning her 40 year tenure at Virginia Commonwealth University. It is a style that we (and others) find to be uniquely effective, people-centered, and decisive.

Women in the Academy

Women's participation in the academy has increased since the 1970s, fueled by greater attention to equal opportunity legislation, affirmative action principles, feminism, women's work ethic, and abilities (Gerdes, 2006). The number of women serving in top administrative positions as presidents, provosts, vice provosts and deans, department chairs, and program directors continues to increase (American Council on Education, 2007).

In spite of this progress, research continues to highlight the challenges and slow progress of women at every organizational level from students (Jacob, 1996; Sax, 2008) to faculty (Zemsky, 2001) to administrators (Glazer-Raymo, 1999; Lafreniere & Longman, 2008). The American Association of University Professors' (AAUP) 2006 Annual Report on the Economic Status of the Profession highlights a number of alarming trends for women in the academy. Although there are signs of rapid increase, the rate is too slow to achieve parity for many of years. Since the passage of Title IX in 1972, women have been solwly integrated into faculty ranks and are still struggling to obtain employment, tenure status, full professor rank, and average salaries on par with men. There is still significant work to be done if women are to be fully and successfully integrated into the ranks of America's faculty in institutions of Higher Education (West & Curtis, 2006).

Barton (2006) suggests that we can begin to address the issues facing women in colleges and universities by applying feminist pedagogical principles to create and sustain nurturing academic communities. Feminist leaders tend to be student-centered, focused on equity and work to build holistic environments in which all constituents can thrive. They tend to be vigilant against oppression and work to ensure that everyone is treated fairly. Feminist educational leadership embraces a political agenda that is motivated by equity. For the participants in Barton's research, feminist leadership entails a micro and macro view of social justice concerns with a desire to move marginalized voices to the center of the conversation, and a willingness to take risks as one strives to enact a transformative agenda. Feminist academic administrators' work toward equitable and holistic social arrangements makes them instrumental in developing more nurturing higher education organizations.

Women, especially feminist women, are more likely to be transformational in their leadership styles (Chin et al., 2007; Eagly, Johannensen-Schmidt, & van Engen, 2003). According to Burns (1978), transformational leadership originates in the personal values and beliefs of leaders and is transmitted to one's followers. The premise is that transformational leaders operate out of deeply held personal value systems that include values such as justice, liberty, equality and integrity. Transformational leaders are able to empower and mentor their followers, addressing each follower's sense of self-worth, thus teaching them to develop a true commitment to their full potential (Burns, 1978).

Transformational leaders have the ability to transform their followers into leaders by broadening and expanding their interests. "The transformational leader arouses heightened awareness and interest in the group and organization, increases confidence and moves followers gradually from concerns for existence to concerns for achievement and growth" (Yammarino, 1992, p. 28). Transformational leaders stand out from others in their force of powerful personal characteristics, ability to appeal to ideological values and expectation of self-sacrifice from others, and intensely personal relationships with others (House & Howell, 1992). The objective for women leaders often includes empowering others through their stewardship of an organization's resources, social advocacy, promoting a feminist policy and agenda, and changing the organizational culture to create an equitable environment (Chin et al., 2007). Transformational leadership can bring about a higher level of performance within the organization than previously was experienced.

Women of Color in the Academy

African American women remain underrepresented as recipients of doctorates and in academic positions within universities. As Table 1 reports, according to the Digest of Education Statistics, 2,445 Black women earned a Ph.D. in 2007, only 4 percent of the 60,616 doctorates awarded that year. Under 4 percent of all tenured or tenure-track faculty are Black females.

Table 1: Black Female Awarded Doctorates in 2007*

Doctorates Awarded	Number	Percentage
All Doctorates	60,616	100%
All Females	30,365	50%
Black Female	2,445	4%

Data sources:
*Table 290, Chapter 3: Postsecondary Education, Digest of Education Statistics 2008

Table 2: Black Female Representation in Faculty Ranks 2007**

Faculty by Rank	Number	Percentage
All Full Professor	173,395	100%
Female Full Professor	45,907	26.5%
Black Female Full Professor	2,193	1.3%
All Associate Professors	143,692	100%
Female Associate Professors	57,032	40%
Black Female Associate Professors	3,745	2.6%
All Assistant Professors	168,508	100%
Female Assistant Professors	79,767	47%
Black Female Assistant Professors	6,035	3.6%
All Instructor[1]	101,429	100%
Female Instructors[1]	54,830	54%
Black Female Instructors[1]	4,552	4.5%
All Lecturers[1]	31,264	100%
Female Lecturers[1]	16,480	53%
Black Female Lecturers[1]	881	2.8%
All Other Faculty[2]	85,175	100%
Female Other Faculty[2]	40,332	47%
Black Female Other Faculty[2]	2,742	3.2%

Data sources:
**Table 249, Chapter 3: Postsecondary Education, Digest of Education Statistics 2008
[1]Non-tenure track position
[2]Includes all non-tenure track faculty lines that do not teach such as researchers and administrators.

Within the academy, few African American women ascend to the highest levels of university professorships and administrative positions. Only 1.3 percent of 173,395 full professors in the United States are Black women. A forthcoming report by the National Association for Equal Opportunity in Higher Education found that Black women were about twice as likely to transfer from a tenure-track faculty position to an adjunct research path as were members of other groups, including Black men. Also, they were substantially less likely than other segments of the population to be retained in tenure-track faculty positions (Chronicle of Higher Education, 2008). Research on Black faculty women cites several external barriers that often stifle their success as scholars, such as an undue burden of nonresearch activities; ambiguous, inappropriate, and unfairly weighed tenure and promotion requirements; lack of access to resources and support for teaching and research; and racism and discrimination (Gregory, 1999).

Much of the research on African American women in the academy focuses on the difficulties they face living with multiple marginality (Berry & Mizelle, 2006; Garner, 2004; Gregory, 1995; Turner, 2002). As Turner (2002) discusses, "Although faculty women of color have obtained academic positions, even when tenured they often confront situations that limit their authority and, as they address these situations, drain their energy" (p. 75). Themes that emerge from her interviews include feeling isolated and underrespected; salience of race over gender; being underemployed and overused by departments and/or institutions; being torn between family, community, and career; and being challenged by students (p. 80).

Yet another line of scholarship examining African American women in the academy focuses on the importance of linkages with their communities, families, and the importance of being mentored and mentoring. In her autobiography, Lynn Winfield (1997) explains:

> In general, African American females in America have not been valued for their femininity or their scholarly work, making issues of personal and scholarly identify problematic. I myself have found few self-affirming images of scholarship, beauty, or success of women of color. (Winfield, p. 194)

Winfield continues,

> Very early, I developed multiple dimensions within my reality that allowed me to function simultaneously as wife, mother, scholar, Sunday school teacher, choir director and other roles in the community. (p. 195)

The positive impact of mentoring is supported in previous research (Blackburn, Chapman, & Cameron, 1981; Eberspacher & Sisler, 1988; Johnsrud, 1990; Moore 1982; Sandlers & Wong, 1985). In their examination of African American female administrators who hold or have held senior-level administrative positions in higher education in the state of New York, Smith and Crawford (2007) found that "mentoring in the traditional definition did not impact the career choices and development" of the women in their study (p. 6). Their study concludes by stating, "Mentoring must be valued as a means to empower African American female administrators in higher education...Similarly, leadership from the board of trustees and the president is clearly a fundamental prerequisite in creating a culture that would allow African America females to flourish" (p. 7).

Looking beyond the specific experiences of Black women in academic settings, Patricia Hill Collins's seminal work on Black feminist epistemology is based on the following propositions:

1) *Concrete experience as a criterion of meaning*—As Collins discusses, "African-American women need wisdom to know how to deal with the "educated fools" who would "take a shotgun to a roach" (p. 208). She continues, "In traditional African American communities Black women find considerable institutional support for valuing concrete experience (p. 211).

2) *The use of dialogue in assessing knowledge claims*— "For Black women new knowledge claims are rarely worked out in isolation from other individuals and are usually developed through dialogues with other members of a community. A primary epistemological assumption underlying the use of dialogue in assessing knowledge claims is that connectedness rather than separation is an essential component of the knowledge validation process (Belenky et al. 1986, p. 18 cited in Collins, 1990, p. 212).

3) *The ethic of caring*—According to Collins (1990), the ethic of caring has three interrelated components. The first component is the emphasis placed on individual uniqueness. "Rooted in a tradition of African humanism, each individual is thought to be a unique expression of a common spirit, power, or energy inherent in all life." The second component concerns the appropriateness of emotions in dialogues. And the third involves developing the capacity for empathy (Collins, 1990, p. 215, 216).

4) *The ethic of personal accountability*—"Not only must individuals develop their knowledge claims through dialogue and present them in a style proving their concern for their ideas, but people are expected to be accountable

for their knowledge claims...Assessments of an individual's knowledge claims simultaneously evaluate an individual's character, values, and ethics" (Collins, 1990, p. 217-18).

Collins's four propositions of Black feminist epistemology can be applied to a variety of settings including an understanding of African American women's approach to leadership.

Methodology

We were interested in learning more about Dr. Grace Harris's leadership style from her directly, as well as from those who had worked with her. We held semistructured interviews with nine individuals. Each interview lasted about an hour. We interviewed the current president and provost of VCU, as well as other senior administrators and faculty (current and retired) who had worked with her over the years. These interviews included the following topics: leadership style, personal influences, administrative accomplishments, institutional legacy, and commitment to social equity and justice. As co-authors, both of us participated in each interview, alternating our roles as interviewer and scribe.

A traditional 360-degree feedback tool is a multi-rater tool that draws responses regarding leadership effectiveness from bosses, peers and subordinates on a wide range of subjects usually within a defined set of themes. Consistent with the literature on 360-degree feedback assessments, we agreed that capturing multiple perspectives provides us with a comprehensive picture of Dr. Harris's tenure at VCU (Chappelow, 1998). Our design is intended to provide a greater awareness of the influence and impact that she had on VCU. We use elements of scholarly personal narrative (SPN) and semi-structured interview methods to present a holistic account of Dr. Harris's leadership.

This exploration is designed to enlighten the reader about the experiences of one woman serving at an urban institution in the heart of the South. As one interviewee points out, "It's easy to tell the story of race and gender, but what makes this story significant are her accomplishments and the lasting impact that they have had on this university." SPN scholarship asks a series of personal, narrative-grounded contextual questions for the purpose of divulging the full range of human experience into formal scholarly writing (Nash, 2004). SPN writers intentionally organize their writings around themes, issues, constructs, and concepts that carry larger, more universal meaning for its readers (Nash, 2004, p. 30). These requirements of SPN render the 360-degree model chosen for this chapter an ideal tool. Consistent with the framework of SPN, this chapter explores the professional life of Grace E. Harris and integrates this exploration with references and insights from other scholarship to examine larger theoretical and practical questions of race, gender, equity, and leadership. We selected Dr. Harris as the focus of this chapter because of our admiration for her, personally and professionally, and her commitment to social equity and social justice.

The Core Elements of Leadership with Grace

Interestingly, Dr. Harris, the individuals we interviewed, and both of us all independently offered very similar themes regarding her leadership style. These themes include advancing administrative vision; putting people first; listening before deciding; and the importance of family, social and community networks.

Advancing Administrative Vision—One prominent theme among the interviewees is Dr. Harris's ability to establish a clear vision and inspire the commitment of others. Dr. Harris is consistently described as a transformational leader. She rose to Chief Academic Officer of the institution and to acting president on two occasions. Her dedication to the university's mission and the students was always clear. The growth of the School of Social Work, her stewardship of the University's first strategic plan and payroll system, her attention to affirmative action policies and procedures, and the development of her community leadership programs are all examples of her vision in action.

The President of Virginia Commonwealth University, Dr. Eugene Trani, described Dr. Harris as a trailblazer who had dramatic influence on the soul of the university, what it is, and the way it relates to people. She is described as keenly aware of emerging issues and developments in the world outside the university. The comments infer that she sees the university as a resource with which to reconcile some of these issues both on and off campus.

Several of the interviewees attributed many of the university's core principles to Dr. Harris. The Vice President for Human Resources and Family Care Services of the VCU Health System commented that Dr. Harris's moral compass and her vision for VCU were needed to help lay the foundation for the university becoming a major force in Virginia:

I think she's been a visionary, a role model. I think she has inspired people to be not only proud of VCU, but also its potential. She genuinely values the unique differences and contributions of a diverse workforce and student body and she wants to make sure that people succeed and I think she fosters trust. She just has a great way of getting you excited about her vision and that helps a team be more motivated to accomplish goals. It's rare that a person can help bring you along, help you accomplish things, helps you through obstacles and then celebrates your successes. Her decisions have had a tremendous impact on our curriculum, our students, staff, and our community image.

Related to this impression, the Provost remarked,

VCU is an institution that has a greater appreciation of values of diversity because of Dr. Harris. The issues that Grace has worked on her entire life are issues that we have to continue to work on. If she weren't there to pave the way, VCU would be an entirely different place.

Dr. Harris's vision was identified across a broad spectrum of activities and ideas discussed by the interviewees. In her role as Dean, she was instrumental in constructing the agenda for the School of Social Work in the late 1980s and early 1990s. Continuing in the footsteps of her predecessors, under Dr. Harris, the School of Social Work became a leading school in the field. The current Senior Associate Dean credits Dr. Harris with the continued growth of the School of Social Work:

She contributed to our momentum on the national scene. The growth of the doctoral program occurred during her tenure as Dean. The program is one of the best in the country. In 1978, we were told that the bachelor of social work (BSW) program had to move in to the school of social work. Grace insisted that "we are all one school," our faculty teach across all three programs. Thus, faculty understand the continuum of the instruction. Grace always supported the BSW program even when some faculty did not. She didn't want any of the programs to feel as second class programs. I have carried out this mantra of oneness. As a School, our strength comes from the three programs.

During Dr. Harris's tenure as Dean, the School of Social Work received reaccreditation, continued to assist in the growth of other programs across the state, increased its enrollment of students and the diversity of the faculty while continuing to elevate awareness of social work and social work education on campus and the School's national prominence.

The interviewees reported similar success in Dr. Harris's role as Provost. According to the President, she oversaw the restructuring of two colleges (the School of Community and Public Affairs and the School of Medicine) and the transition from a commuter institution to a residential university. The president also credited her with enhancing the university's commitment to the community, improving student engagement, and hiring good personnel. There was considerable agreement among the interviewees that her stewardship on the strategic plan and university payroll system were probably her most prominent achievements as Provost. Additionally, her efforts to bridge the divide between the academic and medical campuses were laudable and helped strengthen VCU's future as a single institution. Dr. Harris is credited with fostering good relations between the two campuses and increasing *esprit de corps* at a time when separatist sentiments were strong. The Vice President for Human Resources and Family Care Services of the VCU Health System commented on the dissonance between the medical campus and the academic campus:

> She has fostered a true understanding and collegiality between the two campuses. She set the culture to think about change and VCU in a different way. Dr. Harris laid the groundwork for a lot of what the President made a reality. She was Provost during a difficult time. The fact that she was able to run things so well eased his transition.

The University strategic plan was instrumental in forging the union between the two campuses and setting the tone for the new VCU. The President, Provost and former Dean of the College of Humanities and Sciences all noted Dr. Harris' role in crafting and implementing the University's first strategic plan:

> She implemented and contoured the vision that the President had when he came to VCU. The first five to eight years (of his presidency) were the most dramatic since VCU's inception in 1969. She was chief academic officer at a time when VCU was creating an identity for itself as

a research institution with a strong urban commitment.
She was absolutely instrumental in its implementation
because she had interpersonal and relational skills. (Former Dean, College of Humanities and Sciences)

He went on to discuss the development and implementation of
the strategic plan. He described the completion as the turning
point in university history. Not only was a plan developed, but
she put into place mechanisms for evaluating it, "It was a novel
idea: doing it, assessing it, monitoring it and holding people accountable was really a sea change at the university."

All of the interviewees agreed on the transformative role that
Dr. Harris played at the University.

[While] the symbolic representation is important, it's
what you do while in that position that is more important. What you have here was the most influential provost [in the history of VCU]. That's a pretty substantial
accomplishment. (Former Dean College of Humanities
and Sciences)

She stabilized our university and proved that women and
women of color could be successful in building alliances
and making tough decisions, and just being admired as a
person. (Vice President for Human Resources and Family
Care Services, VCU Health System)

In reflecting on Dr. Harris, the current VCU Provost stated,

We would not be what we are today; we would not have
the kind of commitment to our strategic plan without
that steady, consistent, determined, quiet, leadership.
Her style wins people over in a way that loud, brash, and
demanding leadership does not.

Putting people first: Prioritizing the human side—Without a
doubt, Dr. Harris's leadership style is one that puts people first.
She very carefully considers the implications of policies and decisions on those who will be directly affected. The Special Assistant to the Dean in the School of Education and retired Vice Provost reflected on Dr. Harris's involvement in making new faculty
contracts more user friendly:

When she looked at the contract that we signed, she was
concerned that it invoked a negative image. It was not
user friendly. It was like signing a mortgage, instead of
something that was more welcoming. It needed a lighter

more personal touch. Being a human being was more important than any technical expertise.

Having a background in business, he learned a great deal from her approach. He reflected,

> She made me focus more on the human side [of issues] for sure. I've been in business for basically 30 years of my career where the nuts and bolts were finance and technology, business principles and practices. She helped me step back and see who was affected by this…Most business people, you can blindfold them, put on them a white shirt, tie, and suit and they will make business decisions based on feasibility studies or numbers. She encouraged me to think a bit broader than that and to think about the human side.

One specific example of Dr. Harris's focus on people is when, Virginia Commonwealth University made the switch from 18 pays for 9-month faculty to 24 pays for 9-month faculty. Several faculty were quite vocal in expressing their resistance to the switch. As the Special Assistant to the Dean of the School of Education and retired Vice Provost recalled,

> In the Faculty Senate, there were about 75 people in the room and they were all vocal…She let me get my points across. Then, she just got up from the back of the room and walked to the front and she parted the waters. She said, 'If you don't like it this year, we will give you a grace period, however, we are implementing 24 pays for 9 month faculty… She had a high tolerance for working with faculty members. You wouldn't believe the folks who resented it. We converted the complete faculty payroll system on this campus. Her true understanding of faculty was a part of that leadership package.

Throughout her career, Dr. Harris has led by example and served as a mentor to others. All the individuals we interviewed could readily identify specific leadership skills they learned from her and discussed the way they incorporated these skills into their own approach. A former colleague reflected,

> During my early work with her, one of my best friends was a doctoral student in our program. When I was taking on this first administrative position, she helped to clarify what boundaries are—what is administrative in-

formation and what can be shared with colleagues. I remember that being a lesson.

A former colleague in the School of Social Work noted, "With Grace, it was never 'I want you to hear this.' She taught by example which is the best way to learn. It really did impact how I dealt with groups of people."

As noted in our introduction, Dr. Harris' career path at Virginia Commonwealth University is historic. Having completed

her undergraduate degree in Sociology from Hampton Institute in 1954, Dr. Harris was denied admission into graduate school at Richmond Professional Institute (now VCU) because of her race. In 1967, Dr. Harris joined the faculty of VCU as an Assistant Professor in the School of Social Work and moved up the academic and senior administrative ranks. Although Dr. Harris officially retired from VCU in 1999, she continues to share her talents with the University on a part-time basis as a Distinguished Professor of the Grace E. Harris Leadership Institute.

Grace Harris –
Courtesy of VCU
Creative Services

While all of the individuals we interviewed were familiar with Dr. Harris's early experiences with discrimination, they all cautioned us that it would be narrow to only discuss this aspect of her life in explaining her interest and engagement in issues of social justice. The Vice President for Human Resources and Family Care Services of the VCU Health System reflected

> During a time of racial discord or prejudice, she was able to become a faculty of a program, later become the dean of that program, and as an African American and a woman to be the Acting President of such a large university. That's just amazing. She was a pioneer in so many ways. And, despite all of the accolades and accomplishments, all of the heady things attributed to her, she has remained so focused on students, staff, the quality of VCU and its reputation. Some people would rest on their laurels, but she still stays involved.

Others offered a similar reflection:

> The fact that she opted to come back to a university that did not accept her for graduate school is a statement of what someone can do. It would have been easy to go some place else and assume a leadership role...It says the world about her. (Emeritus Faculty)

> She always set this bar for everybody, that you need to think about everyone in terms of priorities and opportunity, and that you shouldn't just think about yourself. There were also little hints, "maybe you could ask him to do this or maybe you could ask her to do that." She was well thought of by most women and minority faculty. They thought of her as someone they could talk to—they'd get a fair hearing and she would represent their interests. (Former Dean, College of Humanities and Sciences)

Dr. Harris offered a similar sentiment regarding her contribution to women and faculty of color:

> I made sure that these groups were always included in consideration for professional advancement, promotion and tenure, and recognition, that we had an adequate representation of women and minorities on search committees, attending conferences and traveling. . .There are lots of ways that people can help that leaders sometimes overlook.

Key Leadership Approach: Listen and Decide—Dr. Harris's leadership style is one that is participatory, calm, and inclusive. She approaches situations with a patient approach that seeks to sincerely understand the nuances and tradeoffs of alternative viewpoints. She listens and considers opinions from all sides: faculty, administrators, staff and students—always careful to listen to their voices. The Vice President for Human Resources and Family Care Services of the VCU Health System elaborated on her participatory style:

> She has made me see how important it is to be calm in situations and to really listen and to include, (as much as you can), a diverse group of people when you are making decisions. She has this uncanny way of remembering who you are and what your job is, and of bringing diverse interests together to encourage collaboration.

One of her retired School of Social Work colleagues noted,
> In the end, I learned committees are cumbersome and they take up a lot of time, but they are effective. You can get more done than what you can on your own. Grace always appreciated that. . .[She] taught me to keep my mouth shut and to allow people to talk.

Although Dr. Harris places a premium on listening to and understanding multiple viewpoints, she is clearly a decisionmaker. She does not shy away from or avoid tough decisions. A hallmark of her leadership style is standing by the decisions she has made and making sure they are implemented. As noted by the Special Assistant to the Dean of Education and former Vice Provost,
> The thing I found in her leadership style is that she was really great to work for. There were no false starts, switching directions, scrap and start all over like some people do... She knew when she set the direction what she wanted done. She was not one to just up and switch courses.

The former Dean of the College of Humanities and Sciences agreed:
> She is well informed, seeks information from a variety of sources and doesn't make rash decisions. I remember one instance when I knew I was right. She countered with an alternative argument from someone else. She always did a good job at understanding the nuances and complexities of any issue. Her capacity to understand issues in a complex and comprehensive way was unparallel... She had the ability, that when she makes a decision, she made it happen. Others make decisions and then take them back...When she made a decision, she made a decision.

Perhaps Dr. Harris summed it up best:
> As I think about being provost, I recall giving everybody a chance to be heard, even when they weren't very nice. Another characteristic is to be patient; not making a decision too hastily. On the other hand, I do believe that decisions must be made...You have to reach that point of decision making after giving people the opportunity to express their views, after the input has been given. You really do want to get a good sense of the thinking of others of whom you respect.

In any leadership situation, making decisions means there will always be winners and losers on any given issue. Dr. Harris's inclusive leadership style resulted in an acceptance of her decisions due, in large part, to her articulation of her reasoning.

> She had a remarkable way of not antagonizing people... You never felt that you didn't get a fair hearing...(She would say) we reached this judgment for these kinds of reasons. Given you respected the way she went about making judgments, you were fine. There was rationality to it and there was a process that she went through in her own mind. I might have lost, but I was given a fair hearing. (Former Dean, College of Humanities and Sciences)

A former colleague, now the Senior Associate Dean, School of Social Work noted, "She had a great way of dealing with conflict without leaving you feeling defensive. She handled most antagonistic situations behind closed doors."

The importance of family, social and community networks— During our afternoon with Dr. Harris, she revealed the significant role that her family played in shaping not only who she is as a leader, but also the way that she connects and reaches out to others. Dr. Harris attributed her leadership to a well-informed background influenced by a lifetime of learning and experience. She has been married to her college sweetheart, James W. "Dick" Harris for more than 55 years. She is a mother of two children, and a grandmother. For Dr. Harris, a strong sense of family, love, respect, pride, and fun were essential to her success. In her interview, Dr. Harris credits her success to her upbringing:

> It was our family way of life; there's nothing extraordinary about succeeding. It was kind of the norm. We had to do our homework; it was expected that you achieve. It was expected that you go to college, it was expected that you be nice to your sisters and brothers even if you fight. There was closeness and a bonding that has lasted. I come from a family of leaders, compassionate leaders, people who had a little fun in doing what they were doing. My uncle, John "JB" Coleman, was very active in the NAACP and was very sure of himself and had a fun outlook in life...he lived his life...he had great influence... I saw a commitment to certain principles and behaviors and at the same time a joy in living...He always made sure that there was

action about his commitments. He actively tried to make changes personally and professionally.

The power of family was visible to those around her. Many of the interviewees spoke about the influence of her family and recalled stories about her parents, sisters, brother, aunts and uncles. A former social work faculty member noted,

I think her family must have had a big influence. She and her sisters were close. Her parents instilled in them an achievement orientation but one that was, at least as I saw it…gentle. That was the way they were going to approach life and achieve what they were going to achieve.

When asked about the role of social and community networks, Dr. Harris reported that her knowledge of people greatly influenced the connections that she has been able to make over time. She is recognized as being skilled in making and keeping connections with people from all walks of life. These connections were instrumental in accomplishing tasks within and outside of the university. Dr. Harris commented,

Practically, the fact that I know a lot of people and can get people involved has certainly been helpful in the Institute. Keeping in touch with issues and progress being made can help you expand your own way of thinking about people. There are connections to other things. I don't hesitate to call people if I think they can be helpful to the programs or other people.

Dr. Harris continued to maintain a strong presence in the Richmond community beyond her affiliation with the University. She was on the Board of Directors for the Christian Children's Fund (1987-1995). She was a founder of the Women's Bank and served on its Board of Directors (1976-1984). She was involved with the establishment of the John B. Cary Elementary School, a response to the need for a different kind of education for area children. Dr. Harris saw her roles in the community as opportunities for good practice. A former colleague reflected,

On the boards she was on, she was a good thinker. She was involved too, in her own social milieus. There were many women to whom she was friendly, and she maintained a good relationship.

The Special Assistant to the Dean of the School of Education and retired Vice Provost reflected,

People outside would put her on boards that focus on social equity and leadership and that was a real tribute to her. When [former Virginia Governor] Warner was elected, he asked her to help staff his transition team.

Continuing the Legacy

Dr. Harris's legacy and ideals continue to provide an inspiring framework for the University. When asked about Dr. Harris' legacy, the interviewees noted the multiple contributions she has made and continues to make to the entire fabric of the University. Dr. Harris's commitment to excellence and her ability to effect positive change, the establishment of the Grace E. Harris Leadership Institute, and the dedication of Grace E. Harris Hall in her honor were just some of the things discussed when asked about her legacy. A former colleague notes,

She was here at a very fine time in VCU's history when VCU first became a university, when VCU was RPI. The students were pretty homogenous. We didn't have students who were from any place other than the South. She was very steadfast and strong in her need for respect for all people. It's a true respect for diversity. You get rich ideas. She has made an impact. She was in the right place at the right time and she used all of her grace and charm to make things happen.

Courtesy of Grace Harris

The Grace E. Harris Leadership Institute was cited as a major component of Dr. Harris's legacy at VCU. Based on Harris's style of leadership, the Institute develops and implements programs based on principles of transformational leadership, collaboration and partnership, commitment to long-term relationships with clients and participants, and focus on leadership in academic and community settings. The university programs, the VCU Leadership Development Program, and the Department Chairs Program are designed to institutionalize Dr. Harris's leadership style as a means to prepare and retain effective faculty, staff and administrators who are currently (or will likely become) leaders within the university. The community programs, the HIGHER Ground Women's Leadership Development Program and the Minority Political Leadership Institute, which operates as a collaboration with the Virginia Legislative Black Caucus Foundation, honor her commitment to her social work profession and continue the tradition of community service.

Most interviewees felt that the Institute programs create a lasting impression on its participants.

> Clearly a lot of people who have gone through the program have taken on increased leadership roles in VCU and the health system. That's a great testament to the institute and to Grace Harris. (President, Virginia Commonwealth University)

The former Dean of the College of Humanities and Sciences commented,

> The Institute is trying to identify a wide range of aspiring leaders who can take people from different backgrounds and use them to improve the university…it is institutionalized in the institute.

The interviewees also highlighted the significance of Grace E. Harris Hall. For the President, naming the building in honor of Dr. Harris was a fitting tribute. "It was very appropriate to name a major classroom facility to honor her lifelong contribution to the university and its students." The Special Assistant to the Dean of School of Education and the retired Vice Provost noted,

> They named that after her for her total contributions to VCU…roughly 15 years from now there will be some children in that building learning whatever discipline. Fifteen years from now, those students in the building,

they may not even know her or know everything we know about Grace. They are in a building named after Grace, the first African American dean, provost, and the only acting president. To name it after her speaks volumes about her legacy.

Conclusion

Dr. Harris's leadership style was transformational for the faculty, staff, and students at VCU. Her administrative vision and institutional stewardship demonstrated strength and wisdom. The interviews point out key elements of Dr. Harris' leadership style that are consistent with the literature on transformational leadership, including her ability to establish a clear and achievable vision, to move others into collaborative action, to create a learning environment, and to develop leaders who will continue a legacy of compassion and responsiveness to their communities. Dr. Harris's ability to gather and entrench people under a common purpose speaks to her transformative talent to encourage and engage a greater sense of purpose among the community.

Many of the themes that emerged from our interviews align closely with Patricia Hill Collins's Black feminist epistemology. Dr. Harris's "listen and decide" approach includes concrete experience as a criterion of meaning and the use of dialogue in assessing knowledge claims. Similarly, her "putting people first" approach aligns with the ethic of caring and personal accountability. Her emphasis on collaborative partnerships and her results orientation enhanced her ability to effect positive change in the organization in an authentic approach. Her model of exemplary leadership continues to provide an inspiring framework for many, as evidenced by the observations provided.

The interviewees provided a rich understanding of Dr. Harris's role at the university and in the community and her impact on each of us. Though we expected to receive many positive comments about her leadership style, the consistency between every story was astonishing. Even though we each had our own story and experiences with Dr. Harris, our recollections of our interaction with her were characterized with the same themes and, in some cases, even the same descriptors and choice of words. Without a doubt, the central components of Dr. Harris's leadership style were consistently identified and recognized by those who worked with her in a variety of capacities within the university.

Her greatly admired and effective leadership style is truly leadership with grace.

References

American Association of University Professors (2006). *Annual report on the economic status of the profession.* Washington, DC: AAUP.

American Council on Education. (2007). *The American college president: 20th Anniversary.* Washington, DC: American Council on Education.

Barton, T. (2006). Feminist leadership: Building nurturing academic communities. *Advancing Women in Leadership Online Journal, 21.* Retrieved February 6, 2009, from www.advancingwomen.com/awl/fall2006/barton.htm

Berry, T. R., & Mizelle, N. (Eds.). (2006). *From oppression to grace: Women of color and their dilemmas within the academy.* Sterling, VA: Stylus.

Belenky, M. F., Clinchy, B. M., Goldberger, N. & Tarule, J. M. (1986). *Women's ways of knowing: The development of self, voice, and mind.* New York: Basic Books.

Blackburn, R. T., Chapman, D. W., & Cameron, S. M. (1981). Cloning in academe: Mentorship and academic careers. *Research in Higher Education, 15,* 315-327.

Burns, J. M. (1978). *Leadership.* New York: Harper & Row.

Chappelow, C. T. (1998). 360-degree feedback. In C. D. McCauley, R. Moxley & E. Van. Velsor (Eds.), *The Center for Creative Leadership Handbook of Leadership Development.* (pp. 29-65). San Francisco: Jossey-Bass.

Chin, J. L., Lott, B., Rice, J. K., & Sanchez-Hucles, J. (Eds.). (2007). *Women and leadership: Transforming visions and diverse voices.* Malden, MA: Blackwell.

Collins, P. H. (1990). *Black feminist thought: Knowledge, consciousness, and the politics of empowerment.* Cambridge, MA: Unwin Hyman.

Eagly, A., Johannensen-Schmidt, M. C., & van Engen, M. L. (2003). Transformational, transactional and laissez-faire leadership styles: A meta-analysis comparing women and men. *Psychological Bulletin, 129*, 569-591.

Eberspacher, J., & Sisler, G. (1988). Mentor relationships in academic administration. *Journal of National Association of Women Deans and Counselors, 51,* 27-32.

Gerdes, E. P. (2006). Women in higher education since 1970: The more things change, the more they stay the same. *Advancing Women in Leadership Online Journal, 21.* Retrieved February 6, 2009 from www.advancingwomen.com/awl/summer2006/Gerders.html.

Glazer-Raymo, J. (1999). *Shattering myths: Women in academe.* Baltimore, MD: Johns Hopkins University Press.

Gregory, S. T. (1995). *Black women in the academy.* Lanham, MA: University Press of America.

Gregory, S. T. (1999, Winter). "Black Women in Academe: Progress But No Parity" *Advancing Women in Leadership Journal,* 1-10.

House, R., & Howell, J. (1992). Personality and charismatic leadership. *Leadership Quarterly, 3,* 81-108.

Jacobs, J. A. (1996). Gender inequality and higher education. *Annual Review of Sociology, 22,* 153-185.

Johnsrud, L. K. (1990). Mentor relationships: Those that help and those that hinder. *New Directions for Higher Education Series, 72,* 57-66. San Francisco: Jossey-Bass.

Lafreniere, S. L., & Longman, K. A. (2008). Gendered realities and women's leadership development: Participant voices from faith-based higher education. *Christian Higher Education, 7,* 388-404.

Many Black women veer off path to tenure, researchers say. (September 9, 2008). *Chronicle of Higher Education.* Retrieved from www.chronicle.com/news

Moore, K. M. (1982). The role of mentors in developing leaders for academe. *Educational Record, 63,* 23-28.

Nash, R. (2204). *Liberating scholarly writing: The power of the personal narrative.* New York: Teachers College Press.

Sandlers, J. M., & Wong, H. Y. (1985). Graduate training and initial job placement. *Sociological Inquiry, 55,* 154-169.

Sax, L. (2008, September 26). Her college experience is not his. *Chronicle of Higher Education, 55*(5), A32-A33. Retrieved February 16, 2009, from Religion and Philosophy Collection database.

Smith, D. T., & Crawford, K. (2007). Climbing the ivory tower: Recommendations for mentoring African American women in higher education. *Race, Gender & Class, 14*(1-2), 253-266.

Turner, C. S. V. (2002). Women of color in academe: Living with multiple marginality. *The Journal of Higher Education, 73*(1), 74-93.

West, M. S., & Curtis, J. W. (2006). *AAUP faculty gender indicators 2006.* Washington, DC: American Association of University Professors.

Winfield, L. F. (1997). Multiple dimensions of reality: Recollections of an African American woman scholar. In A. Neumann & P. L. Peterson (Eds.), *Learning from our lives: Women, research, and autobiography in education.* New York: Teachers' College, Columbia University.

Yammarino, F. J. (1992). Transformational leadership at a distance. In B. M. Bass & B.J. Avolio (Eds.), *Improving organizational effectiveness through transformational leadership.* Thousand Oaks, CA: Sage.

Zemsky, R. (2001). Gender intelligence. *Policy Perspectives, 10*(2), 1-15.

Easing Our Path:
The Healing Power of Dialogue for African American Women in Leadership

Christopher Anne Robinson-Easley

Introduction

Historically, African American women have had to face ongoing issues of suppression, racism and denigration in their lives, and for many reasons, they struggle when working toward change. When African American women assume leadership roles, these issues can feel like they are magnified tenfold. As a part of their healing ritual, for years African American women have engaged in sisterhood gatherings, which have played an important role in their lives. However, the research suggest that any resulting change effects from these dialogues end with the individual participants and thus far have not served as catalysts for deep, systemic and impacting change within the African American community.

This paper raises the question as to whether or not it is time to move beyond the dialogue and to actually evoke systemic and strategic change, thereby more succinctly address the ills that African American women endure. This paper explores this question from a first-person perspective and is driven by my experiences as an academic in higher education who has also served in leadership positions in academia and in business. Utilizing the first-person perspective, this paper proposes a theoretical change model, drawing upon propositions from interdisciplinary perspectives that suggest a new archetype for addressing issues in African American women's communities.

The Lens from Which I View the Issues

My theoretical sensitivities and perspectives emerge from a multidimensional interpretive schema. When understanding the rationale behind the questions I ask, I factor in that I am an African American woman who comes from a collective African consciousness. I am a mother of two young adults and was a wife for 24 years. Professionally, I am an Associate Professor of Management and a management consultant to public and private sector organizations. I have also served in executive and management roles in higher education. Before my academic career, I spent over twenty years in management and directorship positions in corporate America. My work has been presented nationally and internationally and has primarily addressed social issues that focus on at-risk youth, diversity, leadership development, community and organizational strategy, and culture.

Though my life has been rich, it has also been broken with pain…the pain of loosing my partner of 24 years to sudden death via a massive heart attack. Adding to that challenge has been the challenges that most women of color experience when moving up the ranks of their chosen profession. Throughout my life and studies, I have also learned that when we openly acknowledge our personal qualities and experiences, we concomitantly open space for another level of a consciousness of meaning to enter, which can be subtle yet of significant impact when deconstructing the way we create and manage sense and meaning (Pettigrew, 1979). Consequently, as I have continued to face challenges, I have also questioned what should I be learning from these experiences.

At a latter stage in my life and career, I obtained my doctorate degree in organization development. My orientation to my work is that of a scholar/practitioner. Lastly, but equally important to this stage of my life, I am also a seminarian. Since entering seminary, my guiding praxis toward understanding change and change theories has evolved. My research and studies in seminary have taught me to more critically examine the epistemology, ontology, hermeneutics, and root metaphors of a change strategy juxtaposed against the environments in which we work. I now ask a different subset of questions that challenge the praxis of the change strategies I studied previously. When I see my communities and people continuing to face challenges and hardship, I have to question whether those strategies are successfully impacting my communities and whether there are better or at least different ways to approach the issues?

While many have viewed my family life, career and educational accomplishments in a positive light, each step I have traveled has been against the backdrop of being a woman of color in a world where we traditionally are not welcomed at the top. So what changed in my life in 2004? And why did that change position me to seriously consider the issues and propositions articulated in this paper?

Three weeks before I lost my husband, my daughter and I had just returned from a month in Europe. I had a wonderful series of academic successes, presenting in Italy and Sweden at two international conferences, and engaging in research with colleagues in France. However, in less than five minutes, I lost the man in my life, who was my life and with whom I had spent close to a quarter of a century. When I did not know which way to turn, my husband was always there to listen, guide, and provide support. Whereas my life suddenly changed, my responsibilities did not—they only increased. I had to step back into a classroom immediately after the services. I was committed to a research project that was going to require me to travel extensively, and exacerbating the situation was the fact that my tenure portfolio was due six months later. My daughter had just started high school, and my son was out of state in his last year of college.

What I quickly understood and felt were the limitations of a support system I so desperately needed. My prior successes did not diminish the fact that I was hurting deeply, my children were in severe pain, and I knew I was not always making the most rational decisions. I had no siblings and no relatives with whom I could call upon for support. I have close friends with whom I could dialogue, but they had their lives, and, equally important, none had ever gone through the loss of a spouse. As a woman of color, I was reluctant to open myself up to support groups—after all, I was a Black woman who had national recognition for my work, evidenced by my accomplishments. How in the world could I admit vulnerability? How would I have been perceived by my colleagues if I had asked to postpone my tenure application? Would six years of my academic life go down the drain?

Being vulnerable did not seem to be a viable option at this poignant time in my life. Our lives as African American women appear to be a series of negotiations that aim to reconcile the contradictions separating our internally defined images of self as African Americans with an objectification as "the other" (Collins, 1990). African American women historically have been identified as "strong." For some, it's a badge of honor; for others, it can be burdensome. As a result, we are forced to work through the realities of our vulnerability, which can conflict with the external images imposed upon us. At this time in my life, I did not feel strong. I was crying inside on a daily basis, and I felt abandoned…by the man I had always thought I would spend the rest of my life with and by friends who were doing the best they could to support me. Against this backdrop, my responsibilities as a mother, whose children were clearly suffering just as much as I was, educator, consultant, community leader, and all the other roles that externally defined me did not allow me to show that vulnerability. At home at night I cried, whereas during the day I had an image to maintain.

African American Women: Objectified and Marginalized

So, how do African American women successfully navigate through our own individualities of pain, suffering, and joys, when our day to day existence is grounded in a society where often we are not recognized as equals? Where is our support system? Who understands and supports us? Where is that safe space where we can cry and be vulnerable?

> *"Black people have always been America's wilderness in search of a promised land."*
> Cornell West (1993)

West's statement coins the double-consciousness and issues of duality that, as a race, African Americans face in an oppressive society (Terhune, 2005). It is suggested that to be Black in White American is to suffer, and African Americans may suffer existentially, questioning their value and worth within this society, and/or they may suffer physically from hunger, homelessness, unemployment, illhealth, drug abuse, and countless other issues (Phelps, 2005 cited in Townes, 2005). These issues of duality and suffering are even more exemplified in the lives of African American women.

In an eight-year study comparing the lives and career struggles of successful Black and White women in corporate America, Bell and Nkomo (2001) found that women come to their workplaces not just from separate directions but separate definitions, which are created out of individual junctures of family background, educational experiences, and community values. African American women continue to remain in the shadows and are essentially invisible to colleagues who do not understand or relate to the realities we face in the workplace. Uniquely positioned in this dualistic epistemic standpoint, our ability to find and live as our true selves remains elusive to many. We cope daily with the obvious dual identity of race and gender, while internally struggling within a social context that does not appropriately represent us (Terhune, 2005).

It has been suggested that within the story of African people in this country, there is also a history specific to the experience of African American women that we ignore—a history that is essential to understanding African American women's perspectives on life in America (Watkins Ali, 1999). African American women belong to a unique subculture, which is not entirely shared with Black men or white women (Jones, 1985 cited in Watkins Ali, 1999). Although African American women endured the same physical and psychological trauma during slavery as did Black men, they also endured the trauma of rape, and separation from their families. Even when pregnant, the harsh physical labor expected of them was unrelenting. In far too many instances, African American women suffered even more at the hands of the white slave mistresses, whose homes and children they cared for (Watkins Ali, 1999). Consequently, the current issues articulated by Bell and Nkomo should not be a surprise, because they are shaped by and emerge from a callously designed history—a history that still haunts us.

Although there is historical complexity to our lives that can be debilitating, current issues facing us are just as draining. Professional African American women are still seeing gender disparity in education, business professions, and professional careers, which also impacts our relationships with our men. During the past fifty years, the percentage of African American women between the ages of 25 and 54 who have never been married has doubled, from 20% to 40%. (Compared with just 16% of white women who have never been married today) (NBC Nightly, (2007). Mortality rates for African American women have been higher than for any other racial or ethnic group for nearly every major cause of death, including breast cancer. African American women with breast cancer are nearly 30% more likely to die from it than are White women. African American women are 85% more likely to get diabetes (a major complication for heart disease) and, like breast cancer, more black women than white women die from heart disease (NBC Nightly (2007). Inclusively,

African American women are working through issues of a deteriorating African American family. There are controversial and troubling questions that must be addressed about the link between the declining numbers of marriageable males due to drugs and incarceration, and Black-on-Black crime, which is a circular and systemic connection. Adding to the woes of the decline in the family structure, Bell and Nkoma (2001) found a significant percentage of the professional women they interviewed reporting how African American women felt stressed by the lack of significant personal relationships with men. Climbing the corporate ladder often means going home at night facing a nonexistent personal life and recognizing that the prospects of finding a mate similar in background and stature may be quite slim.

With issues of duality and objectification in the background, how do we understand and heal ourselves, while supporting one another in an effort to strategically and systemically cope with life in general, while at the same time working to ameliorate these debilitating issues? To continue in the manner we have without effecting appropriate support systems, in concert with a dialogical process that works to create deep change strategies is counterproductive to ourselves, our families, and our future. How do we heal the pain we feel on a daily basis?

It has been suggested that African American identity formation in and of itself is a distinctive process within American life. The forces of racism, color consciousness, sexism/genderism, and American religiosity have impacted the formative experiences of persons of color, and have perverted self-esteem, challenged and/or changed social stability, and significantly threatened existential security (Butler, 2006). Yet, when we talk about healing the pain that emerges from issues of duality and objectification, we must also focus on understanding and healing issues of marginalization that manifest and reside within our own African American female communities.

Change without unity can be challenging. Yet historically African American women who have chosen to live their lives as lesbians and bisexual individuals have faced a triple threat of oppression: being forced to work through issues of race, gender, and sexual orientation. And, while it has been posited that living the life of a lesbian is a life that draws its strength, support and direction from women (Reynolds, and Powell, 1981), recent studies suggest that marginalization within the African American community is sometimes higher than that within the white communities, with Black women who regularly attend church displaying higher instances of homophobia than their male counterparts (Negy, Eisenman, 2005; Redmond, 2006).

Human beings have the capacity to change their world. However, to successfully seek understanding as to how a new reality can be constructed, we must first understand how our current reality is constructed and how and why we buy into this reality (Cooperrider & Srivastva, 1987). Yet when addressing issues facing African American women, we are historically placed into locations and roles that do not address our realities, thereby providing limiting answers to looming questions (Mitchem, 2002). As a result, when we try to understand ourselves from traditional streams of research, study, and change, we are faced with Eurocentric psychologies that have been replete with bias of white supremacy, making it extremely difficult to understand who we truly are in order to systemically cope with our realities, which are plagued with multiplicities of issues (Akbar, 2003, Mitchem, 2002). Many African American scholars continue to search for alternative ways of helping African Americans engage in effective "knowing." We have to approach understanding ourselves, our situations, our diversities and our differences from a different paradigm than that which has been our traditional lens. The crisis of identity necessitates liberating activities that can bring about a salvation that extends to the core of one's being (Butler, 2006)—a salvation that can work to heal ourselves from the external forces that threaten us as well as help us bridge the chasms that exist within our own community.

African American Women: Dialoguing to Bring About Change?

So how do we evoke substantive change in our lives and support one another? African American women have always engaged in dialogue with one another. These methods of getting together, which through the years have been coined under the concepts of "sisterhood" or "girlfriend gatherings" appear to be ritualistic forms of bonding and sharing that serve to support a healing process. When examining the dialogues of African American women, the phenomenology of African American women appears to be inextricably linked to the intersections of our psychology and spirituality, which help to frame the existential and phenomenological types of questions that emerge in girlfriend types of conversations—conversations that also address the existential dilemma of cultural oppression (Watkins Ali, 1999). An example of deeply rooted historical gatherings of women, that focus upon support as well as community action and change has been the Black sororities. The purpose of this paper is not to challenge these institutions—they are critical to our existence—but rather to suggest a model that could move their work more quickly toward a broader-based systemic change strategy.

In recent years, there has been a groundswell of sister support groups. African American women gather for a variety of reasons: to share coping strategies for a variety of crisises, to discuss the progress they are making in acheiving their goals, or just simply because they have a need to talk in order to decompress (Villarosa, 1994). It has been suggested that the unique pressures that African American women face makes sisterhood gatherings essential. We understand one another. We know the details of Black female reality, and this "knowing" emerges not only intellectually, but viscerally, because it is in the marrow of our bones (Randolph, 1999). African American women have many shared experiences and ideas that stem from living in a society that denigrates us. We have unique experiences that lead to unique perspectives or standpoints for self-examination. There are characteristic themes that emerge in our dialogues—themes of struggling for independence, self-reliance, and self-definition (Banks-Wallace, 2000).

Yet, when deconstructing the linguistic processes that African American women engage in, a question emerges. Will experiences of oppression impact and affect the way in which women code and decode reality and therefore impact the way we form our respective linguistic representations and resulting realities (Brown, 2004)? Is there a danger in allowing just a free flow of conversation without critical analysis as to the etiology of the expressions and internalized beliefs that result from varying social constructions? How can we begin to socially construct a broader society of physically, mentally, and most important, spiritually healthy African American women that focus on supporting one another for purposes of survival and growth? African American women need to develop an ability to aggregate and articulate individual expressions of everyday consciousness as a self-defined and collective standpoint (Banks-Wallace, 2000). Each woman's theoretical database for making critical decisions about life can be influenced by access to both her personal experiences and the collective experiences of a population of women living with similar issues.

As I reflect upon my needs and continued needs as an African American woman who faced loss and daily deals with challenges to my identity as a professional, I know that the ability of African American women to access and draw upon this data base is integral to maintaining health-promoting behaviors that allow me and others to move beyond behaviors that are barriers to optimal well-being (Banks-Wallace, 2000). However, dialogue without critique and resulting change strategies may lead only to continuation of the current reality.

Moving Beyond Dialogue

Strategies for change that align the mind, body and spirit are important to the African American female community. Strategies for change have to move beyond putting band-aid approaches on profusely bleeding issues. We have to take society, as well as ourselves, to task and drive deep change. Intentional dialogue ensconced with focused change strategies that give credence to our strengths and inner beauty suggests a movement beyond the girlfriend conversational modalities of venting or strategies that may result only in programmatic change. Intentional dialogue enables African American women to move towards strategies that can impact the healthiness and alignment of the mind, body and spirit. A model that suggests intentional dialogue is not designed to replace the work and healing that occurs in pastoral counseling, church ministries, or any other means of evoking change that is grounded in one's spiritual or religious beliefs. The purpose of proposing this model as a strategy for change is to help facilitate creative transformation through systematic and strategic approaches that can be incorporated into existing religious and spiritual modalities of intervention.

Proposition: Strategies for Evoking Change

Postmodern organization development theorists suggest that problem-solving methodologies typically practiced by a logical-positivist orientation fail to build generative theoretical premises and new change theories that could eliminate or at least delimit presumptive paradigms (Cooperrider, 1986). African

Americans have been plagued with change strategies that fall into the categories of empirical analysis or action research, both with a problem-solving orientation. Interventions grounded in traditional streams of sociology and psychology generally focus on changing the value systems of the individuals. However, one must question the legitimacy of attempting to change values. This paper suggests a theoretical model that is designed to move the dialogical process toward visioning and implementing strategic and systemic action.

This posited model is built upon the guiding praxis of a prior model a colleague (also a woman of color) and I developed in 2003, which suggested the theoretical interplay between discourse analysis and appreciative inquiry. The propositions of this applied format in Figure 1 (see next page) suggest that the steps in the model have the potential to move the dialogue of African American women from a conversation or series of conversations to a *dialogical process*, grounded in organizational development theory and practice, that forms the foundation for strategically focused interventions designed to develop deep change in the African American community, with a particular focus on issues prevalent to African American women.

Steps one and two in the model suggest a need to gather and talk. However, the focus of the conversations must be to clearly listen to and deconstruct the linguistic representations that emerge within the dialogue. The ontological framework of discourse analysis begins with postmodern thinkers who for close to twenty years have suggested that what we take for reality is nothing more than a construction of the human mind. Discourse analysis seeks to understand the fundamental nature of the social world at the level of subjective experience (Burrell, 1979) and presupposes that if one really wants to capture the dynamics of life, efforts must be directed on the actors' expressed and hidden representations of the social world in which action is embedded. Action and meaning must prevail in the explanation of human conduct (Giddens, 1987) since fact and value are linked in any form of argument (Parker, 2000). This level of analysis is critical for African American women. The concrete individual and the reality of the Black experience must be the point of departure of any phenomenological analysis of human existence (Cone, 1970). Therefore, if we focus on deeply listening to and analyzing the patterns of our language, we have a chance to break down those

Figure 1

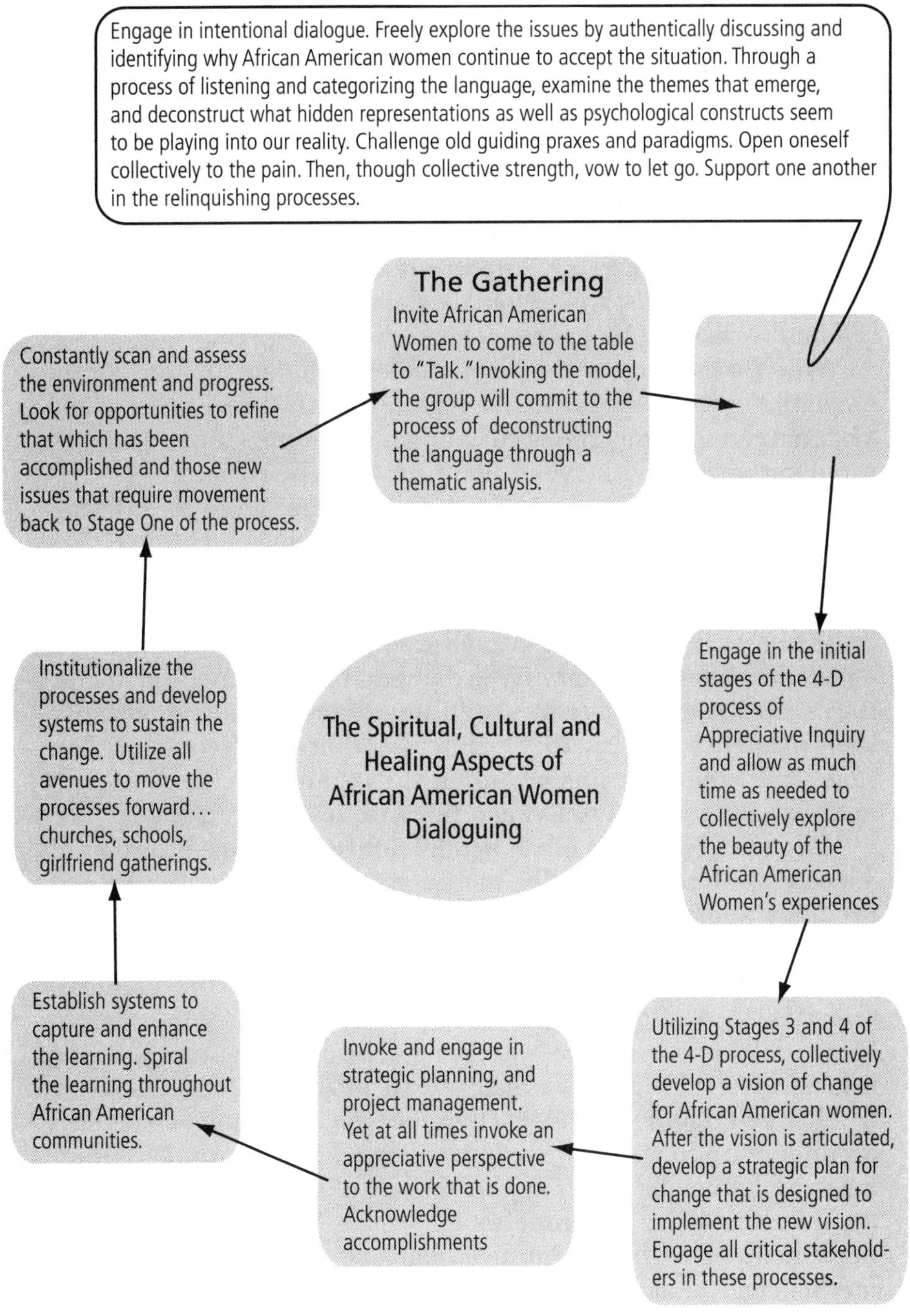

Engage in intentional dialogue. Freely explore the issues by authentically discussing and identifying why African American women continue to accept the situation. Through a process of listening and categorizing the language, examine the themes that emerge, and deconstruct what hidden representations as well as psychological constructs seem to be playing into our reality. Challenge old guiding praxes and paradigms. Open oneself collectively to the pain. Then, though collective strength, vow to let go. Support one another in the relinquishing processes.

The Gathering

Invite African American Women to come to the table to "Talk." Invoking the model, the group will commit to the process of deconstructing the language through a thematic analysis.

Constantly scan and assess the environment and progress. Look for opportunities to refine that which has been accomplished and those new issues that require movement back to Stage One of the process.

Institutionalize the processes and develop systems to sustain the change. Utilize all avenues to move the processes forward… churches, schools, girlfriend gatherings.

The Spiritual, Cultural and Healing Aspects of African American Women Dialoguing

Engage in the initial stages of the 4-D process of Appreciative Inquiry and allow as much time as needed to collectively explore the beauty of the African American Women's experiences

Establish systems to capture and enhance the learning. Spiral the learning throughout African American communities.

Invoke and engage in strategic planning, and project management. Yet at all times invoke an appreciative perspective to the work that is done. Acknowledge accomplishments

Utilizing Stages 3 and 4 of the 4-D process, collectively develop a vision of change for African American women. After the vision is articulated, develop a strategic plan for change that is designed to implement the new vision. Engage all critical stakeholders in these processes.

hidden linguistic representations that impact our behavior and emanate from the self in order to change our worldview and resulting actions.

Change must first occur internally before one can change one's external circumstances, which can be quite a liberating experience. New language and expressions have the power to become the core of our change processes. Through deconstructing our patterns of discourse, we can understand the relational bonds that exist between people and understand the way structure is created, transformed and maintained (Barrett, Thomas, & Hocevar, 1995). Equally important, once we understand these patterns, it becomes easier for us to evoke a change in our internal and external dialogues.

When engaging in this methodology, the size of the group engaging in the dialogue is not germane to the process. In whole systems change, the groups can range in size from small to facilitated gatherings with over 1,000 people in the room.

What is the relevance of intentional discourse for African American women? Is it true that only a thinly veiled line exists between a cry for justice and expressions of hate? Rage has a way of being uncontrollable and unstoppable, and unless its energy is redirected, rage will consume the self (Butler, 2006). Rage will develop when one's humanity is denied and an individual and/or race's existence is controlled by those who attempt to objectify their existence (Butler, 2006). However, there is also a duality in rage—the creative transformation that conquers circumstances and restores the soul to living a life with joy (Butler, 2006).

The next two steps of the model address the need to rebuild ourselves. More specifically, in the stage of *change*, theoretical premises suggest that Appreciative Inquiry (Cooperrider, 1986) requires that participants actively engage in diagnostic assessment in order to exchange on knowledge created via discourse analysis, thus allowing a second level of reconstruction before being able to re-integrate these second-level representations into strategy designed to bring forth effective change (Easley & Alvarez-Pompilius, 2003). Therefore, once we have developed an understanding of how we have allowed our external environment to define our internal perceptions of self, we take that understanding, leave it behind us and move forward. The forward movement, however, is grounded in an organization development methodology that incorporates processes that facilitate our examining our strengths, beauty, and accomplishments that have made us who we are in order to acknowledge, define and plan for the change we desire.

Grounded in social construction theory and practice, Appreciative Inquiry is an approach to organizational analysis and learning that is intended for discovering, understanding and fostering innovations in social organizational arrangements and processes (Cooperrider & Pratt, 1995). While Appreciative Inquiry (AI) is a mode of action-research that meets the criteria of science as spelled out in generative-theoretical terms, it also has as its basis a metaphysical concern that posits that social existence is a miracle that can never be fully comprehended (Cooperrider & Srivastva, 1987; Marcel, 1963; Quinney, 1982). As a methodology, AI seeks to locate and heighten the "life-giving properties" that impact the core values of the individuals participating in the AI experience (Cooperrider & Srivastva, 1987; Thatchenkery, 1996). AI has the capacity to help African American women accelerate the work they do in framing and expressing love and support for one another, while at the same time discovering internalized strengths and goodness that can be strategically garnered toward effecting change strategies. Appreciative Inquiry's hermeneutics situate the participants in a mode of inquiry that can lead to strategies focused on changing the way we live and participate in our various social organizations (Cooperrider & Srivastva, 1987). Therefore, African American women can work toward discovering where they possess *strength and internal power* while visioning the change we desire in our lives at all levels of our existence. The latter stages of the AI processes move us toward developing strategies to actually implement the desired state.

Inherent in the AI process is a search for knowledge and intentional collective action that is designed to help evolve the normative vision and will of a group, a search that begins the real change processes (Cooperrider & Srivastva, 1987). In contrast to traditional action research, Appreciative Inquiry seeks to address the question of how people can engage in dialogue that is focused on the goal of seeking a common positive vision of a collectively desired future (Barrett & Cooperrider, 1990), typically manifested through storytelling and sharing of positive experiences within the organization. Appreciative Inquiry, or AI, thus seeks out the best of "what is" to provide an impetus for imaging "what might be" (Thatchenkery, 1996). Therefore, unlike many other intervention strategies, AI starts from the initial frame of reference that "I'm okay," my organization (or in this case individuals with whom I identify) is okay, and I have potential to impact my environment.

Hermeneutically, AI also includes the anticipatory principle that suggests our future reality is permeable, emergent, and open to the mind's causal influence—that is, reality is conditioned, reconstructed, and often profoundly created through our anticipatory images, values, plans, intentions, beliefs, and the like (Cooperrider and Pratt, 1995). With this is the recognition that every social action somehow involves anticipation of the future, in the sense that it involves a reflexive looking-forward-to and backward-from. This reflexive looking forward and backward for African American women is critical. The way one contextualizes the past is through the understanding of their historical and cultural roots. When we consciously, collectively and collaboratively engage in looking at our history of survival and growth, we recognize the strengths we bring forth from those roots, thereby enabling us to take a reflexive look at our negative images and understand and deconstruct them to ensure that they don't survive in the emerging future.

Lastly, embedded in the hermeneutics of AI is the principle that when engaging in an AI process that moves the participants toward action from a positive approach, the participants can develop their own provocative propositions for change that excites the members of the group, thereby simultaneously creating an anticipation of a new future (Cooperrider, 1986). These provocative propositions lay the foundation for the next three stages of the model which incorporate basic principles of strategic planning, project management and organizational learning.

The key phases of the Appreciative Inquiry process (called the 4-D cycle) include defining the topic choice (e.g., the topic participants will begin discussing), inquiry into the life-giving properties (e.g., sharing stories as to when and where we have been our best) that include data collection and discovery, articulation of possibility propositions (e.g. visioning the ideal), consensual validation/agreement and co-construction of the future (where the participants leave the process with action steps) (Cooperrider, 1986; Williams, 1996). While all key phases of the AI process are critical, the failure to fully engage in the design of implementation processes to effectively roll out the strategy can be detrimental. Visioning without strategic implementation can deplete the spirit. However, understanding how to implement is often an arduous task. Driving change requires planning, and the last four stages of the model suggest strategic, yet systemic planning processes that require full engagement in implementing and institutionalizing the action, in concert with reflective/reflexive activities that require participants to constantly scan the environment in order to effectively progress juxtaposed against environmental changes. Strategic implementation requires participants to define the overarching goals and objectives, carve out the scope of work, identify resources and areas of support, establish responsibilities and sequences of action, identify and commit to a timeline and ensure that communications processes are defined. Equally important, participants must anticipate additional resource requirements and establish areas of accountability and appropriate communications regarding progress while also engaging in periodic results reviews and assessments as they monitor and stay on target with proposed budget allocations. The successful implementation of strategic initiatives also requires a climate free from fear and intimidation. Yet the possibilities that can emerge from the work are endless.

The last phases of the model suggest the importance of developing systems that help move the model throughout the African American community. Therefore, it becomes important to share the knowledge and results gained from engaging in the process with other African American women and/or groups.

Sometimes the thought of engaging in change can be overwhelming. However, what we have to remember is that making a difference can be the results of many ripples in a pond. African American women have many venues to share knowledge and insights in order to encourage new ripples to form. However, we have to be intentional and strategic with our processes for sharing information and encouraging others.

Conclusion

Intentional dialogue, grounded in the postmodern premise of discourse analysis, has the potential to be far more than a gift of fateful nature; it can develop into a social construction of interacting minds (Bell, 1973), which can shift consciousness and facilitate ideas and new meaning on the systems that are problematic, thereby causing a re-emergence of those systems with new life and character: Through the integration of Appreciative Inquiry, positive ideas can be thrust center stage as the prime unit of relational exchange and reality (Cooperrider, 1986), which lead to positive and focused energy which can result in new strategies for change. African American women can create and discover new social possibilities that are designed to enrich their lives. However, this awakening must also be collaborative.

So, where do we go from here? I sincerely hope that as the propositions and resulting model in this paper are more widely circulated, we will work to implement and share results. Change does not have to begin on a massive level. The beauty of this model is that it can be implemented in almost any venue—a group of friends, church community, sorority, etc. Sisterhood is critical, especially in today's unstable environment. Yet, sisterhood that has a fundamental purpose of change can significantly impact the instability of our environment. The collaborative alignment of strengths can overcome deeply rooted issues. However, we have to be committed to action, and the action has to begin with us.

References

Akbar, N. (2003). *Akbar Papers in African Psychology.* Tallahassee, FL: Mind Productions and Associates.

Banks-Wallace, J. (2000). Womanist ways of knowing: "Theoretical considerations forresearch with African American women", *Advance Nursing Science, 22*(3), 33-45.

Barrett, F., & Cooperrider, D. (1990).Generative metaphor intervention: A new approach for working with systems divided by conflict and caught in defensive perception. *The Journal of Applied Behavioral Science, 26*(2), 222-224.

Barrett, F., Thomas, G., & Hocevar, S. (1995). The central role of discourse in large scale change: A social construction perspective. *The Journal of Applied Behavioral Science, 31*(3) 353-372.

Bell, E., & Nkoma, S. (2001). *Our separate ways.* Boston: Harvard Business School Press.

Bell, D. (1973). *The coming of the post-industrial society.* New York: Basic Books.

Brown, M. (2004). *Blackening of the Bible.* New York: Trinity Press International.

Butler, L. H (2006). *Liberating Our Dignity, Saving Our Souls.* St. Louis, MO: Chalice Press.

Collins, P. H. (1990). *Black feminist thought: Knowledge, consciousness and the politics of empowerment.* New York: Routledge.

Cone, J. (1970). *A Black Theology of Liberation.* Philadelphia: J. B. Lippincott Company.

Cooperrider, D. (1986). *Appreciative Inquiry: Toward a methodology for understanding and enhancing organizational innovation* (Unpublished dissertation). Case Western Reserve University, Cleveland, OH.

Cooperrider, D., & Pratt, C. (1995). *Appreciative Inquiry, Relational realities and constructionist approaches to organizational development.* Unpublished workshop presentation. Cleveland, OH: Case Western Reserve University.

Cooperrider, D., & Srivastva, S. (1987). Appreciative inquiry in organizational life. In W. Pasmore & R. Woodman (Eds.), *Research in organizational change and development* 1, pp. 129-169). Greenwich, CT: JAI Press.

Easley, C., & Alvarez-Pompilius, F. (2003). A New Paradigm for Qualitative Investigations: Towards an Integrative Model for Evoking Change. *Organization Development Journal, 22,* No. 3, (Fall 2004) 42-59.

Giddens A. (1984), *La constitution de la société. Eléments de la théorie de la structuration.* Cambridge: Polity Press

Marcel, G. (1963). *The existential background of human dignity.* Cambridge, MA: Harvard University Press.

Mitchem, S. (2002). *Womanist Theology.* New York: Orbis Books.

NBC Nightly (2007), African American women and where they stand. Retrieved from http://dailynightly.msnbc.msn.com/archive/2007/11/20/476352.aspx.

Negy, C., Eisenman, R. (2005) A comparison of African American and white college students' affective and attitudinal reactions to lesbians, gay, and bisexual individuals: An exploratory study. *The Journal of Sex Research, 42*(4) 291-298.

Parker, M. (2000), The Less important sideshow: The Limits of epistemology in organizational analysis. *Organization, 7*(3), pp. 519-523.

Quinney, R. (1982). *Social existence: metaphysics, marxism, and the social sciences.* Beverly Hills, CA: Sage.

Randolph, L, (1999). Girlfriend Greatness-African American women. *Ebony.* June 1999.

Redmond, D. (2006). *The influence of knowledge of homosexuality and religious importance to homophobia among African American students at a historically Black college* (Unpublished doctoral dissertation). Houston TX: Texas Southern University.

Reynolds, L. & Powell, L. (October 31, 1981). Black lesbian bibliography. *Off Our Backs, 11*(9), 9-17.

Terhune, C. P. (2005). Biculturalism, code-switching, and shifting: The Experiences of black women in a predominately white environment, *International Journal of the Diversity, 5* (6) 2005/2006, 9-15.

Thatchenkery, T., (1996). Affirmation as facilitation. A postmodernist Paradigm in Change Management, *OD Practitioner, 28*, Nos. 1 & 2, 12-22.

Townes, E. (Ed.). (2005). *A Troubling in my soul: Womanist perspectives on evil and suffering.* New York: Orbis Books.

Villarosa, L. (October, 1994), Circles of sisterhood. *Essence, 25,* (6), 89.

Watkins, A. C. (1999). Survival and Liberation. St. Louis: Chalice Press.

West, C. (1993). *Race matters.* New York: Vintage Press.

Williams, R. (1996). Survey guided Appreciative Inquiry: A case study, *OD Practitioner, 28*(1 & 2), 43-51.

Workplace Discrimination:
Isn't Education Supposed to be the Equalizer?

Theresa Julnes Kaimanu
Portland State University

Kloshe tumtum mika chako (Welcome to you). My name is Theresa Julnes Keleka Kaimanu. My heritage includes ancestry from Quinault, Quilluette, Lower Chehlis, Satsup and Shoalwater Bay. I am formally enrolled in the Shoalwater Bay Nation, located on the coast of Washington State. I am also an allottee heir to Quinault land. Shoalwater Bay is at the northern-most end of the Chinookian Indians and the southern-most end of the Salish Peoples. My Nation is one of the "fish eating tribes of western Washington," as described by Judge Bolt (U.S. v. Washington [1974]) in his controversial ruling of fish allocation amongst tribes and commercial and recreational fishing rights. In keeping with traditional foods, my diet consists of seafood; I do not eat beef, pork, or poultry.

I am the great-granddaughter of Charles Benjamin Armstrong. My great-grandfather was one of the seven signers of the recognition of our tribal lands with the federal government. My great-grandfather was a part of my life until I was sixteen. I came to know him better through my grandmother's stories for the next couple of decades.

When I was very young, my mother worked for the Cooperative Extension Service in downtown Seattle. This area was where most of the urban Indians lived in Seattle. I remember going to work with her, and one of the women there exclaimed, "how cute; you adopted a little Indian girl." My mother boldly told her, "She is not adopted; she is my little girl." My mother had not inherited her mother's dark hair and darker complexion, but I had. My parents didn't make distinctions about color or class. My mother did not want to talk about her heritage, and she avoided any exposure to the sun. I didn't give this avoidance much thought until I was an adult. I grew up poor, and I thought my life was normal, that is, until I entered the 7th grade when we moved from Seattle to Olympia.

It became apparent to me that I was different by the responses I got at school. I had lived in low-income government subsidized housing, yet they were in neighborhoods that housed families whose parents were pursing an education. I was no longer surrounded by these values but rather judged by what I wore and the family I came from. I did not fit in. And I did not realize that my mother was also having issues of not fitting in. My mother had interrupted her education to take care of her husband and children. Now my father had a government job, and my mother started substitute teaching. She found a full-time teaching job, and then she left every summer (She was a high school teacher) to further her education. My parents had realized the middle-class American dream. So between her work and education, I took on the household and, as before, had my grandmothers as role models. I did not understand my paternal grandmother; she didn't believe in education for women. But she was always there for a hug and smile. Through *talk story* (a term used to describe learning through story telling), my maternal grandmother was my connection to my native heritage and to my strength as a woman.

The value that stayed with me as I was growing up was that going to college was a given and I was expected to finish graduate school. Marriage and other roles e.g. parenting, were not expected but education was. My mother had lived on a reservation for a few years and she lived in several foster homes. She was the parent who told me that education was the way out of poverty. While my father's family did not value education, my father came to the path through my mother. In high school, my mother told my father that if he wanted to be with her, he would have to go to college. His parents were middle class, and he didn't understand how this would eventually impact him, but he loved my mother. So both of them went directly to college after high school (They were married immediately upon graduation). I attended my first college class in vitro.

My father came from a patriarchal family and my mother from a matriarchal heritage. My father had decided that I would become a lawyer, and I shared his vision until I was about to graduate from college. I hesitated in applying to law school by deliberately missing deadlines. The first law school I finally applied to called me at work and asked me to start almost immediately in their summer program. I was a reluctant participant.

It was soon apparent that I didn't fit in, nor did I like my fellow students. It was a private school with no ethnic diversity. With little motivation, and having to drive 30 miles each evening one way to school five nights per week, I didn't feel inspired. Students would hide reference books from each other in the library to compete for grades. These values did not fit the communal life of a Native person. So, I left.

After some searching and taking some writing classes, I found myself back at the University of Washington studying for my Master's of Public Administration degree. There were a few Native students there as they had a Fund for Improvement in Post-Secondary Education (FIPSE) grant for teaching a specialization in tribal administration. The program also had some foreign students in its Humphrey Fellows program. As I was graduating to the Ph.D. program, the dean was Hubert Locke, an African American. While there were no women of color in mentoring roles, I couldn't have had a better mentor than Fremont J. Lyden. He guided me throughout graduate school at the University of Washington and thereafter in my first years at Portland State University. He "gently shoved" me into self-determination.

Dr. Lyden also introduced me to Pat Britz who became my best friend in graduate school. She was like an elder sister or mom. She had Native ancestry, and she formerly studied cultural anthropology and could help me understand some of the awkwardness I experienced. I thoroughly enjoyed being a doctoral student. Since I was in the Special Individual Ph.D. program, it was an interdisciplinary degree that required my participation in five different colleges across campus (Business, Law, Medicine, Public Affairs, and Arts & Sciences).

I collected friends across disciplines and backgrounds. I worked at the Graduate School in Minority Affairs and Technology Transfer. One of my co-workers, Augustine McCaffrey, became another "sister." She is Comanche, and I reconnected with her in my national Indian education work later in my career.

As I was about to graduate from the University of Washington, I reveled in the number of interviews that I was invited to consider. As I traveled throughout the country, I discovered the lack of ethnic diversity at every institution. Then there were few women in the field of Public Administration and even fewer minorities. I watched to judge whether the University really wanted me or they wanted my female minority status. At one institution, the female professors whom I pulled aside to get their candid impressions were actively seeking employment elsewhere. When I "taught" a module for the faculty as one part of the interviewing process, the topic was hiring. The response I got was "we would hire the black one." I tried to prompt a discussion but they only said that they would hire the black candidate in the exercise I used for the teaching module. No prompting could ensue a discussion. I was told they had been ordered by a judge to institute diversity. During the exit interview, the chair of the department did not understand why I wouldn't even discuss an offer. Wasn't education supposed to be the equalizer?

After more than 50,000 frequent flyer miles (and despite my having turned down some interviews), I chose Portland State University (PSU). I would be within three hours of my tribe's reservation and family. Most important, it was the opportunity to make a difference in PSU's Master of Public Administration in Health Administration degree. One third of the student body specialized in health, yet there were no full-time faculty to teach and mentor for this specialization. The program needed my interdisciplinary approach to learning. With my pending offers, I was the only interviewee for the job at Portland State University. I interviewed and they offered me the job within 24 hours. I felt empowered (and wanted). I felt that I was hired on my talents alone.

PSU wanted me for my talent, but being an underrepresented minority helped it with its desire to diversify its faculty. However, I don't think they were prepared for someone who had learned to speak up and questioned equity in application. I was told "don't you know the definition of junior faculty is to be seen but not heard?" When I asked why an incoming faculty member was to be paid 25 percent more than I when he hadn't even finished his Ph.D., I was told "He is ten years older than you and he has a family to support." I learned that PSU would not be an equal opportunity employer. But I hoped that this would change over time.

After five years at PSU, my department was looking for a new colleague in my department. The applicant pool still reflected the lack of racial and ethnic diversity in the field. One applicant was a female and she seemed like a dynamic and highly talented person. My colleagues didn't see it that way and were attempting to choose another person who looked like them. I found the male candidate's qualifications to be lacking and fought hard to change my colleagues' minds. The female candidate was offered the job and hired. To my dismay, the new hire promptly aligned with the dominant culture. She is a talented individual and succeeded well in PSU's culture. It wasn't until five years ago that we hired a tenure track woman of color. I can say that we are very different but we share similar values. Two years ago, another woman of color was switched from fixed term to tenure track. Our departmental statistics now reflect more diverse representation. Yet the allotment of merit pay for 2009 came with the stipulation that "Inequity in salary is not a criterion to be used in the review of exceptional performance." Nothing has changed in twenty years. But I am still hoping.

Commissioner for Accreditation in Oriental Medicine (1993-2002)

One of the greatest rewards in teaching graduate students is generating a future colleague. One of my former students, Liza Goldblatt, introduced me to Oriental Medicine. She nominated me to serve as a National Commissioner for the formerly named National Accreditation Commission for Schools of Acupuncture and Oriental Medicine (NACSAOM), now known as the Accreditation Commission for Acupuncture and Oriental Medicine (ACAOM). The commission was surprised and pleased when I went to interview them rather than have them review my CV for consideration. I was installed as a Commissioner within 48 hours and spent 10 years fulfilling a leadership role in the field.

As a volunteer, I rearranged my life to be available for full commitment. I planned my graduate seminars on Mondays and Tuesdays so that I could travel on Wednesdays for site visits and Commission meetings. The application of standards and continuous improvement complemented my teaching well. And my teaching complemented my ability to help schools to integrate the intent of the standards and to use accreditation as one of the tools for management rather than as a hurdle to be completed.

From my first site visit, I fell into the role of chair and trainer for future chairs. ACAOM's long-term staff person, Penelope Ward, gave me my choice of schools to review as she could always count on me to complete what I had promised to do. So I did a lot of reviews. I served as Treasurer and, part of the Executive Committee. These activities led to my role in creating the first accredited doctoral program for Oriental medicine in the United States.

When I first joined the Commission, the professional group was splintering into two separate groups. The members fought. This didn't help the profession, as it was trying to get its legitimacy established in the United States. The profession had regretted the decision to have a master's degree as the entry point to the profession and desired the distinction of a doctorate.

The Accreditation Commission took on the leadership role to unite the two professional groups—the Council of Presidents which represented the Oriental Medicine colleges, and the Commission (ACAOM)—to create the blueprint for this new degree. I was appointed chair and facilitator of the task force that would speak for the four groups. The history of the groups' efforts had resulted in someone storming out during every attempt to communicate previously. I spent the next two years working to keep them together, and no one walked out. At the end of two years, we had a blueprint.

The next phase consisted of chairing a committee of the accrediting body to write the standards and hold public hearings during the development process. Again, I chaired and facilitated the meetings and hearings. After two years, we had developed the standards. As I was leaving the Commission (it was time), the Commission had approved two schools to start the doctoral program, and several other schools were applying. I chaired another site visit after that, but I knew that I was ready to focus elsewhere.

I had joined the Oriental medicine field in a volunteer capacity because I believed in its value to society. I had watched my grandmothers use natural medicine while I was growing up, so I wanted to help it become more mainstream. I watched it grow in popularity, particularly after the *New England Journal of Medicine* in 1993 published its stunning report that alternative medicine use was mainstream, as more than one in three Americans regularly used alternative treatments. During the second half of my tenure with the Commission, the field experienced the kind of conflict that emerges when power/money exists where it didn't exist before. The field that reflected my tribal values now had power and politics controlling the medicine. People enter the field for their own reasons, and the motivation changes. The culture reflects the mainstream, and the diversity that created it is lost in the power struggle. Can equity exist with these influences?

Tribal Administration Program (1998-2003)

My years at the University of Washington had given me the idea of using my interest in the latest technology to help tribal members who did not want to leave their communities to be in an urban setting for two years and earn their Master of Public Administration degree. Remembering the tribal program at the University of Washington, I looked into the possibility of a FIPSE (Fund for the Improvement of Postsecondary Education) grant to start a Tribal Administration Program (TAP) using the teleconferencing (Polycom) capacity with the online learning management system of WebCT. The FIPSE program supports and disseminates innovative reform projects that promise to be models for improving the quality of postsecondary education and increasing student access. At this time, this technology was at the cutting edge. This would give me the chance to spend time and make a difference in my community.

Programs were emerging in engineering and computer science to use these technologies, but they were highly experimental. The concept of using this approach to connect the tribal communities to education appealed to the Program Officers at FIPSE. I thought that I would get an enthusiastic response from my College (College of Urban and Public Affairs [CUPA]) at Portland State University. The Chair remarked that he signed the application because he thought I would never get funded, and the Dean was not encouraging, as he had his representative sign for him while he was on his annual out-of-country visit. He had other plans for tribal connections.

The Office of Information Technology staff and administration were elated. They provided an amazing amount of support. They wanted to move forward with technology and needed faculty to want to "push the envelope." I had a vision, but I knew the path would be challenging.

The first transmission was a two-way teleconference between PSU and the Confederated Tribes of Grand Ronde. PSU had just completed construction of its first two Distance Learning classrooms. We had the Polycom unit on a box pointed at me with a Smart Board. The bandwidth wasn't wide enough for both audio and video, so we used a speakerphone for the audio.

One of the challenges was the lack of infrastructure for the teleconferencing. The Oregon State Department of Administrative Services (DAS) needed to convince the legislature that this network was possible. My friend, Lois Cohen, was working at the School of Education, and she was a friend of the head of DAS. She arranged for a meeting with Don Mazziotti. He had been authorized with ten demonstration sites for the Polycom teleconferencing network. I proposed that if he would connect PSU with three tribes, he could show the legislators that he could connect anywhere in the state. He agreed. A couple months later, transmitting from PSU with connections to the Confederated Tribes of Grand Ronde, Confederated Tribes of Siletz and Umatilla Nation, I testified before the state legislature's Joint Committee on Technology. Don agreed with my proposal that a picture was worth a thousand words. With that transmission, he received the appropriations to build the state network.

Within two years, we had twenty Native American students enrolled in Tribal Administration Program (TAP) courses. Twenty may not sound like a lot, but when you consider that we had an average of two Native American students per year in Public Administration and a total of twenty Native American graduate students throughout the campus, this was a significant increase. While TAP and its vision grew to include a policy analysis think tank and collaboration with other universities, PSU's support of the program declined.

The Office of Information Technology had been able to get national exposure for its innovations, and we were known among the Ivy League schools and the U.S. Department of Education for our willingness to be creative with technology. We were one of a handful of universities to get National Aeronautics Space Administration (NASA) transmissions, and TAP was getting attention at both technology and education conferences. TAP was used as an example to help raise money for the Distance Learning wing of the College of Urban and Public Affairs. And as usual, when there is an emergence of potential power and influence, it becomes a target.

The future of TAP was in jeopardy. Someone else wanted the program, and that person had more power and influence. In my contacts with potential new tribal sites for the Program, I cautioned them to wait a couple months when I saw the power moves. I wouldn't let my tribal communities become victims in a power struggle. Unfortunately, some people don't like to share power. In December 2002, I was told that TAP would not be able to use the funding it generated to grow and sustain itself (virtually ending the current program). This was a move to allow someone else, (a non-Native, non-academic) create her own program. Her attempts to get funding after the College dropped the TAP failed, and there is no longer any tribal administration program at PSU. Isn't education supposed to be the equalizer?

Chair of Public Administration (2000-2003)

I never wanted to administer anything but my TAP. However, a couple of my colleagues approached me about running for division chair. They were interested in a new leadership style, and we had just organized into an extra level of administration with a School Director's position. (We went from a College with Departments to a College with Schools and Divisions under those Schools). So, after some discussion, I reluctantly agreed. The administrators in the College were taken by surprise when the election was held. The Associate Dean had hired me years ago and knew that I would want to change the culture. I was now Division Chair.

A couple weeks after I started my chair duties and over three months after I was elected Division Chair, the new School Director put a contract in front of me that stated I would accept a buyout of one class (out of seven) for my duties as chair. The normal buyout before this period had been three courses. He told me that I had twenty-four hours to sign or resign as chair. Since the other two chairs in the School had been elected before the change with a School Director, they would continue with the three-course buyout. In my mind, there was no choice. I had promised my colleagues. But I felt the inequity again.

Our faculty meetings changed, thus changing the way we interacted together. At first, the pre-sent agendas with documentation were rarely read. Most of our meetings previously had been informational. I wanted discussion. My tribal background supported decision by consensus. Everyone took a turn to speak, and no one was to criticize or interrupt the speaker. In order to move the meetings to this step, I started to submit prewritten motions. That really released the opinions! After I declined to serve another term as chair, someone else took over as the new chair. However, the faculty were not happy when the next chair went back to informational meetings. Faculty would no longer accept top-down decisions on issues that they felt were faculty governance issues. Since then, we have had two other faculty serve as chair. Though the faculty meetings are productive, the interaction remains guarded by some participants (both junior and senior faculty members).

As with other groups outside the College, I had some great affirmations of my role as Chair and Director of the Tribal Program. I enjoyed University Committee service and projects that I worked on with other Colleges. The School of Education provided the most welcoming interactions. Outside the University, Michael A. Brintnall, the executive director of the public administration accrediting body, was extremely supportive. Working with all the chairs of public policy and administration programs was welcoming and rewarding. Some of my greatest memories come from interactions with others trying to assist Native students in their pursuit for education.

National Institute for Native Leadership in Higher Education

I belong to several native education groups including the Oregon Indian Education Association and Oregon Tribal Contractors Association. On a national level, the National Indian Education Association and Tribal Contractors Association have annual meetings which provide great environments for sharing stories of working with our Native students. I served on the board of the National Institute for Native Leadership in Higher Education (NINLHE) whose mission is "to transform higher education in the United States and Canada in ways that improve the experiences and educational outcomes of Native students, which includes Native American, Alaska Native, Native Hawaiian, and Aboriginal peoples" (http://ninlhe.unm.edu/). The support system that NINLHE provided, in its annual meetings, board meetings and support through the listserv, was instrumental for many of us trying to push for policies supporting our Native students, staff, and faculty at our home institutions. When my Tribal Program was cut, I lost much of that support system because I was no longer connected to a native program. Communication is still nurtured through the listserv.

The Native American Student and Community Center

One of my proudest achievements was helping with the creation of the Native American Student and Community Center at PSU. More than 15 years ago, I joined Native students, staff, faculty, and community members in trying to visualize and establish a Native Center at PSU. The university eventually gave its blessing to fundraising for the project. While we were not a top priority, after about five years of raising money from the tribal communities and the student fund, we broke ground, and the building was finished in 2003. Besides helping with grant writing and fundraising, I personally contributed to the building of the Native American Student and Community Center. I was the only non-philanthropist to make a significant donation. I "adopted" the child play area, and it was named after my nation, the Shoalwater Bay Children's Play Area. The Center provides a home on campus where Native American, Alaskan Native, and Pacific Island students find academic and social support. The Center welcomes the greater Native Community to the PSU campus, providing opportunities for shared learning and understanding.

Personal roles

When my stepson was in the eighth grade, he stated that his academic goal for that year was to be a leader. When I asked him what that meant to him, he stated that he wouldn't be a follower. When I explained to him that a good leader gives credit to his followers when everything goes right and the leader takes the blame when things go wrong. He asked me if he could change his mind. He no longer wanted to be a leader. It was then that my challenge became to show him that leadership had its own rewards. The day he told me that he wanted to go to college was one of those rewards. For now, he has assumed and has been promoted to team leader in his Americorp field work. He rose to that position knowing the responsibilities of leadership.

What would I do differently? When I was offered a job at West Virginia University in 1988, even though it was temporary, hoping to be permanent, I would have taken it because their interest in me was genuine. They told me the next year that it would have been permanent in their genuine pursuit to show me their desire to have taken the position. They also had interviewed me with the expectation that I would be one of their future administrators by arranging interviews with current administration. In 1994, when Washington State University offered me a position at Spokane, in hindsight, I would have taken the position for the same reasons. I was asked to consider working for a tribe, but, at the time, I thought that I could accomplish more for Native students by staying in an academic setting with my TAP and Chair position. When asked to apply for the presidency of a Native college, I couldn't afford to take the cut in pay. Why didn't I make these decisions? My views about a career reflect those of my parents' generation when you served a lifetime at your one and only position. People rarely changed positions. So I chose a career path that conformed to that image.

The State of Oregon revamped our retirement system in 2003. It no longer provides the secure retirement that it did when I started my career. Now I would (and do) encourage others to make sure they are fairly compensated for the work demanded of them before accepting a position as a public servant. It is an honorable career but is also a career that can dominate your life. While I still serve as a role model, I believe that personal happiness is a part of that role. You can't be a good role model if you feel like a martyr.

What keeps me in my current career position? I have been blessed with the number of stories that current students and past alumni have told me. They express that they couldn't have done it without me. I know that they just needed someone to believe in them the way I hope that they now believe in themselves. They tell me that the stories and values I shared with them helped them succeed. I hope they then try to help younger people believe in themselves, as it should be in the circle of leadership.

With a renewed vision in my career, I am now finding myself stretching my wings again. I am hoping to spend my next sabbatical reinvigorating my passion in Native education and health issues. I was deeply humbled to be asked to share my story for this book (*Women of Color and Leadership: Taking Their Rightful Place*) and to be valued for what has colored other peoples' judgment of my worth.

I was brought up being told that education was the most important goal in life. With education, you get out of poverty, and you are recognized for what you know. At 51 years old, as a Native American woman with a Ph.D. from a highly regarded educational institution (University of Washington), I can say that is has always been a struggle for equity in a field that has and is still currently dominated by Caucasian males. I have friends of every color and gender. I enjoy variety and diversity in life. My conclusion in life is that I won't ever fit in the mainstream, but I feel much more blessed with the multitude of experiences that I have had by walking in my own moccasins.

Wawa mahsie hah (Thanks for listening). No Chinookian words exist for good-bye.

References

Eisenberg, D., Kessler, R., Foster, C., Norlock, F., Calkins, D., & Delbanco, T. (1993). Unconventional medicine in the United States—prevalence, costs, and patterns of use. *New England Journal of Medicine, 328(4)*, 246-252.

U.S. v. Washington, 384 F.Supp. 312, 419 (W.D.Wash.1974).

National Institute for Native Leadership in Higher Education Retrieved from http://ninlhe.unm.edu/

Employment Discrimination 21st Century Style

Vidu Soni
Central Michigan University

I Am Not Any Different

As a professor of human resource management, the subject of the prevalence of employment discrimination inevitably comes up for discussion in my graduate and undergraduate classes. My students sometimes wonder out loud if I have experienced discrimination in my career. My answer is how I, as a woman of color, could have been spared from the many forms of workplace discrimination when the phenomenon is so widespread and pervasive. For minority women who have achieved some degree of professional success, discrimination becomes particularly difficult to combat. Complaining about discrimination is not seen as "cool" and does not receive much sympathy or understanding from colleagues or courts when someone has supposedly "made it." Similarly, equal pay for equal work is not seen as a problem if a woman is employed in a high-paying job even if she may be earning 20–30% less than her male and White colleagues with the same qualifications. Discrimination becomes compounded for women of color, and bias and challenges grow both in "kind and degree" when the effects of race and gender are combined.

Over time, I have learned to swim against the current and have spoken against discrimination and advocated for others facing similar challenges in the workplace. The triumph came in the form of insights into what discriminatory behaviors look like and understanding the thought processes behind them, the ability to articulate and to fight injustice, and developing the courage to continue to function and thrive in the presence of discrimination without being demoralized. In retrospect, my career experience has been a story of high aspirations, smashing of aspirations, detours, survival, resilience, finding my path, achieving success, and an ongoing journey in search of organizational justice. What is more disconcerting, however, is to realize that, 25 years later, my two daughters, who are trying to make their way into high-prestige, high-status professions, are experiencing the same issues.

Discrimination persists in a more subtle and sophisticated form. For example, a recent headline in the *Boston Globe* reads, "Brigham neurosurgeon awarded $1.6 million in sex discrimination case" (Kowalczyk, 2009), pointing out that the department chair told the surgeon, who is a minority female, during surgery in 2007, "You are just a girl, are you sure you can do that?" Similarly, a training seminar on "gender equity," organized by *WOMENLEGAL* magazine (2009) states, "Law firms continually hide behind the notion that a high rate of attrition among women is due to their choosing to leave. There is little recognition, however, that many women depart because they feel they cannot succeed in the firm's current environment" (p. 1).

This is not to deny that substantial gains have been made in the availability of opportunities for women and people of color since passage of the Civil Rights Act of 1964. To some extent, we have achieved the goal of greater representation. The research on discrimination now needs to focus on what happens to women and minorities *after* they enter the organizations (i.e., how they are still treated inequitably and how their opportunities continue to be limited every step of the way) (Brief et al., 2000; Heilman et al., 2004; Soni, 2000, 1999; Wolfman, 2007). Sturm (2001, p. 458) argues that in the contemporary workplace cognitive bias, structures of decision making and patterns of interaction have replaced deliberate racism and sexism as the frontier of much continued inequality. She refers to them as "second generation" of discrimination "involving social practices and patterns of interaction among groups within workplace that, over time exclude non-dominant groups." To assume that we have solved the problem of discrimination and deliberately ignore the subtle forms of discrimination would be going backwards in the evolution of achieving workplace equality, access, and fairness.

The More Things Change, The More They Stay the Same

Discrimination in its content and form has changed in many ways over the last four-and-a-half decades since the passage of the Civil Rights Act of 1964, some people even argue that it no longer exists (Kravitz & Klineberg, 2000). However, the academic research, complaints filed with the Equal Employment Opportunity Commission (EEOC) and equivalent state agencies, extensive case law, and personal stories paint a different picture. Roberts (2008) reported that the EEOC in fiscal year 2007 received the highest number of discrimination charges filed in five years, a total of 82,792. Race continues to be the number one issue followed by gender. Often multiple types of discrimination are alleged in a single filing. The EEOC attributes the jump in charge filing to a combination of greater awareness of the law, changing economic conditions, and increased diversity and demographic shifts in the labor force. A review of discrimination claims on the EEOC website shows that in the last 15 years (1992–2007), there has been virtually no change in the number of race and gender based discrimination complaints filed. For example, in 1992, there were of 29,548 race related and 21,796 gender-based discrimination complaints filed compared with 30,510 and 24,826 in 2007 (www.eeoc.gov). But what is more important to note is that these formal complaints do not begin to describe the magnitude of workplace discrimination. For every complaint filed with EEOC, there are many more that are not filed. This indicates that race and gender based discrimination persist despite the progress made due to civil rights laws, affirmative action, and diversity management interventions.

Much scholarship has been generated in the last two decades addressing issues such as equality in employment, the glass ceiling, diversity management, and affirmative action to increase representation of women and minorities in leadership roles (Dipboye & Colella, 2005; Kilian, Hukai, & McCarty, 2005; Wells, 2000; Wolfman, 2007; Soni, 2000, 1997; Frauenheim, 2007). The literature provides accounts of barriers and challenges that are specifically gender, race and ethnicity-based, while pointing out that the situation for women of color is the most dire. The status and representation of minorities and women in professional and managerial positions continue to be affected by social, psychological, and organizational barriers, and to eliminate these barriers we must understand the factors that perpetuate them (Dipboye & Colella, 2005; Kilian, Hukai, & McCarty, 2005; Wells, 2000; Wolfman, 2007). For example, the evaluation of effectiveness of women of color in managerial and leadership positions may become problematic when the positions are ambiguously defined and no objective criteria and standards for evaluation exist (Heilman et al., 2004; Lyones & McArthur, 2007). Additionally, as Gentile (1998) points out "the over-determined terminology of 'merit' and hiring the 'best qualified' persons where the indicators of merit may often include many factors besides observable talent such as, familiarity, comfort level, prior relationship, prestigious schools, and government compliance" (p. 115) complicates the situation further.

This chapter examines how employment discrimination, particularly for women of color in professional and managerial roles, can be understood in the 21st century context. The methodology utilized is a combination of theoretical research and personal narrative approaches. The chapter discusses the many ways in which the contemporary forms of discrimination are manifest. It is a complex phenomenon and is difficult to explain by a single factor. Overt discrimination and open bigotry are now viewed as socially unacceptable in most circles. However, despite this progress, discrimination continues and still harms in a more complex and subtle form. *This is the new dilemma of workplace discrimination.* Recognizing these challenges, making them visible and discussable, and demonstrating that the barriers faced by minority women are much more than a matter of perception (DeAngelis, 2009; Hinton, 2004; Soni 2000, 1997) need to become important strategies for eliminating the "second generation of discrimination." These barriers are real to those who are subjected to them and have real consequences for their careers and the organizations that employ them. Discrimination occurs at many levels: social, institutional, and individual. Because of its multiple sources and manifestations, discrimination continues to be a dominant force within the lives of most minority group members in the United States (Gallup, 2002).

A General Framework for Understanding Discrimination

Title VII of the Civil Rights Act of 1964 prohibited discrimination in all aspects of employment on the basis of race, color, sex, religion, and national origin. Since then, age, disability, and, in some states, sexual orientation have been added to the protected categories. In addition, retaliation and sexual harassment claims are also covered under Title VII. Differential treatment and disparate impact have been the two prevalent theories used by courts in deciding discrimination cases (McDonald, Ravitch, & Summers, 2006). Discrimination traditionally has been defined as unjustified negative actions that deny individuals or groups of people equality of treatment (Dovidio & Hebl, 2005, p. 11).

Dipboye and Colella (2005) define discrimination as "differentiation that can occur against persons on the basis of characteristics that are inappropriate and irrelevant bases of employment decision (e.g., group membership)" (p. 5). Discrimination occurs not only in selection, appraisal, and compensation, but also in the more informal and subtle forms such as social exclusion and lack of recognition for one's achievements. Discrimination can be unintentional or malicious, conscious or unconscious, overt or covert.

Based on the research cited here, it can be argued that discrimination remains a major problem today even though it is not as blatant as in the past. Dipboye and Colella (2005) argue that discrimination today must be defined to include not only blatant mistreatment in the workplace but also covert forms that are influenced by causes that are far removed from the workplace. The subtlety of modern forms of discrimination poses a major dilemma, in that, it is harder to recognize, confront, and overcome. Laws and policies can deal with blatant racism and sexism, but do not address ways of dealing with exclusion from informal networks, ambivalent feelings, inappropriate jokes, attributional bias, and negative nonverbal behavior. Moreover, as bigotry has become less visible, attempts to eliminate discrimination can appear unwarranted and can provoke accusations of reverse discrimination and preferential treatment (Sidanius, Pratto & Bobo, 1996; Swim et al., 1995).

Dipboye and Collela (2005) have developed a general framework for a broad understanding of workplace discrimination. They argue that discrimination occurs in "complex multilevel settings" and involves "reciprocal causation and dynamic process" (p. 445) and can occur at the individual, intergroup, or institutional level and sometimes at all levels simultaneously. It is seen in the most concrete and tangible form at the individual level. Discrimination at the organizational level is an abstraction and is based largely on aggregates of what occurs at the individual and group levels. To complicate matters further, the social psychological models of subtle discrimination add yet another dimension—the role of intrapersonal conflicts (conflicts that are internal to the individual) in the discrimination process (Crandall & Eschelman, 2003). This implies that individuals are often caught among competing and inconsistent pressures to discriminate or not discriminate. For example, an individual

may be personally inclined to discriminate, but cannot do so because of a labor shortage or the legal environment. Conversely,
an individual with egalitarian views and behaviors may be in
an organizational climate that is nonsupportive of diversity and
hostile to minorities.

A general framework of discrimination helps us realize that
even though research reveals unique aspects of discrimination
peculiar to each specific target group that have their own history and context, there are dimensions of discrimination that
cut across target groups. Discrimination can theoretically be understood in terms of minorities and women encountering structural and systemic organizational barriers, inequitable human
resource practices and policies, organizational culture based on
White male norms and models of success, lower performance
expectations, not receiving credit for their achievements, being
subjected to different evaluation criteria and performance standards, and having lack of political capital or constituency within
the organization (Babcock, 2006; Soni, 2000, 1999). Social and
economic inequalities are most apparent along racial and ethnic
lines, and, for that reason, discrimination on the basis of race
and ethnicity continues to attract the most attention.

It Didn't Just Happen in the 1980: Discrimination Persists

While analyzing a case study on employment discrimination in
one of my classes, some of my twenty-something students argued
that discrimination was something that occurred in the 1980s
and that it was not relevant to them. This lack of understanding
and denial of subtle discrimination become major obstacles in
eliminating it (Brief et al., 2000; Lambert et al., 1996; Schnake
and Ruscher, 1998; von Hippel, Sekaquaptewa, & Vargas, 1995).
Although laws, organizational policies, and social norms appear
to be effective in controlling overt forms of discrimination, unless they address psychological bases that underlie intrapersonal and interpersonal level discrimination (e.g., stereotypes, negative affect, microinequities), discrimination will continue (Glick
& Fisk, 1996; Katz & Hass, 1988).

What's Different About Discrimination Today

Many researchers argues that the motivation for and cause of
discrimination at the individual level commonly do not reflect

a malicious desire to harm other groups and that polls and surveys about prejudice and intent to discriminate have shown consistent decline in the past few decades (Schuman et al., 1997). Instead, they argue, discrimination arises out of unconscious psychological processes, making much of the discrimination that occurs unintentional. For example, individuals internalize egalitarian norms and principles but continue to harbor negative feelings and beliefs, often unconsciously (Sears, Henry, & Kosterman, 2000). Or discrimination may frequently be manifested in subtle and indirect ways, in the ways members of majority group interpret the actions of minority groups and the ways they interact with them, which is also not readily recognizable as discrimination (Gordon & Johnson, 2003; Hinton, 2004; Smedley & Smedley, 2005). Subtle discrimination has been labeled as "modern racism" (McConahay, 1986), "symbolic racism" (Sears, 1988), and "aversive racism" (Dovidio et al., 2002). These explanations of contemporary racism, and similar explanations of contemporary sexism, have one central theme—that is, discrimination today is more likely to be disguised and covert, and it frequently appears in a more nebulous and ambiguous form that is difficult to identify and acknowledge.

Dovidio and Gaertner (2000), through several studies, have demonstrated that many well-intentioned Whites who consciously profess a belief in equality, unconsciously act in a racist manner, particularly in ambiguous circumstance. For example, this may occur when hiring or evaluating the performance of a minority woman in a managerial or leadership position where the criteria are not objectively defined. They call this pattern "aversive racism," referring in part to Whites' aversion to being seen as prejudiced, given their conscious adherence to egalitarian principles (DeAngelis, 2009). They found that aversive racism contributes to disparities in the workplace. For example, at the time of hiring, aversive racism can affect the way qualifications are perceived and weighed in ways that can systematically disadvantage Black relative to White applicants. In an empirical study of the diversity climate in a federal agency, Soni (2000) found examples of aversive racism. In a study conducted by her, when asked "if all people have a right to be treated with dignity," virtually all of the respondents agreed with the statement. However, when asked "if supervisors challenge the perceptions that 'less qualified' people are hired or promoted to satisfy diversity goals," only 20 percent of White males and 11–15 percent White females and minorities agreed with the statement.

Modern racism also creates a glass ceiling for women and minorities. As studies (Crampton & Mishra, 1999; Kilian, Hukai & McCarty, 2005) point out, although organizations are seeing an increase in the number of women and minorities in management positions, inequalities persist. For example, women hold 44 percent of managerial and administrative positions but account for only 5 % of top executive positions nationwide and only 6% of line positions (Catalyst, 2002). The situation is substantially bleaker for women of color who face race and ethnicity as well as gender discrimination. Women, particularly women of color are leaving corporations at ever increasing rate because they find it hard to succeed in traditional organizations (Catalyst, 2001; Zeilberger, 2002). Researchers have also pointed out the "double marginalization" that professional women of color face because of their gender and minority status. Some of the barriers standing in the way of minorities advancing to leadership roles include: (1) lack of mentors and role models, (2) exclusion from informal networks of communication, (3) stereotyping and preconceptions of roles and abilities, (4) lack of significant line experience, (5) lack of visible and challenging assignments, and (5) lack of family-friendly HR policies and culture (Giscombe & Mattis, 2002).

Reskin (2002) proposes a theory of discrimination to counter the conventional notions of race and gender prejudice. He argues that the impetus for discrimination is not necessarily animus by White male employers toward people of color and women. Rather, discrimination is fueled by unrecognized employer biases toward individuals "like themselves." People often not only generalize from ideas regarding social groups to individuals, but they tend to perceive those like themselves more favorably. Thus, those with dominant social status benefit from positive attributions. Reskin argues that taken together, these processes induce White men to perceive other White men in more favorable terms than men or women of color. However, regardless of the motives of those discriminating, the outcome and impact of the discrimination are the same on those subjected to it.

Discrimination at the Intersection of Race and Gender

Most sociologists and labor economists acknowledge that any analysis of women that ignores race is incomplete and may simply describe the pattern for White women. Similarly, theories of racial inequality that fail to incorporate gender into their frameworks are equally insufficient for understanding the lives of women of color (Browne & Misra, 2003). Intersectional approaches maintain that gender and race are not independent analytic categories that can simply be combined. Instead, multicultural feminists call for creating alternative theories that can fuse race and gender to describe the unique experiences of women of color. The development of intersectional perspective on gender and race is rooted in the work of scholars studying women of color and this body of work usually falls under the rubric of multiracial or multicultural feminism (Baca & Thornton, 1996; Lorber, 1998). A purely intersectional perspective suggests that there is no gender perception that is race blind and that there is no race perception that is gender blind (Weber, 2001).

Multiracial feminist theorists argue that race and gender are social constructions that are constantly reproduced through social interactions and are designed to create and maintain social hierarchies. The race and gender categories contain inherent power differences which are infused into every aspect of social life—from identities and self-concepts, to interpersonal interactions, to managing of organizations—and create disadvantages for women of color and privilege for White men (Collins, 1999; Glenn, 1999; Weber, 2001). Other explanations posit that social hierarchies are created through perceptual, cognitive, and behavioral processes about which participants are often unaware. However, they are instrumental in influencing the distribution of resources and political power (Reskin 2002, Ridgeway, 1997). Multicultural feminist theories offer an alternative epistemology and methodology to traditional positivist social science by highlighting the subjective experiences of members of oppressed groups as a valid basis for knowledge (Collins, 1999).

Gross inequalities in the labor market persist in which females and minorities are disadvantaged. On many indicators such as wages, job authority, and occupational position, minority women are at the bottom, falling below White women and men of their same race and ethnicity (Browne, 1999). Feminist intersectional approaches assume that discrimination based on the combination of race and gender is operating in the workplace when employers are making decisions about hiring, promotions, training, and wages. Additionally, in high-level, high-status positions, women of color often find themselves in a token status—as sole members of their demographic groups—which leads to a sense of isolation in a culture inhospitable and alien to them. They feel pressure to perform better than their male colleagues and are less likely to have role models of the same gender and race. The theory of intersectionality was supported by an empirical study conducted by Soni (2000) in a federal agency. The study's findings consistently showed that women of color perceived and experienced more discrimination, reported less job satisfaction, felt a need to constantly prove themselves, and were often stereotyped as "incompetent and unqualified." Similarly, I have personally found myself in a token status during most of my managerial and leadership career and felt that I had to work twice as hard and be twice as good just to run in place. These types of pressures are invisible to members of the majority but directly affect the retention, recognition, and promotion of women of color.

Contemporary Forms of Discrimination

Subtle and systemic discrimination faced by women and minorities can be institutional, intergroup, or interpersonal. The following discussion focuses on inter- and intrapersonal forms of discriminations which tend to be subtle in their expression.

Prejudice and Stereotyping

Prejudice and stereotypes are individual cognitive and affective processes that produce discrimination. Prejudice is commonly defined as an unfair negative attitude toward a social group or a person based on his or her membership in that group (Fiske, 1998; Lambart et al., 1996). A stereotype is a generalization of beliefs about a group or its members that is unjustified because it reflects faulty thought process, over generalization, and factual incorrectness (Dovidio et al., 1996). They are both rooted in categorical thinking about others. One of the most basic forms of social categorization is the classification of people into ingroup and outgroup members. People categorized as one's own group are evaluated more favorably than those of other groups. The process of social categorization also influences affective reactions, such as fear, low levels of trust in interactions, and hostility (Davidio & Gaertner, 2000; Fisk, Lin, & Neuberg, 1999; Insko et al., 2001; Soni, 1997).

Besides their expression in overt discrimination, racial stereotypes and prejudice can shape interpersonal interactions in subtle but significant ways, such as through self-fulfilling proph-ecies. Discrimination in the workplace can also occur indirectly through biases in the way people interact with each other, pro-ducing interpersonal anxiety or avoidant behaviors (Dovidio et al., 2002; Heilman, 2001; Hyers & Swim, 1998). Interpersonal discrimination can adversely affect members of minority groups by intensifying their perceptions of discrimination in the work-place and by interfering with efficiency and productivity. Percep-tions of discrimination, in turn, are associated with a range of negative work-related reactions, including negative work atti-tudes, greater job stress, mistrust, and a lack of responsiveness to critical feedback, feelings of powerlessness, greater conflict, and less organizational commitment. In addition, the avoid-ant behavior can reduce the support and diminish the quality of mentorship for minority group members relative to majority group members (Ragins, 1999).

Gender Stereotyping

Eagly and Karau (2002) argue that stereotypes are both "pre-scriptive and descriptive." In other words, in work organizations, men and women are expected to behave differently based on gender-stereotypic behaviors and roles. For example, I was told by a group of women at my workplace that some people harbored resentment toward me because "whenever we had an organiza-tional social event, I brought things that I had purchased rather than cooking them myself." Gender stereotypes not only describe differences in the way women and men actually are but also what the norms of behaviors suitable for each group are, (i.e., how women and men "should behave). For women, these typi-cally include behaviors associated with men that are believed to be incompatible with behaviors deemed desirable for women. Thus, the self-assertive and tough, achievement-oriented, "agen-tic" behaviors, for which men are so positively valued, are typi-cally prohibited for women (Eagly & Karau, 2002; Rudman & Glick, 2001). I have seen this scenario in my college classrooms, where students look at my attempts to maintain civility in the classroom as an affront to them, whereas my male colleagues' aggressive approaches are praised. Consequently, behaviors that violate stereotypic expectations and associated actions, even though they may be positive, can elicit negative emotion (Mc-Conahay, 1986).

There is ample evidence in the literature that women are subjected to gender-biased evaluations, with their performance on male gender typed-tasks often devalued and their competence denied (Heilman, et al., 2004). These biased evaluations have been attributed to cognitive distortions and perpetuate negative expectations of women. The negative expectations result from the inconsistency between stereotypic perceptions of what women are like and the qualities thought necessary to perform a typically male job. To illustrate, I was once asked in a job interview for a director of human resources and labor relations position, "Can you swear?" To the interviewer, this was seen as an important characteristic in order to be effective in that position. Indeed, bias seems to flourish in situations in which ambiguity about performance quality and cognitive distortion can easily occur (Cole, 2007; Heilman, 2001; Lyons & McArthur, 2007). Penalties for women who violate gender stereotypic prescriptions by being successful are apt to take the form of social censure and personally directed negativity.

The way that gender stereotypes manifest and harm was proven by the landmark discrimination case, *Ann Hopkins vs. Price Waterhouse* (490 U.S. 228, 109 S. Ct. 1775, 1989). In order to improve her chances for promotion to partnership, Hopkins was advised by her boss, a managing partner in the firm, "to appear more feminine, to wear more jewelry and make-up, to style her hair...soften her image in the manner in which she walked, talked, and dressed" (Gentile, 1998, p. 218). Another partner wrote in her file, "She is consistently annoying and irritating—believes she knows more than anyone about anything, is not afraid to let the world know it. Suggest a course at charm school before she is considered for admission to partnership" (p. 206). There is considerable evidence in the literature that success can be costly for women in terms of social approval. Research found that being disliked was shown to strongly affect competent individuals' overall evaluations and recommended organizational rewards, including salary and special job opportunities (Heilman et al., 2004; Lyons & McArthur, 2007).

Microinequities and Microaggressions

In recent years, many researchers have labeled the invisible and subtle discrimination as *microaggressions* (Pierce et al., 1978; Sue, 2004, 2005; Solorzano & Yosso, 2000) and *microinequities*

(Feagin & Benokraitis, 1995; Hinton, 2004; Moynahan, 2005; Rowe, 1990). These terms are used to point out implicit bias in the context of racism and sexism and are used interchangeably here. The term *microaggression* was originally coined by Pierce (1970) in his studies of racism. Solorzano et al. (2000) define microaggressions as "subtle insults (verbal, non-verbal, and/or visual) directed toward people of color, often automatically or unconsciously." Similarly, Sue (2007, p. 273) defines microaggressions as "everyday insults, indignities and demeaning messages sent to people of color by well-intentioned White people who are unaware of hidden messages being sent by them." Sue argues that most White Americans perceive themselves as good, moral, and decent human beings who believe in equality and find it difficult to believe that they possess biased racial attitudes and may engage in behaviors that are discriminatory. Thus, the perpetrator usually believes that the victim has overreacted and is being overly sensitive.

Mary P. Rowe at MIT, who has been studying microinequities for the last 30 years defines microinequities as "apparently small events which are often ephemeral and hard-to-prove, events which are covert, often unintentional, frequently unrecognized by the perpetrator" (Rowe, 1990, pp. 153-155). She argues that microinequities occur whenever people are perceived to be different, such as an African American in a White firm or a woman in a traditionally male environment. "These mechanisms of prejudice against persons of difference are usually small in nature, but not trivial in effect. They are especially powerful when taken together," continues Rowe. Similarly, Hinton (2004) points out that microinequities are a form of "subtle messages, sometimes subconscious, that devalue, discourage and ultimately impair performance in the workplace." These messages can take the shape of looks, gestures, or even tones.

The cumulative effect of microinequities often leads to damaged self-esteem and eventually withdrawal from co-workers. These exchanges are so pervasive and automatic in daily conversations and interactions that they are dismissed and glossed over as being innocent and innocuous. Yet to persons of color and women, microinequities are detrimental because they impair performance by sapping the psychic energy of the recipients and by creating material inequities (Franklin, 2004; Sue, 2004). Some argue that the daily racial microaggressions that characterize aversive racism may have more influence on anger, frustration, and self-esteem than traditional overt forms of racism (DHHS, 2001). Microinequities are often difficult to detect or be sure about which makes it difficult for the target to take effective action. The constant experience of being uncertain about whether one is left out or put down inevitably leads to misplaced anger which may then be inappropriately directed. Faced with microaggression, the victim may not be certain of the motives of the aggressor, and may be ambivalent about how to respond (i.e., return the similar hostility or overlook the behavior which may further reinforce the aggressor's position).

Damage Done by Microinequities

The power of racial and gender-based microaggressions lies in their invisibility to the perpetrator and, oftentimes, the recipient. Microaggressions can usually be explained away by seemingly nonbiased and valid reasons. When subjected to microinequities, many people of color describe a vague feeling that they have been attacked, that they have been disrespected, or that something is not right (Franklin, 2004; Moynahan, 2005; Rowe, 2008). Research points out that experience with microinequities result in a negative racial climate and emotions of self-doubt, frustration and isolation on the part of the victim. Moynahan (2005) writes, "Microinequities have the power to erode a person's motivation and sense of worth. The end result costs companies millions of dollars in low productivity, absenteeism, and poor employee retention." Microinequities cause damage because they cannot be predicted and are irrational. By and large, they occur in the context of merit and striving for excellence, but do not have anything to do with excellence or merit, they occur in the context of work but without relevance to performance (Feagin & Benokraitis, 1995). Moreover, because one cannot change the provocation for negative reinforcement (e.g., one's race or gender) it inevitably creates a sense of helplessness. Microinequities persist because they may seem too petty to readdress through formal grievance and lawsuits, which may seem heavy-handed and may carry the risk of loss of privacy and professional image for the aggrieved person.

Microinequities exert damaging influence both by "walling out" women and minorities from male-dominated professions and by making them feel less effective. Microinequities cause dominant group members to see minorities as "invisible" (Rowe, 2008). Being treated as invisible is a major problem reported in the literature which leads to more tangible negative outcomes such as, being underpaid or overlooked for promotion. Women of color may also often be burdened with routine tasks which may prevent them from working on challenging and creative projects leading to promotion. Microinequities also have a negative Pygmalion effect. A lack of expectation of good performance may result in a self-fulfilling prophecy. For example, an Asian American woman who is expected to be docile may later be perceived as insufficiently assertive to be a candidate for promotion to a managerial position (Sue, 2007).

Legal Remedies are Not Always a Choice or Adequate

Many people oppose affirmative action or diversity interventions arguing that these programs are not needed as there are legal remedies available. However, the legal scholarship (Bisom-Rapp, 1999; Krieger, 1995; Schuman & Edleman, 1996; Sturm, 2001), case law, and anecdotal accounts show that "there are significant limitations on the efficacy of anti-discrimination law" (Bisom-Rapp, 1999, p. 1039). Based on an extensive study, Bisom-Rapp concluded that employment lawyers representing management play a significant role in shaping attitudes and perception about employment disputes. They put the complainant at a disadvantage by generating copious amounts of data to convince the public that workplace equality has been broadly achieved. Employers frequently demonstrate their loyalty to EEO law through symbolic rather than substantive actions (Edleman, 1992). Defense lawyers safeguard their clients against discrimination claims by advising workplaces to strategically position themselves by putting in place nondiscriminatory procedures and making seemingly fair, merit-based employment decisions. While these litigation prevention strategies may prompt managers to identify and remedy certain biased actions, they may mask rather than eliminate some discriminatory decisions and reduce the law's effectiveness as a remedial tool (Sarat & Kearns, 1993).

In fact, the central premise of the legal advice is that bias may be eradicated by ignoring race, gender and age, which runs counter to the race and gender conscious remedies that social scientists claim is necessary to correct the effects of prejudice, stereotyping, and microinequities disadvantaging minorities and women. Organizations with workplace cultures favoring White males may make procedural alterations yet fail to significantly alter the status of protected groups. Antidiscrimination law compliance must be substantive as well as symbolic. Formal law is increasingly limited in its ability to remedy workplace discrimination. This is due to the increasingly subtle nature of bias itself and to case law which tends to favor employers (Cain, 1994). Through recommendations, management attorneys attempt to ensure the generation of documentation and oral testimony that would support employers' decision in the event of adverse employment action, such as a discharge or discipline.

Moreover, the above problems associated with legal recourse tell only half the story. Lawsuits once started take a life of their own, and delays, stone-walling, posturing, denial of discrimination and defaming the complainant are tactics used by management lawyers. The personal costs, both financial and psychological to the litigant who has already been demoralized by discrimination is often prohibitive. During my tenure as a human resource director, I have seen these challenges faced by many individuals who tried to fight discrimination through formal channels.

An important question to explore in future research then is who should solve the problem—should it be the organizations, the individuals, peer groups, government regulations, or the legal system? The literature provides many recommendations to counter workplace discrimination. Some of the most popularly used strategies are changing human resource management practices, transforming organizational culture, providing diversity training, mentoring and developing diverse talent, removing glass barriers, and obtaining a commitment from top leadership. Failure to address the problem of modern forms of discrimination has harmful consequences for women and minorities, particularly for women of color, as well as wasted human capital and legal and productivity costs for the employer.

Soni (2000, 1999) proposes several concrete steps organizations can take to decrease the occurrences of discrimination. (1) Organizations must seek to develop non-legal remedies to deal with subtle discrimination and microinequities. (2) Managers who routinely engage in discriminatory behaviors should first be counseled and if that does not improve the situation must be sanctioned. (3) Organizations must monitor retaliatory behaviors following a grievance or discrimination complaint. (4) Organizations must ensure that performance evaluations are valid and job-related in both content and process. Subjecting women and minorities to higher standards, failuring to provide performance feedback, and magnifying their mistakes are the common problems reported by women and minorities (Soni, 2000). (5) A well-established, well-communicated conflict resolution system must exist in organizations to solve discrimination complaints at an early stage. (6) Lastly, the issue of social and organizational justice ought to be a made an important part of the dialogue surrounding the goal of creating equitable workplaces.

Conclusion

While writing this piece, I felt that I can identify with most, if not all, experiences of other people of color in the workplace. Often experiences of one person are dismissed as anecdotes, but when discriminatory behaviors are multiplied by hundreds of thousand times and they take the same insidious forms, it becomes a theoretical question begging for exploration. For the last five-to-six decades, scholars, lawyers, courts, and civil rights activist groups have developed well-recognized theories and models that have significantly increased our understanding of employment discrimination. The most commonly experienced microinequities and discriminatory treatment come in the form of questioning of competence, lower performance expectations, being treated as "invisible," contact avoidance behaviors, lack of access to resources and power, being excluded from challenging assignments leading to career growth, and lack of organizational allies.

A discussion of the way to access power, develop allies, and engage in collective activism is outside the scope of this writing. What this chapter focuses on the myth that discrimination no longer exists, and both the victim and perpetrator's inability to recognize and challenge it in its current forms. Furthermore, an important challenge is presented by the inability of the legal system to redress and provide relief except in the most egregious cases. Therefore, new legal, nonlegal, and institutional approaches to dealing with discrimination must be developed. Institutions need to educate, prohibit, and sanction discriminatory conduct by supervisors and leaders.

Even though appreciating and growing workplace diversity has become the most used "buzzword" in the 21st century, subtle and complex discrimination still adversely influences the status of women and people of color and symbolic declarations of "valuing diversity" often disguise the systemic and subtle discrimination. The barriers to progress of women and minorities and their various causes are well documented in the research reviewed in this chapter. The most prevalent forms of discrimination seem to be manifested in prejudice, stereotypes and microinequities. According to Davidio and Hebl (2005), the research on stereotyping, interpersonal interactions, and avoidance behaviors suggests that "discrimination may be alive and well," even if the blatant discrimination has been eliminated. "It is the small differences or 'molehills' that accumulate to create 'mountains' of differences" (Valian, 1998, p. 110).

References

Babcock, P. (2006, Feb.). Detecting hidden bias. *HR Magazine*.

Baca, Z. M., & Thornton, D. B. (1996). Theorizing differences from multiracial feminism. *Feminine Studies, 22*, 321-333.

Bisom-Rapp, S. (1999). Bulletproofing the workplace: Symbols and substance in employment discrimination law practice. *Florida State University Law Review, 26*, 959-1049.

Brief, A. P. et al. (2000). Just doing business: Modern racism and obedience to authority as explanations for employment discrimination. *Organizational Behavior and Human Decision Processes, 8*(1), 72-97.

Browne, I., & Misra, J. (2003). The intersection of gender and race in the labor market. *Annual Review of Sociology, 29*, 487-513.

Browne, I. (Ed.). (1999). *Latinas and African American women at work: Race, gender, and economic inequality*. New York: Russell Sage.

Cain, M. (1994). The symbol traders. In M. Cain & C. B. Harrington, (Eds.) *Lawyers in postmodern world: Translation and transgression*. New York: New York University Press.

Catalyst. (2002). *Women of color in corporate management: Three years later.*   New York: Catalyst.

Cole, Y. (2007). Why are so few CEOs people of color and women? www.diveristyinc.com

Collins, P. H. (1999). *Gender, Black feminism, and Black political economy.* London: HarperCollins.

Crampton, S., & Mishra, J. (1999). Women in management. *Public Personal Management, 28*(1), 87-106.

Crandall, C. S., & Eshleman, A. (2003). A justification-suppression model of the expression and experience of prejudice. *Psychological Bulletin, 129,* 414-446.

DeAngelis, T. (2009). Unmasking 'racial micro aggressions.' *Monitor on Psychology,* 40(2), 42-48.

Dipboye, R. L., & Colella, A. (2005). Discrimination at work: The psychological and organizational bases. Mahwah, NJ: Erlbaum.

Dovidio, J. F., & Gaertner, S. L. (2000). Aversive racism and selective decisions: 1989-1999. *Psychological Sciences, 11,* 315-319.

Dovidio, J. F. (1996). Stereotyping, prejudice, and discrimination: Another look. In C. N. Macrae (Ed.), et al. *Stereotypes and Stereotyping.* (pp. 276-319). New York: Guilford.

Dovidio, J. F., & Hebl, R. M. (2005). Discrimination at the level of the individual: Cognitive and affective factors. In R. L. Dipboye & A. Collela (Eds.), *Discrimination at work: The psychological and organizational bases.* Mahwah NJ: Erlbaum.

Eagly, A. H., & Karau, S. J. (2002). Role ambiguity theory of prejudice toward female leaders. *Psychological Review. 109,* 573-598.

Edleman, L. B. (1992). Legal ambiguity and symbolic structures: Organizational mediation of civil rights law. *American Journal of Sociology, 97,* 1531-1547.

EEOC (2009). Charge statistics: FY 1997 through FY 2007. http://www.eeoc.gov/stats/charges.

Fiske, S. (1998). Stereotyping, prejudice, and discrimination. In D. Gilbert et al. (Eds.), *The handbook of social psychology, vol 2.* (pp. 357-411). New York: McGraw Hill.

Franklin, A. J. (2004). *From brotherhood to manhood: How Black men rescue their relations and dreams from the invisibility syndromes.* Hoboken, NJ: Wiley.

Gallup (2002). Poll topics & trends: Race relations. Washington DC: Gallup Organization. http://www.gallop.com

Gentile, M. C. (1998). *Managerial excellence through diversity.* Prospect Heights: Waveland Press.

Giscombe, K., & Mattis, M. (2002). Leveling the playing field for women of color in corporate management. *Journal of Business Ethics, 37*(1). 103-115.

Glenn, E. N. (1999). The social construction and institutionalization of gender and race: An integrative framework. In M. M. Ferree, J. Lorber, & B. B. Hess (Eds.), *Revisioning gender* (pp. 3-43). Thousand Oaks CA: Sage.

Glick, P., & Fisk, S. T. (1996). The ambivalent sexism inventory: Differentiating hostile and benevolent sexism. **Journal of Personality and Social Psychology, 70**, 491-512.

Gordon, J., & Johnson, M. (2003). Race, speech, and hostile educational environment: What color is free speech. *Journal of Social Philosophy, 34*, 414-436.

Heilman, M. E., et al. (2004). Penalties for success: Reactions to women who succeed at male gender-typed tasks. *Journal of Applied Psychology, 89*(3), 416-427.

Heilman, M. E. (2001). Description and Prescription: How gender and stereotypes prevent women's ascent up the organizational ladder. *Journal of Social Issues, 57*(4), 657-674.

Hinton, E. L. (2004, March/April). *Microinequities: When small slights lead to huge problems in the workplace.* www.diversityinc.com

Hyers, L. L., & Swim, J. K. (1998). A comparison of the experiences of dominant and minority group members during an intergroup encounter. *Group Processes and Intergroup Relations, 1*, 143-163.

Katz, I., & Hass, R. G. (1988). Racial ambivalence and value conflict: Correlation and priming studies of dual cognitive structures. *Journal of Personality and Social Psychology, 55*, 893-905.

Kilian, C. M., Hukai, D., & McCarty, C. E. (2005). Building diversity in the pipeline to corporate leadership. *The Journal of Management Development, 24*(1), 155-168.

Kowalczyk, L. (2009, Feb. 24) Brigham neurosurgeon awarded $1.6 million in sex discrimination case. *Boston Globe.*

Kravitz, D. A., & Klieneberg, S. L. (2000). Reactions to two versions of affirmative action among Whites, Black, and Hispanics. *Journal of Applied Psychology, 85*, 597-611.

Krieger, L. H. (1995). The Content of our categories: A cognitive bias approach to discrimination and equal employment opportunity. *Stanford Law Review, 47*(6), 1161-1248.

Lambart, A. J. et al. (1996). Private versus public expressions of racial prejudice. *Journal of Experimental Social Psychology, 32*, 437-459.

Lorber, J. (1998). *Gender inequality: Feminist theories and politics*. Los Angeles: Roxbury.

Lyons, D., & McArthur, C. (2007). Gender's unspoken role in leadership evaluations. *Human Resource Planning, 30*(3), 24-32.

McConahay, J. B. (1986). Modern racism, ambivalence, and the modern racism scale. In J. Dovidio & S. Gaertner (Eds.), *Prejudice, discrimination and racism* (pp. 91-124). New York: Academic Press.

McDonald, J. L., Ravitch, F. S., & Sumners, P. (2006). *Employment discrimination law: Problems, cases, and critical perspectives*. Upper Saddle River, NJ : Prentice Hall.

Moynahan, B. (2005, June). *Go ahead sweat the small stuff.* The Conference Board Executive Action.

Pierce, C., et al. (1978). An experiment in racism: TV commercials. In C. Pierce (Ed.), *Television and education* (pp. 277-293). Beverly Hills, CA: Sage.

Pierce, C. (1970). Offensive mechanism. In F. Barbour (Ed.), *The Black 70s.* Boston: Sargent.

Ragins, B. R. (1999). Gender and Mentoring Relationships: A review of research agenda for the next decade. In G. N. Powell (Ed.), *Handbook of gender and work.* (pp. 347-370). Thousand Oaks, CA: Sage.

Reskin, B. F. (2002). Rethinking employment discrimination and its remedies. In M. F. Guillen, et al. (Eds.), *The new economic sociology.* (pp 218-244) New York: Russell Sage Foundation.

Ridgeway, C. L. (1997). Interaction and conservation of gender inequality: Considering employment. *American Sociological Review, 62,* 218-235.

Roberts, S. (2008). Discrimination filings with EEOC the highest since 2002. *Business Insurance, 42*(10), 4. Http://www.crain.com

Rowe, M. P. (1990). Barriers to equality: The power of subtle discrimination to maintain unequal opportunity. *Employee Responsibilities and Rights Journal, 3*(2),153-163.

Rowe, M. P. (2008). Micro-affirmation & micro-inequities. *Journal of the International Ombudsman Association, 1*(1): 2-9.

Rudman, L. A., & Glick, P. (2001). Prescriptive gender stereotypes and backlash toward agentic women. *Journal of Social Issues, 57,* 743-762.

Sarat, A. & Kearns, T. R. (1993). Beyond the great divide: Forms of legal scholarship and everyday life. In A. Sarat & T Kearns (Eds.), *Law in everyday life* (pp. 21-55).

Schnake, S. B., & Ruscher, J. B. (1998). Modern racism as a predicator of the linguistic intergroup bias. *Journal of Languages & Social Psychology, 17,* 484-491.

Schuman, H. et al. (1997). *Racial attitudes in America: Trends and interpretations.* Cambridge, MA: Harvard University Press.

Schuman, M. C., & Edleman, L. B. (1996). Legal rational myths: The new institutionalism and the law and society tradition. *Law & Social Inquiry, 21,* 903-924.

Sears, D. O. (1988). Symbolic racism. In p. A. Katz & D. A. Taylor (Eds.), *Eliminating racism* (pp. 53-84). New York: Plenum.

Sears, D. O., Henry, P. J., & Kosterman, R. (2000). Egalitarian values and contemporary racial politics. In D. O. Sears et al. (Eds.), *Racialized politics: The debate about racism in America* (pp. 75-117). Chicago: University of Chicago Press.

Sidanius, J., Pratto, F., & Bobo, L. (1996). Racism, conservatism, affirmative action, and intellectual sophistication: A matter of principled conservatism or group dominance? *Journal of Personality and Social Psychology, 70,* 476-490.

Smedley, A., & Smedley, B. D. (2005). Race as biology is fiction, racism, as a social problem is real. *American Psychologist, 60,* 16-26.

Solorzano, D., Ceja, M., & Yosso, T. (2000 winter). Critical race theory, racial microaggression, and the campus racial climate: The experiences of African American college students. *Journal of Negro Education, 69,* 60-73.

Soni, V. (1997). A biopolitical view of diversity. In A. Somit, and S. Peterson. (Eds.), *Research in Biopolitics.* Greenwich: JAI Press Inc.

Soni, V. (1999). Morality vs. mandate: Affirmative action in employment. *Public Personnel Management, 28*(4), 577-594.

Soni, V. (2000). A 21st century reception for diversity in the public sector: A case study. *Public Administration Review, 60*(5), 395-408.

Sturm, S. (2001). Second generation employment discrimination: A structural approach. *Columbia Law Review, 101*(3), 458-568.

Sue, D. W. (2004). Whiteness and ethnocentric monoculturalism: Making the "invisible" visible. *American Psychologist, 59,* 759-769.

Sue, D. W., et al. (2007). Racial microaggressions in everyday life. *American Psychology, 62*(4): 271-286.

Swim, J. K. et al. (1995). Sexism and racism: Old-fashioned and modern prejudices. *Journal of Personality and Social Psychology, 68,* 199-214.

U. S. Department of Health and Human Services. (2001). *Mental Health: Culture, race, and ethnicity: A Report of the Surgeon General.* Washington, DC.

Valian, V. (1998). *Why so slow? The advancement of women.* Cambridge: MIT Press.

von Hippel, W., Sekaquaptewa, D., & Vargas, P. (1995). On the role of encoding processes in stereotype maintenance. In M. P. Zanna (Ed.), *Advances in experimental psychology.* (pp. 177-254). San Diego, CA: Academic Press.

Weber, L. (2001). *Understanding, race, class, gender, and sexuality: A conceptual framework.* Boston: McGraw-Hill.

Wells, C. P. (2000). The perils of race and gender in a world of legal abstraction. *University of San Francisco Law Review, 34*(3), 523-535.

Wolfman, T. G. (2007). The face of corporate leadership. *New England Journal of Public Policy, 22,* 37-72.

WOMANLEGAL. (2009, April 16). Advancing gender diversity in legal profession: One day forum. Ark Group.

Zeilberger, R. (2002). Female entrepreneurs of color lead the pack of new business owners.www.DiversityInc.com.

Against All Odds:
Challenging the Ugly Underbelly of Organizational Bias

G.L.A. Harris
Portland State University

Let me preface by saying that this chapter has been the most challenging endeavor that I have ever undertaken during my still relatively short academic career. Academic writing has become my prose, and as such, I have experienced great angst in how much personal detail I should disclose about myself, especially at this pretenure stage. Will there be repercussions in light of these revelations? In the end, I reconciled that, as a woman of color, particularly one who was neither born nor raised in the United States, my contribution to this book should embody an authentic journey of my coming of age. I hope that my candid and sometimes raw accounts of racism and sexism may enlighten others who may face similar situations. This narrative thus chronicles the way that the influences of strong female role models, most notably my mom and teachers, have helped me to combat these adversities and the way institutions like the military have solidified my preparation for such negative encounters.

The Early Years

I came to the academy through a most predictable yet circuitous route. My mom, who was a teacher earlier on in her career, forbade me from pursuing the profession. She scolded me, "Whatever you do, don't teach." Mom was clearly jaded by her experiences as a teacher in Jamaica and wanted to spare me of the indignation. Mom had never apprised me of the details of her journey as a primary school teacher, but there was a sense of foreboding dare I disobey her. Further, at the time, it was the running joke that although teachers in Jamaica enjoyed social prestige, they were paid starvation wages. As twice divorced, my mom had long come to terms with the fact that neither my father nor my sister's father could provide her and her children with the security she desired. Ahough Jamaica would forever remain home, my mom, along with thousands of other professionals, left the beautiful island in the sun for what was believed to be greener pastures overseas. Many emigrated to Canada and the United Kingdom. My mom astutely chose the United States partly because of an older cousin, with whom she shared a sister-like relationship, had emigrated there with her husband a decade.

Meanwhile, in Jamaica, and while my mom was paving the way for my sister and me to join her in the United States at a later date, I attended Whitfield Primary School in Kingston. I had a teacher, Ms. Johnson, who was as much a teacher as she was a disciplinarian. Ms. Johnson was my mom's "bach mate." They had attended teacher's college together. In light of this association, when Ms. Johnson (a spinster who had adopted two children) became my teacher, and in the physical absence of my parents, she became my unofficial guardian. Without explicit declaration by Ms. Johnson, in her eyes I was destined to succeed. Failure was not an option, despite the grave reminders of an educational system rooted in inequities. I remember when I announced my intention to become an air hostess (airline stewardess), it brought about such disappointment from Ms. Johnson that I quickly changed my aspiration to that of a physician without regard to what the profession entailed.

Ms. Johnson was a wonderful teacher, but she drove her students hard. She had a long and thick leather belt that she dubbed "snaky well-bred Johnson" and did not hesitate to wield it to get her students in line. I was fortunate to have never suffered the fury of "snaky" and did everything to avoid doing so. Ms. Johnson had a stellar reputation for producing the largest number of national common entrance examination scholarship winners in the school. If a student was selected for and made it through Ms. Johnson's class, it was equivalent to academic preparation for the rest of one's life.

I did exceptionally well in school. I became the girl spelling bee champion for Whitfield Primary School and subsequently placed thirteenth in the parish (state) of Kingston. That same year, I successfully vied with 22,839 other school children around the island for the coveted 4,000 secondary school spaces. I won a scholarship to the prestigious St. Hugh's High School for girls. I was 10 years old. In hindsight, though I realized the magnitude of my achievements, I regretted the plight of the average Jamaican child in the absence of an advocate. Ms. Johnson, I now know, keenly understood this unfair stacking of the deck and did all she could as an educator to level the playing field for the most disenfranchised children. Another girl from Whitfield Primary School who was in Ms. Johnson's class also won a national scholarship to St. Hugh's High School. I think this girl was older than I but for a child, she portrayed a hard look well beyond her years.

The Jamaican Coat of Arms is "Out of Many, One People," yet this older classmate and I were clearly among the minority at St. Hugh's High School and our presence was noticeably felt. The diverse student body included Caucasians, foreign and Jamaican born; Asians, both Indian and Oriental; light-complexioned Blacks; and a few like my fellow classmate and I from Whitfield Primary School whose skin color was of a much darker hue. The majority of the students were private preparatory schooled while the remaining minority like myself came from Jamaica's version of the public school system. The differences were stark. The preparatory schooled girls were overwhelmingly non-Black, or, if mixed race, were so light complexioned that sometimes only the texture of their hair as the distinguishing feature. One girl, Donna, was an exception in that she was preparatory schooled and a budding pianist. But unlike most of my preparatory schooled cohorts, Donna's skin color was only a tinge lighter than mine and despite her hot combed straightened hair, the natural kinkiness of her mane was undeniable. A respite of mine was my dance classes with Barbara Recquois, a dance contemporary of Jamaican dancers Eddy Thomas and Rex Nettleford. Like Ms. Johnson, Mrs. Recquois was especially strict in rebuking herand likened anyone who failed to properly execute her commands to "digging yams" (an insult).

Life at St. Hugh's High School offered structure and academic challenge. The all-female faculty served as positive role models for me and the other students, especially at that developmentally vulnerable time of our young lives. The races and ethnicities of our high school faculty also ran the gamut. Some of the faculty who resembled me sported afros, donned mini skirts and exuded confidence not only in the way that they carried themselves but also in the performance of their craft. On career day, we had a complement of female professionals on campus. I remember being awed by the credentials of Dr. Mavis Gilmore, a physician who had 16 letters behind her surname and who later became Jamaica's Minister of Health. The girls who attended St. Hugh's

High School resided, for the most part, in affluent communities like Red Hills and were often chauffeured to school by their parents in privately owned vehicles, a rarity reserved for the privileged at the time. In fact, one of those students was Dr. Mavis Gilmore's niece, while others were the children of the island's politicians, barristers and foreign diplomats. The remaining few like me took public transportation to and from home.

Coming to America

Upon emigration to the United States, I entered eleventh grade at New Rochelle High School where I soon found a new sense of belonging. New Rochelle High School represented a rich patchwork of American and foreign students from all races and ethnicities. There was a noticeable constituency of West Indian students with whom I became fast friends, as well as with two African students whose fathers were diplomats. Yet it was the West Indian posse with whom I held the closest collegial relationship and with whom identified.

We formed the Caribbean Culture Club. New Rochelle High School also included a Black Culture Club comprised primarily of African American students. Whenever tension erupted between the Caribbean Culture and Black Culture Clubs, Dr. Gaddy, (then the first Black principal of the school and whom I believe went on later to become the first superintendent of schools for Westchester County), took it upon himself to serve as mediator between members of the two groups. Dr. Gaddy decided that the two clubs should merge. He explained that the only difference between the groups was that Columbus happened to drop us off at different geographic locations. He was right. Yet from then on, though technically we functioned as a club, each group continued to engage in its separate activities.

During that period, my mom had enrolled my sister and me in dance lessons at the New Rochelle Community Center under the direction of Pearl Primus. Mrs. Primus was a Trinidadian woman who headed the Whitney Young, Jr. Theatre Dance Group Company. Mrs. Primus was the only Black woman I knew at the time who consistently donned in African garb from head to toe. It always struck me that this stately and erectly postured woman had a sense of self and clearly reveled in her African-centricness. Yet, I would not realize how well known a figure Mrs. Primus was if not for two subsequent events.

I excelled academically at New Rochelle High School and was one of 16 selected to go to France as an exchange student. I was the first Black student to have been so honored. Although I was proud of this achievement, our group pictures never portrayed me in a favorable light. The quality of the photography was such that I was always featured as a mere black blip on an otherwise normal human body. The school newspaper's photographs were the worst. But the bright spots of my exchange-student experience was that I was twice highlighted in the local newspaper. Our trip even made the pages of the *New York Times*. I was even on French television, albeit briefly, and got to meet and photograph with legendary actor Ossie Davis, Jr. Following these events, Mrs. Primus asked me to record my experiences as an exchange student and during one of our dance recitals, she introduced me as the "first woman of color" to have been chosen as an exchange student from New Rochelle High School. Although the term "woman of color" has now been popularized, before Mrs. Primus's use of the term, I had never heard it used before.

The second memorable event about Mrs. Primus occurred while I was on a trip en route from Philadelphia to Seattle to inspect two subsidiaries for my first food manufacturing employer. During the flight, I read a special issue of *Ebony* magazine that highlighted the lives of notable Blacks. There, in the corner of one of the pages, was a picture of a much younger Pearl Primus who was purported in her hay day to have danced for Queen Elizabeth II of England. Again, I was naïve about Mrs. Primus's stature which extended beyond her role as simply my dance teacher.

My Bouts with Racism

That said, I believe that a disproportionate number of White Americans still harbor a pollyannish notion about the state of race relations, believing that any associated problems with race relations is a thing of the past and/or that the groups that are experiencing such problems are being overly sensitive. Unfortunately, such thinking serves to devalue and hence discredit the discriminatory experiences of nonWhite groups. My repeated encounters, with racism betrayed a certain naiveté. Yet it was this same naiveté, no matter how frequently I encountered these ills, that continually evoked an element of surprise and reaction of bewilderment on my part each time they occurred.

My first recollection of direct racism in the United States was following the completion of my first year at New Rochelle High School. The first job I secured through the school during the summer was with a family in Scarsdale, New York, taking care of a four-year-old boy named Brian. I remember that when I met Brian's mother she repeatedly commented on the eloquence of my English. I was taken aback by this bizarre response, as English is my primary language. During that summer, Brian once remarked that Black people are ugly. With controlled outrage, when I inquired where he had learned such claptrap, Brian replied that he learned it from his father.

Years later when I purchased my first home in southern New Jersey, it was on the heels of securing my first corporate position in food manufacturing. Incidentally, my American-born stepfather, an African American, regularly noted that going to southern New Jersey was like going below the Mason Dixon line. Though I never understood what he meant at the time, the significance of his mantra later became evident. My new home which was situated in a planned community, was charming on the surface, but beneath loomed a sinister and even dangerous undercurrent. The Pinelands, or the Pinies as it is known, is reputed to have been and may still be a haven for the Northeast's version of the Klu Klux Klan. My encounter with some of the residents is emblematic of the region.

Shortly after I moved in, the two White couples who subsequently moved in on the opposite sides of my home soon became friends and the wives began using my lawn as a path to each other's homes instead of the concrete pathways that were provided for such purpose. I took issue with this practice and so at an opportune time visited the home of one of the women while the other was visiting her. I was diplomatic but direct in advising the women that their frequent walks across my lawn to and from each other's homes was creating an almost grassless track in my lawn, and I asked that they use the appropriate pathways. In retaliation, the women made it a habit of blocking the concrete pathways where I walked. But, armed with an adamant streak of my own, I would walk in between them, often brushing against the miscreants in the process. The attacks against me escalated and became more violent in nature when a few weeks later my car was vandalized.

In another incident with the same neighbors, while I worked in New York and commuted to my home in southern New Jersey on weekends, I remember arriving home to the horror of finding the glass of my French doors at the rear of the house shattered. In my absence, the cowards had used my time away to not just break into my home but to deliver a message that they were not to be challenged. I immediately alerted one of my neighbors and contacted the police. I employed a contractor to temporarily place plexiglass over the door until the glass panes of the doors could be replaced. While in New York, I happened to contact the contractor who returned the following week to install the glass that had arrived. He began describing that the plexiglass itself had been shattered. I had to dispatch the southern New Jersey police while I was in New York. My parents, especially my mom, feared for my life. But I was bound and determined not to allow these simpletons to run me out of my own home. There were legal bouts back and forth between these White neighbors and me. I was defiant and displayed no sense of fear whatsoever in dealing with these thugs. I was an enigma whom they were determined to exterminate. Further, I spoke with a foreign tongue and as they saw it, I had no place in their neighborhood, even though I was one of the first residents in the new development.

Quite coincidentally, my employer at the time transferred me to one of its plant locations in Pennsylvania, so it became necessary for me to relocate and rent out my home. On the appointed day of the move, the wife of the couple who was alleged to have vandalized my home came out and denounced me as a "nigger." I fired back that she was the "nigger," as the word simply means lowdown, and that is exactly what she is. I presume that even today this woman is still befuddled and reeling from my intellectual retort. In my encounter with some Whites in the United States, I have been cast as an "uppity nigger," as I clearly do not know my place. And, in all candor, I neither understood nor cared to know where that place was or should be. I took no notice of such slights, as I always believed that my place is wherever I choose it to be.

Following my two-year assignment in Pennsylvania, I returned to my home in southern New Jersey, but the demographic makeup of the neighborhood had changed. Not only had the neighborhood become more racially and ethnically diverse, but many of the homes that were formally owner-occupied became rentals. Probably out of sheer necessity, as he and his family could ill afford to move elsewhere, the one remaining holdout of the gang of racist neighbors soon befriended the Blacks who had now populated the neighborhood. I distinctly remember one day, upon driving into the development, when this racist neighbor who was standing beside his new Black neighbor, waved to me. I was infuriated, so much so, that I parked my car, jumped out, went over to this White neighbor and proceeded to vehemently disparage him in the presence of his Black neighbor about what a hypocrite he was. I forbade this racist neighbor from ever waving to me again.

Challenging "isms" in the Workplace

Though I was, for the most part, successful in my professional career pursuits, I was usually the only Black and/or woman in my capacity in food manufacturing. Though my relationship with many was collegial, I was keenly aware of the potential forces at play (i.e., sexism and racism). At one plant location, the operations manager, in the presence of a subordinate, blew a kiss at me. Recognizing this power play, and with the insight that had I taken the matter to the plant manager, he would have considered the operations manager's overture a harmless prank and that I was being overly sensitive, I approached the operations manager immediately following the incident and told him in no uncertain terms, yet as diplomatically as was possible, to never blow a kiss at me again. My request was poorly received, and the operations manager thereafter did all that he could to sabotage my career in the company. However, as matters of principle and the law, I vowed that because this was an all White male manufacturing environment, it was incumbent upon me, particularly as the chief human resource management officer, to demonstrate leadership by nipping the problem in the bud in an effort to deter the occurrence of similarly biased incidents against any employee, as well as to disallow this incident from defining my tenure with my then employer.

In a second incident, this time with a few more years of experience and wisdom about the industry under my belt, I moved from the corporate headquarters to assume regional responsibilities for the depot and plant locations. My car at the time had Pennsylvania license plates and I was visiting one of the depot locations in the Bronx, to meet with the depot manager and his supervisors. I was well attired and drove my car into one of the enclosed bays. Upon entry to the depot manager's office, I immediately noticed a large poster of a scantily clad woman. I deliberately ignored the poster, choosing instead to focus on the business at hand—the meeting with the depot manager and his supervisors. Following the meeting, I looked up and casually commented, "Now who placed that poster there?" The room erupted in laughter. The poster had been strategically affixed to that location of the wall to command my attention, and the depot manager stated that they wondered when I was going to notice it. Word quickly spread throughout the other company locations that I was "alright."

While to the casual onlooker this incident might seem trivial or perhaps offensive at worse, as the main human resource management professional for the company, passing this test was key to establishing relationships with the predominantly White male manufacturing workforce. Choosing initially to ignore the poster was not to suggest that I condoned the tactic. But at the outset, and as a clear outlier, given the intervening variables that included the constituency served, my role as a transplant from the corporate headquarters, and my gender and race, I was mindful that my acceptance and prospects for future effective leadership in the company were predicated on how well I survived this initial challenge. This situation was characteristic of the rough and tumble terrain of the depot and plant locations, especially those located within the five boroughs of New York City and North Jersey. Despite the reasonable success that I experienced as a Black woman in food manufacturing, the reception in other industries was often a chilly one.

As an independent consultant I periodically partnered on contracts with an older White male colleague who was nothing less than respectful in my business dealings with him. On one occasion, the client, represented by another White male, approached my colleague, shook his hand, and rendered me invisible, even though I was standing next to my partner. I deliberately moved forward, extended my hand toward this client representative, grasped his hand, and shook it firmly while I introduced myself. I was my colleague's partner on the project and was determined not to be ignored. My older White colleague gave me an approving smile following the encounter.

At another company client's facility where I was conducting a series of employment law workshops, one of the participants during one session break jokingly called my attention to a particular company's poster for black bean soup. He, the participant, thought that the poster was amusing because I had once worked for the company depicted in the poster, and now I happen to be the consultant on the project for his employer. But more importantly, the message that this particular participant wanted to convey was that my race was akin to the black bean soup, thus the incendiary nature of the poster. However, I was unable to ascertain whether or not the poster was deliberately placed on the wall for the purpose of evoking an effect on my part.

But this encounter only served to affirm the insidiousness of this workplace culture and to raise serious doubts about whether or not a short-term series of employment law workshops would have been sufficient to address the entrenched problems of discrimination within the company. Besides, the primary reason why I secured this employer as a client was so the client could divert media attention from the onslaught of racial and gender discrimination lawsuits that had been lodged against the company. Regrettably, I suspected that the company only employed my expertise to demonstrate that it was taking steps as a form of redress to either convince the courts and/or the Equal Employment Opportunity Commission (E.E.O.C.) that it was taking such charges seriously.

At the request of an international client company with locations throughout the United States, I travelled to one of its manufacturing plants in the South to investigate allegations of rampant racism by the White management of its largely non-unionized Black workforce. This was essentially a remote part of the state, where any visit to the plant would be for calculated and deliberate reasons. Unbeknownst to the plant manager (or so he led the company's upper management to believe), the operations manager was engaging in unethical, illegal and racist behaviors that potentially compromised the company. The operations manager was using the Black rank-and-file workforce to do his personal bidding. In return, the operations manager was compensating the workers at the company's expense. The plant's time-card system was a holdover from years past, and the crude manner in which the employees were allowed to adjust their time cards by using correction fluid to amend their hours was an indication of how insulated this plant management, and specifically the operations manager, felt from outside interference. To get to the root of the problem, it grew increasingly necessary for me to clandestinely meet with employees off the plant premises, often after midnight. In retrospect, I wonder whether some of the actions that I took while on this assignment were acts of bravery or of foolhardiness and whether it was sheer luck that kept me from disappearing into the recesses of this back country.

The upstairs of the plant facility was surrounded by thick plexiglass that allowed the White managers above to survey the Black workforce below from every angle of the plant. The Black employees whom I interviewed on the plant premises were visibly fearful of jeopardizing their jobs by talking to me. I interviewed the plant manager and asked him what he believed his rank-and-file employees would say about him if asked. The plant manager was clearly insulted, perhaps given a number of factors: the question itself, the perceived intrusion of an outsider and by proxy the company's corporate office meddling in the plant's affairs, because of my race and possibly gender, because I am a foreigner or because I was perceived as a Yankee since at the time I resided on the Northeast. In every respect, my presence was noticeably unwanted by the plant management.

I subsequently submitted a 60-page report to my client's corporate headquarters delineating my findings as well as offering recommendations for corrective action. In the report, I informed my client that the plant's management had engaged in intimidation and held the Black workforce hostage armed with the knowledge that the plant was the largest employer in the area, the highest paying and perhaps represented the only source of employment for much of the largely Black populace in the region. In addition, much of the Black workforce was barely literate and relations between management and the rank and file assumed an eerie aura that seemed reminiscent of a gone by era in the deep South.

The Military

From age 18, I became ensconced in the military way of life. Though I only remained on active duty for four years, I enjoyed the camaraderie of the institution and so continued my service through the Reserve. Upon becoming a citizen, I applied for and received almost simultaneous offers for commission to both the

Navy and Air Force Reserves. I subsequently accepted the commission as an officer in the Air Force Reserve. Given my personal experience with the military, and as one who now conducts research about the institution, I believe that unlike any other American institution, the military goes to extraordinary lengths in ensuring that its diverse workforce is one of harmony and is not distracted from the mission at hand. The military recognizes that race relations is a work in progress, and it regularly tests the cultural climate of its workforce (Evans, 2003). Unlike many employers in both the public and private sectors, the military openly acknowledges that the various segments of its population experiences are different. It considers race and ethnicity to be of a "compelling government interest" and therefore vital to national security (Karabel 2003, p.1).

The military was the first employer to establish such measures as race relations in an effort to protect its Black forces from unwarranted racial attacks (Evans, 2003; DEOMI, 2002). Moreover, the military also recognizes that race and/or ethnicity serve as critical factors in determining the recruiting and retention patterns of its personnel (Bachman et al., 2000, Department of Defense, 1999, Hosek et al., 2001, Segal et al., 1999, Smith, 2001, Segal and Wechsler, Segal, 2004). More than any other organization, it is the military that has prepared me at every stage of my development, both as a person and as an officer, to assume the reigns of leadership and, in doing so, to confront and manage the challenges of race and gender discrimination.

Fortunately, my experience with racism as a career military officer has been limited. This is not to say, however, that I have never experienced racism and sexism in the military. Perhaps the most brazen account of racism was as a civilian visiting an officer's club for the purpose of a meeting in a civil-military organization of fellow officers. While in this officers' club, I joined the food line when an older White woman approached me and declared that she needed spoons. I deliberately ignored her. Another White woman, who resembled this woman, also approached me and said that she needed utensils. What is interesting to note about this incident is that I was not the only person in line, of course, but simply the only Black person in line. I turned to the woman and sternly advised her that I, like her, was a guest of the officers' club. The White waitress in the club, whom neither of the older White women approached, even though she was visibly attired in a waitress uniform, came and apologized profusely to me. The irony is that had I been in uniform, this incident would have never occurred. My rank, regardless of race and/or gender, would have afforded me the appropriate level of respect. What was disheartening, however, is that when I described the incident to a fellow White officer, whom before this day I had considered a mentor, she stated that I should ignore the matter altogether. As a consequence, my mentor-mentee relationship with this officer declined precipitously.

In a second encounter, then as one of 703 other attendees at Squadron Officer School (SOS), I happened to have been in my quarters when one of the housekeepers visited to clean the room. Upon entry, I addressed the housekeeper by saying, "Good morning." However, she appeared to be surprised by the salutation. Upon completion of her tasks, and as she was about to exit the room, I said, "Thank you." She immediately turned around and in her deep southern accent, stated that of all the officers with whom she has dealt in cleaning their rooms, I was the only one who has acknowledged her. She stated that there was also a wager between the housekeeping and janitorial staff to discern where the cadre of foreign officers who were attending the school were from. But, though each staff recognized that I donned the American military uniform, they could tell that like the foreign officers, I was not American born.

I found this revelation uncanny for not only had they not heard me speak before then but at the time of my attendance at SOS, it had been many years since I immigrated to the United States. My conversation with the housekeeper thus settled the wager. She also wanted to thank me for acknowledging her to which I replied, "You do what you do, so that I can do what I do." Little did she know that her life paralleled my mom's in that she too represented the sacrifices that my mom initially made for my sister and I as an illegal immigrant in the United States when her sole source of employment was as a domestic. Additionally, in my former civilian career in food manufacturing, I often befriended members of the various hotels' housekeeping and janitorial staff for they were the only reflections of myself during the course of my travels across the country.

In a third incident, then as a newly minted field grade officer at the rank of Major, I was enrolled in the seminar format of Air Command and Staff College (ACSC), a 10-month professional development training program, as one of many criteria for consideration for promotion to the next field grade level, or to the rank of Lieutenant Colonel. As is customary, the cohort of officers from the three components of the U.S. Air Force (active duty, Reserve, and Air National Guard) convened to discuss relevant topics in accordance with the program's curriculum. I was one of three minorities, all Black women, to enroll in this ACSC training. Unfortunately, by the end of the training program, I was the lone Black officer left in the cohort. The other two Black officers, who were also in the Air Force Reserve, prematurely terminated the training for personal reasons.

The lesson for one day in question was on leadership. The senior Captain responsible for leading that discussion posed the question, "What do you think of when you hear the name George Washington?" All of my White colleagues eagerly raised their hands to give positive accounts associated with the name. I then raised my hand and said, "He owned slaves," to which the questioner countered, "I did not mean that." In essence, my own recollection of this famous American was contrary to the accepted view of the majority, a culture to which she, the Captain, belonged. I, as "other," as deMello Patterson (2000, p.104) terms it, held a view of George Washington that was contrary to the mainstream, or that of White officers, and in effect, that of White Americans in general. For to be an American is to be representative of the White culture and therefore the mainstream. But to be out of the mainstream casts one as other, nonWhite and thus un-American. Consequently, to be other invokes deviance (Ellefson, 1998; Law, 1999,). Incidentally, military women also characterize this departure (Ellefson, 1998).

It was only shortly thereafter that my fellow Black female officers left the group. Interestingly enough, as Black officers, we are all direct descendants from slaves, but my African American cohorts are also Americans by birth, while I am American only by naturalization. So perhaps, despite our common ancestry, we had different experiences growing up, and we essentially processed and felt the sting of the Captain's insult differently. I, as another symbol for "other" as a foreign-born Black woman, and perhaps selfishly so, remained in the group for the sake of my career. I dismissed the Captain's comment as pure folly, or that of an ignoramus, who lacks proper schooling, while my African American cohorts were personally offended by the remark. But, surely, this does not mean that I, too, was not offended by the Captain's remark.

I deliberately reconstructed the situation to make it less about the Captain and more about me. I therefore chose to belittle the Captain by not dignifying her remark with the acknowledgment of a response as a way of putting her in her place. My nonresponse though was by no means a sign that I was silenced. In a sense, I concluded that this was not a battle worth fighting, for the person (the Captain) was worth neither my time nor my energy. I was unidimensionally focused, valued my career more and was not about to have my gallant efforts derailed by the uncouth. So, I pressed on.

So, to suggest that racism does not occur in the military, when the military itself is a subset of American society, would be naïve, if not disingenuous. In fact, for some, sexism in the military has been the more challenging. Yet, although Black female officers, for example, admit to their race as a challenge, they also attribute this gnawing duality to sexism (Hosek et al. 2001). The work of Dansby and Landis (1998) reveal the way the experience of minority female officers makes them the least likely of any group in the military to have favorable views about the institution. In particular, Black female officers are the least likely of any demographic group in the military to be promoted (Hosek et al. 2001). Yet, paradoxically, once promoted, Black female officers remain the most loyal by remaining in the military longer between promotion cycles than do other groups. But this level of commitment by Black women to the military may be borne of a two-pronged reality. First, minorities, especially Blacks, have long viewed the military as "more racially fair" than institutions in the civilian sector (Segal& Wechsler Segal 2004, p. 19). And, second, even as minority women, the military in many ways still represents a better opportunity for a career than do employers in the civilian sector despite what Moore (1991) sees as a double jeopardy for Black women in the military, given their reliance on the military as an employer of choice.

The military traditionally attracts individuals of a certain temperament. Its culture is more likely then to acculturate its workforce over-time to exercise measured approaches to challenging situations like race and gender discrimination or any other potentially and emotionally charged situation. The various required professional development training that military personnel must complete at every stage of their careers makes them more apt to be prepared to function even-handedly in challenging situations, the most challenging of which is combat. For commissioned officers, and especially minority female officers, must craft constructive ways of coping while neither succumbing to nor tolerating any degree of disrespect from subordinates and superiors alike when confronted with these situations. In doing so, the military does an effective job of continually preparing its workforce for any eventuality and, as a consequence, teaches its personnel to keep their emotions in check in the face of adversity. Such display of maturity and levelheadedness in turn characterizes leadership. The research literature, as indicated, shows that minority groups join the military because of the perception of the institution as an equal opportunity employer (Segal & Wechsler Segal, 2004, p. 19). And given my own experience as a military officer, this has certainly been the case.

Academia and Coming Full Circle

I have now come full circle by finding my way to the academy despite my mom's pleas to avoid the vocation. My career pursuits up to now have been largely successful in coping with race and gender discrimination. Although these encounters were more likely to have disproportionately occurred within personal contexts, (e.g., with racist neighbors), I have had my fair share of like experiences in the workplace. However, I credit much of my ability to handle these counterproductive behaviors to my upbringing, temperament; the guidance of strong female role models, like teachers, including my mom; and my leadership training in the military, a communal culture that is intolerant of behaviors that deviate from its institutional norm yet is sensitive to the issues of race and/or ethnicity. A resonating pattern in my life has been defined by the academic medium where I have consistently found a sense of belonging, and now as an academic, I delight in the intellectual exercise.

As for my personal experiences as a woman of color, and particularly as a Black woman in academe, the jury is still out, for at the time of this writing, I had only submitted my dossier for promotion and tenure consideration a few weeks prior. I had naively made the assumption that the academy symbolized rationality and equity and dealt with a constituency that represents the most educated segment of the U.S. population, However, one senior African American faculty member cautioned me of the need to bring to bear the full arsenal of my corporate experience with racism and sexism in dealing with the inherent inequities of academe. Essentially, I should go about the business of the academy with the same ways of knowing and expectations that I had utilized in the corporate world as a woman of color and should never underestimate the level of brinkmanship that is often practiced in the institution. The message was simple—leave nothing to chance and take nothing for granted.

My mom frequently lamented that I am "as hard as nails" given my obstinate nature. Yet, I believe that it is this dogged determination that has served me well in dealing with the travails of life and most notably with gender and racial discrimination. In providing these vivid examples of my encounters with these ills, I hope that my story will serve as a testament to the Black immigrant experience of one who repeatedly encountered and fought against systems of exclusion. Yet, had it not been for the intervention of advocates, surrogates, the military, and my acculturation from childhood to adulthood, perhaps this immigrant girl would not have possessed the intestinal fortitude to succeed despite the naysayers and against all odds.

References

Bachman, J. G., Segal, D. R., Freedman-Doan, P., & O'Malley, P. M. (2000). Who chooses military service? Correlates of propensity and enlistment in the U.S. armed forces. *Military Psychology, 12*(1), 1-30.

Dansby, M. R., & Landis, D. (1998). Race, gender and representation index as predictors of an equal opportunity climate in military organizations. *Military Psychology, 10*(2), 87-105.

Defense Equal Opportunity Management Institute (DEOMI). (2002, February). *Historical overview of racism in the military. Special series*, Pamphlet 02-1.

DeGruy Leary, J. (2005). *Post traumatic slave syndrome. America's legacy of enduring injury and healing.* Milwaukie, OR: Uptone Press.

DeMello Patterson, M.B. (1998). America's racial unconscious: The invisibility of whiteness. In J. L. Kincholoe, S. R. Steinberg, N. R. Rodriguez & R. E. Chennault, (Eds.), *White reign: Deploying whiteness in America* (pp. 103-121). New York: St. Martin's Press.

Ellefson, K.G. (1998). *Advancing army women as senior leaders —Understanding the obstacles.* Carlisle Barracks, PA: Army War College.

Evans, R. (2003, June 26). *A history of the service of ethnic minorities in the U.S. armed forces.* Center for the Study of Sexual Minorities in the Military. Santa Barbara, CA: University of California, Santa Barbara.

Hosek, S. D., Tiemeyer, P., Kilburn, R., Strong, D.A., Ducksworth, S., & Ray, R. (2001). *Minority and gender differences in officer career progression.* Santa Monica, CA: RAND.

Karabel, J. (March 28, 2003). *Race and national security.* Retrieved May 30, 2008. http://www.csmonitor.com/2003/0328/pS01-coop.html.

Law, S. A. (1999). White privilege and affirmative action. *Akron Law Review, 32,* 603-621.

Moore, B. L. 1991. African-American women in the U.S. military. *Armed Forces and Society, 17*(3), 363-384.

Office of the Under Secretary of Defense, Personnel and Readiness. (1999). *Career progression of minority and women officers.* U.S. Department of Defense.

Segal, D. R., & Wechsler Segal, M. (2004). America's military population. *Population Bulletin, 59*(1), 1-42.

Segal, D. R., Bachman, J. G., Freedman-Doan, P., & O'Malley, P. M. (1999). Propensity to serve in the U.S. military: Temporal trends and subgroup differences. *Armed Forces and Society, 25(3),* 407-427.

Smith, M. M. (2001). The military retirement reform act of 1986 or redux: A postmortem. *Journal of Political and Military Sociology, 29,* 305-318.

The Journey of a Black Woman School Principal in a Small, Southern, Rural Town

E. Renée Sanders-Lawson
University of Memphis

Introduction

In 1992, I became the first African American woman principal in my home county's school district since the schools integrated in the 1960s. I write this experience narrative from the perspective of an African American female educational practitioner who is committed to making the educational opportunities for children of color more equal and fair. This chapter focuses on the ways race, gender, and class issues impacted my professional life (specifically at Selma Middle School), my life in general, and my work for social change. Writing this chapter forced me to examine how my personal and professional life experiences have influenced my commitment as the principal of a southern middle school to work for social justice in a learning environment.

I hope that my narrative will help persons who are responsible for recruiting and hiring women of color as teachers and educational administrators to understand the impact of racism, sexism, and classism on the persons in their employ. Moreover, I hope that this chapter gives voice to the many Black women with experiences similar to mine. My narrative connects with the larger role Black women played and are still playing in the struggle for social justice within learning environments. I illuminate some of the issues I dealt with during the tenure of my principalship related to race, class, and gender by sharing my own experience as "the first one" and, often, the "only one" still.

Defining Terms: Social Justice as Distributive and Participatory Justice

Two terms that I will use throughout this chapter need explanation: *distributive* and *participatory* justice. The use of these terms can best be illustrated by their place in the Civil Rights

Movement in the United States. The struggle for civil rights has had and continues to have two social justice dimensions. The first is distributive justice, that is, how social goods and the attending benefits and burdens are distributed. African American history is replete with examples of the distributive inequalities of goods and services to our communities. Social goods include health care, legal services, and, of course, educational opportunities. John Rawls (1971) termed these *primary goods* because they are needed to ensure that a person is able to live the best possible life he or she can. The struggle for a fair and just distribution of social goods has been the hallmark of the Civil Rights Movement. My family has been, and continues to be, active in this dimension of the struggle.

The second dimension of social justice is participatory justice, or the ways distributive decisions are made. Who participates in the making of these decisions? African Americans have understood that, without adequate group representation in those institutions that govern the distribution of social goods, given the racist nature of many social practices, there would still be distributive injustice. Because of this dimension, my appointment as principal at Selma Middle School was about much more than me. It was more about the collective community that I belong to having someone at the table when decisions were being made.

The Journey Begins: My Family and Childhood

My journey to the principalship began years before 1992. I was born and raised in Smithfield, North Carolina in 1960, the younger of two children. My brother is eight years older than I am. My mom was a registered nurse, and my father, a laborer, was disabled as a result of debilitating rheumatoid arthritis. He was diagnosed when I was three years old, and by the time I was eight, he was declared totally disabled. My mom graduated salutatorian from her high school and later received her nursing degree from the Lincoln School of Nursing in Durham, North Carolina. My father did not finish high school but instead left high school and joined the army so that he could help support his family. Even though only my mom graduated from high school (and attended college), both parents had high educational expectations for my brother and me. Both of us were destined to finish high school and college. As a family, in addition to work and school, we balanced our time attending church services and activities between two churches. Additionally, both parents were active, my mom more so than my dad, in the Civil Rights Movement in Smithfield, North Carolina and Johnston County. Their social activism had a great influence on my brother and me. That sense of activism, "rooted" in our upbringing, was only enhanced by our early K-12 educational experiences.

I attended the all-Black Johnston Central School for first and second grades. I have vivid memories of my first grade teacher, Ms. Naomi L. Smith, and my second grade teacher, Mrs. Ann Sanders. As a young child, I always adored jewelry, make-up and fashion. During the first grade, I decided that I would make a fashion statement, so I "borrowed" a couple of my mom's rings from her jewelry box and wore them to school. I was the center of attention for a brief moment. My celebrity status quickly wore off as Ms. Smith discovered that I was wearing my mom's jewelry. She called my mom, and, of course my mom came to school, retrieved her jewelry, and promised to "deal with me" when I got home. In the second grade, I remember the first day of school. As Mrs. Sanders called the class roll for attendance she called my name, "Eleanor Renée Sanders." Not knowing any better, I proceeded to correct her and told her that I was called Renée instead of Eleanor. She responded, "Your parents named your Eleanor, and in this classroom you will be called Eleanor." Mrs. Sanders attended a neighboring church, and for years beyond second grade (until she died) she was the only person I ever remember calling me Eleanor.

Since these were rather fond memories, it's unfortunate that after the second grade I had only one other Black teacher the rest of my K-12 public school experience. Mrs. Mary Leftwridge taught me biology in the tenth grade. Those teachers of the segregated south seemed to have a commitment to education that encompassed a sense of racial pride for their students and an emphasis on academic success as the avenue for a better life (Tyson, 2001). My mom always said, "As a race of Black people, our goal should be for all our children to do better than the previous generation." Ms. Smith and Mrs. Sanders just confirmed what I heard regularly from home. Education is important, so "girl, you better do good in school." These teachers were the guardian angels for Black children before and during the years of school desegregation. They had to be because public education for African Americans in North Carolina was always given a low priority by the whites in power.

The first public schools in North Carolina were built in the 1840s after state legislation allowed counties to adopt taxes for schools. Several private academies prepared students for college and careers in teaching and business before the state established public high schools for whites in 1907. The first high school for African Americans was founded in 1914, with the first graduating class in 1921. In 1920, Johnston County had 99 schools for whites and 35 for Blacks, most of which were housed in ill-equipped, wooden buildings with one or two teachers. In 1922, the new superintendent, H. B. Marrow, expressed a desire to bridge the gaps between whites and Blacks and, between town and county in public education. Within a decade, he was able to facilitate the largest school building campaign in the county's history and abandon autonomous districts in favor of what was supposed to be a more equal distribution of educational resources.

In the 1960s, federal mandates for racial integration led to the consolidation of 18 high schools into 5. At that point, what was first known as Johnston Normal School for Negroes, then Johnston County Training School, and finally Johnston Central School, was no more. Distributive justice was being enacted. Ironically, as I write this chapter, I am making travel arrangements to return to Smithfield, North Carolina for the 40th commemorative celebration of the last graduating class at Johnston County School. Even though I didn't graduate from this high school, my roots were planted there in the first and second grades. All students who ever attended the school have been invited to the celebration.

My story is probably no different than that of any other young, Black child in the South in the sixties, whose family was deeply involved in the Civil Right's Movement. Anticipating forced integration, my parents decided to exercise the "Freedom of Choice" option for the 1968-1969 school year. That option allowed students to attend schools where a majority of the students were of a different race. Because of my grades, my parents chose to enroll me in the formerly segregated white elementary school. Consequently, I was one of two Black students in the third grade at Smithfield Elementary. This was distributive justice at its worst. I could now have truly equal access to the same educational experiences as my white counterparts. I remember the first day of school: my third-grade teacher asked the other Black student and me where we lived. Pam answered, "Pine Acres," and I answered, "Sandy Run." Pine Acres was a subdivision of lower middle to affluent middle class Blacks. Sandy Run was not. Even though I was just eight years old, some 41 years later I still remember that from that point on, the teacher's interaction with me was different from her interaction with Pam. It was if my fate was predetermined. Where I lived defined who I was and maybe, more detrimental, my chance for success. I remember thinking to myself, "I'll show you." I would spend the rest of my life doing just that.

I had to be bussed from my neighborhood to my new school. I remember how much I hated riding the bus. By the time I reached middle school, I had been tagged or labeled "a good student" by the Black students in my neighborhood. Unfortunately, that was like the kiss of death. Bus rides became even less fun because of the label. By high school, I became one of two Black students inducted in the National Honor Society. That meant I took upper-level courses, and so more often than not, I was the only Black student in my classes. If there were other Black students taking upper-level courses, we did not take classes at the same time. At school, it was fine to be known as a good student, and the white students seemed to accept me as such. But the bus ride going to and from school was no fun. I heard everything from "Who do you think you are" and "You think you're better than us" to "You must think you're white!" What a quandary. If I didn't make good grades and remain active in school, my parents would be disappointed, and if I did what my parents expected, my peers verbally abused me. What a choice. It's often said, "be careful what you ask for, you just might get it." We marched, protested, and demanded distributive justice in the form of equal access to a quality education. We got that, or did we? Like many Black students of this era, I survived and made it my goal to show that being Black and being smart were not in opposition. It was also the goal I took to my job as principal.

Coming of Age and to Terms with Distributive Justice

During my junior and senior years I made all of the appropriate preparations for college. I knew early on that college was mandatory and not an optional choice. It was set; a few of my closest friends and I were applying (early decision) to the University of North Carolina at Chapel Hill. As my classmates and I were navigating this process, a friend shared her encounter with one of our school's guidance counselors. My friend, who missed the National Honor Society's grade criteria by a few points, had just met with her counselor. She was told that she need not apply to UNC-Chapel Hill because she would probably not get in. I was outraged. I had a part-time after-school waitress job, so I challenged her to apply early decision with me in spite of the contradictory guidance she had been given. I told her that when we applied, if she was not accepted, I would refund the application fee she had paid. We applied early decision, we were accepted, and we attended and graduated in four years unlike many of our counterparts who took five or more years to graduate.

Upon graduating from Smithfield-Selma High school, I received my bachelor's degree in psychology and a master of science degree in rehabilitation counseling from the University of North Carolina at Chapel Hill. My admission to the University of North Carolina at Chapel Hill coincided with the legislative consent decree, which demanded that all universities in the University of North Carolina system increase the minority presence at each of the then sixteen campuses. This led to persons questioning whether students of color were regularly admitted to the university or whether we were "special admits." Were we simply "affirmative action" cases? We felt the tension as we walked across campus, entered classrooms, the cafeteria, and the libraries. We felt the tension from some professors and classmates as we attempted to actively participate in classroom discussions. Some often felt that persons of color occupied spaces that their own children, children of relatives, or children of friends could have accepted if only they had not been offered to "those people." The fact that I was an excellent student and honor society member at my high school was lost to some. There was little regard to the intellect, talents, and skills that we brought to the campus. (Lawson, Forthcoming) While tensions grew around me, I found refuge in the Black Student Alliance, my sorority, Alpha Kappa Alpha, and, last but not least, my church.

On campus we faced those tensions, but back home our community celebrated us. After all, at one time no Black students were allowed to attend UNC-Chapel Hill, and even though there were still few Blacks attending, this was a small step toward "getting our piece" of what was rightfully ours, a chance at equal and fair distribution of a quality education and the educational experiences that accompany that. After all, did we not have a right to a solid education? Here I should note that my husband (Bill) received his Ph.D. in philosophy from UNC in 1980. He was the first African American to receive the degree from this department and its only recipient until 2000.

My Family's Involvement in the Civil Rights Struggle in the County

Smithfield, North Carolina is a small town that had a reputation of active Klan activity. On the eastern and western end of the county stood a billboard displaying a man on a horse with Klan paraphernalia (a robe and hood) that read, "KKK welcomes you to Johnston County." I remember this vividly as a small child. Our county became infamous as a result of these two "welcome" signs. I was a member of a family that was well known throughout the surrounding communities as community activists for social justice. I remember marching in protest of inhumane treatment of Native Americans as a youngster. I remember participating in a rally organized by my brother denouncing police brutality against minorities while the very police that we were boycotting visibly circled the location of the rally. I remember the worried look on my mom's face as she waited to hear word about my brother and cousins as they attempted to integrate a local eating establishment, or later as two cousins integrated the county public library. I bring these memories to this narrative.

My mom was the first and maybe still is the only Black head nurse at our local hospital. For a number of years, all Black patients admitted to the hospital were admitted to the second floor, where Mom was head nurse. When beds on the other three patient floors filled, white patients were transferred to the second floor, and Black patients, if necessary, were taken out of their rooms and put in the hallway. In those instances, white patients would often refuse to be served by the attending "Nigger/Negro" or Black nurse. This was yet another challenge when all we simply wanted was equal access to health care, just like our counterparts.

My Tenure at Selma Middle School

Upon graduating from UNC-Chapel Hill, I returned to Johnston County to work as a school counselor. I served as a counselor for five years until deciding to return to graduate school to get my

administrator license, which I earned in 1989. At the time I finished the license, no vacancies in K-12 administration existed in
Johnston County. One of my college professors recommended me
to a principal of a high school in Hickory, a small town in North
Carolina. Hickory was located in the foothills of the mountains,
not too far from Asheville and Charlotte, North Carolina and
about four hours from my home. Before I knew it, I had been
convinced to go to Hickory, North Carolina for an interview. I
was hired on the spot and served as an assistant principal at
Hickory High School for two years (1989-1991) and then moved
to Grandview Middle School, another Hickory City School, as an
assistant principal for an additional year (1991-1992).

In 1992, I was recruited back home to Johnston County for
the principalship of a middle school that was in the process of
being built. I remember like it was yesterday, getting the call
from the assistant superintendent for personnel. When she first
called, I was not overly excited in that I had been offered several
similar positions prior to this one, none of which I took. In fact,
I was pretty noncommittal about the position at Selma Middle
at the time I received her last call. Later, when relating the nature of the call and my response to a friend, I was reminded
that I verbalized that I wanted to be a principal, but in fact had
turned down several chances to realize that dream. The friend
then said, "So, do we think they will just keep asking?" As I
thought more about that, I decided to call the assistant superintendent back and made arrangements to travel down to Smithfield, North Carolina to talk more about the position. On the day
of our meeting, I remember walking into her office and, after
the initial exchange of greetings, I noticed several large stacks
of applications on her desk. When I asked what they were, she
said, "Applications for the Selma Middle School principalship."
I almost fainted when she told me that there were 75 rejected
applications for that position. I was not one of them. After all, I
had not yet applied.

During that same time frame, the Johnston County Citizen's
Association. (a grass-roots organization founded to spear-head
efforts for social change in Johnston County) had been in dialogue with the school system officials about the inadequate representation of persons of color in key administrative positions
in the district. Feeling that their concerns were not being heard,
they decided to boycott or "walk out in protest" after expressing

their concerns at the school board meeting. The night of their boycott happened to be the same night that the board appointed me principal of Selma Middle School. My mom was a part of that boycott.

Selma Middle School did not exist previously, so I had the privilege, responsibility, and honor of working with the architects and interior designers in the final stages of construction as the school was being built. Also, as the faculty had not yet been appointed, I had the opportunity to hire the faculty and staff. Given the demographics of the school, with 47% students of color, I proceeded to attempt to hire a diverse faculty. After all, I had been taught that a good school leader was sensitive to the demographics of his/her school and worked to create a climate wherein all students felt comfortable. Sometimes being able to see someone who looks like you will increase the comfort level for students. Unfortunately, there were persons in the community who thought I was hiring too many Blacks and proceeded to tell the superintendent that he needed to do something to correct the situation. I was warned not to "make too many drastic moves." I guess that the community was not quite ready for the type of participatory justice that I was ready to enact. There was now a new player at the table, and I was not sure yet if I was welcome.

I had been offered a principalship in another district in North Carolina and several in Johnston County before accepting the position at Selma Middle School. Selma was the first community that I served as a school counselor upon receiving my master's degree, so I had already developed an awareness and understanding of the community and its needs. The demographics of the student body served at Selma Middle School were diverse: in addition to 47% of the students being Black, more than 40% were exceptional children, and more than 60 % received free or reduced lunch. Interestingly enough, many of my students were children of my previous high school classmates as my middle school was one of the feeder schools for my high school alma mater. I realized that I could be a "voice" for this group that not often heard in Johnston County's educational decisions.

The leadership of our district schools had not previously been diverse. In 1992, about 17 administrative changes were made: of that number three of the five high schools had women appointed to the principalship for the first time in the history of the district. Again, there had not been a Black woman in the principalship since the schools integrated in the 60s. The superintendent was ahead of his time in regard to making decisions beyond the usual political appointment of administrators. He seemed to understand the issues of social justice as they related to Johnston County. The new school afforded him an opportunity to exercise his vision by hiring me as principal.

Selma Middle School was to be completed by August 1992, but unfortunately the construction was not complete until February 1993. Conqesuently, we moved into the new school mid-year, in February of 1993. Some unused classrooms on the nearby elementary campus were renovated as temporary quarters for Selma Middle School students and faculty. One of the first expectations the first year was for each team of teachers to make home visits. I offered to go along with any teams not comfortable doing so on their own. Given that some of the homes were in unsafe, poverty-ridden neighborhoods, this request was not warmly received by the faculty. However, after the home visits were made, the faculty was glad that it was a task expected of them. It greatly enhanced their connecting with our students and with the school community. During my tenure as principal, I dealt with racism, sexism, and classism directed both at me and at other minorities. I bring the memories of those experiences (Biases may be a more accurate term) to this chapter. During one of the home visits, the team of teachers came back surprised at what they learned and the questions, asked of them during their site visits. One of our most active parents asked, "What's it like to work for a Black woman? I've never known Black women to do anything but teach and nurse sick folk, never a school principal." The teachers were upset and surprised that I was not surprised, just better informed.

I remember learning that we would finally be able to move into our new school building less than a week before we were to move. A student dance was planned for the last Friday we were to have school at the elementary school site. My first inclination was to cancel the student dance in order to better facilitate the weekend move to the new building, but a group of parents asked if we could still have the Valentine's day party. In addition to celebrating Valentine, the party celebrated our move to the new school. I agreed, providing that they would do all the planning and that I had to have the final approval on all details.

Our school housed a district program called the LifeSkills Program for TMH (trainable mentally handicapped) students. This program served all TMH students in Johnston County from age 12 until they turned 21. TMH students are the lowest functioning of the exceptional students. Another site in the district housed the program that served them upon their entrance into K-12 and served them until they were 12 years old and could transfer to my school. These students were taught only basic life skills because most would never live independently from their parents and/or guardians.

The parents planning the student dance did not want "those kids" attending the dance. Once they shared that with me, it became apparent that there was much work to be done in increasing the awareness level and teaching of tolerance. My response to them was simple and straightforward: there was only one Selma Middle School, and it included the Life Skills students. No students would be excluded from taking part in Selma Middle School activities. Because of my morals, values, and belief system, I would not allow any student to be treated as anything less than as a "full citizen" at Selma Middle School. I would never knowingly allow what had been done to me and other persons of color or other diverse populations be done to our LifeSkills students.

On another occasion, I recall one colleague, who happened to be white, calling to say that he wanted to come over and visit the new school. As I gave him a tour of the school with all of its state- of-the-art technology and equipment, he remarked, "You know you only got this position because you're Black." I responded "Well after one hundred forty years of us not getting what we were entitled to....don't you think, it's about time?" I surmised that this colleague was not thrilled that I, too, now had a seat at the table. That is participatory justice.

There were often subtle and then not-so-subtle instances when persons were surprised to see a Black woman as principal of the school. Case in point: the secretary and receptionist were white females, and the assistant principal a white male. If all of us happened to be in the front office and someone new to the school came in asking for the principal, I simply became invisible. The principal had to be either the white male or one of the white females. The looks on their faces told the story when one or all of the others pointed to me.

The Road Ahead and Lessons to be Learned

In August 1996, I left my position as principal of Selma Middle School. By this time I had met my future husband, and it was apparent that we would be getting married and moving to Michigan within the next year. He was a professor and chair of the philosophy department at the University of Delaware and was being recruited by Michigan State University. I applied for and received a position in central administration as Director of Human Resources. I was responsible for all classified and certified employment issues of middle and high school personnel. In this position I would still have some sort of influence, so our community celebrated my move to this position. I was still in a position to "give voice" to the voiceless in the hiring of personnel in the district. Many times it was simply being strategically located so that applicants and especially applicants of color were given the same opportunities as their white counterparts. After that one year at the district office, I resigned my position with Johnston County Schools to relocate to Michigan State with my husband. The reaction of the Black community was interesting. I was told, "How dare you leave this position. Do you know how long it took us to get you in that position?" The principalship and director of personnel position were not about me as a person but about me as a member of a collective community that had waited so long for the opportunity.

My husband and I decided that, since I had to give up my position to relocate anyway, this would be a good time to pursue a Ph.D. We both saw it not only as a step forward in my professional preparation and credentialing but also as a chance to further the social justice agenda to which we are both committed. Obtaining a Ph.D. would strengthen my positioning to achieve another position of influence to advance our social justice agenda.

At Michigan State, I became a full-time Ph.D. student for four years. After I completed my Ph.D., I was hired as Director of the Office of Supportive Services at Michigan State University. I directed two TRIO programs: Student Support Services and the Ronald B. McNair Post-Baccalaureate Achievement Program. (TRIO refers to a group of academic support programs for limited income and/or first generation high school and college students.) Every yeary my office staff of 14, and I provided services to 600 new freshmen who were not regularly admissible to the university but were admitted to my programs as special admits. These students would not have been admitted if it had not been for the special consideration given the program participants.

We were at Michigan State University for eight years until my husband was recruited again, this time to the University of Memphis. Because of my varied and diverse experiences, I was able to secure a position on the faculty in the Department of Leadership in the College of Education. Most recently, I was asked to direct the Center for Urban School Leadership in addition to my faculty role. The center prepares teachers to become assistant principals and assistant principals to become principals. Local school districts contract with us provide a more extensive, rigorous, and nontraditional one- or two-year professional development opportunity for their teachers, leaders, and assistant principals. Both positions since leaving Selma Middle School, have allowed me to further advance our social justice agenda.

Conclusion

I was born and came of age in Smithfield, North Carolina during the Civil Rights Movement and, as noted, my family was very active in the movement. Educational programs at Selma Middle School were a reflection and/or extension of my family's involvement in the Civil Rights struggle. The major goal of the Civil Rights Movement, beyond the end of segregation, was to give the all individuals the opportunity to flourish. King's wish was for all children to be judged based on the content of their character rather than race or gender. As educators, we focus on supporting the growth of the individual students in our charge. We are not interested in creating a system that produces uninformed/naive followers. Schools must allow for the individual growth of each child.

Researchers must remember that approaches to social justice are historically and culturally situated. The approaches to social justice taken by women educators must be situated in the civil rights movements of the 1960s. This historical setting provides an important understanding for analyzing our approach to both education and leadership. We bring to our educational programs a strong sense of social justice within a liberal democratic framework. This means that we try to establish an educational system that respects individual differences and fosters individual strengths. Our goal is to produce students who are good citizens, students who are intelligent and self motivated. This conception of teaching and learning is in line with a liberal democratic view of education and, of course, social justice.

The Civil Rights Movement is prominent in our lives as educators. We see education as the instrument with which to achieve some sense of equality for marginalized children and their families. As a result, race, class, and gender are prominent issues in our teaching, and we continue to focus on the empowerment of our students. Our work for social justice is simply to instill in our students and their families the belief and knowledge that society should respect the social and political worth of each individual.

I stand on the shoulders of all of those great Black women educators who persevered because they knew it was the "right thing to do." When I start to get tired, despondent, and weary, I remember the words to one of my Mom's favorite spirituals: "I don't feel no ways tired. We've come too far from where he brought us from. After all, the best is yet to come."

References

Lawson, B. (forthcoming). Philosophical playa hatin': Race, respect, and the philosophy game" In G. Yancy (Ed.). *Critical perspectives on the profession of philosophy: Latin-American and African-American voices.*

Lawson, B.E., & Sanders-Lawson, E.R. (2001). "Violent crime, race, and black children: Parenting and the social contract." In H. McAdoo (Ed). *Black Children: Social, educational, and parental environments.* Thousand Oaks: Sage.

Rawls, J. (1971). A Theory of justice. Cambridge, MA: Harvard University Press.

Sanders-Lawson, E.R. (2001). Black Women School Superintendents Leading for Social Justice. Unpublished doctoral dissertation, Michigan State University.

Smithfield, NC: Official Johnston County Visitors Information. Retrieved February 1, 2009 from http://www.johnstoncountync.org/content/?linkcode=23.2D

Tyson, C. (2001). From the classroom to the field: Teacher, researcher, activist. In R.O. Mabokela & A. Green (Eds.), *Sisters of the academy: Emergent black women scholars in higher education* (pp.138-149). Sterling, NJ: Stylus.

Teaching About Diversity Through Art Education:
A Chicana's Perspective at a Predominantly White Institution

xxxxxxxxxxxxxxxxxxxxxxxxxxxxxxxxxxxxxxxxxxxxxxxxxxxxxxxxxxxxxxxxxxxxxxxxxxxxxxxxxxxx

Adriana Katzew
Massachusetts College of Art and Design

It was my first year back in the U.S.—Dallas, Texas, to be precise. Although I was born in the U.S., I was raised in Mexico City, the land of my parents. But when it was time for me to start high school, we moved back to the U.S. because my mother thought it would provide my sister and me better opportunities in life.

I was ecstatic to be in my new high school, where academics and learning were valued, where I was encouraged to think and study without being called a *matada*—a dead one (an expression commonly used in Mexico to describe kids who "kill" themselves studying). As part of the curriculum in my new school, students could choose an elective course. As I read through the list of electives, quivering with excitement, I immediately settled on art. While art had filled my nonschool life in Mexico (the architecture and colors that surrounded me in the streets and the walks in the neighborhood parks where artists would sell their paintings), I had only had one art class in 7th grade. I must admit, I don't remember much of it, except designing my initials in funky styles, and coloring them in endless ways—never to see them again for the teacher, *el Maestro* Eustaquio, would lock them in a fenced area we used to call *la jaula* (the cage) in the back of the classroom.

So I excitedly jumped at the opportunity to take an art class again, this time in my new high school in my new country. I can still see Mrs. Harrison's face, pale, sagging and softened by the passage of years, yet still retaining a welcoming roundness framed by her white hair, always up in a chignon. What did I paint or draw in her class? What did I learn? I have no memories of any of it, and no artwork saved from that semester to remind me. But what remains engraved in my mind is one particular event in that classroom that would change me forever.

I must have been in the midst of creating a painting because I needed yellow paint, and there was no more in my table. I remember going to Mrs. Harrison and asking her, "Could I please have some yellow?" She barely looked at me as she said she didn't understand me. So I repeated the question. But again, she didn't seem to understand me and walked away, to the back room, where all the art supplies were stored. I followed her, and for a third time I repeated my question, now feeling upset. When again she didn't seem to understand me, I walked toward the shelves and grabbed a bottle of yellow paint as I uttered, with much frustration, "Yellow! Yellow!" Unfazed, she simply responded, "Oh honey. Jell-o is a food. In this country we say 'yellow.'" That was the last time I took art in that school.

This incident, however, would not be the first time that I would learn of, and come across, disdain toward Mexicans in my new school in Texas. But my experience with Mrs. Harrison taught me that the art classroom is not always the safe haven that people associate with it. Many other things happen besides students learning how to mix colors, create self-portraits, or do one-point perspective. It is a place where students can experience social justice or injustice and where diversity may or may not be valued.

As painful as my experience in that classroom was, it taught me two other things: first, that I loved art and would continue to do it no matter what, and second, that I would work so that no person would ever feel as I had in Mrs. Harrison's class because of who they were, where they came from, or how they spoke. This experience has contributed in shaping me and my passion for social justice and cultural diversity. It is this passion that colors my lens as an academic in the field of art education: first in the classes I teach, also in taking a leadership position to bring about changes in an art education program, and finally in reflecting on the importance of recruiting people of color into the field of art education.

Transforming the Curriculum

When I arrived at the University of Vermont in 2005 as an assistant professor in Art Education, I was given the freedom to design some of my courses.[1] At that point in time, the curriculum

---

[1]While the author was at the University of Vermont (UVM) from 2005-2009, she has since left to teach at Massachusetts College of Art and Design. She wrote the first draft of this chapter while she was at UVM.

for students in the Art Education Teacher Preparation Program focused on practicum courses in art classrooms and out-of-school art sites, as well as on the "nuts and bolts" of becoming an art teacher, such as writing lesson plans, assessment, and classroom management. From my perspective, what was sorely lacking in the curriculum was a course that focused on broader issues in the field of art education, so I set forth to design and teach such a course.

When I first designed a seminar style course, titled "Current Issues in Art & Education," I wove in issues of social justice and diversity throughout because of my own experiences as a learner and a teacher in different art education venues. I had previously taught theater and dance to low-income, middle school children and visual arts in after-school programs and community art centers in low-income communities. I had also created a photography and creative writing program for recent immigrant children from Puerto Rico and the Dominican Republic.

As a Chicana (Mexican American) artist and educator who has taught art to low-income children, students of color, and immigrant children, and as a researcher who has studied Latino/a artists who speak of the impact that the arts have had in their lives, I was convinced of the power of the arts in providing a voice or forum for individuals and populations at the margins iofsociety. So I set forth to designing a course that would provide my students—future art educators—with an education that would allow them to understand the power of the arts for diverse populations. This, I hoped, would in turn lead to them providing their students with the means to experience the power of the arts in developing their voices.

During my first semester of teaching the seminar, I came to realize how appropriate this focus was, given the student population at the university and in the Art Education Program in particular. The University of Vermont is located in the second whitest state in the U.S.—96.8% of the population of Vermont is white (U.S. Census Bureau, 2006). Similarly, the university is a predominantly white institution. In the fall of 2008, the total undergraduate enrollment of white students was 92.2%, while students of color made up 7.2% (UVM, 2008a, 2008b, 2008c). In terms of the Art Education Program, of the approximately sixty students enrolled in it from 2005 to 2009, only two have been multiracial, while the rest have been white, and most of these students come from homogeneous communities, with limited exposure to people different from themselves.

The focus on social justice and diversity is also relevant due to the reasons art education students enroll in the program. They often tell me that they enroll in the program because they want to "teach art," which, as I have come to learn, generally refers to art making; they do not initially see art education as a discipline that can, and should, address issues of race and ethnicity, cultural diversity, and social justice. How then would they come to see tackling issues relating to diversity, multiculturalism, and social justice in the art classroom as important? One of the ways, I thought, was for them to become conscious of what they do and do not know, as the following examples illustrate.

We Reproduce What We Know

Back in 1959, when the first issue of the journal *Studies in Art Education* was published, scholar Edmund Feldman stated, "Just as people hold ethical views they have never examined but which nevertheless inform their behavior, unconscious assumptions of an aesthetic character inform art teaching" (1959, p. 22). Indeed I have found this to be the case with my art education students. Their aesthetics are shaped by their experiences, including the courses they have taken in art history and studio art, which largely reflect a Western canon. They echo this canon during their student teaching internship. I have observed them teaching about artists and art styles with which they are familiar, and having their students create artworks that imitate specific artists and art movements such as Picasso, Fauvism, and Impressionism. My pre-service students are indeed reproducing the knowledge they have (and the aesthetics shaped by that knowledge) without questioning how they have acquired their knowledge or questioning its scope. They are not aware of their aesthetic assumptions until they are confronted with them face-to-face.

In my seminar "Current Issues in Art & Education," we address the limited scope of the canon from which they are working through one specific exercise I do with them. I first ask them to "please write the name of an American artist." All students quickly scribble a name without difficulty and look up almost immediately. Next I ask, "Please write the name of a woman artist." They write down a name, almost as fast, and then look up. I go on to ask for the name of a "Black" artist, and it takes them a little bit longer to look up, and only some of them write a name. When I ask for the name of a Chicano or Chicana artist, most pens don't move, and no set of eyes look at me. This same thing happens when I ask for the name of a Native American or Asian American artist.

Once we're done with the questions, we deconstruct the exercise, first by going over people's responses. Semester after semester, the pattern repeats itself—most students write Jackson Pollock or Andy Warhol for the name of an American artist—never the name of a woman artist or an artist of color. As for a female artist, most students name Georgia O'Keefe. Ask about a Black artist and the answer is either Jean-Michel Basquiat or, as of late, Kara Walker, due to her growing popularity and inclusion in contemporary art history courses. As to Chicano/a artists, only occasionally do I get a response, invariably Frida Kahlo (who, I let them know, was not a Chicana but a Mexican artist). No specific names are offered for Native American artists, though sometimes a student will mention art forms (stereo)typically associated with Native Americans, such as basket weaving. As to Asian American artists, I have as of yet to have a student name someone.

We then deconstruct this exercise in terms of my students' scope of knowledge and aesthetics, and the implications for the teaching of art. Most students express embarrassment as it dawns on them how limited their repertoire of knowledge is. Our discussion then centers on how this limited knowledge will translate into their teaching. What art history and artists will they teach in their classrooms? Whose aesthetics will they teach and reinforce? We all agree that they can only teach about the artists and art movements they know about. In other words, they will reproduce the knowledge they have and the aesthetics shaped by that knowledge. Yet we end the discussion with possibilities. We agree on the importance of teachers continuing to learn and expand our knowledge of art and artists from different ethnic and cultural groups in the U.S. and from different countries.

My students, however, are not alone in their reproduction of art knowledge and aesthetics. A recent study (La Porte et al., 2008) examined the curriculum content implemented by K-12 art teachers during their first through seventh years of teaching. The study showed that, "overall, teachers used topics that were similar to those taught to them in undergraduate school" (p. 362). For example, 81% of the teachers surveyed had studied Western European art as undergraduates. When asked about their current usage of this type of art in their curriculum content, the highest response was that they "often used it." Conversely, only 40% had learned about Latino art as undergraduates. Not surprisingly, when all teachers were asked about their current usage of Latino art, the highest response was that they "rarely used" it (p. 369). The study also found that "[teachers] with an undergraduate training in multicultural art approaches or theories to art education reported higher use of Multicultural Art" (p. 362). This study shows how critical it is for students to receive an education that includes multicultural art if they are to bring it into their curriculum when they become teachers. Yet I do not want my students to simply include artists of color into their curriculum here and there, but to think critically and participate in their own thinking process about change. I want them to see multicultural art more as a process or philosophical orientation (Chanda, 1992).

Incorporating Other Cultures in the Art Classroom

While the "name the artist" activity has proven a good way to engage in an important discussion on the reproduction of knowledge, the challenge for my art education students arises when they have to create and teach art lessons that include issues of diversity and multiculturalism during their student teaching internship. I created this requirement because I thought it was vital for them to be able to put into practice what they had learned in theory during our seminar on the current issues in the field of art education.

While students seem ready to take on the challenge, it is also clearly novel territory for virtually all of them. Most of them initially choose to create lessons about cultures outside of the U.S., (and often ancient ones). My sense is that they make this choice either because cultures outside of the U.S. have the lure of the "exotic" or because it is safer to do so than to tackle issues that might touch on race and racism in the U.S.—areas that many students are not comfortable addressing themselves.

I often see my students borrow aesthetic elements or art forms from another culture and then incorporate them into their lessons, frequently failing to contextualize those art forms or elements within their culture of origin (Banks, 1991; Chanda, 1992). For example, one of my students suggested borrowing the idea of the *alebrijes*, the fantastical animal-like creatures created in Oaxaca, Mexico. When I asked her what she would teach about Mexican culture in connection to this art form, she had not considered it. The same issue arose when she suggested teaching brush paintings inspired by the Chinese ink painting she referred to as Sumi-e—the name for this style of painting in Japan. When I asked her to discuss how this artistic style had emerged or what it reflected about Chinese culture, she did not know; nor did she know that ink paintings had originated in China and spread to Japan (Siudzinski, 1978). She also did not realize that she was using the Japanese name for this style of painting, which derived from the Japanese words "black ink" and "picture" (Hirayama, 1979, p. 7)—information she would have learned from the most basic research. She stated that doing too much research on it and sharing it with her elementary school students would turn them off and destroy their joy of simply creating artwork. She added that she would not have wanted too much of that in art class as a kid.

As she said this, I was left wondering if she was reproducing the teaching style of her previous art teachers. This seems to be an area where the theory of multicultural art education is far ahead of its incorporation in practice, for students often want to reproduce what they have seen in the art classroom as students or from their mentor teachers. As Patricia Stuhr has witnessed, "when our students get out into the field for student teaching experiences and/or take their first teaching job, often something happens to them that seems to eradicate this knowledge base (social and cultural content, inquiry, and teaching methods that they learn in their art education program)" (Stuhr, 2003, p. 305). What is it that impedes our art education students from taking the approach to "first familiarize [themselves] with the intention of the 'other' artist" (Bartel, n. d.) and contextualize the art in their respective cultures as opposed to just pick and choose elements they like?

While I do not discourage my students from looking at cultures outside of the U.S. or from the past, I remind them to also look closer to home as a source for our teaching: at the community in which we live. For instance, despite being a predominantly white state, Vermont's landscape is changing. Due to refugee re-settlement programs, there are refugees coming from countries such as Sudan, Bosnia, Vietnam and Iraq. And there is also a large number of Mexican migrants coming to work in Vermont's dairy farms. Yet despite this changing landscape and the fact that most of my students have come across some of these populations in some of their practicum classes, none of them have designed lessons relating to the cultures of these students. This, then becomes a point of dialogue between us and gives me the opportunity to share with my students that "research indicated that when teachers use knowledge about the social and cultural context of their students when planning and implementing instruction, the academic achievement of students can increase" (Banks, 2006, p. 200). As Elizabeth Garber further argues, in social justice education the interests, voices and lives of students are part of the curriculum, and ultimately, "education for social justice is education for a society where the rights and privileges of democracy are available to all. Art education for social justice places art as a means through which these goals are achieved" (Garber, 2005, p. 16).

Yet, my challenge remains finding ways in which my students can (1) better understand their students who fall outside of the "mainstream" either within the classroom or within the larger community, (2) negotiate their teaching and learning with different students, and (3) design a curriculum that takes them into account, as much as it does the other students. As a faculty of color, I share with my students some of my own experiences in school so that they have a more personalized way to think of these issues and understand the ways in which teachers act that make students feel welcome or excluded. I then provide my students with suggestions for their learning and teaching. For instance, one of my students, who was in the midst of her student teaching internship, shared with me and her fellow classmates the challenges of working in an elementary school where a large number of students are refugees from Africa and the Middle East. She said that some of these students pretend not to understand what the teachers are saying to them when they are misbehaving. When I asked her what evidence she had that the students were pretending, she couldn't respond. She explained that she was basing it on what her mentor teacher had expressed. I took this as an opportunity to share with her and my other student teachers my own experience in adapting to English when I first came to the U.S. for high school.

Even though I had taken some English language classes in Mexico and felt rather proficient, the moment I was surrounded by Texan English I often found myself not understanding what people were saying, especially in that first year. Sometimes I could understand parts of what they said, but the more people talked, the longer it took me to paste together the conversation and make sense of it all—usually long after the conversation had ended. My closing words to this student were a request of her: do not jump to conclusions about the children you are teaching who are adapting to the U.S. and to the English language. Give them the benefit of the doubt. And let's get you some literature on language acquisition so you can better understand what your students are going through. Ultimately, though, what I hope my students got out of this dialogue was the importance of treating children with dignity instead of placing them in facile categories.

The Importance of Leadership in an Art Education Program

While I have been fortunate to be able to shape my courses to include issues of diversity and social justice, meaningful change does not happen only at the classroom level. All members of a program, of a department, and, for that matter, of a university, must share a philosophy that values the importance of diversity and social justice and incorporate these issues into the curriculum.

In my case, I was fortunate to be given the opportunity to coordinate and direct the art education program within the first weeks after beginning my position at the University of Vermont. In retrospect, I believe that I was asked to take on this duty because the program was in dire need of consistency and stability, because no full-time faculty members had been able to dedicate themselves solely to the program. So I took the opportunity not only to give the program stability, but also to subtly challenge its status quo by making changes in its philosophy and the contents of the program so that it would reflect a philosophy that embraced cultural diversity and social justice.

The Art Education Program's philosophy back in 2002 stated, "The UVM Art Education Program is built on the belief that it is vital to merge passion and knowledge in both arts and education" (UVM, 2002). I have expanded this philosophy, reflected in the present mission statement: "The Art Education Program provides the tools for our students to become thoughtful and critical thinkers engaged with the broader field of art education, who advocate for the arts beyond the classroom, and who understand the importance of providing diverse populations access to art education" (UVM, 2007). This philosophy now reflects the importance of diversity and social justice in it.

Equally important in my leadership position as the director of the Art Education Program are the changes I have made to the curriculum. For example, once I realized that my students had very little knowledge of non-Western art history, I instituted a new requirement that art education students must take a non-Western art history course. This of course required buy-in from my departmental colleagues in studio art and art history, who supported me in this endeavor.

As I already mentioned, I also created an advanced-level seminar that would invite students to think critically on the broader issues in the field of art education—including multicultural art education, issues of diversity, and social justice. I also made changes to the requirements for students in their semester-long student teaching. In the past, students had to write and teach 8 to 12 lessons, none of which had to be on issues of multiculturalism or diversity. As part of their licensure portfolio, they now teach two lessons that tackle these issues and write an essay that addresses integrating issues of diversity and multiculturalism in the classroom.

While these changes have been important in repositioning the Art Education Program, at the same time, I face the fact that my students come to me in their third year, with little exposure to issues of multicultural art education, diversity or social justice from their previous general education courses and core art education courses. Moreover, I am the only professor in art education who integrates these issues into the curriculum. This, of course, is a problem, because it leaves me, as the sole faculty of color in art education, shouldering the responsibility to teach issues of diversity and social justice in our core courses. The danger, then, is that while I have made changes to the program, this does not mean that these changes have been institutionalized. There is a difference between faculty who agree with these changes philo-

sophically and intellectually but whose curriculum does not necessarily reflect them, and those who are personally vested with
these changes. Inevitably, once in a while the thought crosses
my mind: What would happen to my seminar on current issues
in art education if I were to leave? Would it be eliminated? And
would the requirement that students teach lessons that tackle
issues of cultural diversity also be eliminated? Would the art
education program revert back to its former structure?

Faculty of Color as Role Models in an Art Education Program

While I have invested both intellectual and emotional energy
to providing a curriculum that will make my art education students more aware, and better versed, in issues of diversity and
social justice through art education, there is something else that
plagues me: How come there are almost no students of color in
the art education program? Several studies suggest that "teachers in the field of art education are not ethnically diverse" (Sabol,
2004, p. 530) and that "nationally, *minority* participation in art
education is minimal" (Richards & Kimweli, 1998, p. 51). One
reason for this may be the fact that they do not see a connection between studying art and a successful arts-related career.
Another factor is the perceived lack of job opportunities and potential for making money (Richards & Kimweli, 1998). The third
reason is the lack of minority role models in art, especially in the
visual arts (Chatman, 1993). According to Richards and Kimweli
(1998):

> The absence of *minority* role models sends an implicit
> message to *minority* students that they are not welcome
> in art education. Indeed, *minority* students' preference
> for role models seems to be based on the ethnicity of
> the instructors. Consequently, if art education is going
> to provide the appropriate role models for *minority* stu-
> dents, art instructors need to train more *minority* stu-
> dents to become art teachers in the public schools and at
> the university level. Training more *minority* role models
> in art education can be systematically done...[by] mak-
> ing a commitment to do what is best for art education—
> diversify the faculty and student populations (p. 58).

As a Chicana faculty who sees hardly any students of color in art education, few art teachers of color in K-12 schools, and few faculty of color teaching art education, studio art, and art history in higher education, I find it crucial that this change. We cannot continue to be underrepresented in the field. However, this requires the commitment of many people at many levels of the educational system. In the meantime, I do want to impress students that I do have—mostly white students—with a sense of the responsibility that they have as future teachers. They will have the power to become role models for their students or, alternatively, to turn them away from the fields of art and art education. So while we figure out how to recruit a more diverse body of students into the field of art education, we must inspire all of our students to do right by all of their future students in the art classroom. No student should have a Mrs. Harrison.

References

Banks, J. (1991). *Teaching strategies for Ethnic Studies.* Boston: Allyn & Bacon.

Banks, J. (2006). *Race, culture, and education: The selected works of James A. Banks.* London: Routledge.

Bartel, M. (no date). *Creatively teaching multicultural art.* Retrieved Oct. 22, 2008 from http://www.goshen.edu/art/ed/multiculturalart.html.

Chanda, J. (1992, September). Multicultural education and the visual arts. *Arts Education Policy Review, 94*(1), 12.

Chatman, L. (1993). A bright future awaits minorities in art education. *Art Education, 46*(4), 21-24.

Feldman, E. (1959). Research as the verification of aesthetics. *Studies in Art Education, 1*(1), 19-25.

Garber, E. (2005). Social justice and art education. *Visual Arts Research, 30*(2), 4-22.

Hirayama, H. (1979). Sumi-e just for you. Traditional "One brush" ink painting. Tokyo: Kodansha International.

La Porte, A., Speirs, P., & Young, B. (2008). Art curriculum influences: A national survey. *Studies in Art Education, 49*(4), 358-370.

Richards, A. & Kimweli, D. (1998). Encouraging minority participation in art education. *Journal of Multicultural and Cross-Cultural Research in Art Education, 16*, 49-60.

Sabol, F. R. (2004). An overview of art teacher recruitment, certification, and retention. In E. Eisner & M. Day (Eds.), *Handbook of research and policy in art education* (pp. 523-552). Mahwah, NJ: Lawrence Erlbaum Associates.

Siudzinski, P. (1978). *Sumi-e: A meditation in ink.* New York: Drake.

Stuhr, P. (2003). A tale of why social and cultural content is often excluded from art education: And why it should not be. *Studies in Art Education, 44*(4), 301-314.

U.S. Census Bureau (2006). State & county quickfacts. Retrieved Oct. 20, 2008 from http://quickfacts.census.gov/qfd/states/50/5010675.html.

UVM, (2002). *Art Education Program-R.O.P.A. (Results Oriented Program Approval)* Report.

UVM, (2007). *Art Education Program Handbook.*

UVM, (2008a). *Headcount ALANA enrollment by student level by race/ethnicity fall 1990 to fall 2008.* Retrieved Feb. 25, 2009 from http://www.uvm.edu/~isis.sbinfo/alaenr.pdf.

UVM, (2008b). *Undergraduate Enrollment by College by Major: Fall 2002-Fall 2008.* Retrieved Feb. 25, 2009 from http://www.uvm.edu/~isis/sbinfo/ugfive.pdf.

UVM, (2008c). *Headcount multicultural and international students by units.* Retrieved Feb. 25, 2009 from http://www.uvm.edu/~isis/sbinfo/fy09p13.pdf.

Part III

*Medicine and
the Natural Sciences*

Keeping the Dream Alive

Evelyn Lewis
Worldwide Public Affairs & Policy

Faith is not believing that God can, but knowing that God will.
    –Ben Stein

This story is an abbreviated account of my journey through life thus far. It recounts choices I have made about work, love, enjoyment, service to others, and personal aspirations. My intent is to inspire your raw determination, stir your passion for living your best life, and motivate you to take action. In the words of a dear friend, Pastor Gerald, "God's blessing is not to replace man's initiative to do work. God's blessing is to empower."

I am the eldest of two children. I was born in Wilmington, North Carolina in the mid-1950s. I have few memories about Wilmington, as my family moved to Tampa, Florida when I was very young. Tampa was really my home because it was where many of my aunts, uncles, cousins, and grandmother lived. My grandmother, Pearlie Welch, was one of my favorite people, a best friend and teacher; she was truly the matriarch and center of our family. Her house was the gathering place in times of happiness and sadness, celebrations and family meetings, and Sunday dinners after church. It was a time for catching up with everyone because we didn't often see much of each other during the week.

In my family, education was highly valued and kindergarten is where the emphasis began, if not well before. My teacher, Mrs. Wimberly, was a sweet, caring woman She shared my parents' healthy respect for learning and dedicated herself to the profession. All of my postkindergarten to 12th grade education was in Catholic schools, which is why I was considered by many to have been born into privilege. My first three years were spent at St. Peter Claver, where nearly all the students were African American. This was a stark contrast to the schools where I completed grades 4 through 12. It was these years that brought clarity and understanding to the life's lessons that my grandmother shared with me.

I had great advice and words of wisdom from many brilliant women. "You're a pretty little black girl" are words that I would hear from my grandmother, one of the most beautiful women, inside and out, that I have ever known. She was a strong, proud, black woman who instinctively knew that if I was going to reach my full potential, I had to know and love who I was. These words set the tone. They provided a framework for me to receive, understand, appreciate, and implement further words of wisdom that were to come. My grandmother made sure I knew and loved who I was and who I had the potential to become.

In West Tampa where we lived, my father was a general practitioner in private practice, and my mother was one of two registered nurses in his office. Aside from my brother and me, the practice was the mainstay of my parent's purpose in life. Care was provided for anyone who signed in regardless of how long it took or whether they could afford to pay. Early on, my parents instilled in me self-accountability, discipline and determined work ethics.

One of my first experiences to better understand these qualities was participating in the Girl Scouts. I became a model scout early in my 12 years as a Scout. During my years as a Brownie Scout, one year in particular stands out. Because I had done exceptionally well selling cookies and earned the highest number of badges, I was to be honored at a father-daughter banquet sponsored by our troop. I was proud to tell my parents about the planned recognition (I was the only African American in the troop) and couldn't wait to attend, especially being escorted by my dad. The day finally arrived, and I rushed home from school, changed into my crisp and newly pressed uniform, and headed to my dad's office.

We were scheduled to leave around 5:30 p.m., but as I waited, and waited 5:30 became 6:00, and 6:00 became 7:00. While I sat waiting in his office, my mother looked in on me periodically and even offered to take me, but it would just not have been the same….so, I didn't attend. It took many years to get through that disappointment. But during those years that I observed my parents work and witnessed the appreciation from their patients, I was assured even through my disappointment that this was not just a job or profession, it was what they were called to do.

Tampa Catholic was one of the best co-ed high schools in the Bay Area. With a commitment since fourth grade to become a physician, I was a focused and studious young student. However, this did not prohibit my involvement in student government, social and science clubs, and sports or serving as the drum major for our high school band. During several of my early visits to the school's administrative office, I was often assisted by a young African American woman, Ms. Sirmons, who was stern but always helpful. It was wonderful having someone to truly care about me and ensure that everything was in order. I don't quite remember who adopted whom but whether I was a success or fell short; she never let me go, never let me fall, and never asked for anything in return, then or now.

After graduating from high school with honors in 1974, I continued my trajectory of middle class education with my acceptance into Spelman College. Those four years at Spelman were exceptional. By now, my hunger for knowledge had taken hold of me, and there couldn't have been a better place for me to feed it. It was an environment where I was nurtured and challenged and where being a leader was expected. Any inklings of fear and doubt were overwhelmingly replaced by self-confidence and accountability, in an environment where my culture was shared and appreciated. It was a place where I could dare to be different, where I could dream and acquire the tools to make them come true, and where the true value of faith, family, and friends was re-enforced and respected.

As in any college or university, there are professors who go above and beyond. I had several while I attended Spelman, but one stood out above the rest. Dr. Jones was the chair of the Department of Biology throughout my years at Spelman College —also fondly referred to as the "Yard" by the men of Morehouse College. A connection was made that I can't explain, but I'm forever thankful that it happened. She has seen me through many occasions when I thought what I had wasn't enough. Her letters of support and encouragement during medical school continue to impact my decisions today.

During my years at Spelman, I was known for my participation in everything from academic clubs, to civic and community events, to my job as a teaching assistant, to protests outside the Board of Directors meeting room. Everyone knew I was preparing myself for medical school and that I wanted to be a practicing physician. Although applying to and financing medical school was always in the back of my mind, the close of my junior year brought it front and center. As I consulted with my professors, friends, other applicants, and my parents, I began to construct my list of potential medical schools. One day, while on the phone with one of my advisors, I was asked which medical schools I applied to. I ran down the list of 12 schools without hesitation. Then she asked about graduate schools. I paused and thought, "Why is she asking me about graduate schools?" She must not understand that I'm only interested in medical school. Therefore, my response was "I didn't apply to any because I'm going to medical school." Whether this was childlike enthusiasm or sheer Spelmanite confidence, I never considered that I wouldn't be accepted; therefore, there was no need for graduate school as a back up plan.

After considering several options to pay for medical school, I applied for and was awarded a Health Professional Scholarship (HPSP) from the U.S. Navy. This obligated me to military service but removed any worries about how I would pay for medical school and allowed me to focus on my studies. When all the votes were counted, I elected to attend Brown University Medical School in Providence, Rhode Island. In the midst of my second year, news came of my grandmother's sudden death.

Ms. Pearlie and my aunt were leaving her house for a routine medical appointment when she suffered a heart attack in her front yard. The news was devastating. Memories of our special times together filled my thoughts. Memories of sharing a spoonful of coffee from her cup, of sitting still with the lights off and windows closed while rain poured and lightning flashed on a hot summer afternoon, of spending summers at her house, picking up pecans off the ground and oranges from the trees in her back yard, and of those wonderful Sundays after church at her house. Yes, they all came rushing back, much like the summer thunderstorms that ended as abruptly as they began. However, unlike the hot, humid, sticky, uncomfortable feeling you experience after the rain, I experienced a sense of peace and reassurance as the rush of memories would always end with her favorite words for me: "You're a pretty little black girl."

Shortly after her death and the end of my second year at Brown, I transferred to the Chicago Medical School in North Chicago. After completion of my required clerkships, a number of which were at the famous Cook County Hospital, I applied to do an elective at the Royal Northern Hospital in London, England.

Several letters were exchanged before I received approval from my school and the hospital in England. In the last note from my sponsor in England, there was a peculiar line that read, "with a last name like Lewis, I know you're of Welsh background and I am looking forward to meeting you." I thought to myself, someone is in for a big surprise.

Once all the final arrangements were made, I was off to London. Because I was traveling across the ocean for six weeks, I convinced a couple of my friends from Spelman to join me at the end of the rotation. They agreed, and we made plans to explore Europe for three more weeks. I arrived in London for my new assignment, and yes, I was correct—they were surprised. Unfortunately, this made for a rocky beginning. When the attending physician realized I was student doctor Lewis, the hair on his neck stood straight out. Our initial relationship can be described as strained at best. Because of this, he took every available opportunity to embarrass or insult me, even in the presence of patients.

On my first day of clinic, a patient with hypertension was assigned to me for evaluation. There was no nurse immediately available, so I was left to check his vital signs. I reached for the blood pressure cuff. It looked like nothing I had ever seen or used before; in fact it was quite archaic. This required that I solicit assistance to ensure it was used correctly before my attending joined us. Unfortunately, no assistance was available and I was left to ask the attending. Instead of demonstrating how to use it he seemingly relished in the opportunity to berate me in full view of the patient and loud enough for others to hear. Over the next few days, the incidents and insults persisted. The straw that broke the camel's back was his quizzing me on the history of Wales while in the treatment room with a patient. Responding to some of the questions, I quickly made him aware that Welsh history was not my specialty nor was it the reason I came to London. I believe I took him by surprise when I informed him that if he continued to show such disrespect for me that I would leave. I told him I could go home and get the same treatment in my own country for free. His attitude changed significantly, and the following five weeks were some of the most interesting training experiences ever.

When the rotation ended, my friends arrived, and we had an amazing time touring England, Scotland, Venice, Paris, Rome and Pisa. This was the beginning of my growing curiosity about other countries and foreign travel. Upon my return to Chicago, I was greeted with the news that I was selected for residency training at the Naval Hospital in Jacksonville, Florida, which was my first choice. After graduation from medical school, I had only a few weeks to relish in my achievement, pack, identify housing, move to Jacksonville, and establish a home. It was pure excitement and adrenaline that pulled me through and had me ready on day one of my residency where it became quickly apparent that I was one of two black physicians in the entire hospital. Medical training, in general, is a very grueling process. However, military medical residency training was known to be even tougher, particularly in family medicine. I had learned that the best place to acquire superior obstetrical skills as a family physician was definitely in the military. Whoever told me that was right on target.

Each of the services has a slightly different process in place for training. In the navy, after completion of your first year of residency, you are sent out as a general medical officer (GMO). You are given a number of site selections from which you create a dream list of your top choices. It can take weeks before everyone is notified where they are going. If you get one of your top three choices, you are viewed as very lucky. I took the risk, asked for a ship because it meant that I would be out of training for only 12 to 18 months, and was assigned to the *USS Simon Lake*, a submarine tender. Being an African American woman, a new physician, single, and assigned as the Senior Medical Officer (SMO) (to a crew of 1,500, of which 500 were female) was a challenging role. Many stories emerged during my year on board but none could rival the feeling of finally feeling 'accepted' and respected by my shipmates. I had become a member of the inner circle.

My assignment to the *USS Simon Lake* ended the summer of 1981, and I returned to Naval Hospital Jacksonville to complete my residency. The year out as a Senior Medical Officer was excellent preparation for my upcoming roles as a manager for interns and assistant chief resident. When you are working eighty or more hours a week, time passes quickly. Before I knew it, two years had come and gone, and once again it was time for another assignment and "dream list." This time, as risky as it was, Okinawa was my first choice, and again I hit the jackpot. Within weeks, I was communicating with my sponsor and making arrangements to move to Japan. For the first few weeks after I arrived, I lived in the bachelor officer quarters located on base. Soon after, I located housing downtown, in a new apartment complex. It was owned and operated by a Japanese couple and their daughter. When I met with them to survey the apartment, we became instant friends. Their daughter had just returned from the States where she had attended college. The complex seemingly met all my needs: parking underneath the building; a disco in the basement; coffee shop on the third floor which was managed by the daughter; restaurant on the eighth floor managed by the mother. The owners made their home on the entire ninth level. Before I signed the lease, they treated me to a full Japanese lunch and a tour of their home. This was a match made in heaven; I liked them and loved the apartment.

While stationed in Okinawa as the Medical Department Head of the Dependent Care Clinic at Camp Kinser, I was assigned to provide care for all the active duty marines' families stationed on the base. When I arrived, I was the only physician in the clinic and there were three corpsmen assigned as my staff. We provided comprehensive care including prenatal care, delivery, school physicals, adolescent sports physicals and counseling, preventive and chronic care management, and same-day surgeries. When not working at the clinic, I staffed the emergency room, providing coverage for labor and delivery. Somehow, I still found time to engage in a vigorous exercise routine to round out my day.

The assignment to Okinawa provided a great backdrop for my growing interest in different cultures and international travel. Inexpensive flights and military "hops" were readily available, and I took full advantage of them whenever the opportunity presented itself. There were frequent trips to Korea, Hawaii, Tokyo, Kyoto, Hong Kong, Taiwan, and Bangkok. I traveled with friends and sometimes solo but always had an unforgettable experience. With a little under eleven months left on the island, my thoughts turned to the next stage of my professional career. I knew I wanted to get back to the resident training environment, but I also wanted to enhance my knowledge and skills in obstetrics, research, and the executive medicine arenas to expand my credentials.

This focused my attention on the widely respected two year Faculty Development Fellowship at Madigan Army Medical Center in Tacoma Washington. Leadership skills in practice and organizational management and graduate medical education were the cornerstone of Madigan's program. There, I knew I could teach residents, gain research experience, earn a master's degree and refine my clinical skills. I was told that competition was stiff, but that had never deterred. I completed the application, contacted the appropriate people, put it in God's hands, and continued my pursuit of excellence.

In the last weeks before leaving one duty station for another, the military celebrates those who are departing for new horizons and welcomes those who are newly arriving. That tradition is known as a "Hail and Farwell" and can serve as somewhat of a roast for those leaving. As expected, my colleagues roasted me during my hail and farewell but, to my surprise they were exceptionally complementary. Until recently, the Navy's tag line was, "It's not just a job, it's an adventure." To show their appreciation for my work and the enjoyment I demonstrated while doing it, they presented me with a plaque in the shape of the island that read, "It's not just an adventure, it's a job."

When my departure day arrived, I found myself racing to the airport because I insisted on one last indulgence of one of my favorite activities, shopping. I took a deep breath, boarded the plane, and was caught by a moment of sadness. I was leaving a place that inspired me to get in the best physical shape of my life. It afforded me lifelong friends, enormous opportunities, professionally and personally, and lots of shopping. As the plane began to taxi down the runway, it quickly gained speed and within minutes we were in the air. I settled in, closed my eyes, and began my long journey back home. Because of the time difference, it was a journey that would actually have me arrive in Washington state before I left Okinawa—what an adventure.

After arriving in Seattle, I headed directly to Madigan Army Medical Center, my new duty station. The relationships I developed in Okinawa and Korea lead to great connections and fast friendships in Seattle. They immediately welcomed and helped me comb the Tacoma area to once again locate a great new apartment. Orientation to the new hospital was quite the task. It was significantly larger and older than the facility in Okinawa. It had numerous extended hallways and was spread out.

The faculty development program provided core training in qualitative and quantitative research, teaching methodologies, and program evaluation. However, the specifics related to our chosen areas of research were fulfilled by the program's University partners, Washington and Pacific Lutheran Universities. My interest in adolescent pregnancy steered me toward the Pacific Lutheran University track for a Masters in Social and Behavioral Sciences. Classes were three to four evenings a week from 5:00 to 10:00 p.m. With this new schedule, because of patients and class, I could no longer workout after my morning or afternoon clinics. Therefore, an adjustment was needed to fit in a daily workout. Weekdays now started at 4:00 a.m. and typically ended around 11:30 p.m., but allowed me to include all of my activities. As I became a more senior fellow, I was often asked to provide seminars for residents and faculty at Bremerton Naval Hospital which was about an hour north of Tacoma. Many of them were attended by the Chair of the Department of Family Medicine, Captain Johnson. As I learned later, he was quietly taking notes on me and the scope of my presentations. This laid the foundation for my next assignment.

Upon completing of my fellowship at Pacific Lutheran, I was recruited to join the teaching faculty at Bremerton. During this next assignment, I met with countless people and school administrators and volunteered in a number of teen organizations. My experience conducting research at an outstanding teen pregnancy center in Puyallup, directed by Ms. Yamone convinced me that I was not only interested in my topic, but passionate about it. For me, passion is that reserve fuel that keeps you going when all other energy resources are depleted. Time was getting short—only three weeks to go to complete and defend my master's thesis.

My good friend and former navy pediatrician, Dr. Nash, whom I met while in Okinawa, asked if I wanted to join her for the 'Pina Colada of Pediatrics" conference in Mexico. With everything on schedule and most of the writing complete, it seemed like a great place to take a break, attend the sessions, apply the finishing touches to my paper, and catch up with an old friend. I had not taken much leave during the fellowship because of classes and research demands. So I requested five days of leave and was off to Mexico. Off I went with manuscript in hand—literally, because I wrote everything before entering it into the computer.

During the four-day meeting, I attended a number of sessions and used the remaining time to study and refine my paper. Although it wasn't a true vacation, it was relaxing and I felt prepared for my defense. As the conference came to an end, we said our goodbyes and boarded our flights to head to our separate destinations. As my flight departed, I closed my eyes to pleasant memories of a brief but wonderful visit with my friend. Just as I was drifting into a nice nap, my eyes abruptly popped open, and I was struck with a sinking feeling of panic. Those pleasant thoughts had been replaced by a picture of my files in a folder, on a table, somewhere on the hotel grounds...in Mexico. That folder contained the finished paper for which there was no other copy. Of course there was nothing I could do until we landed. Once on the ground, I called the hotel in a calmly frantic voice to see if they could locate it. I was switched from person to person, most of whom spoke little English, and didn't quite understand what I was referring to. Nonetheless, they tried, as I held onto the call for what seemed like forever. Unfortunately, the files were never located.

Exasperated but not defeated, I knew I needed a plan if I was going to be able to rewrite my paper with the few notes and references I had available in the two weeks left. The good news was that I had completed all my class requirements. The bad news was that my days were about to get even longer. As part of my plan, I removed my watch because it seemed to symbolize how rapidly my time was running out. To reduce distractions, I stayed late to work at my desk and many times those late nights collided with morning. *The day* arrived, and with hard work and God's grace, I was ready. The presentation went as smoothly as if I were a duck floating in a lake on a quiet and calm spring day. My committee was very impressed with the presentation and the supporting science. They never had any inkling of the peddling required the previous two weeks for that duck to float as gracefully as it did that day. Graduation was a welcome celebration of accomplishment even though my mother and brother could not attend. We spoke on the phone, and, as always, they were my biggest cheerleaders. I could always feel their presence around me.

In addition to the fellowship, my assignment at Madigan led to two additional opportunities. An army physician I met while attending the 38th Medical Parallel Conference in Korea also landed at Madigan several months before me. We connected again and became great friends. She was a member of an organization known as Women of Vision, a nonprofit organized to create opportunities to effect change for women of all nationalities. Women of Vision collaborated with international women's groups to sponsor conferences that addressed women's issues. In 1991, Women of Vision organized and sponsored a conference in the USSR. There was a delegation of thirty-two women: eight in medicine, business, education, and the arts respectively. At the last minute, my friend Gloria was unable to make the trip and asked if I could attend in her place. All the stars aligned and there I was, on my way to the USSR. We flew overnight from Seattle to the sister city of Moscow and traveled to the conference city of Makhachkala the next day.

My presentation was entitled "The State of Women's Health in America." Fortunately, my topic was well received. Meeting, sharing, and collaborating with women in attendance at the conference and other events, and traveling to several other locations like Stockholm, Helsinki, Copenhagen, and St. Petersburg, was an unforgettable experience. After our return, I became a member of Women of Vision, and we made a similar trip to Cork Ireland in September 1993. On this trip we also visited Tipperary, Kildare and Dublin. We were all heroes when we returned from this adventure.

Although Bremerton was just an hour north, I needed to find housing closer to the hospital. My friends and I searched several communities and took a closer look at four possible places. Our first stop was a nice house whose backyard served as the channel for trident submarines entering and exiting from Bangor submarine base. Those massive boats were surreal sights as they floated by that house just as the sun began to set. I could have easily resided there but my friends voted it down. The house was slightly isolated with several large trees and with my schedule of leaving before sunrise and returning long after the sun had set, they were worried about my safety.

Another excellent find was an apartment on the sound. When we arrived, the agent/owner seemed less excited than when we spoke on the phone. Nonetheless, he gave us the grand tour. This apartment was fabulous with a breathtaking view of the sound. Although the rent was a little more than I wanted to pay, the place was worth it. I turned to the agent/owner and said, "I'll take it." He replied, "Sorry, it's not available". My friends and I looked at each other and immediately understood. They knew I wanted to question his response, but I resisted. It was evident that this location would pose a safety concern, albeit for a different reason. Disappointed, we proceeded to our final two locations and selected a nice, quiet apartment in Port Orchard. Looking back, at that place and time, it was the perfect location for me.

Naval Hospital Bremerton is a community-based hospital located on a wooded, 49-acre campus. Assimilating into the culture of my new setting was made easy by the staff, faculty, sailors, and families we served. At the time, I was the only African American physician at the hospital, and that prompted interesting conversation from staff and patients. I heard comments such as "It's great to see you" and "you are the first black physician I have ever met." A number of veteran sailors expressed the best sentiment when they smiled and said, "I'm so proud." Although I always give my all, words like those made it impossible for me to ever consider anything less. Although I had no way of knowing, at the time, there were other comments generated from the supervisor of the hospital lab. He engaged other hospital staff to assist him in his fact finding mission about me. During routine conversations, I could be asked anything from what my favorite food was, what I did for fun, my past experience, and on and on.

After months of intelligence gathering, the gentleman I referred to as the "secret operative" exposed himself. With the knowledge acquired from his covert operation, he knew I really enjoyed racket ball and struck up a conversation that lead to an invitation to play. After the game, we had dinner, and through small talk (and I mean really small talk; he is a man of few words) discovered that our mothers were nurses, we grew up forty-five minutes from each other in Florida, we enjoyed many of the same activities, and most of all, we enjoyed each other. We began dating and were together every chance we had.

Bremerton is one of those facilities that is often called upon to execute its mission to provide care anywhere in the world in time of crisis. I faced this head on at the end of a long Friday evening clinic when my department head appeared at the door to my office with an interesting look on his face. Consequently, I knew something out of the ordinary was about to happen. He told me he had been notified that we, Bremerton Family Medicine, had to send a doctor to naval Base Guantanamo Bay, fondly referred to as GITMO. He said he placed our names in a hat and had his last patient pull one out…then he looked me directly in the eyes. At that point he didn't need to say anything else.

U.S. Naval Base Guantanamo Bay is the oldest U.S. base overseas and the only one in a communist country. In November 1991, thousands of Haitians fled their country following a violent military coup. Many were intercepted by the Coast Guard, and 40,000 Haitians passed through GITMO, where a Joint Task Force (JTF)—members of the army, navy, air force, marines, and coast guard—operation was established to provide healthcare and other needed services. The news that I was the one who would deploy created enormous chaos for me, a single woman, who would have only one business day to get my affairs in order, sign blank checks, and give friends access to my bank account and apartment. Thank God for my trusted military family and friends.

On our approach to the landing strip, the hundreds of tents used to house my new patients and colleagues, seemed to consume the land below me. Before I knew it, I had landed at my home for the next three months. Within a few hours, I was introduced to my personal space, one of a hundred medium tents with about 20 other members of the JTF. There was no time to transition; I was simply immersed into the circumstances, treating patients with common diseases and medical conditions such as otitis media, infections, cellulitis, HIV, ectopic pregnancy and stillborn births, as well as diseases I had only read about, such as measles, active tuberculosis, syphilis, elephantiasis, malaria, filariasis, and loa loa.

Cultural competence, a subject considered by many to be one of my areas of expertise, refers to an ability to interact effectively with people of different cultures. It is comprised of four components: (a) awareness of one's own cultural worldview, (b) attitude toward cultural differences, (c) knowledge of different cultural practices and worldviews, and (d) cross-cultural skills. Developing cultural competence results in an ability to understand, communicate with, and effectively interact with people across cultures. Upon seeing my patients with JTF colleagues, this academic term took on untold clarity and provided concrete evidence of its value.

During just another day on the island, a strange set of events began to evolve. I was in the clinic with a number of the corpsmen when we noticed a large gathering of my friends, referring to my Haitian patients. They were all dressed in white clothing or wrapped in white sheets. The crowd continued to grow. Before long there was a full-fledged protest in progress. They were protesting treatment they were receiving from us. Unfortunately the misunderstanding between the Haitians and Joint Task Force security members erupted into a clash of cultures. One of our HIV positive patients sustained a laceration to his scalp and was brought in for me to examine. After cleaning his bristly bleeding wound, it was apparent that he needed sutures. Although I explained what I was about to do and warned him of the needle stick, he moved abruptly, causing the needle to pierce my finger after going through his scalp. In that moment, even with his apology, I had many feelings, and fear was among them. However, caring for my patient prevailed. Afterwards, the appropriate incident report was filed and protocol followed. My tests remained negative.

I extended my assignment several weeks to assist with repatriation and to care for the remaining HIV and AIDS patients that remained. My return to Bremerton was associated with two "positive" changes that remain with me today; when screened for TB, my test was now positive (I did not have TB; I would just be known as a converter, which sometimes warrants treatment), and my life...it was changed forever.

The definition of integrity is often said to be what you do when no one is watching. I think it should perhaps be altered to say that it is what you do when you *think* no one is watching...because there is always someone watching. I found this to be the case when I was considering my next move. Somewhere in this process, I was contacted by Jeannette, one of DOD's finest and most respected family physicians. I had heard of her and perhaps seen her, but we had not had any extended conversations; after all she was army, and I was navy. However, this did not deter her from seeking me out to discuss my career goals. You see, she had been *watching* me. Thus began the conversation and what would become a complex process to get me to the Uniformed Services University (USU) as faculty at the medical school. The usual tour of duty or assignment averages three years. I was just under two years at my current base when this dialog began. Before success was achieved it would involve two admirals, a general and the absolute unselfishness of my department head and mentor, Dr. Johnson. He could have blocked my early transfer to USU for any number of legitimate reasons, notwithstanding that my departure would strip his department of its only woman and all of its diversity. But he didn't; he acted in my best interest to ensure the best for my career.

My arrival in Maryland was greeted by one of the worst ice storms the area had ever experienced. Fortunately for me, I did not have to worry about finding housing right away. I had remained in contact with my military "family" and good friends from my days in Okinawa. Rich and Val had my room ready, and, together with Jim and Linda, they met every imaginable need. I remained with them for a few weeks and although they insisted I could stay longer, it was time to find my own place. The first few months at USU required plenty of adjustments. Although this was an academic military environment and not a hospital, it possessed an air of sterility all its own. Little did I know that this would be the lynchpin assignment that would test my intestinal fortitude and link all of my past training, experiences. It would take me to such places as Africa, India, China, Philippines, Spain, Russia, London, Scotland, Japan, and Italy. It was an experience that cast the mold of the person I am still becoming. My tour of duty at USU spanned ten phenomenal years and was peppered with peaks and valleys.

After my transfer from Bremerton, Carl and I continued our relationship, accumulating frequent flyer points flying between Washington State and Washington DC over the next five years. Both families were smitten with us as a couple, making the announcement of our engagement one of the happiest times of our lives. Unfortunately, this would also be a time when my mother's health would take a downward turn. My brother and I worked diligently to accommodate her needs, but living in different states made it difficult even with other family members assisting. After months of pleading, she finally agreed to move in with my brother so that we could have more direct oversight of her care. Although her health improved, it was temporary. Ultimately, it lead me to make the most difficult decision I have ever made as a daughter and as a physician. At the age of sixty eight, life support was discontinued, and we lost our mom in late June 1999. I strongly considered postponing our wedding, but with the support and encouragement of friends, family, and my matron of honor Stephanie, the "secret operative" and I were married four short months after my mother's death.

I began my tour of duty at USU in February 1994 as an assistant professor in the Department of Family Medicine and also served as Deputy Vice President for Minority Affairs. Several months later, I responded to an invitation by a new faculty member from the Department of Medical and Clinical Psychology searching for a primary care physician research partner. We were very successful at landing a number of internal grants but the jackpot came by way of a major grant, from the National Institutes of Health (NIH) to thoroughly investigate weight management challenges in women, particularly African American women. This resulted in a secondary appointment for me to the Department of Medical and Clinical Psychology.

My role at USU began to evolve and expand. I was asked to serve on the medical school's admissions committee and participate on various dissertation and masters' defense committees. Although both required a considerable amount of time, it was wonderful working with and mentoring future physicians and scientists. I also joined other volunteer physicians at Mobile Medical Care, a sponsored clinic for the underserved. As you can imagine, this deepened my commitment to expose and eliminate the untold inequities in health and healthcare. Soon there were more opportunities: Director of Family Practice Clerkship, which included management and quality control for our thirteen sites across the United States; Director of the University Health Center, where we provided the full spectrum of care for our students, their families, and eligible faculty; Vice Chair of the Department of Family Medicine, and Associate Chair for Research. Each new opportunity came with its unique challenges which were eagerly met by me and my ever-increasing "network of mentors."

In the midst of my ninth year at USU, the Vice President for Research summoned me to his office. He presented the call for proposals from the Center for Minority Health and Health Disparities for my review. With my expertise in the area of health and healthcare disparities and the successful implementation of the co-developed cultural competency curriculum for the medical school, he thought this was an ideal project for me. I agreed with him on all but one disconcerting point. He wanted me and another colleague to write the proposal, but have someone else be the principal investigator (PI) because of their track record with grant awards at the NIH. While his point was historically supported, my feeling was that if we wrote, it we should be co-PIs. After several discussions, the co-PI and I submitted our first proposal, but we were not funded. However, on resubmission, we were awarded six-and-a-half million dollars through the NIH Center for Minority Health and Health Disparities to establish the Uniformed Services University Center for Health Disparities Education and Research (USUCHD). The USUCHD's mission is to promote health-related change and ultimately reduce health disparities among racial and ethnic minorities through research, education, training and community outreach and information dissemination.

After twenty-five years serving in the Navy, my time had come to look ahead. My choices were not as broad as in the past, and being asked to move to Texas caused me to pause. There were long discussions with my husband; my brother, Command Sergeant Major Lewis; and his wife, Sergeant Major Lewis, as well as other mentors and friends, before I decided to retire. Within a few weeks, I was interviewing for civilian positions. The two final contenders were Director of Diversity at an academic medical center in Chicago and Director Medical Alliance Clinician with a large pharmaceutical company headquartered in New York. Although my husband was in support of whatever decision I made, he was not fond of having to move. Since the position in New York was field based; I accepted the position with industry.

The transition from service organization to industry was an enormous change. During the span of my six years with the company, I held positions including Director, Medical Alliance Clinician, Director, Government Regional Medical Research Specialist, Director, Managed Markets, and Director, Medical Policy. The common thread running through each position was the ability to collaborate and partner with my medical colleagues as well as community organizations and their leadership. Every level provided an opportunity for tremendous growth, refinement and supplementation of skills, and additional areas of expertise. However, it was my position as Director of Medical Policy in the Division of Worldwide Public Affairs and Policy that I found most challenging yet rewarding.For me, this position completed what I called the "Victory Triad." While there are no easy solutions to the inequities in health and healthcare, the Victory Triad is the mortar that will ultimately hold everything together. Although they are not always viewed this way, the company and the people with whom I work are unrelenting in their desire to assist in making people's lives better with products that decrease, eliminate, or prevent suffering, pain and disease. It is a place where I learned why talent alone is not enough, why highly talented people are not necessarily highly successful people and the message behind the words:

If you think you are beaten, you are; If you think you dare not, you don't; If you would like to win, but you think you can't, It's almost certain you won't...... Life's battles don't always go to the stronger or faster [wo]man, But sooner or later, the [wo]man who wins is the [wo]man who knows [she] can.
(Walter Wintle, "The Man Who Thinks He Can")

Having discovered the invigorating independence of free enterprise, my season for renewed passion and tenacity in life, relationships, and work is in full force. One of many benefits of this new season is having more time to participate in the academic and sporting achievements of my nieces, Alyse and Jazmyne, and other events in the lives of family and friends. Strategic alignment with organizations, like the National Business Group on Health and the American Medical Association/National Medical Association and the National Hispanic Medical Association Commission to End Health Disparities, fortifies my commitment to actively engage in the war on health and healthcare disparities and to mentor students interested in the biomedical sciences.

I also have the opportunity to channel my enthusiasm, passion, and other attributes into running a new consulting business that has been in the planning stage for some time. The company's name is Evelyn L. Lewis International. One of the major offerings, the PECAN (Physically Empowered Communities Across the Nation) Chronicles, borrows a portion of its name from Evelyn's Ultimate Pecan Pies and More Inc. The word PECAN underscores my passion for cooking/baking and health/wellness and denotes both an authentic southern dessert and a program dedicated to working with individuals, families and communities in concert with our healthcare system to transform the health of our nation. Other company programming includes health education presentations, town hall health forums, advocacy development, cultural competency, health disparity training and education, and community outreach and engagement. With the public outcry regarding healthcare for our veterans, service members and their families, resurgent interest in healthcare reform, and health and healthcare inequity the company is destined to grow. Nonetheless, knowing that there are significant challenges lying ahead, I find it re-assuring that many of the characteristics contributing to my success as a military officer—hard work, self-accountability, attention to detail, and service to others—are collectively the trademark of successful entrepreneurs.

Through the years I have often been asked whether there is anything about my life that I would change or do differently. Preceded by a smile, my reply is a resounding "no!" The premium ingredients that make Evelyn's Ultimate Pecan Pies the best this side of heaven, are much like the ingredients that have paved my pathway for a purposeful journey. It is the lessons of love and promise from my grandmother; self-accountability, discipline, work ethic; and service to others from my parents; unconditional love from family and friends; support and the "pay it forward" words and actions of my mentors that have made it all possible...together with the peaks and valleys. I think Leo Rosten stated it best when he said, "the purpose of life is to be useful, to be responsible, to be honorable, to be compassionate. It is, after all, to matter: to count, to stand for something, to have made some difference that you lived at all."

All Things Work Together for Good

Cynthia I. Macri
Special Assistant (Diversity) to the Chief of Naval Operations

"The views expressed in this article are those of CAPT Cynthia Macri and do not necessarily represent the views of the Department of the Navy or the Department of Defense."

My decision to join the U.S. Navy in 1979 was made purely out of curiosity and necessity. I attended college and medical school in Pennsylvania, a state in which I had never lived or worked, and to which I had no ties. I am the third of five children, all of whom were in college or graduate school in 1979, and the Navy offered a full scholarship for medical school. I had grown up overseas in developing countries, where our community leaders and role models were State Department personnel, military attachés, and Marine Security Guards. Needless to say, I wanted to be a Marine and was advised that I would have to join the Navy in order to serve the Marines as a doctor. I also wanted to be a doctor on a ship and to be stationed in San Diego. I was accepted as a Navy Health Professions Scholarship (HPSP) student, and after 26 years of active service, I've never been stationed with the Marines, never been on a ship, and never been stationed in San Diego. So why do I stay in? My story is long, and the "lessons learned" are many, and recently I have had the opportunity to reflect on the decision points that led to more challenging assignments and more personal and professional fulfillment.

In my early days, it was really all about survival, although, compared to my parents and grandparents, life was pretty easy and my path was already paved. Both sets of grandparents immigrated from Japan to Hawaii, but to different islands. In those days, it could have been different continents. My parents were born in Hawaii as younger children of many, resulting in a group of over 40 first cousins spanning more than 20 years. Due to my grandfather's position within the school system on the Big Island, he was arrested after the Japanese attack on Pearl Harbor and scheduled for deportation to Japan. But my grandmother intervened, and instead he was sent to Louisiana, while my grandmother, father, and aunt were sent to Camp Jerome in Arkansas where they remained until they were released at the end of the war. Interestingly, one of my aunts was attending Tokyo Women's College at the same time and was staying with her uncle, a Lieutenant Colonel in the Japanese Army, who was later killed at Iwo Jima by the U.S. Marines. Another uncle had enlisted in the U.S. Army and was serving in South America.

My mother's family, on the other hand, lived in Wahiawa, Hawaii, on the island of Oahu. They owned a poultry farm and supplied poultry to Schofield Barracks. In fact, my mother attended both school and church on Schofield Barracks, one of the larger U.S. Army bases in Hawaii. My mother later attended Southwestern College in Winfield, Kansas and earned a bachelor's degree in the early 1950s and went on to receive a teaching certificate and taught grade school in Hawaii. My father went on to serve in the U.S. Army during the Korean War, and graduated from the University of Hawaii with a degree in botany. After they married in 1953, they moved to St. Paul, Minnesota, where the three middle children were born while my dad was getting his Ph.D. in plant genetics.

I attended Kindergarten and first grade in Hilo, Hawaii. My dad taught at the University of Hawaii in Hilo and worked on a corn breeding program. I don't remember that much about elementary school in Hawaii, but I do remember the day President Kennedy was assassinated and the fact that I could not cut in a straight line with scissors. In 1965, my dad took a sabbatical to Cairo, Egypt with the Ford Foundation. Picture this—a family of seven, Japanese, with five kids traveling by air from Hawaii to Portland, Oregon; St. Paul, Minnesota; New York City (for the World's Fair); London, England; and possibly Frankfurt, Germany, until finally landing in Cairo, Egypt. It must have been a nightmare for my parents.

At first, we lived in a flat (apartment) in Cairo in a tall building in the middle of the city. It was hot all the time, and there were frequent electrical outages resulting in our being stuck in the elevator. We were enrolled in the American school, which was called Cairo American College, and the three middle kids attended elementary school in Digla. All three of us skipped grades here, so we ended up in 1st, 3rd, and 4th grades. My oldest sister was on the main campus in 5th grade, and the youngest was not in school yet. We moved to a big house in the American community in Maadi, Egypt, much closer to our school at the end of the summer. My memories of Egypt are unshakably positive, up to and somehow including the air raid drills and our emergency evacuation to Greece due to the Six Day War. I remember multiple trips to the pyramids, and not just the ones in Giza. We also took trips to the Sphinx, the Valley of the Kings, Tutankhamen's tomb, the museum in Cairo, the Muhammad Ali Mosque, Nubia, bazaars, food markets, feluccas on the Nile River, Luxor and Karnak, the Avenue of the Rams, and the Abu Simbel. I remember the Red Sea, Alexandria (Egypt), and the Suez Canal. I remember our trip to the Holy Land—the Church of the Holy Sepulcher, Bethlehem, the Grotto of Mary, the Via Dolorosa, the Mount of Olives, the Dome of the Rock, and a multitude of landmarks that you only read about in the Bible.

In May 1967, women and children were flown to Athens, Greece to await the arrival of husbands and fathers. We were at the Athens Hilton for three glorious weeks; I mean we were kids, so we did not have the same fears and apprehension that the moms had. In fact, our biggest regret was that we had just received our semi-annual food shipment from the United States and had not had enough time to eat that great American food that was so scarce while living overseas.

We moved back to Hilo, bought a house, and prepared to dig in for the long haul. This is the first time I was faced with the realization that being different was not always a good thing. At the time in Hawaii, elementary school classes were broken down into levels based on either grades or test scores. I was in the A class, and there was an abundance of children, like myself, of Japanese descent. But unlike myself, the great majority of my classmates had never been away from Hawaii and had been together since kindergarten. Recall, I had skipped a grade in Egypt, so I was now in what was formerly my brother's class. I might as well have been a different species. I befriended the two white kids in the class because they, too, were new. The boy was only half white, and his dad worked with my dad at the University of Hawaii. The girl was not that friendly. In fifth grade, I found that, I was already bigger and more athletic than all of the girls and most of the boys and was typically chosen early on a variety of teams before many of the boys. So, that, plus being new, plus having white friends, put me in a category by myself. Even my cousin, in the same class, seemed to shun me. My dad spent most of the year away looking at other job opportunities, and when he proposed that we return overseas to Lahore, Pakistan, I could not wait to leave.

We attended Lahore American School, and it was here that I established my reputation as an athlete. I played basketball with my brother and his friends in the backyard shooting at a net that was six or eight inches above the regulation height on a homemade backboard. I was good enough to play on the Varsity girls' team when I was in 7th grade, but my sister was against it, and my parents agreed with her, so I ended up playing soccer on the junior high school boys' team. Our three years in Lahore were not without political strife—we were unwittingly involved in the riots when the power shifted in the Pakistani government and when India started threatening. When the ammunition dump not far from the airport and the school blew up, we were sent home and returned two days later to find our school guarded by big scary men with machine guns. That did not inspire confidence or any sense of safety whatsoever. But my soccer career was launched and my reputation as an athlete secured. I actually withdrew to athletics because I felt persecuted by my older sister, who was the smartest kid in the entire school—and every school she attended thereafter. In reality, I was just not that smart; everything was kind of a struggle, and I used all kinds of diversionary tactics to avoid the obvious —that somehow I managed to be part of a family full of academic superstars.

In 1971, my dad had to move. He gave us all kinds of choices, like the International Rice Research Institute in the Philippines and Molokai, Hawaii. We visited Molokai, a small island, one coast of which was once the world famous Leper Colony. It took about 30 minutes to drive from one end of the island to the other. We had just come from a city in a big country on a big continent At that time you, could go anywhere from Holland, to Korea, to Turkey, to the entire African continent, from where we were. Molokai seemed so tiny and so remote. Thankfully, he ended up in Islamabad, Pakistan, the capital city of West Pakistan. It was touted to be just like Washington, DC —a planned city with city blocks, cultural and historic buildings, and paved streets with traffic lights, and it was clean. The reality was that the principal mode of transportation was still the bicycle, and there was no industry in Islamabad. The first year was kind of a blur. School started late because of the new school building, then the toilets backed up through the sinks in the classrooms, then came Ramadan, Thanksgiving, the big evacuation due to the war against India and the secession of East Pakistan, now Bangladesh.

Our evacuation from Pakistan in 1971 was even more eventful than the one from Egypt. We drove up to Kabul, Afghanistan and stayed at the Intercontinental Hotel, waiting for our names to be called to board the evacuation flight out. My dad had to drive the car back across the border to Pakistan, then take a bus back from the border. Meanwhile, we were called up, so we had to leave, and his name had to go to the bottom of the list. We spent several anxious days waiting for him in Minneapolis until Christmas Eve, when he called us from Boston to say he had arrived in the United States. It was bitterly cold, and, our first experience with the discomforts of snow, but we also experienced Christmas shopping for the first time. After the New Year, we went to Mexico, where we spent the next few months.

I had left my algebra book in Oslo on our evacuation journey, thinking that I wouldn't need it again, and really, if you had all your worldly possessions in one suitcase, why would you waste the space with an algebra book? So while everyone else in my family was brushing up on their studies, I was not. Imagine my surprise, when I found out that there was an entrance examination for the American high school in Mexico City for the next quarter. If I didn't get into the American school, the alternative was the Spanish immersion Catholic school next door. Unfortunately, my 9th-grade language was Latin, and I only had two years of junior high Spanish and three years of beginning Urdu, spanned across two schools. No one was concerned that my siblings would get into the American school, and there were plenty of other American families that had only one of their kids in the Catholic school, so it seemed like destiny. Fortunately, I scraped by, scoring well below my younger sister in reading comprehension, as usual, but passing nonetheless.

The American high school in Mexico City was my only experience with a large school, large classes, and a choice of what classes to take. Naturally, there was little correlation between classes we had in Islamabad and classes we had in Mexico City, except for Algebra I. I ended up in Spanish II, World History, Greek Mythology, Algebra I, International Physical Science, and Typing. In my World History class, no one knew there was a war going on in India and Pakistan. I was not behind in any of my classes, and I ended up typing 50 words per minute on a manual typewriter in less than 8 weeks. After that quarter, the war was over, and we were going back to Pakistan via Hawaii, our home of record. We ended up back in Islamabad by mid-April and rejoined our classes which were now much smaller and less international. In fact, our Latin teacher had left, so now my only choices for foreign language were German and French. By mid-May it was 117 degrees at the school, and there was no air conditioning and no shade. The School Board decided to close school early because of adverse weather conditions, and there was a suggestion that we should all be held back a year because we didn't have enough days of school, but my mother prevailed, and we were all promoted to the next year. I could just imagine her thinking that we could all FIVE be at home for another year!

That summer, we could not go back to the States because we had already been there in April. When you live overseas, the biggest events in the summer, besides the 4th of July celebration, were waiting and watching as the new people showed up. There were a lot of kids who were Washington Redskins fans. I did not know at the time that the State Department was in Washington, DC. A lot of older, high-school age kids were only visiting their parents there for the summer. In the fall, they returned to boarding schools in the States or Europe for the school year. Since we were not with the Embassy, State Department, USAID, or the military, we met most of the new kids through church, movies, or our motorcycle "gang." By the time school started in September, we had already welcomed and thoroughly indoctrinated the new kids.

Tenth grade for me was the first time I really felt I was able to assert myself without being just one of the Izuno kids. It was striking because I was so different from the others in terms of my primary interest, namely athletics. I tried out for and made every team and was recognized at each tournament banquet. I played volleyball, soccer, basketball, softball, and flag football. Team members were also encouraged to be cheerleaders for economic reasons, so I did that, too. In the spring, I did the "brain bowl," table tennis, and, in my senior year, the one-act play. I quit piano in 11th grade—my family put a lot of emphasis on music, but I personally had no patience and no talent, so I resisted mightily. At some point, I told my parents that I was not like everyone else—that they never bothered to come to any of my games, and they did not even know how good I was as an athlete. Ultimately, my dad came to most of my soccer games during my senior year, including my last game, where I kicked a potentially tournament-winning penalty kick over the cross bar. Okay, so where were they my junior year when we won every single game?

I graduated from high school at the top of my class, gave the valedictory speech, shared the stage with the U.S. Ambassador, and went off to college. My parents dropped me off at Lehigh University, walked up all the stairs to my room, bought me a comforter and bathrobe, and put some money in a checking account for me. Then they drove off to the airport and went back to Islamabad. So here I was in Bethlehem, Pennsylvania in a class of 1,000 students and did not know a single person. My roommate was from New York, wanted to be a lawyer, was incredibly smart, and had a boyfriend. We could not have been more different.

I could not recall the last time I brushed my teeth with tap water, showered in a community shower, walked around the house other than fully dressed, or eaten in a dining hall with total strangers and extra food. And to top it off, not only were a good one third of the students also valedictorians, but they also placed out of several credits or even semesters of classes because of their high school curricula. And about the checking account—whatever money that was there was of no use to me because I had never walked into a bank or written a check. I did chemistry with a slide rule because I could not afford the calculator, although I have to admit that I did have friends who let me borrow their stuff.

It must be true that survival requires that you forget the really awkward moments of your life so you can focus on the outcomes, because my memories of college do not include the reasons I got so many Bs and Cs and how I finally got a grade rather than an incomplete in Physical Chemistry. I chose Lehigh University because the standardized test score means were higher for math than verbal and because Lehigh had a soccer team. I knew I wanted to be a doctor and major in Biology but did not know that, at the time, Lehigh did not have a Pre-Medicine or Pre-Health major. I also did not know that Lehigh's soccer team was a men's team. I was walking on this huge college campus, looking the wrong direction before crossing the street, completely flustered by the crowds of students who seemed to have shared or similar experiences growing up, all of whom knew who the Beach Boys were when I saw a sign for "Soccer Tryouts – 3 p.m. Saucon Valley Fields." Soccer, unlike calculus, was a word I knew, so I got into my shorts and t-shirt, got on the bus, and rode over to the fields. It was not until I got over there that I realized there were no other girls on the bus. To their credit, the guys were great, and I think that as an engineering school, with primarily engineering majors, Lehigh was not that competitive athletically except in wrestling and later, football. I attended every practice and team meeting, and ultimately, when it became clear who the starting eleven would be, the high school superstars who did not want to sit on the bench left the team, leaving me a spot. So I traveled with and actually played in a few of the freshmen men's team games.

I remember my first road trip to the U.S. Naval Academy, where I did not have anywhere to stay because the visiting team spaces were not yet configured to accommodate women. I nearly missed the game, but my wonderful, loyal teammates came and got me and took me to the training meal. In case you don't know what a U.S. Naval Academy training meal looks like, I will explain. We went to a huge room with rows of tables and chairs and thousands of men who, to me, all looked exactly the same. We were served from vats of scrambled eggs and sausage with other offerings I did not even recognize. It was loud and hot, and all I could think about was how anyone could run after eating even a fraction of what was on their tray or could ever be hungry again. My understanding was that every midshipman had to either play a sport or attend the game that was going on, so this was the only school where we actually had fans.

It was exhilarating to be on the field somewhere I was comfortable and actually to be playing soccer. I have to stress here that I am not an activist of any kind; I did not stick with the men's JV team because I wanted to make a statement or lead a Title IX crusade. In fact, I did not know anything about Title IX (the Act which, among other things, helped promote the participation of women in intercollegiate sports) until much later. The truth of the matter is that I did not even get to play unless we were way ahead or way behind. Back in those days, there was only one division for soccer, so we traveled from as far as upstate New York to Annapolis, Maryland, to more remote places such as West Point, New York, all by bus —an 18 passenger van, actually. We played against "soccer schools," like Hartwick College, the current national champion and perennial contenders. I tried to play both men's JV soccer and women's JV volleyball, but I really loved soccer, and I needed the training so I could continue to run up South Mountain, upon which Lehigh was built. I tried out for JV basketball as my winter sport. Basketball was my strongest sport in high school. I was the highest scorer, most valuable player, a tournament all-star, and team captain in high school. And so was everyone else trying out. And most of them were taller and much more skilled. So when the opportunity came to play indoor soccer in the winter, I abandoned the small pool of athletic women who played multiple sports and concentrated exclusively on soccer year-round.

I honestly do not know how I got through college. Academically it was a disaster my first two years, and it improved only slightly. I remember only two professors well—David Cundall, my faculty advisor, who taught Comparative Vertebrate Anatomy and who could draw every embryologic development since the beginning of time, and Barry Bean, my genetics professor who gave me my first A in college. There was little guidance for premedical students because we had not yet achieved critical mass. Or maybe there was critical mass, but I just didn't know it. I had never witnessed the "cutthroat" pre-med mentality, but now, in retrospect, it was most likely because I was not viewed as a threat. I did not know that you were supposed to take easy electives so you could keep your grade-point average up so you could get into medical school. I just took courses I thought were interesting. So despite my pitiful grade-point average and average standardized test scores, I was probably invited to interview for medical school because they wanted to see what kind of person thought it was a good idea to take, as a biology major, two civil engineering and two molecular biophysics courses.

When I look back at my Navy scholarship application, there are multiple leadership roles and scholastic and academic honors that I did not remember. However, I now believe that there were two things that may have made me an interesting person when reviewed by medical school admissions committees. The first was actually not something I started in college, but something that was very important to me in high school. When I was living in Islamabad, Pakistan, I was offered a volunteer position at the Rawalpindi Mission Leprosy Hospital. I assisted the missionary doctor and nurses in examining patients, documenting lesions, and working with patients undergoing physical therapy. I also played with the children whose disfigurements precluded them from returning to their villages despite their complete medical cure. When I returned to the United States for college, I galvanized my friends from the various residence halls and from one fraternity, Zeta Psi. I decided we would do a knit-a-thon, where the students would pledge a certain amount of money per hour, and my family and friends from the American community in Islamabad would knit bandages for the Leprosy Hospital over Christmas. With the support from the Lehigh University community, we raised over $500 for the Leprosy Hospital and knitted over 20 reusable bandages for the physical therapy department paraffin heat therapy program. The second thing I did stemmed from the implementation of Title IX in 1977. After one year on the JV men's team, I moved up with my teammates to Varsity, where I played even less but was able to participate in a more rigorous training schedule while continuing to play year round. I also assisted the coaching staff with scorekeeping, substitutions, and statistics, a position I retained until graduation.

In 1977, a new group of very talented soccer players arrived at Lehigh University, and many from the old team were cut. However, we still wanted to play. So, with the help of two of my teammates, I started the Lehigh University women's soccer club with $100 of Athletic Department funds and some soon-to-be discarded soccer balls. Bethlehem Sporting Goods gave us a good deal on socks and cleats, and I drew a logo for our team shirts. We had to buy our own uniforms but the Lehigh University bookstore put the numbers on and silkscreened the design. We actually had a schedule of games between "real" schools such as Princeton and Penn State that already had bona fide varsity women's soccer teams, and naturally, they beat us pretty badly. But we persevered, and I was able to play soccer on an intercollegiate level throughout my four years at Lehigh University.

It certainly was not my grades or self-confidence that got me into medical school. In fact, when I declared my intent, the health professions advisor at the time told me that she could not recommend me for medical school because my grades were too low, and it would soil their reputation. I had no alternate plan, so I asked several professors to write letters of recommendation on my behalf, applied to four schools in Philadelphia that I saw everyone else applying to, and followed up on an application from Harvard Medical School that was sent to me. I now realize that the only reason I received an interview from Harvard is because I checked the "Other" box under demographics. Recall that I had no money and no car, so I had to borrow both a car and a volunteer to drive up to Boston for this interview.

When I arrived in Boston for my interview, I was the only candidate who owned neither a suit and leather shoes, nor the alternative, sandals and a broomstick skirt. I had no fashion sense and had not prepared for either an institution like Harvard or for my interview. I took the tour of the medical school, ate lunch with the group, and did not say a single word. I felt like a curiosity more than anything else. When I finally met the admissions office personnel and the person who was to interview me, he took one look at me and said, "Oh! You're not the sort of minority we are looking for!" Perhaps he thought I wouldn't understand English or something. The interview deteriorated from there, especially because it was clear that I did not have the proper amount of reverence for the institution. The truth of the matter is that I knew some people from my high school overseas who got into Harvard and Radcliffe, and they did not have the high school portfolio that I had, so my view was that Harvard and Radcliffe were really not all that competitive.

I also received a two-page rejection letter from the University of Pennsylvania. No one told me that Penn was a private, Ivy League school. The letter read something like this, "Dear Miss Izuno, This year we had over ten thousand highly qualified applicants to our venerable institution, and you're not one of them…" But the nice thing about not having a back-up plan is that you keep beating your head against the same wall. Just before Christmas, I received a letter inviting me for an interview at Temple University in January. This was the last Christmas vacation I would travel overseas. It was also the last Christmas that I would otherwise have had nowhere to go. Everyone else got to "go home for Christmas," but my home was halfway around the world, and every holiday and vacation throughout college was colored by the anxiety of deciding where to go or even where to live for the summer. My family had moved to New Delhi, India by this time, so I took full advantage of the opportunity to travel to Agra to see the Taj Mahal, the Red Fort, and many other ancient works. When I returned, I found another friend to drive me to Philadelphia for my interview.

If you have never been to North Philadelphia, you may be shocked by Temple's location, but honestly, I was so exhilarated to even be invited to visit, I did not notice the fact that the patch of grass that looks like an expansive lawn in front of the medical school on the brochure was actually about 6 by 12 feet, and no one actually sits outside on North Broad Street. My interviewers were welcoming, interested, and knowledgeable about my background, Lehigh University, Leprosy, and international agriculture. They did not seem to mind that I was Asian or female. But I did notice that I had a blue folder and that I was being interviewed for the Minority Recruitment and Retention program. I left my interview with mixed feelings. I really wanted to go to Temple, and yet, I knew my credentials were not strong. This was further enhanced by rejection letters from the Medical College of Pennsylvania and Hahnemann Medical College.

By the end of the following week, however, I received a letter of acceptance from Temple University. I sent my parents an aerogram that same day and a month later received the reply, "Congratulations, how are you going to pay for it?" My baby sister was planning to attend Carleton College in Minnesota; my younger sister was a sophomore at the University of Chicago; already planning to attend graduate school, my brother was in a Ph.D. program at Colorado State University; and my oldest sister was also in a graduate program in Indiana.

So I walked into a Navy recruiter's office and asked for the Navy's Health Professions Scholarship (HPSP) to attend medical school. The Navy bent over backward to help me out, including picking me up and driving me to the Philadelphia Naval Hospital to get a waiver for scoliosis (curvature of the spine), with which I had been diagnosed at age 16. With waiver in hand, we returned to the Lehigh Valley, where I was later commissioned as an ensign. I still have that polaroid picture taken with LT Bullock in Easton, Pennsylvania.

I spent the summer after graduation working at Colorado State University where my brother was attending graduate school. I also had to get my driver's license so that I could drive my car from Harrisburg to Roxborough and from Roxborough to school. I remembered nothing about the neighborhood around Temple University School of Medicine because I had been there only once for the interview. I think we even parked in the parking garage. But when you are a student, you get to park on the street.

The first two years of medical school were extremely difficult, and I think part of it was because I had not been previously indoctrinated into the culture of competitiveness in the classroom, and part of it was because I thought civil engineering was more interesting than biochemistry in college. I also found out that some of the other minority students were on campus before school started, had met the professors, and actually had old tests to study from, so I finally went over to the building that housed the Minority Recruitment and Retention Program and asked where my old tests and faculty advisor were and was told that I was put in the program only for statistical reasons. I hoped it was not to improve the retention rate, because I was struggling in everything except Anatomy and Histology.

I reflected on what I was told, and the urban legend that half of the minority students (meaning Black students) were expected to fail (and repeat the year) or drop out during the first year. I had to applaud Temple for instituting a program that was designed to assist students of color, even though it did not include my color. It turns out that there were two Black men in the top ten graduating from my class, and I was still on the upward slope of the bell curve. I did poorly in Pharmacology and was told that I had to pass the National Board Part I exam to advance to the third year. I was threatened by someone else in the HPSP program from the year ahead of me that if I didn't pass the exam, I would end up in the Navy as a pharmacy technician for four years. I studied a lot after that and ended up passing the exam and moving on.

The third year was a huge relief. Now all the book learning had relevance to my patients. I started off in Psychiatry where I had the best resident ever, named Nelda Mendez. She was wonderful and compassionate and made me present my patient to the visiting professor. This was long before I had any self-confidence; in fact, I was still licking my wounds from the "Conditional" in Pharmacology. I wanted to like Psychiatry so I could work with her forever, but I was not to be deterred from surgery. The rest of the third year was a complete blur, and I did well in everything except Family Medicine. An interesting thing happened during these required core clerkships. I stopped fear-ing the neighborhood around Temple but rather began to appreciate the wide racial, ethnic, and cultural diversity of the people living there because as patients they taught us much more than what we could read about in books.

Extracting historical information, counseling patients, and giving discharge instructions were not rote-memory exercises but rather an opportunity to listen to their concerns and to understand their environment. On my psychiatry rotation, for example, I encountered a huge Black man with a head that was tiny relative to his body. I was stuck in a room with him to do his intake physical. He was somewhat delusional and very hard for me to understand, but when he said that he knew people could read his thoughts because the doctors put needles in his head and out came his thoughts on paper and the doctors could read them, I realized that brain waves on an electroencephalogram (EEG) could look like cursive writing to someone who was illiterate. Understanding this one thing changed my fear to compassion and probably affected the way I viewed patients for the rest of my career.

During our fourth year, we were allowed to rotate outside our hospital, so I arranged Orthopedics rotations at the Mayo Clinic, the National Naval Medical Center (NNMC), and some other private hospitals. It was only then that I realized how much value the indigent and uninsured add to our medical education and was even more grateful to have been given the opportunity to train at Temple and its affiliate hospitals.

I applied for and matched to the General Surgery internship at NNMC. I did not remember anything from my 6 weeks of officer training in Newport, Rhode Island three summers earlier, but neither did any of the other incoming interns. I think there were 13 general surgery interns, and at least one third were female. I do not recall if there was any diversity otherwise, since your main concern during internship is getting to the end of the year. I learned three rules from the general surgeons: 1) Trust no one. 2) If you want something done right, do it yourself. 3) Always remember you are surrounded by a team of well-trained assassins. This was later supplemented by Rule #4: If you are only on call every other night, you miss half the cases. These were rules I adopted and lived by, especially #4.

It was after yet another night of every-other-night call on Cardiothoracic Surgery that a big fat Navy nurse with a clipboard came up to me on the Cardiac Stepdown Unit, 3 West, and told me, "Your stockings are too dark." In the Navy we switch to winter uniforms around October 1 and into summer uniforms around May 1. So this was October, and I was wearing the service dress blue skirt for some reason. So I said, "My skin **is** this color, and I conform to the height and weight standards of the United States Navy." I learned many things from that remark. First of all, honesty is not the best policy when dealing with senior nurse corps officers, especially when they have a clipboard and can write down your name, which is emblazoned on your name tag, which you also wear everyday on your uniform. Being of Japanese descent did not help either, because I was instantly recognized everywhere I went.

As a result of this encounter I got to spend many hours with a variety of senior individuals including the surgery department head, the cardiology department head, director of nursing services, and commanding officer himself. In addition, this totally trashed my "getting along with others" grade on my officer fitness report (fitrep) which is like a report card for military personnel which goes in your permanent file and which is seen by every promotion board throughout your career. So I had to go to the behavioral equivalent of safe-driving school for first offenders, which consisted of speaking to one of the Navy's senior psychiatrists for several months—maybe even years. Meanwhile I witnessed other doctors throwing things at nurses, swearing in front of patients, and even swearing *at* patients. Why weren't they meeting the same important people I was? The only things they had in common with each other were their race and gender.

My plan was to finish this interminable internship and go out to the Fleet as a doctor on a ship or General Medical Officer (GMO). At the time, the Navy would only allow women on support ships, so I lobbied hard and got myself penciled in for the *U.S.S. Yellowstone*, a Destroyer tender. I had originally planned to apply for Orthopedics, but the rule was that returning GMOs got priority over interns. The interns were ranked by what their contributions had been thus far. One of my internship classmates was a prior-service, U.S. Naval Academy fighter pilot who had flown several missions over Vietnam prior to going to medical school. There were many other interns who had either distinguished themselves prior to internship or during internship as well, so I knew my chances were zero or less. So I rearranged my schedule so that I could do some OB/GYN, a specialty that I had never considered because of my experience in medical school. In fact, I viewed my OB/GYN experience at Temple as one big abortion service. I only did pelvic exams on women who were getting either a first trimester abortion or a second trimester saline termination. It was barbaric and ethically challenging for me, even as an observer. But OB/GYN in the Navy was completely different, and I met gynecologic cancer patients for the first time.

I learned the most from my cancer patients; I learned the limitations of medicine and surgery and developed a deep understanding of the drive to do the best possible surgery and offer the most effective therapy without killing the patient. It was harmony and peace, really. Patients who died were, for the most part, prepared to die, and you, as the doctor, could provide as much comfort as you were capable of. On the obstetric side, I saw fat, healthy babies who were not withdrawing from drugs or affected by alcohol, and, for the most part, babies who had mothers *and* fathers. I could handle even the 18 months on the Obstetrics service if I could ultimately become a gynecologic oncologist, so I put in my application for residency in Obstetrics and Gynecology in San Diego following my GMO tour.

In March, the medical officer on my ship had his appointment extended for another year, and I was left with no billet. But, not to worry, the people at the Bureau of Naval Personnel know everything about you before you do. So I got a phone call from my assignment officer, who offered me the choice of the Administrative Support Detachment in Bahrain or the Marine Corps Air Station in Yuma, Arizona. You never want to get the last set of orders in the drawer, and these two choices were definitely looking like the last two that no one else wanted. So why would I want it? Growing up I had lived overseas in the Middle East for 9 years. Wasn't it someone else's turn? And 117 degree desert heat, even dry heat, was already something I'd experienced. Besides it was a two not one year tour. I had to have time to think about this, and thankfully while I was thinking, the OB/GYN department head called me and asked if I wanted to stay on in the residency at NNMC. I knew that if I took this residency now I'd never get to San Diego. But considering my other two choices, I accepted the residency position.

From Day 1, I was far behind the three guys in my year group. At least two of them were pretty supportive, but unfortunately we were never on the same team. We were all on teams with one resident at each year level, and of course the interns all reminded me that they knew more about obstetrics than I did. My new tactic was that on the rare occasions I was right about something, I made sure not only that everyone knew I was right, but that everyone knew they were wrong. This did not help my "getting along with others" grade, and led to more visits to the psychiatrist, now for recalcitrant offenders. But by the end of my second year, I had pretty much caught up with my peers and had found refuge in the operating room. I had great surgical skills, far out of proportion to my reading comprehension skills, and I loved the long hours and complicated cases. I also found a local soccer team and played at least one game per week and, trained for the 1986 Marine Corps marathon.

Life was good, but you can never fully recover from a reputation like mine unless you go away. The fraction of the world population that hates you for making them work like a dog even if you are working alongside them is huge, and the number who appreciate you is small, but not zero. And with time, some of the people who hated you will come to admit they learned something from you. On the other hand, I also learned that you cannot be an effective teacher if you are hated and despised. So I needed a fresh start, and fortunately, the Navy was happy to accommodate.

I met my husband when he was assigned to NNMC for his last tour before getting out. He was a runner and had previously been stationed as a general OB/GYN physician at the Naval Air Station in Adak, Alaska. The Navy's practice of sending young doctors out for a period of time to be general doctors for the smaller units in the Fleet, which did not require the expertise of a full cadre of specialists, meant that the residents were, for the most part, older, married, and with children. In the Navy, they were also mostly men. So imagine my surprise when someone arrived who was actually fit, had time to exercise, and understood the demands of the OB/GYN residency. Because he was a superior officer and the Chief of the Gynecology Service at NNMC, and I was still a resident, we had a stealth relationship, a relationship made easier by the fact that NNMC provided consultant services to a geographically wide variety of hospitals and clinics such as Iceland, Patuxent River, Okinawa, Guantanamo Bay, and two places in South Carolina. As the junior staff person and a generalist, he was the person who provided that coverage. In 1987, upon graduation, we were married and received orders to the Naval Hospital in Jacksonville, Florida. It was glorious. We worked out and ran 6-10 miles per day and did a 5K, 10K, or half marathon every weekend. And we both were accepted at top-tier fellowships in Southern California, sponsored by the Navy.

I arrived at my fellowship visibly pregnant, bearing a striking resemblance to Fred Flintstone. This was not good timing, but I soon realized that no time was "good" or "bad" to have a baby, because regardless of when you had one, it was going to be yours for at least 18 years, so there would be some management issues that you would have to address regardless of what age the child is. Since we were both in fellowships, he at the University of Southern California (USC) and I at the University of California, Irvine (UCI), our days were long and the commute highly variable. So we decided to hire a live-in babysitter, an older woman who had come over from the Philippines to be with her son in Maryland. She was loyal, energetic, and never complained.

I would typically leave the house at 5:30a.m. and return after 10 p.m. Since I did not know any other mothers and certainly did not interact with any neighbors between 10 p.m. and 5 a.m., I had no one with whom to compete with about my child's amazing development and milestones. She started walking and talking when she was around 7 months old(May 1990). If she wanted something she had to ask for it or get it herself. During her first year of life, I had to complete a research paper and get it published; take my oral board certification exam in Chicago; cover the inpatient service for the senior fellows when they went on vacation; attend meetings; interviewing for jobs; and somehow figure out how to raise a baby who rapidly became mobile and inquisitive, with my mom out of the country and everyone else I knew on the East Coast. I don't know of any books out there that gives you even the tiniest suggestion on how to manage these competing responsibilities. But when my daughter started asking for things in Tagalog, I thought perhaps I should be spending more time with her.

I decided I would test the patience of my peers, residents, and faculty. I started bringing her on rounds when I did not have sick patients or procedures I knew I had to do. I also started bringing her to parties and declined to attend those at which she was not welcome. I even took her to a few meetings with whomever was willing to travel, including meetings in Maui, San Antonio, and Orlando. She became a fixture at my side, and everyone remembers her to this day. I learned then that my daughter would always be a part of who I am and that I would not present myself as someone less than that, nor would I behave in a manner that would exclude or embarrass her, regardless of what I was told would define success. I think she also learned that she had to be well-behaved and respectful of others or this relationship would not work. I never had to punish or discipline her to make her comply. On the other hand, I was firm on what the rules were and, what constituted acceptable behavior, especially in public.

My fellowship years were some of the best in my memory. We, the UCI Gyn Oncology Fellows, were all treated like we were the best fellows any specialist had ever had, and I think we responded to that. We were welcomed as colleagues, and our goals were well defined. I owe an infinite debt of gratitude to my three primary attending physicians at UCI. They were fiercely loyal to us, and we to them. When the time came to leave, I asked for orders to San Diego, since really I was already almost there, but San Diego was not available, so we accepted orders back to NNMC.

I privately feared that I would pick up where I left off at NNMC but was surprised by how much time had healed many old wounds and in fact was welcomed back by a wide range of surgical specialties. I was also surprised by the way I was treated by my own division. I had done many complex cases and had already performed a number of procedures effectively and safely with little or no supervision. However, when the first opportunity came to do a pelvic exenteration at Walter Reed Army Medical Center (WRAMC), I was completely ignored, and they paid for a colleague to come up from Naval Medical Center Portsmouth to assist them. Since I was relatively new in the National Capital Area, I chose to employ some of my new "people skills" and ignore this.

Instead, I marketed myself and became the primary gynecologic oncology consultant to both NNMC and Malcolm Grow U.S. Air Force Medical Center at Andrews Air Force Base. Numerous lifelong friendships and mutually respectful relationships grew out of this decision. However, when the OB/GYN residencies from NNMC and WRAMC combined, there was nothing anyone could do to save me from the next five years of covert and overt harassment by the leadership of the OB/GYN Department at WRAMC.

When the programs combined, I was the program director of the only fully accredited OB/GYN program in the National Capital Area, yet the WRAMC program director used intimidation, threats, and unsubstantiated lies about my performance to undermine my authority. I had spent the entire previous year arranging rotations at outside hospitals to enhance my Navy residents' experience in routine gynecologic surgery and to increase the amount of time they spent in the operating room. As a result, my third year residents had done more cases and were more confident in the operating room than the Army chief (fourth year) residents. The decision was made to have the Army residents do all the cases until they caught up with my residents. Everyone thought this was a good idea, except me and, of course, all my residents. But you can't reason with an old man who had painted himself into that corner, although I have to admit, I did aggressively point out the obvious flaws with his thinking.

As a result, a "search" was done for a residency director for the integrated program, and another Army Colonel was brought in to fix the whole situation. I remained fiercely protective of my residents, especially since I had selected them to come to NNMC, and I did learn that loyalty to yourself and to your people is more important than conforming to unfair, unhealthy, and discriminatory practices. I was counting the days until another group of gynecologic oncologists would graduate so that one of them could come to WRAMC and replace me. It would be about five years before someone could relieve me, but in my last two summers there, I was approved to try out for the All Navy Women's Soccer team and played All Navy Soccer for one month each year for the next three years.

When the opportunity arose to take over the HPSP program for the Navy at the command that was then called the Naval School of Health Sciences (NSHS), I immediately accepted and left WRAMC in March. Within a year, I was informed that I had been selected to my current rank, Captain, despite all efforts by the Army to discredit me. Perhaps only they were more surprised than I. My time at NSHS and, later, the Naval Medical Education and Training Command (NMETC), was almost entirely positive. I learned a great deal about educational disparities, learning styles, management, career development, cultural differences between civilians and military personnel, and team cohesiveness. My mentors and colleagues at this command were men of great integrity and fairness. And their management styles combined to prepare me for the next step in my career.

I was appointed Vice President for Recruitment & Diversity at the Uniformed Services University of the Health Sciences (USUHS) in Bethesda, Maryland by a former Navy Surgeon General, who was then serving as President of the military medical school. He felt that diversity was important enough a priority to give it Vice President status, or a seat at the table. Looking around that table, it was obvious that there was work to be done. This was my dream job, I thought. I always wanted to be on the faculty or executive staff of a major university, like my father and brother before me. And here I was unencumbered by tenure and other rules designed to maintain the status quo, and even better, I was already a Captain in the Navy and I now had nothing to lose or to gain by taking this position. Plus, I already knew all about recruiting medical students. I had been doing that for three years, studying trends, reviewing statistics, and visiting a wide range of undergraduate schools. I knew less about recruiting a diverse faculty, however, which I viewed as the biggest challenge.

I did not realize how big a challenge this would be until I found a Latino, Harvard-trained cardiologist who had ties to NNMC and who would be willing to consider USUHS in his career plans. I also knew that the Navy cardiologist had just left to take a post at the Naval Academy. So I presented the candidate's Curriculum Vita, and was told by three people, including the Cardiology Department Head and the Dean of the Medical School, that I would have to find funding for him if they were to consider him for a full-time faculty position at USUHS. It was then that I realized that the School of Medicine was, in fact, not interested enough in diversity to put out any collective effort, and I was clearly completely on my own.

Further, when I presented my report to the Board of Regents regarding the issues and what we were doing in my department to address them, I was cut off by one of the Regents who was then working for industry and not at a medical school and was told that he was tired of listening to excuses. He just wanted to see our numbers. This told me that he had no idea how big the problem of diversity was in higher education and how much other schools and the private sector were paying to enhance their own diversity, without making a significant impact on the overall national outcome. No one on the Board stopped him, so this interaction told me that it was time to hunker down with my loyal staff of one (and later two) and my $44,000 budget and to create low-cost innovative programs that would somehow address the issue of increasing the number of qualified students in the pipeline.

Since my first recruiting visit to Tennessee in 2002, I was stunned by the low numbers of qualified students of color interested in medicine and in the collective efforts of medical schools to compete for them. Programs with greater diversity seemed to have more funding and summer programs and internships. They also had retention programs and well staffed and equipped Multicultural Affairs offices. I applied for a grant at USUHS for $10,000 to develop a summer program. It was denied. So, not to be deterred, I used personal funds and creative (but legal) financing with other departments and institutions to develop the summer program I envisioned. Now in its sixth year, we have touched over 300 high school students from a wide variety of economic, racial and ethnic, experiential, and geographic backgrounds. The physicians and ancillary health professionals at NNMC and the Navy's Bureau of Medicine and Surgery have been steadfastly supportive.

These experiences, including the failed grant application, have prepared me for my new job as the Special Assistant for Diversity to the Chief of Naval Operations. The fact that there is such a position, as well as a hard-working, totally committed diversity directorate under the Chief of Naval Personnel, should be a clear indicator to both internal and external customers of the Navy's commitment to diversity, not just regarding numbers, but also to enhancement of the work environment, job and promotion opportunities, cultural competency, and community outreach. In retrospect, every barrier I have stumbled over, every door slammed in my face, and every swing I did not take, were part of my personal development and the choices I made have, prepared me to tackle the responsibilities of the road ahead. I picked my battles and made lots of mistakes but turned every adverse word or action into something I could defend.

The fact that my daughter, now a sophomore at Case Western Reserve University, shares my passion for improving health and educational disparities is one of the accomplishments of which I am most proud. As I said earlier, my lessons learned are many, but my regrets are few. Joining the Navy was the best decision I made, and being a Naval Officer is something that I believe stripped away many of the initial stereotypes and allowed me to start one step ahead as a woman of color in a white, male-dominated world. And now, with the charge to each of the Navy's enterprises from the Chief of Naval Operations, and the support of the Chair of the Joint Chiefs of Staff, I am confident that what lies ahead for the Navy is an environment that is a true reflection of the richness of America's diverse cultural heritage.

Women of Color and the Formation of a Science Identity

Fayneese Sheryl Miller, Regina Toolin, and Robert Biral
University of Vermont

Very learned women are to be found, in the same manner as female warriors; but they are seldom or never inventors.

–Voltaire, *Dictionnaire Philosophique.Women*

There are some systematic differences in variability in different populations....So my sense is that the unfortunate truth—I would prefer to believe something else, because it would be easier to address what is surely a serious social problem if something else were true—is that the combination of the high-powered job and the differing variances probably explains a fair amount of this problem.

–Lawrence W. Summers

How little has changed in the 250 years separating Voltaire's comments about women and Summers's remarks, made in 2005, explaining why women have not excelled in STEM (science, technology, engineering, and math) areas to the same degree as men have. While both acknowledge the fact that there are women who are "learned" and who have the ability to excel, neither view women as *capable* of contributing to the development of new knowledge in the "sciences." Summers's argument that there are "systematic differences" between men and women that affect the probability that women will contribute to society or science to the same degree as men do, echoes Voltaire's distinction between learned women and female warriors. There are some but few in number, and therefore even fewer have the capacity for independent or creative thought.

Voltaire seems to be arguing that women are inherently inferior to men. It is unclear whether Summers is arguing the same. On the one hand, it seems that Summers is arguing that women lack the aptitude; on the other hand, it seems as though he is attributing the lack of aptitude to the many different competing demands, such as work and family, on women's time and to societal expectations that women be the primary caretaker and caregiver. For example, he states, "it is the general clash between people's legitimate family desires and employers' current desire for high power and high intensity, that in the special case of science and engineering, there are some issues of intrinsic aptitude, and particularly of the variability of aptitude, and those considerations are reinforced by what are in fact lesser factors involving socialization and continued discrimination."

Summers uses 80 hours a week as the amount of time that scientists must devote to their careers if they want to be among the top in their field. Is this realistic, regardless of gender and/or race? It is certainly based on a stereotypical view of men and women's role and place in the home, community, and work. What is clear from his remarks is that he holds to the societal myth that men are the traditional providers and "must commit more than 100% of time and energy to the workplace" (Valverde, 2003, p. 103). What is also clear is the implication that only women who are unmarried or childless can compete at the highest levels with men. He says, "And the relatively few women who are in the highest ranking places are disproportionately either unmarried or without children." It is the belief that scientists, regardless of race and/or gender, can engage in high-powered and high intensity work only if they are less committed to family than to work. This belief reinforces the cultural barriers and adherence to societal norms that hinder the advancement of women in the sciences and, to some degree, the willingness of women to continue in the sciences and engineering beyond college.

Summers's statement that women are unwilling to put in the 80 hours a week he deems necessary to succeed in the sciences and engineering was met with a great deal of anger. On the other hand, his remarks created renewed interest in the reasons why women were still not enjoying the same degree of success as men in STEM (science, technology, engineering, and math) areas. While Summers seems to minimize the role that gender and race discrimination plays in who advances in the sciences and engineering, others propose that it can not be relegated to a minor role. Nancy Hopkins, a professor at MIT, when explaining why women were not reaching the level of full professor in higher education, stated, "We all thought that women getting the jobs was all you needed to achieve equality. But it turns out that the experiences of different people are not necessarily the same, or equal, in the same place" (MIT News, 2002, para. 18). Holmgren and Basch (2005) describe the experience of women scientists confronting a glass ceiling. They refer to a 2001 report from the National Council for Research on Women, *Balancing the Equation*, to argue that women in the sciences experience the glass ceiling when attempting to gain access to laboratories, disseminate their research, participate as members on key commissions, and gain promotion to full professor. Regardless of as to why there are so few women, and particularly women of color, in the sciences, the disparity in rank, salary, opportunity, and access points to the reason that men in the sciences and engineering enjoy more success relative to women.

Questions about the ability of women to do science have long been answered. We no longer need to focus on whether or not women have the ability to excel in the sciences. Research (Holmgren & Basch, 2005) has shown that females, especially during the secondary education years, are as competent in the sciences as are males. In the 1970s, only 25% of females were finalists in the National Science Talent Search; each year since, the percent of females has continued to rise. In 1999, for example, 45% of the finalists were female and, in 1999, 2000, and 2001, females won top honors in the Intel Science Talent Search. In 2009, the Nobel Prize in the sciences was awarded to two women. Clearly, women have the *right stuff* to succeed in and contribute to knowledge production in the sciences.

Yet the number of women who pursue science at either the collegiate or postgraduate level does not reflect the trend at the secondary level. As the degree level becomes more advanced, the number of females pursuing a degree in the sciences deceases, remaining low relative to men. The number of women pursuing advanced degrees in the sciences for the past 30 years in higher education represents about one-third of the PhDs in the sciences. The number of assistant professors in the sciences has grown over the years, but the number of women who are full professors remains around ten percent.

Although females are among the top in the science talent searches, they are less likely than males to continue with science beyond high school. Women earn more than half the degrees in the life and social sciences, yet they earn only one-fourth of the degrees in physics (NSF, 2007). The number of women who attain degrees in computer science is equally low and steadily declining (Spertus, 2004). The decline might be explained by research (AAUW, 2000; Margolis & Fisher, 2002) showing that females, during the early years, show less interest and are less skilled in computers than males. And although females earn 35% of the degrees in chemical engineering, they earn only 14% of the degrees in electrical engineering (NSF, 2007).

If the picture for women in many of the disciplines of science and engineering is bleak, the picture for women of color in the sciences is even bleaker. The proportion of women of color in science, engineering, technology, and mathematics is not only small compared with that of nonminority women, but the higher the degree area the more precipitous the decline (NSF, 2007; CPST, 2007). As a case in point, of the 69,300 science and engineering full professors in 2006, only 600 (or 1%) were African American females. The number is even smaller for women of Latin American descent and Native American and Alaska Native women. These numbers run counter to the data on the number of women of color who declare science or engineering as their major.

In 2006, the number of African American females enrolled in science and engineering graduate programs was 15,884 (NSF, 2006). Of this number, 16% were enrolled at one of the HBCUs (Historically Black Colleges and Universities). The number of Hispanic females enrolled in graduate science and engineering programs in 2006 was 12,839. Of this number, 38% were enrolled at an institution with a high Hispanic student body (NSF, 2007). Interestingly, during the same time period, first-year African American (32%), Hispanic (32%), and American Indian (31%) female students indicated that they were more likely to major in the sciences or engineering compared with 24% of the white females (cited in NSF, 2007).

In addition, in a study conducted by Hansen (2004) on girls and science, African American females were found to have higher levels of interest in science than white females. Why, then, are females of color among the least likely to pursue a career in either the sciences or engineering? Does the glass ceiling occur earlier for females of color than it does for white females? Does something occur to females of color during the K-12 years that negatively affects behavior but not interest?

Social distance theory may help explain the differences in the experience between women and women of color in the sciences. According to this theory, white women are less likely to be perceived negatively by white males than are minorities because they are recognized as sharing a similar cultural or racial experience. In other words, white males are more likely to be positive toward white females and to see white females rather than female of color as acceptable colleagues. In theory, then, the argument is that because the experiences of white women scientists are perceived as being closer to those of their white colleagues, they are therefore more acceptable than are women of color who find themselves in an unenviable double-bind position of gender and race. In other words, not only do women of color have to endure the stereotyping of women that serve to discriminate against them, but they have to suffer racial and ethnic stereotypes about their ability as well. This double bind has implications for the employment status of women of color.

Employment Status of Women Relative to Men

African American males and females have experienced some gains in their employment in the sciences over the last 25 years, with their numbers increasing from 2.6% of the jobs to now approximately 6.9%. On the other hand, all women saw their numbers increase from 12% to a little over 25% of the jobs in the sciences (NSF, 2007). Of the total percentage of women working in the sciences, white women comprise 20%, those of Asian descent 4%, African Americans 2%, and Latinas 1.2%.

Women in Science and Engineering (WISE) can be found on virtually every major research and most small liberal arts college/ university campuses in America. Science and engineering fellowships for women and/or people of color are still being offered, and although there has been an increase in the number of women and people of color pursuing careers in the sciences, the numbers are not close to reaching parity with men in the field. Women still have not moved into higher education at the rate necessary for systemic change to occur. According to a study done by NSF (2007), women accounted for 31.7% of all faculty in higher education. Of this number, 39.4% were at the assistant professor level, 32.9% at associate professor, but only 20.6% at full professor. When the data is disaggregated according to race, the disparity is startling. While white women comprise 23.9% of all faculty, African American women make up only 2.3%, with Latinas and American Indian and Alaska Native women trailing at 1.3% and .2% respectively. The percentages are even smaller for women of color who hold faculty positions in the sciences or engineering.

The purported glass ceiling for women in the sciences is not limited to the United States, but is a global problem. In Sweden, women with postdoctoral fellowships in the sciences have to score five times higher during the merit process than men in order to receive a similar merit rating (Wennerås & Wold, 1997). In Italy, women researchers with national laboratories advance at only half the rate of their male colleagues (DeWandre, 2002). And in the United Kingdom, women, while receiving more than half of the degrees in biology, hold only 9% of the full professorships (DeWandre, 2002).

A major difference between the experience of women scientists and engineers in the Unites States compared with women in Europe is that the culture in Europe is perceived as less amenable to discussions suggesting discrimination against women and people of color. This places women of color or ethnic minority women in a double bind, similar to that of women of color in the United States. Specifically, Pain (2009) argues that it is perceived as impolite for women and ethnic minority scientists to speak openly about race and gender discrimination in Europe. Consequently, Pain proposes there is little help to be received from others when European women of color attempt to fight back against what appears to be discriminatory behavior or practices.

These differences, however, beg the question of whether the disparity in rank and opportunity has to exist between males and females. France, for example, produces three times as many female physicists as Germany. But unlike Germany, France provides state-supported childcare. Is this the reason female physicists in France are able to succeed at the same rate as males? Summers (2005), in his remarks, gives credence to this presumption by raising the question, "what do we actually know about the incidence of financial incentives and other support for child care in terms of what happens to people's career patterns?" Looking to France's example might provide the answer. What would happen if higher education offered compensation packages that would attract women who have the interest, desire, and aptitude to succeed at the highest level in the sciences and engineering, but who without compensation for childcare might not be able to do so. If university compensation packages included childcare, or if there was state-supported childcare in the United States, would the gender disparity in the STEM areas disappear? And the most tantalizing question of all: would more women of color persist in their science careers to increase their numbers in relation to the overall number of women in the sciences?

Sharon's Story

The experience of women of color in higher education differs from institution to institution, but many females of color who hold academic positions in science or engineering departments seem to share a common story that suggests that, at some point in their career, they perceived themselves as having been treated differently than their colleagues. In the following paragraphs we share Sharon's story. In the tradition of narrative inquiry, Sharon's story is a composite of several actual stories told by women of color in their journey to becoming a scientist.

Sharon is a full professor at a highly-ranked university, and her story is not unlike that of many "smart" girls interested in math and science. Sharon's story begins in high school where she is one of two African American females in the honors geometry, algebra, and science classes. Sharon recalls that she and her classmate were not the only African American females capable of excelling in the honors math and science classes, but they were the only two, she says, who are recommended for the honors courses.

Sharon does well in the algebra class she takes in the 9th grade. It is in the 10th grade when she takes geometry that she begins to have problems. One day she asks her teacher for help and is told, "Maybe you don't belong in this course." Though she is able to learn geometry well enough to get a decent grade, her math confidence has been shaken by her geometry teacher's insensitive remark. Since she has fulfilled her math requirement, she decides not to take any more courses in math.

Sharon starts her freshman year in college as an undeclared major. She has her heart set on majoring in science, but doubts she will be able to pursue her goal, feeling little confidence in her ability to do the math classes essential to her major. The college she attends had a general education curriculum, and she is required to take a math and science course during her first year in college. To her surprise, she not only does extremely well in the math class but, more importantly, enjoys the work of the class. Feeling good about her math skills again, she decides to follow her interest and majors in biology.

The students at Sharon's college are assigned a mentor when they enroll. Sharon is assigned to the only African American female faculty member in sociology. She encourages Sharon to do well and is available to meet with her during scheduled office hours and at other times. Sharon takes full advantage of the professor's willingness to meet with her, and bolstered by her advisor's belief in her ability, she follows her advice when she encourages her to apply to graduate school. Interestingly, none of her science professors ever mention graduate school as a possibility to her. Overall, Sharon enjoys her college science experience, finds work in one of her professor's labs, works hard on her senior thesis, and graduates among the top students in her class.

Sharon is accepted to a graduate program and quickly learns that she has to work harder if she wants to become a successful scientist. Sharon begins to spend as much time in the lab as possible, working on a research project she has designed and undertaken, her hard work and long hours paying off when her results look good.

It is in the classroom and hallways, she experiences problems. Sharon does not know that she is the first African American female admitted to her graduate program until she arrives. Some professors are not ready for her. One in particular puts a toothbrush in his mouth when he meets her in the hallway rather than take the time to say hello. Another refuses to believe she is as good a student as her peers. He repeatedly grades her papers and exams lower than anyone else's in his course. At first, Sharon believes that she is not testing well or does not understand what her professor is asking the class to do.

Then a couple of things happen. She shares her work with her advisor, who (unknown to her) removes her name from her work and gives it to another colleague to assess. That professor gives her good grades on every paper, even raising her grades on her multiple choices exams when errors are found in the grading process. This finding surprises Sharon when her advisor tells her what might be occurring. Next, he asks Sharon to see some of the work of her peers, which when looked at, confirms her advisor's suspicions when she notices that answers she gives are similar to those of her peers. Armed with her new knowledge, she approaches her professor and, without mentioning to him what she has learned, mounts an argument for him to change her grade on each paper and exam. Confronted with the "possibility" that he has made some mistakes in reading her work, he reluctantly changes her grades.

Sharon also discovers that the other students in her cohort have copies of sample exams for the course but do not share the exams with her.

Sharon applies for and is a successful recipient of a National Science Foundation Graduate Fellowship, becoming the first person in her graduate program to receive one. Not surprisingly, the professors in her program begin to view her as one of their star students. What does not change, however, are the underlying attitudes displayed toward her when she began the program. Only now the faculty make comments like "Sharon is different" and "She is not like the rest." To Sharon the meaning is clear. She is now viewed by the white faculty as more like them and not like "those other" African Americans who are interested in doing science as a career

Sharon receives her PhD and moves to a two-year postdoctoral fellowship at a well-known university, where she continues to excel. However, she discovers that the other fellows working with her advisor meet with him for breakfast once a week, whereas she has never been invited. When she decides to accompany one of her friends in her fellows group to a breakfast meeting, her advisor conducts the breakfast meeting as though she has never been absent from the previous meetings. She continues to attend the meetings every week until her fellowship ends.

When the fellowship ends, Sharon, who is now highly sought after for assistant professor positions, accepts a job offer and soon has no difficulty receiving tenure and promotion to associate professor. After this, she begins to branch out and apply for science grants that are focused on education at the K-12 level and encourages collaboration with her education department colleagues, soon becoming the most successful grant writer in her department. She continues to publish in science journals and is now publishing in science education journals as well.

When she considers going up for promotion to full professor, she finds herself in a situation strangely reminiscent of her
high school math experience. She is told by the senior faculty in
her department that she is not doing the right kind of scientific
work. Rather than fold her tent and capitulate to their demands
that she do the "right" kind of research, she decides to put her
dossier forward for review despite the negative feedback she has
received, knowing that she will most likely receive a negative
vote from the senior faculty eligible to vote, all of whom are white
males. When she receives the expected negative vote, she challenges it and eventually wins the right to go forward with her
promotion dossier. Winning full support from the college-wide
promotion and tenure committee and the university committee,
Sharon is promoted to full professor.

Analysis of Sharon's Experience

Sharon's experience is not unique. She fits the typical profile of
an African American female interested in science at an early
age. More importantly, she proves at every level that she has the
ability and aptitude to excel in the sciences. Why then does she
meet with challenges and obstacles? An obvious response might
be that she was not expected to succeed in the sciences. A second
response might be that she was not expected to pursue a career
in the science because of a belief that females of color are more
likely to get married and shift their attention away from their
work to their family. Both of these are based on stereotypical
views of women.

During high school, Sharon was not perceived as having a
science or math identity. Carlone and Johnson (2007), in a paper
on the experiences of successful women of color in science, argue
that the perception of a *science identity* is a key factor in whether
or not women of color are able to succeed in the sciences. They
define a science identity as "accessible when, as a result of an
individual's competence and performance, she is recognized by
meaningful others, people whose acceptance of her matters to
her, as a science person" (Carlone & Johnson, 2007 p. 1192). Sharon did not acquire a science identity until she was in college,
when she began to succeed in math and science classes and her
advisor made her feel as though she had a future in science. The
belief that she is competent in science persists throughout her
graduate experience, receiving further confirmation when she is

awarded a prestigious National Science Foundation Graduate Fellowship. The confirmation of her science identity is not tested again until she attempts to present herself for promotion to full professor.

Carlone and Johnson use a model of science identity that incorporates three concepts—performance, recognition, and competence. Performance is defined as "social performances of relevant scientific practices—e.g. ways of talking and using tools" (p. 1191). Recognition involves "recognizing oneself and getting recognized by others as a 'science person'" (p. 1191). And competence is defined as "knowledge of science content (may be less publicly visible than performance)" (p. 1191). When Sharon presents herself for promotion to full professor, her performance as a scientist and her recognition as such by others is called into question. Since Sharon is now writing as many grant proposals for practice-based science as she is for lab-based research and is receiving funding for both types of work, the level of her science intensity is called into question by her male colleagues. Summers argues that high intensity is one of the key components for a successful scientist. Sharon is more productive than ever. Why, then, do her male colleagues question her level of intensity?

According to Carlone and Johnson (2007), women of color experience a double bind in that their gender and racial identities affect whether or not they are readily perceived as a scientist. Aptitude and success in the sciences are simply not enough for women of color. Sharon experiences disparate treatment in graduate school. That she does not seem at all surprised that this happens certainly accounts for her "boldly" inviting herself to her graduate advisor's breakfast research meetings. Because Sharon has a strong science identity, seeing herself as a scientist serves as a buffer against the negative impact of disparate treatment. That she also has a strong racial identity serves her well. For when she receives an NSF award and observes that her professors accept her success as a scientist because they view her as an exception, she co-opts their attempts to neutralize her race and gender and uses it as strengths to advance her career. Carlone and Johnson (2007) propose that it is "much easier to get recognized as a scientist if your ways of talking, looking, acting, and interacting align with historical and prototypical notions of a scientist" (p. 1207). With an NSF fellowship, Sharon looks more like a scientist.

In sum, Sharon's persistence and her need to be perceived as a scientist are key factors in her success. In addition, the support she receives from others and the confirmation she gains from external agents—like grant-making entities—are important to her identity development.

Conclusion

Access and opportunity to succeed in the sciences remains a challenge for many women of color interested in the sciences. Success in the sciences for women of color is dependent on their ability to contextualize experiences in science classes, with science professors, and with colleagues through the development of a strong science identity that will allow them to be perceived as scientists. For women of color, this is not an easy thing to do. One of the participants at the conference where Summers spoke questioned whether access to science opportunities is truly objective. Referring to the Swedish Medical Council project as a case in point, the questioner challenged the notion of a completely objective process in selecting applicants for positions. The Swedish Medical Council, in trying to identify "very high-powered research opportunities" for postdoctorates, selected them from what were perceived as the top emerging scientists in Sweden. When the selected group turned out to be primarily male, two of the women chosen were able to access the data used to choose the post-doctorates and found that different standards were used to pick the males over the females. Women, to be considered, had to publish in more select journals than men. Males who were part of a centrally identified network were more likely to be selected than females with comparable work but fewer connections.

As the questioner concluded with a point germane to our discussion here, the Sweden experience provides more evidence that the process used to determine who has a science identity is more subjective than objective. Given that women of color are the least connected in the sciences, their efforts to be perceived as scientists will most likely force them to confront one or more of the several challenges that Sharon in our case study had to meet and overcome.

The way women of color experience science needs to be addressed at every level of the educational process, from middle to secondary to higher education. Sharon's experience, where she was made to feel as though she did not belong in the honors class when she sought help, is not unique. Johnson (2007), in a study of the experience of 16 Black, Latina, and American Indian women science students, found that women of color feel conspicuous in classes where they are one of a few and, therefore, choose not to ask questions for fear of being perceived as not knowing the material or not having done the assigned work for the course. It is ironic that a science identity, for some—especially males—is built by not asking questions (Seymore & Hewitt, 1997). To not ask questions, for males, is presumed to be a measure of their innate intellectual abilities. Males find other ways to draw attention to their science knowledge. Women of color are afraid to ask questions in class and are less likely than others to be selected to be part of a research team. They therefore are again in a double bind, because they have fewer opportunities to show that they can or have developed a science identity.

Johnson (2007) raises the issue of meritocracy when discussing the way science professors discourage women of color in their quest to develop a science identity. Johnson says that "race, ethnicity, and gender may not be permitted to play overt parts in who succeeds in science classes, but they are certainly affecting the experience of students of color in those classes" (p. 817). Sharon, not being told of the breakfast meeting, is an example of race not playing an overt part, but certainly being part of her experience. Johnson provides the reader with another example. One of her students raises the issue of who is expecting to partner with whom in the lab. Johnson visits the lab class mentioned by the student and observes white females ignoring the teaching assistant's suggestion to partner with four Latinas in the class because there was a shortage of laboratory equipment. The white females chose to wait for equipment to become available rather than work with the Latinas. The experience of women of color in the sciences will be slow to change unless it is acknowledged that their race/ethnicity and gender play a considerable part in the formation of a science identity

In sum, it has been shown that women of color are interested in studying science and having a career as a scientist. In order for more women of color to be successful in the sciences, the challenges and obstacles they face need to be acknowledged and addressed. If initiatives to increase the number of people who choose to major and work in one of the STEM areas are to be successful, all who are interested in the sciences must be given the opportunity to access classes, laboratories, and professors. To do otherwise will certainly result in many qualified young people of color, both female and male, not achieving their dream of become scientists.

References

American Association of University Women (AAUW). (2000). *Tech-savy: Educating girls in the new computer age.* Washington, DC: AAUW Educational Foundation. www.auw.org.

Carlone, H., & Johnson, A. (2007). Understanding the science experiences of successful women of color: Science identity as an analytic lens. *Journal of Research in Science Teaching, 44*(8), 1187-1218.

Commission of Professionals in Science and Technology (CPST). (2007). Four decades of STEM degrees, 1966-2004. The devil is in the details. *STEM Workforce Data Project, Report no. 6.* www.cpst.org.

De Wandre, N. (2002). Women in science: European strategies for promoting women in physics. *Science, 295,* 278-279.

Hansen, S. (2004). African American women in science: Experiences from high school through the post-secondary years and beyond. *NWSA Journal, 16*(1), 96-115.

Holmgren, J. L., & Basch, L. (2005, January 28). Encourage, not gender, key to success in science, *San Francisco Chronicle,* B-9.

Johnson, A.C. (2007). Unintended consequences: How science professors discourage women of color. *Science Education,* DOI 10.1002/sce.20208, 805-821.

Margolis, J., & Fisher, A. (2002). *Unlocking the clubhouse: Women in computing.* Cambridge, MA: MIT Press.

MIT News (2002). *MIT completes ground-breaking study on status of women faculty.* Retrieved from http://web.mit.edu/newsoffice/2002/genderequity.html

National Science Foundation (NSF). (2007). *Women and minorities, and persons with disabilities in science and engineering:* NSF 07-315. Division of Science Resource Statistics, Arlington, VA.

Pain, E. (2009). *A double bind: Minority women in science in Europe.* http://sciencecareers.sciencemag.org/career_magazine/previous_issues/articles/2009_02_27/caredit.a0900030.

Seymore, E., & Hewitt, N. (1997). *Talking about leaving.* Boulder, CO: Westview Press.

Spertus, E. (2004). *What we can learn from computer science's differences from other sciences. Women, work, and the academy: Strategies for responding to 'Post-Civil Rights Era' gender discrimination.* http://www.barnard.columbia.edu/bcrw/womenandwork/Spertus.html.

Summers, L. (2005). *Remarks at NBER conference on diversifying the science and engineering workforce.* http:///www.Wiseli.engr.wisc.edu/archives/summers.php.

Valverde, L. (2003). *Leaders of color in higher education.* Walnut Creek, CA: Alta Mira Press.

Wennerås, C., & Wold, A. (1997). Nepotism and sexism in peer-review. *Nature, 387,* 341-343.

Part IV

International Scholars

Practicing Postcolonialism:
A South Asian Woman in the Academy

Shakuntala Rao
State University of New York

In this chapter, I discuss my experiential location as a South Asian woman, immigrant, educator, and scholar who is deeply dedicated to questions raised by postcolonial theorists; this autobiography details my experiences in the American academy and my discovery of postcolonial theory and practice. Postcolonial theory has helped me to locate myself and to critically rethink the canonical texts of my discipline, Communication Studies. In the 1990s, scholars in the humanities like me, interested in questions of race, gender, ethnicity, and empire, gained immensely from dialogue with the emergent field of postcolonial studies, which provided comparative historical analyses of these issues from global or transnational perspectives. Postcolonial studies as a disciplinary approach began with critiques of existing methodologies and by recognizing various forms of marginality, unmasking of imperialism's ideological guises, and marginality in cultural production, narratives, and popular culture. As a South Asian woman teaching and researching in a discipline—Communication Studies—which has historically been narrow in its epistemological stance and therefore unwelcoming of critical interventions, introducing questions of postcolonialism has been both challenging and rewarding. This chapter is about the privilege and freedom of being able to speak and write (as a tenured full professor at a four-year state university) and also about the silences—the unsaid and what-cannot-be-said. After struggling to overcome such silences, and to seek and assert authority, I have found a place in the academy, which has been profoundly empowering.

Theorizing Postcolonialism

Orientalism (1978), by Edward Said, considered by many as a foundational text of postcolonial studies, helped me to first think through my location as a South Asian immigrant female intel-

lectual. In the book, Said, himself a Palestinian American scholar, writes:

> I think the major choice faced by the intellectual is wheth-
> er to be allied with the stability of the victors and rulers
> or—the more difficult path—to consider that stability
> as a state of emergency threatening the less fortunate
> with the danger of complete extinction, and take into ac-
> count the experience of subordination itself, as well as
> the memory of forgotten voices and persons. As Benjamin
> said, "to articulate the past historically does not mean to
> recognize it 'the way it was'"…It means to seize hold of a
> memory (or a presence) as it flashes up at a moment of
> danger. (p. 43)

In this work, Said charts the Western world's construction(s) of
"an inferior East" by underscoring how the authorizing/authori-
tative Occident continues to produce an objectified and negatively stereotyped Orient (p. 31).

Drawing from Michel Foucault's definition of discourse and
Antonio Gramsci's conceptualization of hegemony, Said traces
the evolution of European power/knowledge paradigms and
their Western epistemologies—which he collectively labels as
Orientalism—and links them with imperialism. These Western
paradigms and epistemologies are invested in various forms and
modes of representation, writes Said, including films, paintings,
journalism narratives, and art. In his analysis of textual representations of the Orient, Said clarifies that "in any instance of at
least written language, there is no such thing as delivered presence, but a re-presence, or a representation. The value, efficacy,
strength, apparent veracity of a written statement about the
Orient therefore relies very little on the Orient itself" (p. 33). For
Said, Orientalism perpetuates an image of the East that determines and re-asserts Europe's understanding and justification
of its territorial accumulations. Moreover, "European culture
gained in strength and identity by setting itself off against the
Orient as a sort of surrogate and even underground self" (p. 31).
In Said's view, the Orient's attempts at self-authentication have
become problematic due to the West's hegemonic discursive practices beginning with the 18th century and especially since the In-
dustrial Revolution. More insidiously, the imperialistic gaze that
has coexisted with the growth of Eurocentric epistemologies has
been internalized by the non-Western Others to such a degree

that there is a real danger that the East's perception of itself has been permanently altered. Not unlike hooks (1994, p. 211) who, in her preference for the use of the term "white supremacy" over "racism," gives herself room to critique the complicity of black people in the pervasive institutional structures that maintain their second-class status in the U.S., postcolonial theorists like Said have commented on the effects of Euro-American constructions of the former colonies on the self-images of individuals and societies so defined.

Orientalism's epistemological challenges to colonial and imperial hegemonic discourse have compelled a whole body of work taking into account the impact of colonialism on immigrant and diasporic experiences, especially in the works of scholars like Bhabha (1994) who have initiated research in mimicry, complicity, and hybridity. In his analysis, Bhabha stresses the interdependence and mutuality of subjectivities that mark the relations between the colonizer and the colonized. Particularly thought-provoking is his analysis of mimicry as a process by which the colonial subject mimics colonial authority and is "at once resemblance and menace" (p. 11). Mimicry subverts the colonizer because, Bhabha argues, it becomes a threat or menace to colonial authority, and it highlights the colonial subjects' differences from the colonizer. This double-edged aspect of mimicry —as in the idea of the "brown-skinned Englishman" eloquently fictionalized in Naipaul's novel (1967), The *Mimic Men*—both challenges and resists dominant colonial political, epistemological, and cultural powers.

Beyond Bhabha, scholars like Anthony Appiah, Henry Louis Gates, Inderpal Grewal, bell hooks, Ketu Katrak, Trinh T. Minh-ha, Chandra Talapade Mohanty, Jose David Saldivar, Sara Suleri, and Gauri Vishwanathan also manifested a postcolonial awareness and focused their scholarship on race, immigration, ethnicity, economic displacement, and challenges to bourgeois white feminism. In the humanities, influenced by Said's work, we have seen the maturation of the field of postcolonial studies with several anthologies and books, prominent such as Ashcroft, Griffiths, and Tiffin's (1995) *Postcolonial Studies Reader and the Empire Writes Back;* Cooper, Chrisman, Brennan, and Menon's (2005) *Postcolonial Studies and Beyond*; Gandhi's (2001) *Postcolonial Theory;* (2003) *Postcolonial Criticism;* Young's (2001)

Postcolonialism; and Williams and Chrisman's (1994) *Colonial Discourse / Postcolonial Theory.*

In the United States, the focus of postcolonial theorists has been on the experiences of immigration, diasporic identity, and cultural and political borderlands (Singh and Schmidt, 2000). Understanding American national identity had historically been focused exclusively on color-line (particularly in the influential works of Frederick Jackson Turner and W. E. B. Du Bois) and the Western frontier but is now taking a more global character. The recent incursion of scholars of color has shaped the study of ethnicity, race, and borderlands and lead to a significant rise in transnational exchanges of ideas on how exilic or diasporic consciousness poses a challenge to traditional nation-state narratives of identity and majority-minority dichotomies. In this context, Du Bois' (1906 p. 22) concept of "double consciousness" has been expanded and metatheorized by postcolonial studies scholars to accommodate the vast amalgam of immigrant, diasporic, and racial identities that it attempts to empower.

Postcolonial theorists have also sought to develop a critical understanding of globalization and the way it impacts local, regional, and provincial identity practices in terms of the dynamics of power. As argued in the works of scholars like Friedman (1982), Fukuyama (2006), and Sachs (1993), globalization does not merely open up world markets and impel straightforward laissez-faire economies, but somehow, necessitates democracy. A postcolonial analysis of power relations can show that multinational capital profitably and cleverly aligns itself with local elites to reinforce preglobalization inequalities in a society and market and to justify new present inequalities. Contemporary capitalism can both undermine and reinforce national hegemonies and the structural economic, political, and cultural divisions within nation-states. Pointedly refuting the *telos* of mere economic globalization, postcolonial scholars like Appadurai (1990, p. 18) have postulated that "new" ethnicities are produced in and by transnational and diasporic sites that appropriate older models of nationalism, that are historically situated within the experiences of colonialism (whether Western or Ottoman). Moreover, these new ethnicities can counter nation-centered narratives of identity. Older rhetorics of identity politics and racial affiliations, do not disappear, but take on new meanings and require new modes of understanding in the new global order.

Being a South Asian Woman and Practicing Postcolonialism in the Academy

During the last 200 years, due largely to the geographic influence of the British Empire, South Asians migrated (in some cases, taken as indentured laborers) to many parts of the world. As a result, the South Asian diaspora is incredibly vast. Many South Asians living in the United States have an established history in countries such as Fiji, Kenya, Uganda, British Guyana, South Africa, Trinidad and Tobago, Jamaica, Canada, England, and Australia. While some South Asians, in particular small groups of Sikh and Muslim farmers, arrived in the U.S. in the early 1900s and settled on the West Coast, the majority arrived in the past 40 years.

A beneficial effect of the American Civil Rights movements of the 1950s and 1960s was the passing of the Hart-Celler Immigration Bill in 1965. The Act changed the history, demographics, and political and cultural life of the United States. Prior to 1965, admission to the country was largely dependent upon an immigrant's country of birth. 70% of all immigration slots were allotted to only three countries—the United Kingdom, Ireland, and Germany. Most of these slots remained unused, while there were long waiting lists for the small number of visas available to those born in Italy, Greece, Poland, and elsewhere. The 1965 Immigration Act eliminated the nationality quota system and substituted it with a more humane family-reunification and skills-based system.

In the 1920s, more than 80% of the people migrating to the United States came from Europe By the 1970s, there was a steady stream of immigration from South Asian. By the 1990s, 39% of immigrants to the United States came from South Asia which includes India, Pakistan, Bangladesh, Nepal Bhutan, Sri Lanka, Burma, and the Maldives. The Immigration and Reform Act of 1986 eased the requirements for South Asians to receive work visas, particularly in the technology industry, and to enter the country as foreign students. According to the United States census data, between 1990 and 2000, the Bangladeshi population increased by 385%, Pakistani by 151%, and Indian by 133%.

While many South Asians have found employment in service industries (especially immigrants from Bangladesh and Pakistan, who have lower English language proficiency), the influx of South Asian students has allowed for their presence to be felt in academic institutions. Although no exact numbers exist, South Asians constitute about 3% of academic faculty positions with the highest representation in science and engineering disciplines (Institute of International Education, 2006). The Humanities and Social Sciences have not historically seen a large number of South Asian graduate students and faculty members, though the trend is definitely changing. Since 2001, the number of Indians on American campuses have come to comprise more than 15% of the total international student body (Institute of International Education, 2006). The increasing presence of South Asians as immigrants and in American higher education opened the door for changes that were to follow and would impact my own presence in the American academy.

Can a South Asian Woman Speak?

Reading postcolonial critiques of Eurocentric ideologies and representations by Said and other scholars has helped me understand my position as a marginalized and minority intellectual and, most inspiringly, has helped me *speak again*. I had to rediscover my voice through practicing postcolonial scholarship and teaching. The title of this section is a take on South Asian feminist and postcolonial writer Gayatri Chakrabarty Spivak's influential essay, "Can the Subaltern Speak?" (1994, p. 66). As Spivak's work has testified, feminist and postcolonial discourses have had several overlapping trajectories. Both discourses have sought to decenter the hegemonic and recuperate the marginalized, both open possibilities of rereading canonical texts and subverting patriarchal cultural forms, and both are practical in their orientation in seeking social justice. Within this juncture exist bifurcations that problematize feminist studies, especially the issue of authority and who has the right to speak for and against minority women. In her paradigmatic essay, "Under Western Eyes: Feminist Scholarship and Colonial Discourses," Mohanty has critiqued Western feminist writings that "discursively colonize the materials and historical heterogeneities of the lives of women in the third world, thereby producing/re-presenting a composite, singular 'Third World Woman'—an image which appears arbitrarily constructed, but nevertheless carries with it the authorizing signature of Western humanist discourse" (1991, p. 52). What, then, is the specific pivotal point of ethnic self-reflection for South Asian women? Spivak has addressed this question forcefully.

In her academic work, which has historically focused on comparative literature, Spivak appropriates the Gramscian term "subaltern" because it could flexibly accommodate social identities and struggles (such as the woman and colonized) that did not fall under reductive terms such as *class*. Spivak uses the term *subaltern* to describe people who are invisible to colonial and Third World national-bourgeois historiography alike. She is especially preoccupied by subsistence farmers, unorganized labor, tribal societies, and communities of workers on the streets or in the countryside. In particular, her analysis is directed at the location of the female subaltern, whom she describes as doubly marginalized by virtue of relative economic disadvantage and gender subordination.

In the essay "Can the subaltern speak?" Spivak equates 20th century French intellectuals such as Michel Foucault and Gilles Deleuze with self-righteous British colonialists who "spoke" for the disenfranchised native women who needed to be saved from the "barbaric" practice of Hindu widow sacrifice or Sati in 19th century India. The point of this juxtaposition was to emphasize how benevolent, radical Western intellectuals can paradoxically silence subalterns by claiming to represent and speak for their experiences. Spivak argues that despite the intellectual energy Foucault and Deleuze invest in showing how subjects are constructed through discourse and representation, when it comes to discussing real, historical examples of social and political struggles, Foucault and Deleuze (like many Western intellectual theorists) fall back on a model of representation in which the oppressed subjects' voices are marginalized.

Within South Asian history, Spivak concludes that "the subaltern cannot speak" because the voice and agency of subaltern women are so embedded in Hindu patriarchal codes of moral conduct and the British colonial representation of subaltern women as victims of the savagery of Hindu culture that their voices are impossible to recover. Spivak's discussions of disempowered subaltern women serve to highlight the limitations of applying European theories to the lives and histories of disempowered women in the Third World. "Can the Subaltern Speak?" has been read as illustrating Spivak's own position as a postcolonial intellectual who is concerned to excavate the silenced voices of the past from the political context of the present. Spivak does not offer any perfect solutions or theoretical formulas for emancipating subaltern women but rather exposes the limited and potentially harmful effects of speaking for marginalized groups. Her articulation of the shifting and complex location of the subaltern and her critique of Western feminist theory and colonial representation helped me sift through my academic political location as I began to ask a version of her essay's title question: I wondered, within the U.S. and global academy, "Can the South Asian woman speak?"

When I first read Spivak's essay in 1988 as a required reading for a graduate school seminar (The essay was originally published in 1985), I was struck by Spivak's delineation of her own location as a postcolonial intellectual. In asking the question, "Can the South Asian woman speak?", the answer remains for me as complicated as the question. Spivak asserts that one cannot use general terms such as "woman" or "worker" to simplistically categorize experiences. Therefore, our experiences cannot be read through ethnic, class, racial, or gendered prisms alone. I must here recount some of my experiences in graduate school which was not only my first entry point into the American academic world but also helped shape my perspective towards teaching and researching postcolonial theory.

I grew up in Delhi, India, in an upper-middle class home in a well-educated family. My father was part of the first group of Indian students recruited and sent for engineering training to Germany after India's independence in 1947. He finished his Ph.D. from Heidelberg University—then called Heidelberg Technical Institute—and returned to India in 1960 to work for the American company Union Carbide. My mother was one of the first women to receive an M.D. from Dhaka University and started her medical practice in post-independence Calcutta. My parents were upper-caste Brahmins but their marriage was not arranged, as was customary in those days, and they came from different ethnic backgrounds. My father was from South India and his mother tongue was Telegu. My mother came from East Bengal and spoke Bengali. My brother and I grew up in a highly secular, cosmopolitan, but nevertheless strictly gendered world.

I had the privilege of attending an all-girls school called Lady Irwin School, named after Lady Dorothy Onslow Irwin, the wife of the British Viceroy of India in the 1920s, Lord Irwin.

The school was located in a beautiful and wealthy neighborhood in New Delhi, lined with old deodar trees, called Canning Lane (named for another British viceroy, Charles Canning). It was an English-medium school where academic instruction was conducted in English, although we took required Hindi and Bengali language courses. Although my education took place in an elite setting, early in my life, it had been made clear to me that most of the resources of the household would go towards my brother's upbringing and education. When my brother decided to attend graduate school, first in the UK and then in the United States, my parents invested much of their savings in his education. A few years later, when it was my turn to make plans to go to College, my parents had little money to pay for my education.

I had watched my brother struggle with his applications to Ivy League Colleges and seen him spend hundreds of dollars applying to places like Brown, Yale, and Princeton—which sounded exotic and distant. I was mesmerized at the bulky application packets that arrived from these far-off places; life in these colleges seemed lavish in color photographs of Tudor-style buildings, students blissfully walking past brightly-colored fall trees, and students smilingly working on computers (which were, in the early 1980s, a luxury for most of us in India). But the numbers listed at the back of catalogs made my eyes pop: $15,000 every year to attend Brown and a whopping $18,000 for a year at Columbia. During my first visit to the United States Education Foundation office in Delhi, which is a federally-funded clearing house for international students interested in education in the United States, I asked the woman at the front desk if she could suggest "the cheapest school possible" for me. Thus, during the Fall of 1986, I applied to schools such as University of Southern Illinois at Edwardsville, Clarion University of Pennsylvania, and California State University at Stanislaus. I paid application and testing fees mostly from my savings from having worked odd jobs during my undergraduate college years.

When I finally enrolled for the Ph.D. program at University of Massachusetts, the only College to offer me financial assistance, I was thoroughly unprepared for the racial and gender politics of graduate school at an American university. South Asian feminist writer Alexander (1999, p. 23) observes: "The questions that are asked in the street, of my identity, mold me…Appearing in flesh, I am cast afresh, a female of color—skin color, hair texture, clothing, speech, all marking me in ways that I could scarcely have conceived of." As Algerian writer and political activist Frantz Fanon had discovered while walking in a white Paris, I soon found myself "marked" (and remarked upon) by my sudden "difference" from others. I often experienced the deep emotional dissonance as an immigrant who spoke English with an accent, a woman whose parents had little money to offer for her education, and a woman untrained to speak in a competitive classroom. Hegde (2004, p. 156) writes, "As I talk to my friends in the South Asian community, I notice how our social locations are marked not only by the sudden loss of familiarity but by continuous reminders of one's status as the foreigner; the outsider; or the other."

I did not always understand the cultural cues; when a white male faculty member and a young white female graduate student would flirt openly, I did not understand the full implications of such dynamics and what effect it had on me. The classroom was an intimidating environment. For someone who had attended an all-girls school and later a women's college, where (as is typical in Indian education) one stood up in deference every time a professor walked in or out of the classroom and maintained a strict distance between oneself and teachers, the mixed-gender setting was difficult to adjust to. The style of instruction was equally disconcerting. The American system was both mysterious and appallingly abrasive. American students would interrupt professors and sometimes address them disrespectfully; I would hear professors joke in the class and talk about their personal lives. Whenever a male teacher and female student would openly flirt in class and in the hallways, I felt desperately uncomfortable.

As a student, I couldn't get a good grade, however hard I worked, despite my being one of the few students in the department who, at the time of her graduation, had already published research articles. I had no teacher who was a woman of color or South Asian in those years. Early on, I realized that middle-class white men were particularly hostile toward my presence in the academy. I was not surprised when one of them mentioned to me that I had little to worry about finding a job because of "affirmative action." He was ignorant that as a foreigner with a non-immigrant visa, I did not technically qualify as an affirmative action candidate. If white men were openly hostile, white female faculty members and peers often conspired against women of color in order to consolidate their precarious state within the hierarchical academic system. A fellow student whom I had seen suffer through severe depression and several nervous break-downs, and who was never being able to fully participate in the department's life, returned after her oral comprehensive exam defense to tell me that she had "passed with distinction." I too had passed, but no one had mentioned the word distinction, only that they had been surprised as to how much I wrote in the few hours I had; certainly the volume of writing did not qualify me for distinction.

When I decided to pursue teaching jobs in the American academy, one faculty member, a white woman, wrote me a nega-tive letter of recommendation, which I discovered only after a South Asian friend working in the career services alerted me. I had done well in her class, and she had often confided in me about her experiences of being marginalized in the department as a woman. I had sympathized with her. I could not fathom her motives for writing a negative letter, or her attempts to sabotage my career. I dealt with these cultural shocks and moments of alienation by remaining silent, especially in classes. I had never been a quiet person before moving to the United States. As a girl, I had often been sent to the principal's office for "talking too much" and my mother regularly reprimanded me for "talking back." I can count on my fingers the few times I spoke during my five years of graduate schooling. Visweswaran (1994, p. 69) observes:

> Gayatri Spivak has asked the question "Can the sub-altern speak?" and answered with an unequivocal no. Speech has, of course, been seen as the privileged cata-lyst of agency: lack of speech as the absence of agency. How then we might destabilize the equation of speech with agency by staging one woman's subject refusal as a refusal to speak?

Following the logic of Spivak's argument, Visweswaran challeng-es the equation of speech with agency and suggests that the si-lence of the subaltern could be interpreted as a refusal to speak in the dominant terms of political representation. While mine was not a conscious act of destabilizing the representational pol-itics of graduate school pedagogy, Spivak's question of "Can the subaltern speak?" became relevant for the first time on multiple levels: I had *become* a subaltern. The silence was to become an important pedagogical lesson for me as a teacher. I have since been cognizant of the fact that "talking" alone does not imply a student's ability to address and analyze deeper epistemological questions. Similarly, I do not equate a silent student with one who lacks critical thinking or is disengaged.

Within the first few months of having arrived in the United States, I had read Friedan's (1963) *The Feminist Mystique*. My first encounter with feminism moved me. Friedan's ability to articulate the various historical contexts that shaped the biological signifier of being "female" impressed me, but I could not relate to the experiences of white middle-class American women. Spivak and postcolonial feminist critiques of Western feminist theory spoke to me during those turbulent years. The works of South Asian writers like Partha Chatterjee, Mrinalini Sinha, Jenny Sharpe, Gayatri Spivak, and Sara Suleri helped me recognize the subalternization of nonwhite women by colonialism and whiteness.

A woman of color, unlike her white counterpart, these authors argued, was marked "doubly other" by her race and sex (Suleri, 1992, p. 756). Echoes of this dilemma resounded in Suleri's (p. 761) urgent observation that there was no available dichotomy that could redefine postcoloniality as necessarily sharing "feminism's most vocal articulation of marginality, or the obsessive attention it had recently paid to the racial body." In "Can the subaltern speak?" Spivak unmasks attempts of Western ontology to *create* the native informant and examine postcolonial women's experiences within their specific historical and material contexts rather than as extensions or minor illustrations of Western feminist theories. In postcolonial critiques of Western feminism I found the explanations of my day-to-day experiences in graduate school. I developed the *consciousness of identity* as a South Asian woman through the process of migration and through my gendered and racial location. I could have easily become despondent and returned to my parents' home in India. Instead, I stayed and found a way to speak.

When (and Where) Can the South Asian Woman Speak: Teaching Postcolonial Theory

When I first started my teaching job, I began to understand the privilege of being in the classroom as a teacher, particularly as someone who could control both the classroom's curriculum and the way students are taught. I increasingly began to reflect on my own location as a South Asian immigrant, a member of a growing diaspora, and a woman of color in the classroom. The first step I took was not to shy away from addressing the questions that postcolonial theory posed for the humanities and social sciences. I encourage students to critique the intellectual spectrum that produces the dominant discourses of multiculturalism; to understand the shifting terrains of dominance and resistance; to "read" the significance of race, class, gender, and sexuality; to understand the "new world order" as historically situated; and to analyze the enduring ideal of nation and varied forms of nationalisms. In my undergraduate classes such as "Media Culture and Society," "Global Media and Communication," and "Media and Popular Culture," I integrate the issues of postcolonial theory into wide-ranging topics. For instance, in the syllabus for the course "Media and Popular Culture," I write:

> When one studies culture politically one has to look at the various political elements of culture and the cultural industries. In this regard, race, gender, class, sexual orientation, national origin, and ethnicity become defining elements of media representations...

In "Media and Popular Culture," I teach a difficult article by Henry Yu (2005, p. 197) titled "How Tiger Woods Lost his Stripes," which focuses on global capitalism, consumer culture, and the articulations of race framed within cultural and national differences and transnational connections (one of the key analyses provided by postcolonial theorists). In discussing this article, I encourage students to understand the complexities of human migration and intermingling and question older classifications of race as used in media rhetoric. In teaching Yu's and similar articles, I don't shy away from some of the thorny issues of multiculturalism, the flawed concept of pinning ethnic origins (Yu cleverly questions our categorization of Tiger Woods as an African American when he writes that Woods is "a quarter Chinese on the father's side, plus a quarter Chinese and a half Thai on the mother's side, for a total of one-half Asian in Tiger, versus only half African American on the father's side, for a quarter black in Tiger"), and questioning race as a biological category represented by and in individuals.

Theoretical questions aside, I tried not to replicate the same classroom dynamics that I encountered in graduate school. It was important for me to be sensitive to the dynamics of majority and minority voices in a classroom setting. I encouraged participation of students from a range of political perspectives, some significantly different from my own and others in the class. In one of my classes, for instance, I ask students to write questions about the readings they do (it is the questions that are graded, not the answers). In the class, I call upon individual students to ask their questions to the rest of the class. Such an activity allows for more cooperative learning where students are less likely to feel cornered for saying the "wrong" answers. The challenge for teachers teaching postcolonial theory is to encourage students to think and critique the language and terminology of colonialism and oppression as well as to avoid students' feeling disempowered in the classroom where the teacher is perceived as an authorial figure.

In a world where one is painfully aware of being different, a persistent ambivalence surrounds many South Asian women as inhabiting the borderlands or the realm "in between." Such feelings of alienation and dislocation as a South Asian woman student and postcolonial scholar have made me enduringly conscious not only of my "otherness," but also my privilege of having been brought up in a multicultural, multiethnic, and gendered society and having seen alternatives in my travels around the world. I try to remember that each student must find his/her voice, as I did, and that education can shape a search into debilitating struggles *and* euphoric openings into new worlds.

As a teacher and student, my most satisfying experiences have revolved around the powerful impression that, in the strange spell of a discussion or lecture, it is possible to see the world differently. I continue to believe that it is possible to think outside our sphere of ideas, habits, and rituals. In this sense, my teaching philosophy is akin to what West (1993, p. 98) describes as the "teaching of philosophy," which demands an "awakening" and a belief that every time a teacher stands up in front of the classroom, she can impact the world of our students in profound ways.

In every class I have taught, I assume that all students are capable of managing the most critical, complex, and difficult intellectual labor. This means that I prefer not to "dumb down" instructional materials. I, therefore, assume and expect a level of intellectual rigor from each student without judging his or her history and from where they arrived in the classroom. The best classes that I ever took as a student were those in which teachers were not afraid to take responsibility for their materials. I was thrilled to find professors who would undertake their own readings, which were inevitably more passionate, and ones that empowered students to raise objections and to begin to read "for themselves."

One has to learn to be able to "speak" for oneself as I did as a South Asian woman, a woman of color, a figure of authority in the classroom, and a postcolonial intellectual and critic. Maggio (2007) rephrases Spivak's question to ask, "Can the subaltern be heard?" He argues that limits of the Western discourse to speak of and about disparate cultures and experiences can be overcome and that "a dialogue with the subaltern can be opened with an emphasis on both speaking and listening." In my teaching career, I feel particularly privileged to have been given the space to "speak" by a college willing to hire me on a tenure-track position and promoting me to full professor and for having been "listened" to by colleagues open to intellectual plurality and students open to pedagogical diversity.

Researching Postcolonial Theory in Communication Studies

My challenge as a new faculty member in the early 1990s was also to establish a scholarly record in my discipline. While my home institution did not require a substantial research record to be granted tenure, the requirements asked for "new contributions to the discipline." Communication Studies as a discipline did not have an established history of interdisciplinary and critical research when I started graduate school, but within a few years, I was in the midst of sea changes: the U.S. Civil rRghts Movement, global decolonization efforts, migration and mobility of populations, and the rise of multinational corporations began to influence a number of intellectual movements in the academy and strikingly challenged the paradigms of the previous generations. In Communication Studies, suddenly scholars were studying feminist and poststructural theory, doing critical ethnography in audience studies, and examining the advent of studies in media globalization, with new questions about nation and ethnic nationalisms. In one of the first published critiques of the Communication Studies "canon" Shome (1996, p. p. 43) reexamined the discipline in relation to issues such as imperialism, neocolonialism, and race and suggested "unlearning" a lot of the older rhetorical and Communication theory traditions and to evaluate critically the kinds of knowledge that have been (and continue to be) "privileged, legitimated, and displaced" and the configurations of sociopolitical and racial interests that are thus served. My own research in postcolonial theory, similar to Shome's work, was increasingly welcomed by a number of journal editors who published the articles with a realization of the significance of expanding the Communication Studies canon at that historical moment.

By the mid-1990s, a group of South Asian postcolonial scholars like Sanjay Asthana, Radhika Gajjala, Dilip Gaonkar, Radha Hegde, Satish Kolluri, Divya McMillan, Radhika Parameswaran, Hemant Shah, Raka Shome, myself, and others emerged. We came to Communication Studies academic conventions armed with the new knowledge of postcolonial theory which gradually began to change the complexion of the discipline. We organized and participated in panels and took over chairpersonships of various committees, which allowed for greater visibility of postcolonial theory's contribution to the discipline. *Communication Theory*, one of the most significant and selective journals in Communication, published a special issue titled "Postcolonial Approaches to Communication"; National Communication and International Communication Associations began to recognize the influence of critical theory on communication, including postcolonial theory, and started publishing a range of new journals like *Critical Discourse Studies* and *Communication, Culture, and Critique*.

Such celebration also came with the recognition that the battle for South Asian scholars continue, in and outside of the classroom, and in integrating postcolonial theory into traditional disciplines. There continues to be a need for more studies focusing on transnational cultural exchange within and among specific ethnic groups, the comparative history of ideas of nationalism within particular racial/ethnic groups, histories of South Asian feminism, and development of a critical history of contemporary theories of globalization. Other difficult issues remain: South Asians are hardly a unified cultural group in the Indian subcontinent, much less in Asia, except perhaps under the colonial gaze. As their presence expands in and outside the American academy, do such diasporas have the capacity to develop their own brand of elitism based on caste, gender, and class? The task for scholars in postcolonial theory remains to analyze the texts, discourses, absences, and silences that construct complex social relations to ultimately undertake the collective project of social justice in the "new" global order. Our work is just beginning.

References

Alexander, M. (1999). *The shock of arrival: Reflections on the postcolonial experience.* San Francisco: A. K. Press.

Appadurai, A. (1990). Disjuncture and difference in the global cultural economy. *Public Culture, 2*(2), 1-23.

Ashcroft, B., Griffiths, G., & Tiffin H. (Eds.). (1995). *Post-colonial studies reader.* London: Routledge.

Ashcroft, B., Griffiths, G., & Tiffin, H. (1989). *The empire writes back: Theory and practice in post-colonial literature.* London: Routledge.

Bhabha, H. (1994). *The location of culture.* New York: Routledge.

Cooper, F., Chrisman, L., Brennan, T., & Menon, N. (Eds.). (2005). *Postcolonial studies and beyond.* Durham, NC: Duke University Press.

Du Bois, W. E. B. (1906/). *The souls of Black folks.* Valley City, UT: Walking Lion Press.

Friedan, B. (1963). *The feminine mystique.* New York: Norton.

Friedman, M. (1982). *Capitalism and freedom.* Chicago: University of Chicago Press.

Fukuyama, F. (2006). *The end of history and the last man.* New York: Free Press.

Gandhi, L. (2001). *Postcolonial theory: A critical introduction.* New York: Columbia University Press.

Harrison, N. (2003). *Postcolonial criticism: History, theory, and the work of fiction*. Malden, MA: Blackwell.

Hegde, R. (2004). Hybrid revivials: Ethnicity and South Asian celebration. In A. Gonzalez, M. Houston & V. Chen (Eds.), *Our voices: Essays in culture, ethnicity and communication* (pp. 153-158). Los Angeles: Roxbury.

hooks, b. (1994). *Outlaw culture: Resisting representations*. New York: Routledge.

Institute of International Education Report (2006). *New enrollment for foreign students climb*. Retrieved October 11, 2008, from http://opendoors.iienetwork.org/?p=89251

Maggio, J. (2007). *Can The Subaltern Be Heard? A (re)examination of Spivak*. In Southern Political Science Association Conference publication. Retrieved November 8, 2008, from www.allacademic.com/meta/p143726_index.html

Mohanty, C. T. (Eds.). (1991). Under Western eyes: Feminist scholarship and colonial discourses. In C. T. Mohanty, A. Russo, & L. Torres (Eds.), *Third world women and the politics of feminism* (pp. 51-80). Bloomington, IN: Indiana University Press.

Naipaul, V. S. (1967). *The mimic men: A novel*. New York: Vintage.

Sachs, J. (1993). *Macroeconomics in the Global Economy*. New York: Prentice Hall.

Said, E. (1978). *Orientalism*. New York: Vintage.

Shome, R (1996). Postcolonial interventions in the rhetorical canon: An 'other' view. *Communication Theory, 1*,. 40-59.

Singh, A., & Schmidt, P. (2000). On the border between U.S. studies and postcolonial theory. In A. Singh & P. Schmidt (Eds.), *Postcolonial theory and the United States* (pp. 2-46). Oxford, MS: University of Mississippi Press.

Spivak, G. C. (1994). Can the subaltern speak? In P. and L. Chrisman (Ed.), *Colonial discourse/postcolonial theory* (pp. 66-111). New York: Columbia University Press.

Suleri, S. (1992). Woman skin deep: Feminism and the postcolonial condition, *Critical Inquiry, 18*, 756-769.

Visweswaran, K. (1994). *Fictions of feminist ethnography*. Minneapolis: University of Minnesota Press.

West, C. (1993). *Beyond eurocentrism and multiculturalism*. Monroe, ME: Common Courage Press.

Williams, P., & Chrisman L. (Eds.). (1994). *Colonial discourse/ postcolonial theory*. New York: Columbia University Press.

Young, R. J. C. (2001). *Postcolonialism: A historical introduction*. Malden, MA: Blackwell.

Yu, H. (2005). How Tiger Woods lost his stripes: Post-nationalist American studies as a history of race, migration and a commodification of culture. In R. Gines & O. Z. Cruz (Eds.), *Popular culture: A reader* (pp. 197-209). London: Sage.

Leadership from the Bottom:
A Case Study of the Women of Matlaquiahuitl

xxxxxxxxxxxxxxxxxxxxxxxxxxxxxxxxxxxxxxxxxxxxxxxxxxxxxxxxxxxxxxxxxxxxxxx

Martha Bárcenas-Mooradian
Pitzer College

The invisible women of Matlaquiahuitl are the grandmothers, mothers and daughters that get up at 4:00 am to grind the corn, prepare the masa (corn dough), and make tortillas for the family. They are the women who at dawn make fresh coffee with chili on winter days. They can be found behind the comal (rustic stove) preparing bean soup for the family and carrying buckets of water from a precarious spring for use in the kitchen or to give the kids a bath. They are the women who harvest the coffee in tenates (baskets) that carry 20 kg or more. The women of Matlaquiahuitl have a pleasant smile and a simple disposition. They have accepted their poverty and their fate as women, although they hope for a better future for their children and grandchildren. They have not yet been given the opportunity to vocalize their thoughts and dreams. Through this chapter they hope that their voices can be heard outside of their community.

Hidden Leadership

The story of the women of Matlaquiahuitl has important implications for leadership roles in developing and postcolonial societies, as well as underserved communities in developed nations that face economic and political disenfranchisement. In the case of Mexico and many other postcolonial societies, ethnicity, gender, politics, and religion, create a context for women's lives that makes them third-class citizens, not only as women, but also as indigenous/mestizo persons in a rigidly stratified social order. The roles that the women of Matlaquiahuitl play within their community exemplify some of the many shapes that leadership can take, especially for persons excluded from formal leadership roles within structured hierarchies.

The women whose voices will be heard in this piece manage to make contributions to the leadership of their community despite the hardship they endure and the difficult conditions they face. They do so by virtue of their roles as both economic and cultural actors who participate in virtually all facets of community life. Although their pervasive, though quiet, agency might be underestimated and underappreciated, the women carry with them an integrative knowledge of their community's economic and social system, which allows them to take informal leadership roles in key decision-making functions. Informally, but effectively, they use this knowledge to preserve and transform their community in the face of broader social disruptions such as unemployment and migration.

Before I discuss the leadership roles that the women of Matlaquiahuitl are increasingly assuming in their community, I will provide a brief description of various conditions that affect this community and that directly affect their situation. Geographically, the community has no easy access due to the mountainous terrain and precarious roads. Politically, the community is situated on the border of two municipalities, one more affluent than the other. Historically, the villagers have lost track of their own origins, having only vague information about great-grandmothers and great-grandfathers coming from the state of Puebla. Culturally, many traditions are directly shaped by the Catholic Church, whose presence is materialized in two big churches, strategically located to serve the villagers of the two municipalities. Linguistically, the Náhuatl language, once spoken by the founders, has been lost. Ethnically, members of the community are either indigenous or mestizo.

Matlaquiahuitl is a rural community of 450 inhabitants located in the mountains of Eastern Mexico, or Sierra del Gallego, at 1250 meters above sea level, in the state of Veracruz. This community is fairly close to the City of Córdoba (20 km), but the poor roads and difficult terrain make it approximately a two-hour drive on a rural bus, which is the only means of transportation available. The geographic location of this community allows for a variety of ecosystems to subsist and for a range of agricultural practices to be employed. A recent study has shown (Bárcenas, 2008) that Matlaquiahuitl was a sustainable community that inherited an ecological-friendly conscience, which allowed the community members to survive for over a century with the resources available in their environment. Matlaquiahuitl, however, is at risk of losing its traditional way of living as globalization reaches its enclave.

Main road dividing municipal jurisdiction
Photograph courtesy of author

The villagers have accumulated a great deal of empirical knowledge of the region. Their agricultural practices allow them to eat what they grow: beans, corn, chilis, various vegetables, coffee and citrus fruits. Livestock is limited to a few chickens per family and a couple of goats for milk (especially for the children) in certain cases. To improve their economy, the villagers travel to nearby towns to sell their produce. This has been the only way to bring in revenue. In general, the inhabitants of this community have survived in their natural environment due to their closeness to nature and immense respect for it.

Younger generations are leaving the village to find better opportunities in nearby cities, mainly in positions of domestic service or as low-paid manual labor. Interaction with the outside world is visibly transforming some customs, traditionally respected by all members of the community, such as ways of dressing and speaking. The native language, for example, has also been lost, possibly by this interaction.

Matlaquiahuitl is underserved in areas such as healthcare, education, transportation, roads, potable water, drainage, law enforcement and trash collection. A medical clinic is open once a week with one or two doctors and one or two nurses attending. In the event of an emergency, the closest clinic is in the city of Córdoba, where inhabitants can be treated using universal health insurance (*Secretaria de Salubridad y Asistencia*). However, many inhabitants cannot afford to travel to Córdoba. Because of educational policies requiring certain numbers of students, Matlaquiahuitl does not have a middle school. Children who attend middle school (age 12 to 15 years old) need to walk for at least 3 km to the nearest community, Guzmantla, to attend a *tele-secundaria* (middle school via TV with an instructor as a guide). The road is not paved, and it presents some difficulties for the children, especially during the rainy season and the winter. Because of this, many children drop out of school at a very early age and instead join the workforce. Most of the children will never attend high school. According to parents, the educational level is very low, in large part because of the lack of teachers and resources. As will be seen in the conversations below, these conditions add to the plight of the women as they struggle to bring change to their communities. (See Stephen, 1992 for a more general history of women's struggles in Mexico.)

Conversations

The women of Matlaquiahuitl volunteered to speak when informally approached, while, coincidentally, the head of the family, (the husband, son, or nephew) was absent. The conversations took place while the women were cooking for their children, getting the bath ready for their children, breastfeeding their babies, making tortillas and bean soup for me (the visitor) or feeding the animals. All the women freely accepted to share their stories as long as they would remain anonymous. Below I present one narrative that is representative of the voices of the women of Matlaquiahuitl which brings to light the foundational leadership roles they play in maintaining the equilibrium of a small community in which ethnicity, social class, education and gender define the individual. None of them consider themselves leaders; however, it is because of their invigorating participation in the community that Matlaquiahuitl has been able to function despite the enormous challenges it faces. As I will indicate in my concluding analysis, this participation has positioned the women to play significant though informal leadership roles.

A typical kitchen. Tortillas are the staple of Matlaquiahuitl's diet. *Photograph courtesy of author*

"Men and women should be equal"

For most women in Matlaquiahuitl, the day starts at dawn when the roosters sing. And without hesitation, the routine of every day emanates from the household under the direction of the women. All the women recognize the same list of unending chores: making coffee from scratch, preparing the *nixtamal* (first stage of corn masa) to make tortillas, carrying water in buckets from the spring, washing clothes; watching the children, helping in the harvest of corn and coffee, taking the children to school, picking them up, selling the produce in nearby cities, participating in church activities, helping in the school, taking care of the sick and needy, feeding the chickens, and on and on.

All agree that there is poverty; however, everyone finds happiness in the family, their children, and their partners. Riches do not give love, they say. Women become mothers at an early age (estimated at 15 or earlier), and the unions with their partners are said to last for many years, influenced by Catholic beliefs. Most women know what it is to have a miscarriage or to lose a young baby. They all agree that the clinic is not sufficient for their needs, as it is open for only a few hours once a week. Most women deliver their children in their own homes. Children are considered a blessing but also an impediment to participating in other activities. Most husbands are not supportive, with a few exceptions. There are some cases of abusive relationships. The most important role for the women is to be mothers and to guide their children to become good people. Many women would love to have more children, but due to the economic crisis they are refraining from having more. Women feel respected by their children, especially their sons. In general, women believe they are respected in their own community.

Women claim that the daily tasks are divided by gender and that, for example, men do not participate in the rearing of their children (with a few exceptions). Nevertheless, women, when need calls, take on men's tasks as well. This simple fact of carrying double duty limits the choices women have with respect to their own well-being. They wait patiently for their children to grow up, and they look forward to the times when they will be liberated from the demands that the community sets on them. Even girls as young as nine take their mothers' roles when the mothers have to be absent. Women work in the fields alongside their male companions; however, it would be rare to see a man grinding the corn in the *metate* (grinding stone) or making tortillas.

"There is no other option but to migrate"

More recently, many women have been seeing their children (some as young as fourteen) leave the village in search of better job opportunities. Some have left for nearby cities, others have traveled to Northern states, and others have migrated to the United States. Approximately ten young children have left in the last five years, something unheard of in the past. Those children are now contributing financially to the family household. At the writing of this chapter, more adult men are traveling or considering traveling to other states in search of work, as they see the economy of their own community deteriorate. As a consequence of this forced departure, women's responsibilities are expanded significantly in an effort to perform their partners' tasks. At the same time, some of the young people who left a few years ago are returning to the community due to the economic crisis in the United States. Their re-integration into the community has proven difficult, as they drive full-size trucks with American license plates on a dirt road where the beasts patiently stroll.

Young girls have also left the village for nearby cities, thus adding to the number of domestic workers exploited. While their financial contribution to the household is appreciated, their participation in the village is missed. All adult members of the village are concerned about how the urban influence will affect the young girls. Some apparent influences are related to ways of dressing and of speaking, for example.

"No one hears us"

The women of Matlaquiahuitl have support mechanisms that allow them to survive the stress of their daily hardships. Casual gatherings and participation in school or religious groups are important events in which women are able to discuss their problems and concerns. Not surprising is the fact that women's concerns are generally more inclusive of the problems that affect the community as a whole. They generally agree about the impoverished state of their community. They all agree that their community suffers a lack of basic resources (water and drainage), proper health services, descent housing and education. Also, there is a collective feeling of impotence to change or eliminate the malevolent foreign forces (political, social and cultural) that are intruding on their space and affecting the way of life they have kept for decades.

"Women are not leaders here because we lack education"

The women of Matlaquiahuitl do not consider themselves leaders, although many occupy important roles in the community, and their participation is recognized by most members of the community. The women interviewed had no formal education, and none of them had finished elementary school. Only a few of them had finished third grade, and they were ashamed to disclose this information. Furthermore, because of their lack of formal education, they consider themselves incapable of taking on roles of importance in their community. Paradoxically, all religion teachers or catechists are women, and no males participate in the Parent Teachers Association (PTA). However, women have taken positions as presidents, vice-presidents and secretaries of the PTA and have weekly meetings with the school teacher to plan the operations of the school. Some other women have been involved as active members or coordinators in programs such as *Oportunidades* (Opportunities), that helps needy families by providing their children with scholarships, food and medical services.

Other women have participated in training workshops when they have been available. However, due to Matlaquiahuitl's geographic isolation, many programs have failed because they were not able to retain teachers. In general, women genuinely believe they have no leadership roles in their community and firmly consider that their participation in the programs mentioned above is only necessary for the continuation of the life of their community. In their many informal gatherings, they insist that they organize to support each other in ways that go from sharing food and taking care of the sick, to addressing issues relating to agricultural practices and politics. Organizing, to them, is about surviving or, to put it in their own words, *más o menos vivir* ("to more or less live").

Most women who actively participate in the community do so at great cost to themselves and with real difficulty. In the first place, these extra domestic activities take a tremendous amount of time that they literarily do not have. So, women who get involved in other groups or programs need to get up earlier to do their respective chores before they leave the house. They also face being reprimanded by their partners or other family members for being outside the home, which is considered their primary, if not only obligation. In cases when the meeting is extended for a few minutes, being late is a cause for censure and verbal or physical scolding. More stressful for most women is to leave their small children unattended or under the supervision of relatives or neighbors while they take their respective roles as "leaders." Support mechanisms might prove helpful to alleviate the tensions created from being outside the household when cultural tradition demands that they should stay home with their small children. In the face of these tensions, many women choose to return home and wait patiently or impatiently for the time when their children are more independent and they themselves are freer to a certain extent.

"The land is there for a middle school"

Some years ago, the community agreed to select a piece of land for the construction of a middle school. So far, the land is there, at the top of the hilly road, but the middle school is alive only in the dreams of many women. The closest middle school is in Guzmantla, a small village approximately 45 minutes walking distance from Matlaquiahuitl. The closest high school is in either El Bajío or Ixhuatlán, much farther away. The bus service is very mediocre (two buses a day visit the community), and most families cannot afford the fare, so their children can attend school. According to most women, a middle school in Matlaquiahuitl would guarantee that their children have more educational opportunities. Most children drop out of school due to a lack of resources and extreme poverty, not because of apathy. Preadolescents have no option but to work in the fields or migrate in search of manual labor or domestic jobs instead of continuing their studies. This reality is bringing instability to many families and the community at large.

A PTA member with some of her children (who range in age from 2 to 21 years old).
Photograph courtesy of author

Most women know that their own children will have access to only limited educational opportunities. They hope that at least their grandchildren or future generations might enjoy what their children have been deprived of. Recently, leaders of the community have had conversations with governmental educational agencies about the construction of the school, only to be informed later that because of the limited number of potential students, policies forbid the building of such school. If Matlaquiahuitl patiently waits for the Mexican educational system to provide a school, it will be at least three generations before they enjoy one of the most basic human rights according the Universal Declaration of Human Rights access to education.

"Having children is not good any more"

Influenced by Catholic principles and a lack of medical services, including family planning, the women of Matlaquiahuitl tend to have many children. All the young women that participated in our conversations had children, some as young as three years of age. However, there were also mothers of children as old as twenty four. Some of them were already grandmothers of one to four grandchildren, with daughters who had found partners at the age of twelve. As far as I know, no formal census has been done in this community, but the index of infant mortality must be high, if we consider the fact that most women who participated in our conversations had lost at least one child at birth or at a young age. According to many, having children now is not good anymore because resources are scarce. At the time of our conversations I sensed a desire on the part of the women to have fewer children.

Because this community is being affected in so many ways and is losing its viability as a sustainable community, men (old and young) have had to leave to serve as cheap labor in nearby and not-so-close cities and leave the fields in charge of the women. In some cases, when the father and adult son leave, young women have moved in with the in-laws to maintain the family balance. Again, women have created a social network to support each other and protect their possessions (fields, animals and food), as well as their values. This most recent trend carries implications at both the family and the community level. More specifically, it brings into question the formal leadership roles traditionally granted by gender.

"The problem that everybody has is poverty"

"What do you do with 70 pesos [approximately 6 US dollars] a day?" A woman asked me after she had summarized in a very optimistic way how friendly the environment of the community was and how, in spite of poverty and adversity, all children attended school (by this she meant elementary school). She then explained how living without money and without resources from the land is making their lives almost impossible. The situation has been made worse by a number of conditions, some environmental, some having to do with inadequate or corrupt governmental policies. For example, there was a decree issued by a governmental agency prohibiting the people of Matlaquiahuitl from growing certain crops on their lands. The women of Matlaquiahuitl, along with the men, took leadership positions to present complaints to the authorities. However, it seems that the case has closed and the villagers will have to face the consequences of such an economically devastating policy.

In addition, from the summer 2008 to January 2009, the area of Sierra del Gallego experienced an extreme drought that left the lands under distress. On January 2009, the harvest of corn was reduced to a minimum and to the point that these long-time corn producers will have to purchase it from other markets. Although I had not seen previous harvests to compare this one to, the anguished faces and dismayed eyes of the men and women of Matlaquiahuitl told what many words cannot tell. In fact, nobody said much as we saw the harvest collected by one family and carefully stored in a small dark room. This was the day of my last visit, a cold and clear afternoon in January 2009. As I left the village behind, I realized then that this tragedy will certainly force more men to leave the village, leaving behind women, children and the elderly to decide for the future of this community. I believe that the leadership roles of this community will be redefined not only by ecological catastrophe and political factors but also by the global economy.

The women of Matlaquiahuitl have not directly identified the system that is responsible for their plight and that of their community as a whole. Instead, they quietly accept their fate and accepted that their geographical isolation is a factor that interferes with the proper responses governmental agencies might make to satisfy their needs. Women know they are at the bottom of the list and that their needs are the concern of no one but themselves. Despite this, they give priority to their children and husbands' needs before theirs, and they dedicate to the community whatever remains of their time and energy after attending to their families. The level of resiliency they demonstrate is immense, as in spite of their precarious living conditions, they still envision a better future, not for their children, but for their grandchildren.

Third-Class Citizens

Various authors (Freire, 2006; Mutua & Swadener, 2004; Smith, 2006) have identified systems of oppression that have affected native and minority populations, colonialism being the most repressive of them. I consider the case of Matlaquiahuitl a microcosm of the struggle many women suffer in México as a whole as a result of Spanish colonialism and the unique conditions it created. Historically, the collapse of indigenous civilizations under colonialism brought not only disease, and an imposed religion and culture, but also the creation of a new mixed race, usually recognized as *mestizo.*

Colonizing mechanisms have been part of the Mexican system in disguised forms and have contributed to the stratification of the Mexican population until the present, into what Esteva and Prakash (2001) have denominated as the social minorities (the masses) and the social majorities (the elite). Incidentally, throughout history, the Mexican government has always supported an elite group (in its majority white) that is proud to acclaim its relationship to the European system. The rest of the population, whether mestizo or indigenous, has limited political influence and representation and no real identification with the European. This is exactly the situation that the inhabitants of Matlaquiahuitl experience at the present, and it is manifested in the feeling of isolation and invisibility and expressed in the phrase often repeated in our conversations: *"Nadie nos escucha"* ("No one hears us").

Women, in the context of a colonized and exploitative system, appear to be the most marginalized and affected individuals. Deprived of their natural resources, native language, and even their self-esteem, women become sexual objects to their partners and submissive agents to all other members of their community and the society at large (when they leave their community for domestic labor). Paradoxically, the women of Matlaquiahuitl, mestizo and indigenous women, serve as the most valuable agents in society who have the capacity to guide the destiny of their community for the well-being of all its members.

The Mexican government, for a variety of reasons noted above, fails to serve equally all of the citizens of the country, especially those living in rural areas and isolated villages, such as Matlaquiahuitl. Women in such isolated regions are left to fend for themselves and their children. In the face of such isolation, the women of Matlaquiahuitl are characterized by their persistence and problem solving and organizational skills. Their resiliency and capacity to envision alternative ways to solve the problems the community faces is one of the reasons they have been able to participate and lead (though informally) in communal projects and programs. For example, a community effort, initiated under the leadership of the women, led to the construction of a modest aqueduct, the purpose of which was to provide a station for them to do their laundry in *"lavaderos"* (wash basins). While the project failed to meet its objectives, the women remained optimistic about future projects.

Concluding Lessons: Emergent Leadership

From the interviews documented above and much that could not be included in this article, it is clear that the women of Matlaquiahuitl bear many burdens and carry many responsibilities. Not only are they charged with the affairs of the household and the care of the children, but they are also required to work alongside or in place of men in many of the productive activities that make up the economic system of their community. They educate the children of the community and oversee the educational system. They also play a crucial part in the Church and its affairs. Finally, in their multiple roles, they are also the source of stability in a community that has seen increased migration inside and outside of Mexico. For all these reasons, women have begun to assume leadership roles, even though these roles are informal and not fully appreciated. They provide advice and counsel and participate in decision making. They do so based on their comprehensive knowledge of the community: its economic, educational and cultural systems, and cultural issues.

First, as the interviews document, the women engage in numerous productive roles in their community in addition to their productive roles within the household. They work alongside men in the fields, raising the animals, as well as selling the products of their land in the nearby villages and cities. They sometimes, though to a lesser extent than the men, sell their domestic labor services in the nearby cities. When they do, it is usually on a temporary basis to make up for financial shortfalls. As a result of their broad participation in their productive system, women have a more comprehensive knowledge of the economic affairs and are able to make significant contributions to decisions regarding economic matters, both in the home and in the community at large. They do so without occupying more formal positions, but their effect is felt nonetheless.

Second, the interviews show how deeply the women participate in the educational life of the community. They do so based on their conviction that an education is essential to the betterment of their children and grandchildren's lives and the community as a whole. They are therefore involved in running the schools as members of the PTA and in other positions. They also are chiefly responsible for educational activities within the household. Finally, they constitute the majority of volunteers in the Church in a variety of roles, not least of which is that of teacher. Hence, as with the economic affairs of the community, the women have comprehensive knowledge of the community's educational system and engage in a significant measure of decision making. While this leadership role is not explicitly acknowledged, it is clear that the women are respected by the children, whom they motivate and encourage to pursue educational goals, and the men cede most of the responsibility and authority in educational matters to them.

Finally, though the women will, on an ad hoc, temporary basis, work outside the community, they are still the most stable and constant members of the community. By contrast, men often work outside of the community for months and even years. Some migrate to the United States in search of work. They thus cease to participate in guiding the affairs of their community and leave a vacuum for women to fill. Women thus gain knowledge of how to fill the roles left vacant, and they maintain, uninterrupted, their experience of community life. As a result, they become repositories of cultural knowledge as well as knowledge of folkways, events, and technical matters. This makes them the principle source of cultural transmission and the guardians of community values and traditions. This knowledge, in turn, makes them critical in the governance of the community. While the men may occupy more formal roles, especially as representatives of the community to the main municipality, the women exert significant control over community affairs by virtue of their knowledge and the authority it affords.

The women of Matlaquiahuitl are minorities in their own country and are considered third-class citizens, peasants or *indias*, (pejorative term used to refer to rural women with indigenous traits). They are at the bottom of the social hierarchy. Their situation demonstrates, however, that certain forms of leadership do, in fact, come from the bottom. This form of leadership is based in knowledge of the full range of activities that make up the life of the community and that can be seen only by those who participate in them. This type of leadership is also informal. However, it is effective. Further, though it is limited by being informal, there is potential for transformation into more formal and recognized roles. Opportunities for such transformation come when the need for real problem-solving skills takes precedence over ingrained prejudices. There is reason to hope that this will happen in Matlaquiahuitl and other communities like it.

Today, most of the stories told about Matlaquiahuitl have been told by the men. The men have spoken on local radio programs, have been interviewed by the local newspapers, and have met with politicians to demand basic services for their community (though with no positive results). However, behind the scenes, the voices of the women of Matlaquiahuitl are loud and strong. They await a hearing from those outside the community. This paper is a small step in that direction. "Maybe," as they said, "something good will happen."

References

Bárcenas, C. (2008). *Sustentabilidad en el Matlaquiahuitl?* Unpublished manuscript.

Duran, J. (2001). *Worlds of knowing: Global feminist epistemologies.* New York and London: Routledge.

Esteva, G., & Prakash, M. (2001). *Grassroots post-modernism: Remaking the soil of cultures.* London & New York: Zed Books.

Freire, P. (2006). *Pedagogy of the oppressed.* New York & London: Continuum.

Mutua, K., & Swadener, B. (Eds.) (2004). *Decolonizing research in cross-cultural contexts: Critical personal narratives.* Albany, NY: State University of New York Press.

Paz, O. (1987). *El laberinto de la soledad.* México: Fondo de Cultura Económica.

Ramos, S. (1994). *El perfil del hombre y la cultura en México.* México: Espasa-Calpe Mexicana, S. A.

Smith, L. T. (2006). *Decolonizing methodologies: Research and indigenous peoples.* London & New York: Zed Books Ltd.

Stephen, L. (1992). Women in Mexico's popular movements: Survival strategies against ecological and economic impoverishment. *Latin American Perspectives, 19*(1), 73-96.

Vasconcelos, J. (1948). *La raza cósmica.* México: Espasa-Calpe Mexicana.

Part V

Practitioners and
Community Activists

Help Me Help You:
Finding a Niche in an Overcrowded Nonprofit Community

Karin Pleasant
Trade&Row Corp

Understanding Ownership

There are many reasons not to start a nonprofit organization, let alone any business. The questions of viability, competitive position, cost-benefit analysis, and overall will to succeed lead either to building a business plan or more mind wandering for the next big idea. In the nonprofit world, the same questions are raised as in the for-profit world but with a different focus. Whether or not someone starts a hardware store or a jewelry business depends on the buyers in a given community. Either business could thrive in different areas. For a nonprofit, there has to always be a need, not just a want, and the need has to be externally focused. According to Peter Manzo and Alice Espey (2001), "A nonprofit organization, in a sense, is 'owned' by the public. No private person can claim ownership or control of the organization. The assets of a nonprofit organization are irrevocably dedicated to charitable, educational, literary, scientific, or religious purposes" (p. 3). I had established for myself that moving into the nonprofit world was not about personal fulfillment and that whatever I did and whomever I worked with, I needed to find a way to build a purpose that complemented existing organizations while meeting an expectation in the community that was not being met— either because of a lack of resources or sub-par quality of currently available services.

When Aldo Puicon and I started planning to form a nonprofit in the Fall 2007, we were clear on the idea that ultimately this was not our organization. When we were recruiting a board of directors in February 2008, we knew that the members would have the right to remove either one of us if we did not fulfill the organization's mission and follow the basic ethical guideline that "you must be faithful to the public good above your personal interests" (Manzo & Espey, 2001, p. 2). What follows is my journey I had toward becoming involved in the nonprofit world and the lessons I learned in creating a sustainable organization.

Inspirations for a Bigger Idea

One of the most interesting experiences I have had was for my thesis project in the MFA writing program at California Institute of the Arts (CalArts). During the Summer 2000, I interviewed several of my parents' friends, as well as my father and his sister, to talk about different aspects of Black culture. The goal was to see what similarities existed in what they were taught about Black history, the tools they used from youth to adulthood to cope with the restrictions of Jim Crow, and their attitudes toward the current trends of younger generations. About a year and half after the interviews took place, one of the interviewees died. He had concluded, "We weren't taught Black history." It was one of the statements that stuck with me because I had the option to take a Black history class in college and connect with a tradition of survival that gave license to anger that my parents could not understand. I learned a lot about all the interviewees' lives that even their children may not know. I realized it was a privilege to have the time to create this space for them to share with me the changes they had been able to witness from the 1920s moving into the 21st century. I thought there was a bridge we could build to develop better tools for future generations, but at that time, I was not sure how to do that.

After finishing at CalArts, I worked with artist/photographer Isabelle Lutterodt under our partnership name, M.U.L.E., to develop art exhibitions in our free time. We spoke briefly about the idea of starting a nonprofit organization, and I bought a guide on how to become a nonprofit in California. After advisement from a mentor who ran a nonprofit for many years, we put the idea on the back burner and focused on independent projects. One of the most important projects we worked on was an art exhibition we co-curated in 2004 at the California African American Museum called *Through the Gates: Brown v. Board of Education*. The experience involved putting together an art exhibition that commemorated the 50th anniversary of the *Brown v. Board* Supreme Court ruling, which "dismantled the legal basis for racial segregation in schools and other public facilities" (http://brown-vboard.org/summary). The process was intense because there were so many discussions in the media about the state of education in 2004 versus 50 years prior. All reports concluded that segregation and disparity in the quality of education received by children of different racial/ethnic backgrounds were actually worse in 2004 than in 1954.

Although it seemed to be an achievement to have artists of different ages and races develop work that touched on so many different aspects of education, what was lacking in the exhibition space was a place for parents, teachers, administrators and children to discuss what was happening in schools on a daily basis. They were observers/patrons like everyone else, who saw the exhibition and listened to panel discussions, but they are the ones who live in the school system and know its challenges first hand. That was what we really wanted to be talking about because if we could not celebrate *Brown v. Board* as a triumph 50 years later, then we needed to know why. There was no space for that joint discussion in that instance, but I knew from that point forward I wanted to make sure that if we had a similar opportunity, there would be.

What I wanted was an experience reminiscent of the interviews I had done for my thesis project, where people were comfortable talking about their lives in relation to the sociocultural issues they face. With the *Brown v. Board* exhibition, I had a framework where art could speak to everyday issues like education and could bring people into a discussion where they had something to respond to. Ideally, the discussion would naturally evolve outside of the artwork into the issue itself. It was not enough for people to see the work. We had to lead people into a discussion that allowed for a personal point of entry.

After *Brown v. Board*, I thought it was important to try and build something outside of a gallery space, as that environment seemed to draw a limited audience. I also wanted to continue working with Isabelle and the two designers who worked on the exhibition: Aldo Puicon and Sencee Tagami, who partnered under the name WORKER. The space design WORKER produced is what made M.U.L.E.'s ideas a reality. The effect of walking into the space and being drawn into an emotion or conjuring an idea without reading any of the wall text was something that made it easier to facilitate a discussion. I asked Isabelle, Aldo and Sencee about their long-term goals—anything and everything they had ever thought about doing, what they had already accomplished, and ideas they had seriously considered for which they had already started making an outline. I thought we could create a business and wanted to see if there was any common ground. To initiate responses, I made my own list, and it made my goals more real after they were documented. The emphasis on community outreach became an ongoing theme. Although our group communication faded between 2004 and 2007, Isabelle, Aldo and I continued to discuss ideas in passing, wanting to work on the connection between art and social issues.

Four years after finishing art school, I enrolled in the MBA program at the Graziadio School of Business at Pepperdine University. During one of my last classes in my last term, an alumnus came to talk to our class about his post-MBA experience. This was timely not only because we were about to graduate but also because people had started talking about the time limit on the value of an MBA. The speaker talked about the opportunities of which fellow graduates in his class took advantage. But the person the speaker focused on for most of his time with us was someone I'll call "Bob." Bob probably started at Pepperdine much the same as many people I met during orientation. He wanted an MBA but did not quite have a step-by-step diagram of how he was going to use it. He just knew it was something he wanted to pursue. The problem with Bob was that by the time he graduated, he still had no plans for himself besides attending graduation and waiting for the certificate in the mail. Bob stayed in the same job and used the certificate as wallpaper. Of all the stories, this one affected me the most. The idea of becoming the person who did not use her degree disgusted and scared me.

While the presenter was still talking, I started an e-mail to Isabelle saying we needed to stop waiting and talking about the idea of pursuing something and actually put plans in motion. Within a few days of corresponding, she sent me information about Make It Your Own, sponsored by the Case Foundation. They had a contest where they were offering grants to people who submitted ideas for community outreach projects. Anyone who wanted to work with others to develop solutions for problems in the community could apply. The timing of this was not lost on me—us putting a plan in motion and having a viable opportunity to apply for funding right when I was finishing my degree.

I focused the grant application on a specific cultural issue in the Los Angeles metropolitan area, and I was encouraged by the goal of the grant to make people feel more empowered to develop solutions in their community by working with others. I wanted to work in partnership with others because it had always been a beneficial experience. I also wanted to challenge myself and other people to feel obligated to be more conscious of the way our decisions affect other people. I had the framework of art speaking to social issues and the goal of creating an intimacy whereby people would feel comfortable relating personal experiences. I reviewed my idea with Isabelle, and we were clear on the fact that regardless of the response, we would keep the momentum going to build an idea for our own organization.

When we found out we did not make it to the second round, we started from scratch by figuring out who would be part of the organization we wanted to create and what ideas each person had to develop a unified focus. As Isabelle was living out of the country at the time, it became clear that she could not be a part of the organization on a day-to-day basis. After contacting Aldo, and Sencee, who had worked with us on the *Brown v. Board* exhibition, it came down to me and Aldo who would be dedicating time to forming an organization.

Starting the Organization

Based on these prior experiences, the two concepts that were common threads and became the focus for developing an organization were (1) creating spaces for discussion where people could feel comfortable expressing their opinions and (2) having a person (subject expert or facilitator) and/or an object (artwork or film) guide the theme of the discussion, serving as a stabilizing factor to keep the discussion on track. People needed to feel comfortable sharing personal information and realize they are part of something larger —that there is common ground to build on, possibly leading to a call to action. At the base level, we would be sponsoring a themed event that would be purely entertaining (like an art performance). Maybe some people would think the performers are interesting but not really see any unifying theme, but others would be searching for the thread we were trying to create and would have a basis for thought and discussion. Whether or not we could get people to "take action" after attending an event would be the next phase. We had to first see if anyone would show up if we had a time and a place to do something.

I still had the "how to become a nonprofit in California" book I had purchased in 2001. With this in hand and with my experience as a backdrop, Aldo and I talked in September and October 2007 about different themes for the organization we wanted. Although there were common threads, I felt we could use the help of an experienced nonprofit leader to refine our ideas, and reached out to Doug Semark, Executive Director of Gang Alternatives Program (GAP). I met Doug during my second-to-last semester at Pepperdine while doing a group project with GAP. In November 2007, with guidance from Doug, Aldo and I founded Trade&Row Corp (Trade&Row) with a vision and mission of "raising awareness of current issues." Although there are many organizations that strive to get citizens to support different causes, what we decided to do differently is to try to reach the people who are like a lot of people we know—people who will donate money to a good cause or even occasionally volunteer for an organization but do not think about what they can do that is more personal, that could have an impact on their own lives as well as the lives of their neighbors. The intention was to make the mission for the organization clear and basic enough so anyone who encountered it would feel welcome to be a part of it.

The independent curator in me wanted a space because that was usually the obstacle in producing a program—we have this idea, but where can we show the work? It was the one aspect of the organization that I initially saw as freeing, but upon further evaluation, came to be a limitation. If we had a space, where would it be? What people in the community did we want to reach? If they were in multiple locations, would they all willingly come to this space to engage in our projects? One of the things we were saying in forming Trade&Row was that people do not engage in what's happening in their own communities, let alone neighboring communities. With a space, we would be creating a financial burden and physical limitation on our activities. The clarity in that discussion and the resulting feeling that we could do anything in any part of the metropolitan area was relieving because it meant that we defined ourselves as flexible, and we could be whatever a particular community needed in order to generate dialogue.

The biggest challenge we were advised about by Doug was financial support. Manzo and Espey (2001) state:

Most nonprofits survive with diverse sources of support, of which grants are often a small percentage. Most financial support comes from individuals. Further, grants are not easy to come by. Funders usually look for broad community support and an established track record in organizations they consider funding, and many foundations do not fund on a multi-year basis. (p. 5)

We needed to have a founders' commitment and to require board members we recruited to raise a minimum amount of funds to secure support. There could be the hope for an "angel" —a deep pocket who had so much faith in what we were doing that he/she would give us a large sum of money, but more realistically, we needed to find a way to raise funds through the programming we offered or through a designated fundraising event. What was of greater concern for us personally was that we both work full-time in other fields and Trade&Row would be managed on a part-time basis. Our ability to commit whatever time we had to the organization to produce quality programming and to find the support needed to make it sustainable would be our dual focus.

In January and February 2008 we developed two election-themed projects for our first fiscal year to take place between mid-July and early November 2008. At the same time, we researched all the state and federal paperwork needed to achieve 501(c)(3) status to become tax-exempt. With our first board meeting at the end of March 2008, we decided to officially start the organization's fiscal year in April. While waiting for the confirmation of tax-exempt status we were able to find a fiscal receiver, Side Street Projects, to offer potential donors tax-deductions for their donations and moved forward with the business of building a network. It never crossed our minds that we should test the reception of our idea before filling out paperwork. We were driven to bring people closer together—we felt the need to "do" rather than watch.

The Downs and Ups of Partnering

Every conversation about the direction of the organization came back to the idea of "partnering." Whether having an artist participate in a project we initiated or working with another non-profit to produce an event, we felt that partnering was an ideal way to mitigate costs and build our network. We did not want to work in isolation. We also did not want to pretend we were doing something new. At the core, we were attempting to do things that other groups do that have a specific cause of support, but would be using our flexibility to be a connecting organization. There was also the basic reality that I had encountered in the nonprofit art community of budget cuts and competition for funding. Aside from ourselves, how could we get people to work in conjunction with one another and not duplicate efforts? Figuring out how to build these relationships was our primary strategy.

Our first venture into partnering was just setting up meetings with different groups. Some of these were based on suggestions from board members or associates who knew of organizations that were trying to do community-oriented work. Through these meetings, we hoped to get advice, build a connection and get a better understanding of what other people thought was missing in the community. This would help us hone in on what we needed to incorporate into our future projects. We would also be spreading awareness about our developing organization in the nonprofit community. In several meetings, people were open to talking about their organization's goals and programming and the reason they started their nonprofit ventures. Though the conversation flowed somewhat easily, the question that inevitably arose, explicitly or not, was what did we want from them? To counter that, I often had an outline of the way Trade&Row and the other organization could work together and produce an event that reflected both organizations' mission statements. However, even with specific examples, there was sometimes bewilderment or uncertainty about what both organizations could really offer one another.

What Aldo and I realized is that as much as nonprofit organizations like the idea of "support" in whatever form it comes, some organizers still want a reason to reciprocate support to someone else. People thought our ideas were interesting and wanted to be kept abreast of our progress, but if we were going to ever "partner," we had to have a reason beyond common interests. Francie Ostrower (2005) notes that "partnerships are tools; they are not ends in themselves" (p. 40). Several people confirmed that in the world of nonprofit art organizations, there had been many discussions about joint projects and collaboration but talk never resulted in action. If we had a very specific project in the future and wanted to collaborate with another organization, we needed to figure out precisely what the *benefit* would be for them. Also, if organizations really want to collaborate, whether on one project or more, they need to share their goals and budget each other into their process. Ostrower (2005) states:

> Partnering is warranted, when two or more organizations have complementary missions, when they can bring different resources to the table, and when those resources are crucial for achieving the objective. Partnering may also be warranted when an objective can only be achieved through collective action and when the partners are truly committed to the objective. (p. 40)

We were eager to share ideas, but maybe it was because we were so new that we had this view. If we were five years in or more and had set programming, would we be as willing to be dependent on another organization? It was independence, after all, that so many organizations strive for—whether breaking even or having enough surplus to support additional equipment or part-time support—independence was a mark of "success."

We stopped initiating meetings with organizations for the sake of meeting people because there are just the two of us working on a part-time basis, and we needed to see our election-themed project, *Campaign Trail*, and our film festival, *We, the People* to completion. The former was based on a premise of soliciting proposals from performance artists to do projects that would require the audience to consider their involvement in the political process. This was a method of artist recruitment I was familiar with through M.U.L.E. The film festival was a new venture for Aldo and I, as we did not have many contacts in the film industry when we developed the idea of showing documentaries about different parts of the country. We wanted to speak to the diversity of people that we were expecting the President to represent, and question whether or not we consider this diversity when we vote. While I was responsible for composing our ideas into calls for participation and Aldo for designing our website and the marketing, we still needed to find venues to hold artists' events and to screen our film festival, which went from one evening of films to three.

While searching for films for our festival, I contacted Scott Beibin of Lost Film Festival, Hollywood Can Suck It and Evil Twin Booking Agency regarding access to a film. He realized this was a new venture for me and near the end of our discussion asked if he could offer me some advice. He said I needed to be more casual. The formality in my voice made it sound like I had more resources than I really did and, being a nonprofit in the stage we were at the time, that was the exact opposite impression I wanted to give. Although now based back east, Scott had lived in Los Angeles and offered specific suggestions of locations and contacts to make that would be more suitable for Trade&Row and the theme of the festival. He went on to suggest websites and other festivals to review, and in the course of 45 minutes, offered me advice at no charge that made a difference in who we were going to approach and why.

From that point on, Aldo and I made more targeted attempts to have well-cemented organizations host an event based on the audience they served and the audience we wanted to reach. In terms of space, we received support from organizations like Armory Center for the Arts, the Department of Cultural Affairs, Echo Park Film Center, eighteen-thirty, and Self Help Graphics, as well as individuals like artist Kim Abeles. They offered space and/or an audience and allowed our goal of venturing into different parts of the Los Angeles metropolitan area within the course of four months to become a reality. The variety of these resources also allowed us to have a better understanding of how to reach out to different types of organizations. Five of these resources came through some personal reference and from following Scott's advice of trying to expand our resources by tapping into smaller venues through fields we had worked in before, which for me was the art experience of M.U.L.E.

In the process of organizational outreach, we realized that we needed to follow another bit of Scott's advice by having pre-screenings for the film festival in order to spread awareness. I made requests to two board members, Ana Craven and Traci Durfee, to organize small gatherings of friends and associates in their communities and host small-scale prescreenings. While connecting to established organizations' audiences is an efficient way of getting broad exposure, we also needed to make sure our board felt equally connected to the organization's goals and were modeling the kind of dialogue we wanted to create through our programming with their friends. We felt that the best way to do that was in a setting of their choice. In addition, we were asking the audience for their feedback on the films, so they came into the event with the knowledge that participation was expected.

These small events were helpful in creating a greater understanding of the organization for board members who had never served a nonprofit organization before. It also brought Aldo and me back to the guidelines Doug Semark had advised us in forming a board of directors, which we followed. Trade&Row's board members are all of different ages and racial/ethnic backgrounds, and do not all live in the same area—two lived outside of Los Angeles County. Their experiences in corporate, educational, nonprofit, and art institutions were meant to give Trade&Row a guiding force that would not allow the organization to be pigeonholed. Organizing these smaller events also allowed us to gauge the appeal of our planned programming and to more easily get feedback on what draws people into discussions about social issues.

By mid-summer, Trade&Row had developed a newsletter subscriber list that was significant enough to make the projects viral. (What was especially helpful was my father's subscribing our family's e-mail addresses to Trade&Row's list, as my family lives in all different parts of the country.) For artists whose projects were difficult to place in the community, either because of cost or timing (as we wanted all of our events to conclude by November 4, 2008), we promoted their work through an online campaign.

With space and costs managed primarily through individual donations and film festival submission fees, we produced a variety of events that others told us was a mark of success. However, the overall attendance did not meet our expectations. By mid-November, we were exhausted and relieved but knew we needed to prepare to evaluate each event for overall content, participant feedback and how well the content/feedback matched Trade&Row's stated mission of bringing people together, facilitating dialogue, and promoting multiple perspectives. Following our final event in November 2008, we started a strategic planning process. One request from the board was for Aldo and me to evaluate each other as executive directors.

Evaluation

When Aldo and I talked about the organization's strengths, weaknesses, opportunities, and threats, we could easily find our weaknesses. We noted that regardless of where events had taken place, we often had some of the same audience members. Although some people would assume we were developing a "following," we knew none of those people converted to Trade&Row supporters. They were supporters and associates of artists we had worked with. It was clear that in the process of moving quickly to develop programming, we had reached out to a pool of contacts who know many of the same art professionals who, during an election year, were collaborating on several of the same politically-themed art projects in the area. Subsequently, they attracted many of the same audience members with them to our events. This ultimately revealed a flaw in our project management, as we had expected different artists to help us attract a diverse audience.We had not reached out enough to the residents surrounding each venue as well as a wider audience of people outside the art community genuinely interested in talking about the way each of us can play a stronger role in our communities.

We initially related this to the fact that we are not event planners by trade and do not personally engage with a large network of people. After further evaluation we realized that the best events we had were ones that were more intimate, with a group of 15 or fewer people who truly engaged the topic at hand. They brought up ideas that others had not really thought of and shared personal stories that otherwise would not have come up in casual conversations with their neighbors. They had lived out our mission and came together because they were supporting a board member or another organization that sponsored an event. It was personal. This mirrored who Aldo and I are as people— preferring intimate settings for people to feel comfortable, where most people had an opportunity to speak without judgment. Moving forward, the primary strategies we were going to employ would focus on creating these moments using our strengths of one-on-one relationship building.

In mid-2008, Doug Semark had initiated an exchange of in-kind services with Trade&Row based on our stated goals and GAP's desire to expose its Alternative Services for Youth program participants to art as a means of personal expression. However, we did not start the planning process for the project until after the school year started and our final preplanned program was completed. At this time, we were close to starting the strategic planning process for Trade&Row, deciding on the appropriate strategies and programs for the next three-to-five years of the organization's life. Doug identified in the memorandum of understanding a list of deliverables for each organization, following a standard process. A study by the United Way of Greater Milwaukee (2004) noted that "partnerships that made the most progress had a specific plan for how each organization would contribute its unique services to achieve mutually identified goals" (p. 6). The memorandum of understanding allowed us to have a structure for building strategies that fit our original goals while having ways to identify complementary partnerships and developing projects with other organizations.

Combining event planning experience we gained with our experience of meeting other nonprofit organizers, we knew that the goals should be written down, not just to have a contract but to have a clear understanding of the obstacles we faced. Misinterpretation could be alleviated by identifying steps needed to achieve each goal. "If the collaborative is driven by a written agreement … it has a higher likelihood of survival" (UWGM, 2004, p. 11).

While still in the midst of the strategic planning process, there was a basic issue that we tried to address in talking with other people about the organization. With a name like Trade&Row, people ask what it stands for and how it was developed. Although we had the idea of exchanging ideas (trade) and propelling forward (row), it did not give people a clear idea of what we were about. We wanted to bring people together to discuss social issues, but this did not always resonate with people. If the community was hesitant about attending events without knowing someone personally connected to the organization, what did we need to say in talking about Trade&Row that made it welcoming and clearer?

An important lesson came at a gathering to launch the redesigned GAP website. Doug noted the website address includes the words "gang free." Doug said he understood the difference between being free of something versus being "anti" something. There is a difference between being "anti-smoking" versus "smoke-free," or being "anti-drug" versus "drug-free." It is the positive approach, which is always harder than the "anti" approach because many people can state things they are against. Being "anti-gang" is a given, but the organization's goal is to prevent gang activity. Preventive measures mean imagining a world where gang activity does not exist and teaching kids who live in at-risk communities what they can pursue when you foster productive habits. This is not only a statement of GAP's values but also what makes the organization unique. It is not reactionary (e.g., more police, tougher sentencing for gang-related crimes) as many other "anti-gang" community programs are.

We needed to be able to say what Trade&Row stands for—our core values—and what specific activities we would undertake to make those values come to life. We needed to distinguish ourselves based on our actions and learn to explain what we want the organization to become. We are a community organization whose programming is entertaining while creating a space for people to talk about the personal effects of social issues.

We decided we had to reach out at different levels of the community to show that collaboration is something we believe in and that dependence on community involvement and ideas would be the only things to really sustain the organization. The United Way of Greater Milwaukee's (2004) study concluded:

> Real collaboration has the potential to reduce duplication, decrease competition, and enhance problem solving. However…real collaboration takes time, is difficult to achieve, and cannot be created by funders. [R]eal collaboration is voluntary and should not be inspired by a grant opportunity. [I]n its most authentic form, collaboration can help organizations work together to advance their missions. (p. 11)

We made a conscious decision to keep the organization small and to build one partnership per year–carefully measuring the quality of the programming and the strength of our partnerships.

Leadership

There was a project in one of my introductory classes in business school about how to define leadership. We broke off into groups and tried to develop the characteristics of a leader through a series of reference texts and personal experience. My group noted that some people are charismatic but do not want the responsibility, only the power. Others are thoughtful decision makers and methodical in their approach to problem solving, but cannot garner the respect needed to have others believe in their abilities. We talked about humility, taking responsibility when things go bad and sharing praise when things go well. Ultimately we found that the best leaders had a balance of several characteristics but not always the same ones. For example, many people have noted that Jimmy Carter is a great ambassador but a horrible president. Aldo and I needed to find out how our personal attributes outside of our strong convictions suited Trade&Row.

For myself, there is a fear of falling into a stereotype—I want to be strong without seeming overbearing and proud without seeming obnoxious. This consciousness was partially generated from the fact that art would be an important part of Trade&Row's mission, and my relationship to art was focused in the community I was exposed to at CalArts—racially mixed, with a few prominent Black faces. In addition, the organization's goal was to work throughout the Los Angeles metropolitan area, and race consciousness in Los Angeles is not optional. The ghettoization that exists throughout the metropolitan area makes it relatively easy to start an organization with the goals of Trade&Row solely focused on one's own racial/ethnic group as reflected in the reality of such organizations' existence. History makes these organizations viable. But we were not going to focus on one area and we needed to learn how to navigate these different spaces and sometimes imaginary boundaries in order to be successful.

I had seen the uproar in Los Angeles in 1991 and the national presentation of so-called "White" versus "Black" opinions generated by the coverage of the first O.J. Simpson trial in 1995 on television. Yet when I visited Los Angeles for the first time in 1996, I felt this was the place to be in order to be exposed to people, music, and culture that I would never find in southeastern Michigan. When I moved to Southern California, I didn't need to look up government statistics to find out where different types of people lived. I found out through many hints in casual conversations with coworkers. However, I moved forward personally to forge relationships with people who were not driven by finding friends who only looked like them. Aldo, being of Peruvian descent and having grown up in San Bernardino County, is one of these types of people. The decision to be a leader of a nonprofit organization, however, forces me to consider what other people feel is important and relevant.

We were tested with this question on the last night of our film festival. We were in an area in East Los Angeles that is predominantly Latino. Walking into a restaurant next door, the employee was surprised when I came in to order and couldn't speak Spanish. It wasn't until the evening of the event that it was clear that expectations for certain audience members were not met. An attendee asked Aldo why more works by Latino filmmakers were not being shown. A couple people left early in the program. With a theme for the evening of "community," and showing films that we thought reflected the way people come together locally to make a change, it was discouraging to think that we would have to show people of a certain race or ethnic group for audience members to be comfortable with the message. But this is the reality in some areas, and we would have to think about how to combat this. We will do another program in this area, but the answers to why and what will need to be different.

Overall, I have become comfortable with the fact that there will never be a solution that works across different neighborhoods. The lesson in that came from a restaurateur whom Isabelle and I interviewed for our thesis project. He noted how certain parts of Los Angeles had changed since he moved in the area many years before. What had been Black neighborhoods were now Black and Latino neighborhoods, and he related the change to a shift in power. When there were more Black people, he knew Black leadership hadn't reflected much consideration for the Latino minority. Now that there were more Latino residents, he lamented whether or not they would have the Black minority's interests at heart. This story was related in 2000, and nine years later, this story continues in different parts of the Southland. Our organization's mission is designed to combat this point of view, and inclusiveness through diversity of outreach, network contacts, and program themes are what we will aim for to achieve it.

Always Learning

With cultural challenges like the individualistic sensibility that is often revered and the increasing use of technology that requires less interpersonal interaction, finding ways to build a community and not just reside in one is growing in importance. Aldo and I know this because our outlook for Trade&Row is stronger with the support and personal investment from people outside of the board and from employees of the organization. Some of the most important input I received came through advice from individuals when it was not expected, and their interest in the organization's success is what you hope for a community organization. Our external focus for the organization has been reflected back on us and is what enables Aldo and I to create a stronger position in the nonprofit world for Trade&Row.

References

Espey, A., & Manzo, P. B. (2001). GET READY, GET SET: What you need to know before starting a nonprofit. Retrieved February 2, 2008 from http://www.faithincommunities.org/GetReadyGetSet.pdf

Ostrower, F. (2005, Spring). The Reality Underneath the Buzz of Partnerships. *Stanford Social Innovation Review, 3*(1). Retrieved November 7, 2008 from http://www.culturalpolicy.org/commons/comment-print.cfm?ID=24

United Way of Greater Milwaukee (2004). Nonprofit collaboration & mergers: Finding the right fit. A resource guide for nonprofits. Retrieved November 3, 2008 from http://epic.cuir.uwm.edu/NONPROFIT/collaboration.pdf

Leadership Through the Lens of Disability and Identity

Carolyn Bailey Lewis
Ohio University

The Leadership Challenge

Few women of color, who are leaders, encounter quadruple challenges. As a widow and woman of color with a disability, I embody all four. Moreover, I have a fifth challenge—one of providing leadership in an ever-evolving media industry while balancing the issues of life.

I have been employed in public media since 1972, working my way up from writer/announcer to general manager. Setbacks along the way made my journey even more difficult when, in 1995, life as I knew it came to an abrupt halt. In his 1987 work, Robert Murphy labeled this disruption "the body silent." My body, like Murphy's was quieted by an intrusion to the spinal cord that made bodily functions cease. I could no longer walk or use my arms. I was paralyzed by a spinal cord tumor.

Following a battery of tests and imaging, 11 hours of surgery, and six months of physical and occupational rehabilitation, I regained much of what was lost and was able to return to the workplace. Diminished was my vibrant, mobile lifestyle, as the wheelchair became my primary method of transportation. With the loss of mobility came the loss of identity. I was a shell of my former self.

Telling one's story, however, is therapeutic and healing. Through researching and writing my dissertation, *Identity: Lost, found, and (re)constructed through healing narratives–An autoethnography of tragedy, travail, and triumph* (2007), I regained a sense of self and reconstructed a lost being. The *tragedy* was my paralysis and the diagnosis of the tumor—thankfully benign; the *travail* was the intense therapy and working to regain my functions; and the *triumph* was my finally coming to terms with the reconstructed identity. By overcoming obstacles and never giving up, I refused to let my wheelchair define me personally or professionally. Coming to this point was a five-year quest.

There are daily challenges for a woman of color who provides leadership in any organization. Having a disability compounds the challenges. Yet, the triumphs are immeasurable.

The Altered Self

Living with illness alters the illness survivor's sense of self. When the body breaks down, so does the life.
(Frank, 1991, p. 8)

I had a choice: accept what life dealt me or forge a new identity following the disabling spinal cord tumor. My life was broken and my sense of self shattered. A new story is created when one is diagnosed with an illness. The old story does not disappear, but rather remains dormant until it can be reframed with the new. Much can be learned by reframing illness less as a catastrophe and more as an opportunity to create a new story (Frank, 1991). When illness strikes, what emerges from the patient, in addition to fear, is a shaken sense of self and uncertainty.

I was asked by a member of my dissertation committee to expound on the way that being a woman of color shapes the way I view disability. I had to explain that, actually, it is the other way around. Color is not the first thing I think about when getting up in the morning, taking a shower, maneuvering in the workplace and other spaces, or traveling. What I ponder is the perpetual issues of dealing with disability as they relate to the time it takes me to get up, prepare for work, prepare to travel, or prepare a meal. Those are my real (dis)ability confrontations. Color is secondary.

When illness strikes, one's standpoint is radically changed. *You* become the situation others look upon with fear and disdain. When I became a leader with a disability, I had to come to terms with my new condition and the physical structures I would come to introspectively review and use. I was awakened to a new sense of responsibility and to what it means to have a disability in an able-bodied world, particularly in a leadership position.

Leading Through Pain

My incredible journey began in 1972 when I was hired as a television writer/announcer for WWVU-TV at West Virginia University in Morgantown. I slowly climbed the corporate ladder with promotions to positions in community relations and public information. After 22 years at the station (now WNPB), my persistence, perseverance, and patience were rewarded in 1993 when I was named interim general manager and finally permanent general manager several months later. That was no easy task. As a woman of color, I was frequently not perceived as credible and had once been passed over for the position of general manager. This achievement took years of working long hours, proving my worth, and being chastised for mistakes that were overlooked when made by my white co-workers.

As general manager, I was actively engaged in the local and public broadcasting communities. My children's activities, committee and board meetings, travel to conferences, and church involvements kept me busy. I always believed I could get everything done in a day, even if it took me all night.

On my 47th birthday, September 19, 1995, I changed from being an active, vibrant, independent professional, providing leadership as the only woman of color serving as general manager of a public television station in the United States, to one who was paralyzed. On that day, I woke up to go to the bathroom and fell on the floor, unable to move.

However, already in the summer of that year, life had began to blur when I experienced months of incredible arm and back pain. I ignored the signs. My family doctor treated the symptoms with medication but never got to the root of the problem. I did not let this stop me. I continued to work through the pain for fear that my supervisor and colleagues would perceive me as an ineffective leader. What I was doing was wearing my body down to the point where my immune system was weakened and, when sickness silenced my body with complete paralysis on that fateful fall day, I had nothing left with which to fight.

The diagnosis was a spinal cord tumor. The prognosis was dismal. Following surgery on September 22, I was alive, yet I was unable to move and was bound from head to toe. A neck brace kept my head aligned and stable, a back brace protected the stitches and the spinal cord, leg supports helped with circulation, and braces on the feet kept them from turning inward. The doctors predicted that I would not live and, if I did, would be a vegetable for the remainder of my life. I defied the odds by living. I faced uncertainty with paralysis.

The physicians at that medical center had never seen a spinal cord tumor, so seven days following surgery, 30 doctors and nurses assembled at my bedside to ask questions about my condition: "Have you traveled out of the country?" "Have you been around diseased pets?" "What have you been eating?" "Have you been under an undue amount of stress?" "What is the history of your family's health?" After nearly 30 minutes, they finished. Lying flat on my back and unable to move, I looked up to the ceiling and said aloud, "By the grace of God, I will walk out of rehabilitation." My doctor later told me that he was certain I was delusional and that he felt very sorry for me.

What my doctor might not have known at that time was the depth of my faith in God. I had seen miracles in the lives of others and had no doubt that He would do the same for me. My husband, children, and friends became my strength, and I leaned on the Scripture from Isaiah 40:31, "But they that wait upon the Lord shall renew their strength; they shall mount up with wings as eagles; they shall run, and not be weary; and they shall walk, and not faint." My pastor read Scriptures of healing to me which saturated my body and spirit, and said, "You will come through this and your life will be a living testimony, and a blessing to others." I held on to that with the little strength I had left in me. Not only did I want to get restored for my own well-being and to continue my career, but also for my husband and my children. They were my inspiration.

Returning to My Rightful Place?

The next step was rehabilitation, where I spent two months as an inpatient working to regain mobility. Rehabilitation was not easy. Many days I dreaded getting out of bed. The nights were long and the days intense. When asked about my goal, it was always "to walk out of rehab and return to work." Indeed, I did walk out of there and, in six months, return to work. The doctors were amazed at the level of intensity I put into the rehabilitation process. Daily activities ranged from learning how to sit up and turn over to squeezing rubber balls and placing pegs in holes. What they did not know was my history, my work ethic, and the way I had to persevere for every inch of professional success.

After facing death with the tumor and pushing myself to the limit, I vowed that life would be different—that I would slow down, take it easy, and give my body time to heal. For nearly a year, I did. Over the months, however, I started to travel again, attend meetings, and take on more responsibilities. A year after the surgery I was careless and had a terrible fall on my back. My body started to slow down, and I was back in rehabilitation, even though I was scheduled to start a new job in another state at Ohio University. I had to begin two weeks later than originally planned. I interviewed for the position walking and returned in a wheelchair as a result of the fall. Starting the new job was daunting. I was the only person of color on the staff, and here I was in a wheelchair! The chair—the dreaded seated position—shattered my identity. How could I take my rightful place from a less postured view?

Finding Voice and Identity

In addition to losing mobility and identity, I lost my voice. The wheelchair silenced and embarrassed me, giving me only the desire to go to work and return home. I did not want to interact with anyone outside the office except my family. It was difficult enough being an African American woman providing leadership as general manager of a public television station, but having to lead from a wheelchair initially made me feel voiceless and powerless. I had my own stereotypes about people with disabilities. Who would listen to me or take me seriously? During meetings my ideas were dismissed, and I experienced lessened eye contact. However, when I began to write my illness narrative through the dissertation, I developed a renewed self-worth and realized that "the chair" was not definitive of who I am. I found my voice when I heeded what my son said: "You've got a good mind, Mom, use that. Your body will catch up."

The wheelchair is a symbol. This form of transportation is a blessing and a curse. The chair provides a mode to get from place to place. On the other hand, it confines, stereotypes, and signifies "not capable or fit." The chair is perceived as limiting the one in it to a person without intelligence or ability. Occasionally, a waiter will ask a companion dining with me "What does she want?" as if I am unable to speak or place my own order. The counterstory (Polkinghorne, 1988) occurs when I articulately place my order and amaze the server by asking for the bill, figuring the tip, and paying with my own credit card or cash. I had to reclaim and maintain my voice.

Polkinghorne (1988) described "self-identity" as two countering notions—self (ipse) which is the opposite of otherness and strangeness, and "identity" (idem), meaning that which remains the same, the extreme singular, the opposite of change. "The idea of self-identity holds the two notions of difference and sameness in tension" (p. 146).

Where identity formerly meant who I was as a woman of color, my identity has expanded to mean more. My identity as a person with a disability became a central issue in my health experience (Vanderford, Jenks, & Sharp, 1997). I came to terms with exploring health, sickness, illness, and disease through different lens, each having its own meaning and role. Each of these things changed the way I viewed leadership and the manner in which others viewed me.

Narrative analysis is particularly salient in the study of the impact of illness on personal identity. As argued by Frank (1995), illness, disability, and trauma are *calls for stories* (see also Coles, 1989). From Frank's perspective, and I concur, individuals experiencing serious illness are wounded storytellers who have lost a primary resource that most storytellers depend on—a sense of temporality. By telling stories and creating illness narratives, the self is able to be (re)constructed in order to find meaning and figure out the standpoint in light of bodily malfunction and change.

Humans are always telling stories, and most have narrative themes such as health and healing, abuse, drugs and alcohol, family life, jobs, and careers. Other themes are tragedy, destruction, disaster, travail, and triumph. Stories relating the intricacies of human social interaction make emotional connections.

Narratives and identity can intersect at almost any crossroad at nearly any life situation or crisis. In my autoethnography, narrative and identity intersect with health and disability. Each day, my narrative is being shaped by experiences with mobility and by other issues that help define my moral fiber, will, and perseverance.

Narratives, according to Bochner (2002), are characterized by five central concerns: the self and the other(s), the authentic researcher's voice, cultural transmission of narrative practices, new modes of representation, and relational connections between writers and readers of social science texts. The pendulum of my life with a disability has yielded personal stories of people's ignorance about what it means to have a disability; stories of invisibility and stories of marginalization, misunderstanding, and misrepresentation. Interwoven throughout each of Bochner's concerns are issues of work, health care, uncertainty, disclosure, dependence, and voice. Nelson's (2001) counterstory serves to put the narrative fragments back together again—"a story that resists oppressive identity and attempts to replace it with one that commands respect" (p. 6).

For instance, on a national television program, "Judge Hatchett," a teenager was being reprimanded for using drugs and for skipping school. To give the young woman a reality check, the judge introduced her to a woman without arms who had drug problems beginning in her teen years. Amazingly, this woman, who was born with no arms could use a pen or pencil to write with her mouth and toes. She could brush her teeth with her toes, and perform other tasks, compensating for not having any other way to do so. She was trained as a baby to use her feet as hands. In 1981, as a senior in high school, she became addicted to crack cocaine due to peer pressure. Her addiction lasted 10 years, but after intensive rehabilitation, she became clean and is now a motivational speaker. The teenager was so impressed with the narratives of a woman who is armless that she vowed to turn her own life around. The armless woman overcame many obstacles, never let her disability be disabling and wrote two books. This counterstory underscores Nelson's (2001) notions of oppressive identity and the oppressed person's perception of herself.

It is an understatement that along with appropriate methods of treatment, narratives have become important tools in the daily work of health care providers in understanding the experiences of patients. Patients who are active interpreters, managers, and creators of their health-care experience can better understand the context in which they come to be treated. Initially, I was not an active participant. Faced with a new challenge, I felt like a bystander and a detached object, as others were determining how my life would be (re)defined. The ideology of health care has been detachment. Powerful physicians make decisions, and patients do what they are told, without question or discussion, creating a chasm and loss of the patient's identity. As argued by Vanderford, Jenks, and Sharf (1997), "Identity must be one central focus of patient-centered research. Conceptions of health, illness, sickness, and disease relate to each individual's sense of what is normal and what is not, which role behaviors to assume, and what changes are experienced" (p. 15).

Carr (1986) analyzed the role of narratives in the making of personal meaning and value, and argued that we create ourselves by telling ourselves a story about who we are, what has happened to us, what we plan to do, and how all of it fits into the big picture. When a person experiences a serious illness and/or crisis, it calls into question the person's very sense of self. Where does one go or what does one do to rebuild identity and regain moral agency and self-definition? Nelson (2001) argued that identities are "narrowly constructed and that, within limits, narrative constructions can be narratively reshaped" (p. 67).

The storied nature of identity (re)construction cannot be understood in isolation from the intertextual web of organizational and societal narratives. Personal narratives are both medium and outcome of broader scripts that shape and are shaped by the material and social nature of communal life.

The Storied Nature of Institutional and Public Life

> Within the organization, stories function in a number of ways. They serve as a storehouse of organizational information, supply reasons for organizational events, and promote or suppress motivation in the workplace.
> (Brown, 1985, p. 28)

Co-constructed frames of reference compose institutional life—active, breathing, living phenomena through which members create their worlds. Narratives, among other frames of reference, bring individuals together into a whole through processes Burke (1945/1969) termed *identification*, allowing them to develop shared assumptions called *culture*. Yet Burke also drew our attention to the ways discourses can simultaneously function to divide and separate individuals living collective lives. Through narratives, members learn institutional expectations, values, customs, and rituals.

Brody (1987) posited that telling a story aids in the process of healing, restoring the disrupted connectedness of the pre-illness story. "We are, in an important sense, the stories of our lives" (p. 182). Members engage in shoptalk and develop the organizational climate, drawing on symbolic and storied resources from their surroundings. For one with a disability, shoptalk is an exception rather than the rule. For them, the organizational climate does not always lend itself to shoptalk simply because of the small number of people with disabilities who are employed. Moreover, co-workers experience a level of discomfort discussing issues of disability because of their limited knowledge base. In fact, the subject is avoided in order to avert shame and embarrassment. Women of color are particularly disadvantaged in this position and victimized due to constraints of cultural expectations.

A disability magnifies the difficulties women of color face carrying out day-to-day activities and the trauma of not being heard by health-care professionals, family, and co-workers. For example, stereotypes still exist that women with disabilities should work in traditional female occupations if they work at all. Hollingsworth and Mastroberti (1983) noted there are two career issues that women with disabilities share with able-bodied woman, role conflict and career aspiration.

Caring for a family and stress in the work environment heighten the conflict for women of color with disabilities. Concerns at home, barriers in the workplace, and being invisible in public heighten the perception that people with disabilities do not have the mental or physical tenacity to lead (Richie, 1992).

When I was hospitalized for surgery and for rehabilitation, I had enough sick time to be away for several months, but my position was in jeopardy because of hierarchical conflicts. The agency for which I worked was moving in a new direction, and there was conflict over new roles and responsibilities. I was completely out of the loop. My husband and the doctors wanted it that way so that I would not have undue stress. For over two months, I knew little about what was occurring at the office or in the community.

Women of color with disabilities face intentional and unintentional discrimination at home, in the workplace, and in public. Management gurus relate strategies of how one should stand to exert and/or exude a position of power. For persons with disabilities in wheelchairs, the power stance is not an option. I had to learn a different form of power through a strong command of the language, a firm handshake, the look in the eye, and an organized work space. In Western culture, the wheelchair signifies "handicap" before it is thought of as being a useful vehicle for transporting individuals from one place to another. As a woman of color who uses a wheelchair in the workplace and in public, I feel the long glances, hear the whispers, and watch the crowd as they part for my mobile transit. I observe dogs on leashes being jerked by the collars when they almost come face to face with me.

More than two million people in wheelchairs are dwarfed by some 42 million people with disabilities who do not have to use wheels for movement from place to place (Bryan, 1999). "The moral generosity that seeks to compensate for physical differences makes cultural outcasts of its recipients by assuming that individual bodies must conform to institutional standards, rather than restructuring the social environment to accommodate physical variety" (Thomson, 2001, p. 51). The fight is constant to ensure that accommodations are made in the workplace and other spaces. Most spaces I am able to negotiate. I manage the other spaces with assistance from co-workers and friends as some areas have more structural barriers than others.

As an American with Disabilities Act (ADA) consultant, I am frequently called upon to advise on new and renovated facilities. It is clear that those who design spaces for persons with disabilities have never had to use a wheelchair for any length of time. Organizations and institutions need to allow the stories of persons with disabilities to be told and to communicate those stories to others. Just as companies engaged in diversity sensitivity training in the 1980s and 1990s, corporations should have a foundational principle to educate supervisors and those with hiring authority on the importance of employment opportunities for persons with disabilities.

Companies do not want to venture into what they perceive as the unknown. That is, to hire a person with a disability and make the appropriate accommodations. Companies are often reluctant to go beyond what the ADA basically requires, and to make physical accommodations in the workplace which provide actual utility. Part of the human resource officer's job should be to obtain knowledge of the ADA and, subsequently, diffuse that information to others within the organization.

Staff meetings should allow time for training, role play, and hearing from persons with disabilities about their illness narratives in order to help dispel myths about those with different abilities and to clearly understand the needs. Organizational publications could feature persons with disabilities and include the stories of their lives.

Storied institutional life is dependent on the community of individuals and joint citizenship, which demands not dependence but interdependence. This interdependence within an organizational culture shapes my and others' stories of institutional life as we co-construct and reconstruct the ebb and flow of human discourse by engaging in narratives. A case in point: Boje's (1991) study of storytelling in an office-supply firm reveals how stories are conceptualized as joint performances of tellers and hearers. "Studying the storytelling episodes themselves offers several advantages because the stories are contextually embodied, their meaning unfolds through the storytelling performance event" (p. 109). Thus, stories should no longer be considered something one person tells another; instead, stories, like any discursive interaction, are fluid and indeterminate experiences that both narrators and audiences use to make meaning.

Everyone has a story to tell, and everyone tells stories. Yet these stories are co-constructed and reconstructed across time and place as multiple parties enter into the story from their own unique standpoints (Frank, 2005). Boje (1991) argued, "As listeners, we are co-producers with the teller of the story performance. It is an embedded and fragmented process in which we fill in the blanks and gaps between the lines with our own experience in response to cues, like 'You know the story!'" (p. 107).

In order to understand my own storied experiences of leadership, disability, and identity, I must consider the way my stories are shaped by and shape the organizations with which I identify. As argued by Harter (2005), "Institutional settings of all sorts, including health care contexts, supply the narrative auspices under which selves come to be articulated" (p. 191). Meanwhile, individual and institutional stories reflect and contribute to broader sociohistorical conditions as expressed in grand narratives.

Conclusion

Those who hear my story say I am inspirational. I believe the terms that best describe me are survivor, conqueror, and overcomer. I am surviving in the media industry—over 37 years now —and learning to conquer by using a wheelchair in a world designed for the able-bodied. Through determination and perseverance, I overcome by refusing to allow anyone to minimize me because of the disability. In addition to providing leadership for two television stations, six radio stations, a cable channel, distance learning services, online services, audio and video productions, media distribution, technology consulting, community outreach, and student professional development, I manage to stay intricately involved on several committees within the university, and on the local, state, and national levels. I am well read and stay current on changing trends and technologies. I mentor numerous students each year and earned a Ph.D. in 2007 while working full-time.

The spinal cord tumor changed my environment, my daily existence, and the lives of those who co-construct my life. Leading through disability and identity as a woman of color has myriad challenges. My mission is to changing attitudes about women of color with disabilities in positions of leadership. Instead of finding negativity and complaining about my situation, I find purpose and realize that every day is a gift. Overcoming barriers (real and perceived) enabled me to create a paradigm shift from passivity to social action and advocacy. Using my voice, and the power of the written word, more accommodations have been made on the university's campus and in the city where I reside. When I travel, hotels and other facilities hear from me if spaces are not navigable via wheelchair. Unfortunately, spaces that appear to be ADA compliant are often not practical for use. I am certain to let the establishment know when they are not.

Below are excerpts from letters sent to leading establishments where I have lodged, normally unaccompanied. My tag line always is, "I might not ever return to your facility again but I urge you to correct these issues for the next person who comes."

There is too much furniture in the room, most of which is unusable for a person in a wheelchair.

The couch near the bed had to be moved so that I could get to the bathroom and the bed is too high.

I had to sleep in my wheelchair since you had no other accessible rooms available.

I called maintenance to remove the bathroom door because the configuration of the door made it impossible to get in.

The only accessible rooms you have are on the 10th floor and above.

What would I do in case of a fire?

The first obstacle at your business was a trash can along with a bucket blocking the wheelchair ramp.

The seat of power created by my leadership position affords me the opportunity to be a role model as a woman of color, with or without (dis)abilities, and to be a voice to affect change for persons whose abilities are different and for persons whose bodies transform over time.

References

Bochner, A. P. (2002). Perspectives on inquiry III: The moral of stories. In M. Knapp & G. R. Miller (Eds.), *Handbook of interpersonal communication* (pp. 73-101). Thousand Oaks, CA: Sage.

Boje, D. (1991). The storytelling organization: A study of story performance in an office-supply firm. *Administrative Science Quarterly, 36,* 106-126.

Brody, H. (1987). *Stories of sickness.* New Haven, CT: Yale University Press.

Brown, M. H. (1985). That reminds me of a story: Speech action in organizational socialization. *The Western Journal of Speech Communication, 49,* 27-42.

Bryan, W. V. (1999). *Multicultural aspects of disabilities.* Springfield, IL: Charles C. Thomas.

Burke, K. (1945/1969). *A grammar of motives.* Berkeley: University of California Press.

Carr, D. (1986). *Time, narrative, and history.* Bloomington: Indiana University Press.

Coles, R. (1989). *The call of stories: Teaching and the imagination.* Boston: Houghton Mifflin.

Frank, A. W. (1987/1991). *At the will of the body: Reflections on illness.* Boston: Houghton Mifflin.

Frank, A. W. (1995). *The wounded storyteller: Body, illness, ethics.* Chicago: University of Chicago Press.

Frank, A. W. (2005). What is dialogical research and why should we do it. *Qualitative Health Research, 15,* 954-974.

Harter, L. M. (2005). Section III: Narrating and organizing health care events and resources. In L. M. Harter, P. M. Japp, & C. S. Beck (Eds.), *Narratives, health, and healing: Communication theory, research, and practice* (pp. 189-195). Mahwah, NJ: Erlbaum.

Hollingsworth, D. K., & Mastroberti, C. J. (1983). Women, work, and disability. *The Personnel and Guidance Journal, 6,* 587-591.

Lewis, C. B. (2007). *Identity: Lost, found, and (re)constructed through healing narratives—An autoethnography of tragedy, travail, and triumph.* Doctoral dissertation, Ohio University.

Murphy, R. (1987). *The body silent.* New York: Henry Holt.

Nelson, H. L. (2001). *Damaged identities, narrative repair.* Ithaca, NY: Cornell University Press.

Polkinghorne, D. (1988). *Narrative knowing and the human sciences.* Albany: State University of New York Press.

Richie, B. S. (1992). Coping with work: Interventions with African-American women. *Women and Therapy, 12,* 97-111.

Thomson, R. G. (1997). *Extraordinary bodies: Figuring physical disability in American culture and literature.* New York: Columbia University Press.

Vanderford, M., Jenks, E., & Sharf, B. (1997). Exploring patients' experience as a primary source of meaning. *Health Communication, 9.* Mahwah, NJ: Erlbaum.

Pittsburgh's Hill District:
Valued Land and the Community Benefits Agreement

Emma T. Lucas-Darby
Carlow University

Social Justice My Way

My understanding of social justice can be traced to my youth during the 1960s in Meridian, Mississippi, a segregated Southern city where African Americans often experienced racism and discrimination. Somewhere deep in my soul, I knew I was a worthy individual and had to do whatever was necessary to overcome the view that so many in the South held of African Americans (During that time we were referred to by the "n-word," Negro or Black).

I would come to know that my church, St. Paul United Methodist Church, was supportive of civil rights activities during the 1960-70s. The local NAACP was active in Meridian. Charles Darden, the local leader, would make announcements in church on Sunday about nonviolent protests in Meridian and throughout the South. Whenever he spoke, I heard something that resonated with me about my value and worth as a human being. Later, mom and dad would emphasize how talented we were and how they wanted us to accomplish as much as we wanted in life. The phrase "We are working as hard as we are so that you can make something of yourself," was shared weekly and sometimes daily. "I will work hard," I thought, but "I will also have to fight the ugly and nasty attitudes and behaviors toward my race that I observed daily." This notion of "fighting" racism, discrimination, and bigotry rose to new heights as I became involved in the Civil Rights Movement, first in Meridian and later while attending Tougaloo College, known for its academically-talented students and their activism in the Civil Rights Movement. My Tougaloo years convinced me that acquiring an education and joining the civil rights struggle was one way I could lift myself up and work for my people. I would hear the words of my mother and father and remember their continuing struggles to make a living for themselves and our family.

My parents emphasized the fact that acquiring an education was imperative. It became clear to me that this was true if I was to contribute meaningfully to the movement toward freedom by becoming a professional and serving as an example for southern Black children. Fighting for constitutional rights, studying to be a successful college student, and participating in protest marches and sit-ins were all ways of increasing and exercising my belief in social justice. Social justice activities provide venues for engaging in actions that I firmly believed in and that became for me a means of expressing my growing belief in the sanctity of basic human rights.

My commitment to social justice was formed early during these years in Mississippi and continued to evolve years later, after I relocated to continue my education in the North. At the heart of social justice are inherent rights of equality and fairness, as well as the right to exercise our inherent constitutional rights and equal access to opportunities. Rawls (1971, cited in Wakefield, 1988) identified the notion of distributive justice that addresses the value of each person. He argued that in a democracy it is imperative that each member of society be given a fair share of the benefits, and participate in bearing the burdens resulting from social cooperation, both in terms of material goods and services and also in terms of nonmaterial social goods, such as opportunity and power (p. 193). This definition is most closely aligned with my past efforts to address social justice concerns and my current focus on nonmaterial social goods.

According to *Pittsburgh Post-Gazette* columnist O'Neill (2008), Robert Lavelle) the Hill District icon and founder of Dwelling House Saving and Loan) stated that the Hill District is the most valuable land in the city. This statement has more meaning today than it did before I moved to this community, and has become more poignant in recent years as eager property development players have begun to invest resources into sections of the neighborhood.

Admittedly, 10 years ago, I allowed the negative comments I heard about this community to sway my attitude toward the area that had been neglected by investors for years. However, a new spirit was gathering and with my daughter's encouragement, I relocated to this area known as "The Hill." The area was not an immediate sell for me, but after many lunchtime "drive-through tours" I realized the convenience this community offers by being within walking distance from Downtown, Mellon Arena, Mt. Washington, and the South and North Side. In addition, the neighborhood provides access to public transportation and, thus, access to many additional areas surrounding the city of Pittsburgh. For me, this meant that I was only one block from a bus stop or a 10-minute drive to work.

This community had been devastated by failed 1950s redevelopment and 1960s riots after the assassination of Martin Luther King, Jr., and is now—in the early years of the 2000s—experiencing redevelopment efforts that include affordable housing. I fell in love with my new community and soon became active in community groups. References were often made to what "The Hill" used to be—a vibrant community that could satisfy all human wants and needs, from clothing to groceries, from fresh poultry to fresh seafood, from great cooked food to baked goods, and from great jazz to memorable dancing. My Aunt Jo still shares stories of her shopping treks along Centre Avenue from Mahon to Crawford Streets. Her recollections are so vivid that I can actually picture the scenes she describes.

However, I realized that many of the new developments being considered, such as a casino and new arena, would have a major impact on my community. Consequently, although I often found my schedule filled with professional activities, I also felt an urgent need to join those concerned Hill residents who were determined to have their voices heard and to have meaningful input into any development efforts that directly impacted our community.

Through the scholarly personal narrative (SPN) methodology and case study, I examine several critical components of the Hill District's organizing strategies around the negotiation of a community benefits agreement. My views and interpretation offer one perspective on a multifarious, sometimes eccentric, eclectic, and convoluted process. Many meetings, challenges and activities are not included in this brief narrative. Starting with historical eminent domain actions by government officials who did not value the Lower Hill community and destroyed a large portion of it, I move to organizing actions by the present-day community that are directed toward stopping a recurrence of an action that previously neglected and voided community input. Nash (2004) notes SPN is an alternative form of intellectual inquiry that draws on the truth of what is out there through the

Figure 1. The area in the rectangle shows the Lower Hill District with original buildings. The overlay pattern identifies the renewal plans that were actually implemented. Photo courtesy of T. Baltimore.

Figure 2. Mellon Arena (formerly Civic Arena) is on the right. Construction of the new arena can be seen on the left. The parking area is part of the yet undeveloped 28 acres. Photograph by author.

documentation of reality (p. 7). According to Ellis and Bochner (2003, cited in Fries-Britt & Turner) this form of self-research provokes, challenges, and illuminates rather than confirms and settles (p. 224). This methodology is used to tell my story of an important period that has and will continue to shape the Hill District as many once knew it, as I and many others know it now to be, and as the Hill District that our grandchildren will come to know, enjoy, and hopefully continue to build upon as they learn about and capture the spirit of my current community activism.

Historical Background of the Hill District

Writer August Wilson; musicians Art Blakely, Mary Lou Williams, Billy Eckstine, George Benson, and Stanley Turrentine; and sportsmen Josh Gibson and Cool Papa Bell are names that immediately come to mind when talking about the rich cultural history of the Hill District of Pittsburgh. Well-known cultural establishments and jazz venues included the New Granada Theatre, Hurricane Lounge, Savoy Ballroom, and Crawford Grill. These individuals and places enhanced an already vibrant community with national and international notoriety. The Historic Hill District was previously a thriving community filled with a variety of stores on Centre Avenue, most of which were owned by Jews and Italians.

The riots of 1968 left many of the stores looted and in shambles. Racial unrest was spearheaded by young African Americans who were angry about the assassination of Martin Luther King and the many social ills they were facing. This devastation was preceded by a property massacre in the 1950s and 1960s. More than 8,000 residents were displaced, valued churches were leveled, and approximately 400 businesses were uprooted for the construction of the Civic Arena (Toker, 1986). Long-time residents still recall the shock that families experienced when relocating and the difficulty of keeping families together as a unit.

Today's Hill District has been my community for 10 years. Its needs are many. This community has been without a grocery store and drug store for 20 and 10 years, respectively. Economic development along the Centre Avenue corridor has stalled, yet communities around us, specifically the South Side Works and East Side are enjoying unprecedented economic growth. So, the announcement of a new arena for the Pittsburgh Penguins in the Lower Hill District moved residents to declare that they had been ignored for too long and that no development would come to the area that did not consider the community in which it would occur. At this point, I saw the need to consider aspects of social justice that were being ignored, as well as unfilled promises from prior years. I could not stand by and allow the needs and interests of my community to be ignored. I first became involved in a concerned residents' group and later in One Hill Coalition (OHC). Each group was organized to fight for input into any new development affecting their community. The Lower Hill District was displaced once for redevelopment purposes, specifically for the building of the Civic Arena that later became the home of the Pittsburgh Penguins. The massive, yet failed, urban redevelopment of the 1950s would not repeat itself.

Community Activism and the Importance of the CBA Process

A community benefits agreement (CBA) for the Hill District was initially discussed by the Hill District Gaming Task Force, which had developed its own Ten Point Key-Reinvestment Proposal which was given to each gaming applicant interested in building a casino in Pittsburgh. This proposal was the result of a process that analyzed and summarized the impact of gambling on the community. A community awareness campaign that addressed the physical structure, and the decision-making process to be used regarding the award of a gambling license, was also organized by Representative Jake Wheatley's office, and meetings were held throughout the community. These meetings and Task Force sub-committee reports identified recommendations that should be givebacks to the community (Hill District Gaming Task Force, April 11, 2006). These recommendations were similar to those that were later identified in the One Hill Coalition's CBA.

A CBA, I came to discover, is a necessary tool that enables groups to communicate. A CBA is a legally binding agreement that leads to a documented contract between a developer who has proposed a project and a community coalition. The underlying concern of community coalitions is that developers of major projects make reasonable commitments and contributions to regional equity that will positively benefit local communities (Baxamusa, 2008; Beideman, 2007; Mulligan-Hansel & LeRoy 2008). Generally, a community coalition supports proposed projects in

exchange for the developer's support of such community benefits as workforce development, living wages, affordable housing,
smart growth, livability, community services and improvements
(Gross 2005; Salkin 2007). Developers are often willing to ac-
comodate such community demands because developers realize
that community support is leverage when seeking government
subsidies and project approvals. Community groups and organizations realize the importance of having their voices heard
even when government and other funding entities have not recognized or responded to critical community needs. The hope of
many community coalitions is that developers will be aware of
the impact a major development project has on their community. LeRoy and Purinton (2005) note, however, that community
coalitions must intervene early in the development process as
CBA discussions generally involve an evolutionary process. The
births of a concerned citizens group and the One Hill Coalition
(OHC) and the sculpting of a CBA are discussed in detail later.

Social Justice and Evolving Tensions in the Hill District Community

The hope of the Hill District is to be treated justly by those
entities—forces and individuals—that have not always done so
previously. The disenfranchisement and underrepresentation of
certain racial groups and economically disadvantaged individuals in matters that directly impact them can also stall community
competence (Fellin, 2001; Rothman, 2001). OHC was formed in
April 2007, and the concerned Hill residents group—later known
as the Hill Faith and Justice Alliance (HFJA), which formed in
January 2007 before OHC, offered the possibility of creating and
completing visions, embracing hopes, and challenging a community to think strategically and futuristically while correcting and
preventing injustices experienced in the past. Residents knew
the community could not stand by while the new arena plan was
moving forward without recognized and deliberate input.

Another recent battle fought by the Hill District was the protest that began in 2006 against the construction of the Isle of
Capri casino in the Lower Hill District. The location of a casino
in a struggling and economically depressed community was not
viewed favorably by many Hill residents. Community activist,
scholar, and actress Dr. Kimberly Ellis organized and led efforts
against a casino being built in the neighborhood. Many residents

felt that the casino would bring no benefits to the community and that casino patrons would drive through the neighborhood to their destination to spend money while many locals struggled to meet basic human needs. However, taking a stand against the casino meant opposing positions taken by some local elected officials. The impact of the casino on the Hill was explored in-depth through the work of the Hill District Gaming Task Force. In addition, Representative Jake Wheatley served his constituents well by sharing his concerns for the location of a casino in his district.

The protest efforts of concerned community residents helped to defeat plans to locate a casino in the Lower Hill, when on December 20, 2006 the State Gaming Commission granted the Pittsburgh slots license to the North Shore Majestic Star Casino. This decision was a victory for advocates who wanted to protect the Lower Hill as a community asset. However, this decision did not alter plans to keep the Pittsburgh Penguins hockey team in Pittsburgh with the promise of a new "home" arena. At this point, discussions of development rights for the Lower Hill continued with sole participation of government officials and the Pittsburgh Penguins. Elected officials including Pennsylvania Governor Ed Rendell, Allegheny County Executive Dan Onorato and Pittsburgh Mayor Luke Ravenstahl were moving with urgency in an effort to craft an attractive deal that would keep the Pittsburgh Penguins in town with their new stadium located in the vicinity of the existing Mellon Arena.

The certainty of a new arena energized Hill residents to act. Similar to the insights of Reisch and Andrews (2001) regarding the discipline of social work, Hill residents have lived the consequences of unjust social arrangements at the local and macro levels and now are proactive, refusing to stand by idly. Concerned residents were now ready to challenge injustice, having recognized attempts to silence their voices through pacification and having repeatedly found their contributions and reconciliatory actions neglected.

I often thought about the social justice framework that could provide a context for advocacy actions of Hill residents. Citizens of a community deserve what is best for them as persons in their environment. Finn and Jacobson's (2002) model of social justice identifies five key concepts—meaning, context, power, history, possibility—that Hill residents would struggle with in the months to come. According to Finn and Jacobson, questions that should be asked when moving through a process such as Pittsburgh faced are:

> How do we give meaning to the experiences and conditions that shape our lives? What are the *contexts* in which those experiences and conditions occur? Who has the power to have their interpretations of those experiences and conditions valued as "true?" How might *history* and a historical perspective provide us with additional contextual clues and help us grasp the ways in which struggles over meaning and power have played out and better appreciate the human consequences of those struggles? And how do we claim a sense of *possibility* as an impetus for just practice? (p. 23)

The concerned Hill citizens (HFJA) and OHC increased my understanding of the social construction of reality—the way beings use their human capacities to give meaning to social experiences. During the past three years of involvement, these experiences generated questions for me, such as: What are the conflicts of power between and within Hill residents and leaders, local elected officials, and the Pittsburgh Penguins? Are the notions of domination and inequality present to such an extent that the way knowledge is acquired is skewed and/or monitored? What is the intracommunity power structure? Who participates in and supports this structure? I often found myself with answers; however, actions and decisions repeatedly called those answers into question as circumstances shifted. The actions of many actors (leaders) were inconsistent at best. Reasons for this inconsistency were most often ambiguous.

In the Beginning: Two Community Groups

I found myself actively participating in grassroots organizing efforts that gave Hill residents a voice. On a cold Sunday, January 28, 2007, approximately a dozen Hill District residents stood in front of Mellon Arena and declared their interest in whatever actions the Pittsburgh Penguins would undertake after having been given many concessions, including a new arena, to stay in Pittsburgh. The concerned citizens met the prior Saturday to discuss the government officials' egregious oversight that excluded input from the Hill District community regarding future development plans. Group participants were residents; stakeholders; leaders from the religious community; and political, social services, and advocacy organizations whose collective mission was to preserve, protect and develop the Historic Hill District. This position is best understood in the context of an urban renewal history that destroyed the lower Hill District in the 1950s. The negotiation of development rights for the Lower Hill property was moving forward with the exclusive involvement of government officials and the Pittsburgh Penguin Hockey franchise.

The Saturday group discussed the best strategies for informing government and Penguins officials that we would not be idle bystanders while they determined the future development of our neighborhood—a neighborhood where we live, work, and play daily. Representative Jake Wheatley and Rev. Johnnie Monroe, a civil rights activist and pastor, were instrumental in sharing information about the activities of the Governor, Mayor, Allegheny County Executive, Sports and Exhibition Authority and Pittsburgh Penguins. Although many group members knew negotiations were moving forward, little was known about details of behind-the-scene actions and decisions. The group agreed to hold a press conference on January 28, 2007 at Mellon Arena to voice their concerns regarding Lower Hill District development rights. Government officials and developers were moving forward with new arena development plans, and in an effort to keep the Penguins in Pittsburgh, the City Sports & Exhibition Authority authorized a $325 million bond issue for the new arena (Belko, 2007). The group formed out of this initiative and whose meetings I attended identified itself initially as concerned citizens and later as the Hill Faith and Justice Alliance (HFJA).

The group's mission was clear and their energy high. I was reminded of the sage strategies used by Civil Rights activist Ida Wells Barnet as she reported the horrific lynchings that were occurring in the early 1900s and urged her Progressive Era comrades to engage in fact-finding and research before moving forward. She commented that people must know before they act, a precondition for preparing for battle (Holt, 1982, p. 47). HFJA acted in much the same way. They, along with Rep. Wheatley, engaged in a process of educating themselves with credible information and developed a listing of facts that supported their collective mission:

1. The Penguins have not been good neighbors and are not entitled to development rights to the land in the Lower Hill.

2. Hill residents and citizens expect to receive proper representation from the elected Mayor and County Executive in any decision-making process that reflects past injustices and affects present and future directions.

3. The designation of a seat at the decision-making table addressing Lower Hill District development.

No matter who or what entity obtains development rights, the Hill District should receive community equity, and the extent of these considerations must be documented in writing. HFJA continued to meet and emphasize to elected officials the importance of Hill community engagement. Over the months, this group's membership grew, as more ministers and residents became involved. This group never altered its original mission and stayed the course to get elected officials to recognize the need to be inclusive in all development decisions. On April 4, 2007, OHC held its first meeting. Unfortunately, OHC failed to recognize the early efforts of or to collaborate with the concerned citizens group (HFJA), even though leaders of OHC were actively involved in this group's early activities.

The Hill District Consensus Group and Pittsburgh United were the lead organizations in the formation of OHC. From the beginning, OHC's purpose was a duplication of that of HFJA. The purpose of OHC was identified as:

A coalition established to capture the collective power of community residents and institutions in order to gain community benefits from the millions of dollars of our tax dollars that are to be invested in the Penguins' new arena and the re-development of the current Mellon Arena site. Through our work we are reclaiming part of what was lost in the original construction of the Mellon Arena. OHC is mobilizing the community residents and institutions to identify the types of benefits the community needs and to decide which asks will go forward to the Penguins and SEA (Sports and Exhibition Authority). (OHC 2007)

Clearly, both HFJA and OHC were organized for the same purpose, yet the latter declared itself as the only open and democratic group with a process by which community residents and stakeholders could discuss and craft an agreement. Their focus was on the community's wants and needs in relation to the public subsidy for the new arena and the proposed 28-acre arena development. OHC leaders were charter members the earlier group and worked to identify a mission statement for that group.

Recognizing the need to be inclusive and democratic, the HFJA invited representatives from throughout the Hill to open community meetings. One such meeting to discuss the commonalities of the two groups was held in April 2007. After lengthy discussions, those in attendance decided to identify the group's purpose and, appointed a subcommittee to craft a mission statement. I served as secretary of the subcommittee and, together with other residents, crafted a mission statement:

> Concerned Hill Residents exist to protect the collective interests of Hill District residents and to protect and preserve the historic, cultural and aesthetic integrity of the Hill District by ensuring that any and all development projects have full disclosure regarding the prospective impact upon Hill District residents. The Residents expect full involvement in such projects from design conception to final approval and any proposed plans for development must contain a clear articulation of community benefits and a comprehensive evaluation of quality of life issues as they are contemplated and set forth by residents and their leadership.

This statement was never approved, mostly due to intervening factors surrounding the organizing of OHC and the inability of the two groups to compromise. A unified community agenda would be a more effective strategy when negotiating community benefits with the city, county and Penguins. Continuing efforts to bridge the gap between the groups were futile. The refusal of OHC to recognize the work that had begun on a memorandum of understanding was unfortunate for all involved. The underlying reasons for this refusal seemed to stem from the expectations of the labor union that received funding for OHC. Nevertheless, the leadership of OHC could not see the benefit of the two groups joining together for the common good of the Hill District community and could not reconcile their differences. I often wondered if power, distrust and classism were driving the tensions between the groups.

Both HFJA and OHC identified common issues, including a master plan for the community, a community development fund and money reinvested, preservation and reparation, community representation/support, public safety/interest, school/education, affordable housing and home maintenance, funds and technical assistance for businesses (including a grocery store), local hiring and training of Hill residents (OHC, 2007).

OHC engaged in a priority identification exercise and, based on community issues receiving the most votes, documented this in the *Blueprint for a Livable Hill*. The priority "planks" replicated those of the Gaming Task Force and the HFJA. One issue or "ask" identified by the HFJA was reinvestment monies in the amount of $10 million, and this excited concern among some OHC members. Dissidents felt a financially strapped City of Pittsburgh, and the Penguins hockey team would be unable to respond favorably to this while supporters believed these two entities had a responsibility to give financial support to the community.

Unify or Bust: Community Disintegration

OHC's failure to recognize HFJA's work that had begun on a memorandum of understanding was very unfortunate. As late as August 2007, an OHC organizer made the following comment: "The sudden rise of a group of ministers wanting to negotiate their own agreement concerning the development is not a distraction for the One Hill group" (Belser, 2007). This is further evidence of OHC leaders' failure to accept the work of the HFJA and their unwillingness to meet to reconcile differences.

Several efforts were made to bring the two groups together, and the timing was optimum. CBA experts were invited to meet with OHC. During a presentation sponsored by OHC on June 20, 2007, Rev. William Smart, senior community organizer with the community group Los Angeles Alliance for a New Economy (LAANE), stressed the need to form an inclusive neighborhood coalition to maximize community input for a CBA. Rev. Smart brought his years of experience with CBAs and notoriety as a chief negotiator of the largest CBA in history to this meeting. This $500 million agreement, the most comprehensive to date and the first negotiated with a government entity, was between the city of Los Angeles, the airport authority, and a coalition of community organizations, unions, environmentalists and residents as part of a $9 million airport expansion (LAANE Newsletter, 2004). Rev. Smart underscored the interests of both Hill groups when he commented that the community should be at the table so that economic development could work for all. He encouraged all Hill groups, churches, and civic organizations to come together; appealed to OHC to communicate with the HFJA; and lauded ministers as a vital segment of any African American community. He also noted that everyone has to understand that all community groups bring self-interest to the table.

The passion with which Rev. Smart encouraged a unified community coalition reminded me of Saul Alinsky's Chicago Back of the Yards organizing. Alinsky valued the participation of the religious community and credited organized Catholic parishes as one of the basic social forces that pressured major meat packers and averted a strike. This type of organizing centered on a single vehicle that was sufficiently powerful to effect social change (Engel 1998, p. 643). A unified Hill group, inclusive of the religious community, would be more powerful than each group separately. During Rev. Smart's Q & A, I stood in front of the group and pleaded a case for unity. I expressed my concerns about the divisiveness and unwillingness of OHC to meet in earnest with the HFJA and reconcile. The fixed looks on some faces signaled unchanged behaviors. During succeeding meetings, my appeals, as well as those of others, were repeated. The importance of all community groups working together for a CBA was further emphasized by Daniel Tabor, a community activist, who stated, "The community benefits agreement has given disparate groups an opportunity to come together and work out differing opinions about how the development should be" (LAANE Newsletter, 2004).

Several weeks later at a subsequent meeting, an East coast scholar was present who spoke briefly to OHC. I was shocked to hear her say that OHC should move forward without attempting to hold out an olive branch to the HFJA. This was fuel on an existing fire from someone who did not fully understand the struggles of the two Hill District citizens groups. I could not contain myself, and I responded with an appeal to Hill residents, stressing the need for all to unify around a critical issue that impacted our community's future.

Local pastor Rev. Johnnie Monroe realized the need for Hill groups to come together to resolve their differences. He helped organized the *Come Let Us Reason Together Meeting* on May 17, 2007, and a *Build the Hill Praise & Unity Service* on October 24, 2007. More than 30 Hill residents, concerned citizens, and elected official were invited to the former meeting whose purpose was:

> [We will gather] to talk and fight about our differences and then put them aside so that we can work for the good of the Hill District. In the end it does not matter whether we are Religious Leaders, Hill CDC, Consensus Group, Raise Your Hand, Hill House, Elected officials and Ward Leaders. What does matter is how we unite to speak with ONE VOICE FOR JUSTICE....Some of you may ask the question, "What is this for, Johnnie Monroe?" The answer —the peace of knowing that we as an African American people can come together and do what people say we can't" do—work together for the good of the community. (Monroe, May 7, 2007).

My attendance at this meeting and the one described below is evidence of my continuing hope for reconciliation among HFJA and OHC.

A *Praise and Unity Service* on October 24, 2007 was another effort to forge one unified group. Ministers throughout the Hill community participated and a joint Hill District church choir sang spirited songs of praise and anthems. The prayers and speeches given by the speakers were reminiscent of those I heard by local ministers and civil rights workers in Mississippi during the 1960s. Attendees represented the membership of Hill District churches, the concerned citizens group, and a few members of OHC. Again, an effort to obliterate the barriers that separated us was not supported. The ugly head of divisiveness had re-appeared.

In an August 30, 2007 statement, a leader of OHC is quoted as saying, "there is inter-squabbling and there is an entirely separate group purporting to represent the Hill District, but the negotiating team has specific goals it is charged to pursue. We're close to being in the same book, but that's to be expected. That kind of dynamic actually moves things forward" (Morrow, 2007). The two groups did not reconcile.

Community Meetings, Conflicts and Strained Relationships

Attending OHC meetings on a weekly basis sometimes felt like going into a battle zone. I did not know what the atmosphere would be at a meeting because there was never consistency of attendance among official OHC members, and those who did attend sometimes tended to cluster along political and philosophical lines. In fact, political constituencies would exhibit unfriendly facial expressions and make snide, malicious and divisive comments that raised the level of existing tensions in meetings. On more than one occasion, I observed members of one political group refusing to speak to individuals who opposed their positions. This noticeable level of animosity continued, caused unnecessary factionalism, and impacted the interest and attendance of residents who did not want to be in this atmosphere. Although OHC claimed more than 100 official members, attendance at most meetings was scant.

The interest and concern of all concerned residents undergirded the fervor of their activism and mine as I continued to encourage inclusiveness for OHC. Although they vowed not to allow history to repeat itself, they also claimed staunch political alliances. This sometimes interfered with the intended progress of OHC. Engagement in community concerns may also be punctuated with emotions that have historical and political origins. Community engagement around a communal issue should create spaces of common interest, hopefulness and respect for each other's contribution to the cause. Finn and Jacobson (2003) suggest engagement as a first step to building trust, which should expand as more knowledge of the issue is acquired. From this knowledge, more discoveries and strategies for action flow. The atmosphere of OHC early in 2007 was one of engagement around development in the Lower Hill. However, the focus of OHC meetings often waned as groups from outside the Hill District joined, divergent community issues surfaced and intergroup conflicts heightened. This was very apparent when an elected official and other community residents were verbally attacked because of their positions regarding the strategies being employed in talks with city and county officials.

The Signed CBA

A negotiating team was identified by OHC and battled with the city, county, and Penguins for one year, with specific benefits and outcomes in mind. Finally, on August 19, 2008, a CBA was signed by OHC, the Penguins, Mayor Ravenstahl, and County Executive Onorato identifying the terms under which the economic development projects would be undertaken. Among the benefits are $2 million in community development funds, with $1 million earmarked for a full-service neighborhood grocery store; a Hill master plan; and a first-source job center (Belko, 2008). These terms are far short of the priorities identified by Hill residents and documented in the *Blueprint for a Livable Hill*. However, no commitment was obtained for development of the 28-acre Mellon Arena site. This is considered by many Hill residents to be an egregious oversight. The 28 acres must provide a seamless connect for the Hill and downtown Pittsburgh. The need for follow-through is critically important. The fulfillment of the terms of the CBA requires monitoring and continued engagement of Hill residents. Community groups and organizations are as strong as their members and, thus, active citizen engagement is imperative.

The true benefits of the CBA to the Hill community can only be determined in the future. Every entity involved in this development should want to be a good neighbor and recognize the Hill District as a valued and necessary asset for the City of Pittsburgh. I will continue to be involved in my quest to advocate for social justice in my community, especially with the encroachment of huge development projects at the Hill District's boundary.

References

Baxamusa, M. (2008). Empowering communities through deliberation: The model of community benefits agreements. *Journal of Planning Education and Research, 27*, 261-276.

Beideman, C. (2007). Eminent domain and environmental justice: A new standard of review in discrimination cases. *Boston College Environmental Affairs Law Review, 34*(2), 273-302.

Belko, M. (2007, June 8). Arena gains on several fronts: Authority OKs bond issue, signs lease with Pens. *Pittsburgh-Post Gazette*, B1.

Belko, M. (2008, August 20). Hill leaders see a new beginning as arena agreement is signed. *Pittsburgh-Post Gazette,* B1.

Belser, A. (2007, August 30) Hill group outlines benefits it expects from new arena. *Pittsburgh Post-Gazette*, B1.

Engel, L. (1998). The influence of Saul Alinsky on the campaign for human development. *Theological Studies, 59,* 64.

Fellin, P. (2001). *The community and the social worker* (3rd ed.). Itasca, IL: F.E. Peacock.

Finn, J., & Jacobson, M. (2003). *Just practice: A social justice approach to social work*. Peosta, IA: Eddie Bowers.

Fries-Britt, S. & Kelly, B. (2005). Retaining each other: Narratives of two African American women in the academy. *The Urban Review, 37*(3), 221-242.

Gross, J. (2005). *Community benefits agreements: Making development projects accountable.* Retrieved from http://www.goodjobsfirst.org/pdf/cba2005final.pdf

Hill District Gaming Task Force. (2006, April 11). Greater Hill District Proposal to City of Pittsburgh Gaming Applicant. Pittsburgh, PA.: Hill District Gaming Task Force.

Holt, T. (1982). The lonely warrior: Ida B. Wells-Barnett and the struggles for Black leadership. In J. Franklin & A. Meier (Eds.), *Black leaders in the twentieth century*. Urbana: University of Illinois Press.

LAANE Newsletter. (2004, December). Coalition wins landmark 500 million community benefits agreement for LAX modernization. Retrieved January 9, 2009, from http://74.10.59.52/laane/newsletter/2004_12.html.

LeRoy, G., & Purinton, A. (2005). *Community benefits agreements: Ensuring that urban development benefits everyone.* Washington, DC: Neighborhood Funders Group, 3.

Monroe, J. (2007, May 7). Letter to community leaders re Come Let Us Reason Together Meeting. Pittsburgh, PA: Rev. Johnnie Monroe.

Morrow, C. (2007, August 20). One Hill or one hot mess? *The New Pittsburgh Courier,* 1.

Mulligan-Hansel, K., & LeRoy, G. (2008). Community benefits: An idea on a roll! *NFG Reports, 1*(15), 4.

Nash, R. (2004). *Liberating scholarly writing: The power of personal narrative.* New York: Teachers College Press.

One Hill Coalition. (2007, June 17). *Preliminary Asks for inclusion in Community Benefits Agreement for the Hill District.* Pittsburgh, PA.

One Hill Coalition. *(2007, June 27). What is a community benefits agreement?* Pittsburgh. PA.

O'Neill, B. (2008, January 13). The Hill District's destiny. *Pittsburgh Post Gazette,* 2.

Reisch, M., & Andrews, J. (2001). *The road not taken: A history of radical social work in the United States.* New York: Brunner/Routledge.

Rothman, J. (2001). Approaches to community intervention. In J. Rothman, J. Erlich, & J. Tropman (Eds.), *Strategies for community intervention: Macro practice* (6th ed.). Itasca, IL: F.E. Peacock Publishers.

Salkin, P. (2007). Understanding community benefits agreements: Opportunities and traps for developers, municipalities and community organizations. *Planning and Environmental Law, 11,* 19-34.

Toker, F. (1986). *Pittsburgh: An urban portrait.* University Park, PA: Pennsylvania State University Press.

Wakefield, J. (1988). Psychotherapy, distributive justice, and social work: Part I—Distributive justice as a conceptual framework for social work. *Social Service Review, 62*(2), 187-210.

Chapter Contributors

Judith A. Aiken is Associate Professor at the University of Vermont where she teaches courses in organizational leadership. Dr. Aiken's research interests focus on the preparation of ethical educational leaders, gender and leadership, leadership and emotionality, and staff supervision and evaluation. Her professional publications include a number of book chapters, including a chapter in the *Handbook of Research on Supervision* and journal publications that have appeared in the *National Association of Secondary Education NASSP Bulletin, Journal of Leadership Studies, Educational Leadership Review, Journal of School Leadership*, and *Planning and Changing: An Educational Leadership* and *Policy Journal*. She holds and Ed.D. from Rutgers University.

Martha Bárcenas-Mooradian has a Ph.D. in education from The Claremont Graduate University. She also completed a doctoral program (ABD) in Latin American Literature at the Ohio State University. She has spearheaded various action research projects and service learning programs in relation to indigenous and underserved migrant populations. Her research includes second-language acquisition, indigenous literatures and preservation of indigenous languages and culture. She is a social activist in the field of immigration and is currently teaching as Adjunct Assistant Professor of Spanish at Pitzer College, where she is also the Director of the Language and Culture Center.

Lora Battle Bailey is Professor and Dean of the School of Education at Brenau University. She holds a doctorate from Auburn University.

Robert Biral is a communication specialist at the University of Vermont. Prior to his position at the University, he was a professor of English at the Naval Academy Preparatory School. He has also been a high school English teacher. Mr. Biral was a Yale University/New Haven Teaching Fellow. He is interested in the impact of technology on student writing. He is a graduate of the University of Connecticut.

Kathleen Ja Sook Bergquist is an Associate Professor in the School of Social Work at the University of Nevada, Las Vegas (UNLV). She completed her master's degree in social work at Norfolk State University, doctorate in counselor education at the College of William and Mary in Virginia, and JD at the Boyd School of Law at UNLV. Adopted from Korea into a Scandinavian American family, Dr. Bergquist spent her early years in Korea, Hawai'i, India, and England positioning her uniquely at a young age to consider the societal and familial impact of poverty, colonialism, and racialized formations of identity.

Fred A. Bonner II researches topics addressing academically gifted African American males in postsecondary contexts, college student development, faculty of color in predominantly White institutions and, high-achieving Blacks and Latinos in science, technology, engineering and mathematics. Dr. Bonner is Professor of Higher Education at Texas A&M University and serves as Associate Dean in the College of Education and Human Development. He is also an active member of Alpha Phi Alpha Fraternity.

Melba Joyce Boyd is Distinguished Professor and Chair of the Department of Africana Studies at Wayne State University in Detroit, Michigan. She is a filmmaker, editor, author of thirteen books and over 50 essays on African American literature and film. She is a Fulbright Scholar and has received many awards for her work, including the 2005 Black Caucus of the American Library Association Book Honor for Nonfiction. She was a Finalist for the 2010 NAACP Image Award in poetry, a Nominee for the 2010 Kresge Eminent Artist Award, and the recipient of the Michigan Council for the Arts Individual Artist Award.

Gloria Holguín Cuádraz is an Associate Professor of Sociology in the Division of Humanities, Arts, and Cultural Studies at Arizona State University. She received her doctorate in Sociology from University of California, Berkeley in 1993 and began her faculty career at ASU's Department of American Studies in 1994. She is a member of the Latina Feminist Group, co-authors of *Telling to Live: Latina Feminist Testimonios,* Duke University Press, and publishes in the areas of Chicana/os and higher education and oral history. She is one of the founders of the Ethnicity, Race, and First Nations Studies Program at ASU.

Marsha J. Tyson Darling is Professor of History and Interdisciplinary Studies and Director of the Center for African, Black and Caribbean Studies at Adelphi University. Much of her published work examines the intersection of race, gender, class and Eugenics. Dr. Darling is a native of New York City.

Nakeina E. Douglas is the Director of the Grace E. Harris Leadership Institute. Douglas earned her Ph.D. in Public Administration and Public Affairs from the Center for Public Administration and Policy at Virginia Tech. Previously, Douglas served as a research and evaluation associate at the National Science Foundation. In addition, she was Adjunct Professor at George Mason University in the Department of Public and International Affairs. Douglas's teaching and research focus on public policy processes, analysis and evaluation, program evaluation, comparative state politics, social research methods, women and leadership, and the intersection of race and social policy.

Yolanda Flores is an Associate Professor at the University of Vermont. Her areas of research, teaching, and publication are the comparative study of literature and culture of the Americas, with a focus on challenging hegemonic representations of knowledge in regard to gender, "race," class, language, and nationality. Professor Flores has authored many articles in these areas and the book, *The Drama of Gender: Feminist Theater by Women of the Americas.* She is currently writing her memoir, *Brown-eyed Daughter of the Sun* and is co-editing *Defying the Odds: Testimonies in Higher Education from California's Agricultural Heartlands.* Dr. Flores holds a doctorate from Cornel University and master's degree from the University of Chicago.

Susan T. Gooden is the Executive Director of the Grace E. Harris Leadership Institute and Professor and Director of Graduate Programs in the L. Douglas Wilder School of Government and Public Affairs at Virginia Commonwealth University (VCU). She has published numerous scholarly articles and book chapters in the areas of social equity, welfare policy and postsecondary education. She has conducted several research studies for MDRC, as well as other national research organizations. She teaches courses in public policy and administration, social equity and public policy analysis, research methods, and social welfare policy. Dr. Gooden is a member of Delta Sigma Theta Sorority and obtained her Ph.D. from the Maxwell School, Syracuse University.

G. L. A. Harris, an Assistant Professor in the Mark O. Hatfield School of Government at Portland State University, received her Ph.D. in Public Administration with concentration in Public Management from Rutgers University. Widely published, Dr. Harris's research lies in civil rights, recruiting and retention in the military, gender equity, organizational performance and unionization. She held managerial positions within the food manufacturing industry and was the principal/founder of her consulting firm specializing in human resource management and employment law. She is also a Commissioned Officer in the U.S. Air Force Reserve and formerly served on active duty in the U.S. Air Force.

Wanda Heading-Grant, Ed.D currently serves as the Associate Provost for Multicultural Affairs and Academic Initiatives at the University of Vermont. Her most recent appointment has been as Associate Dean in the College of Education and Social Services at the University of Vermont. Dr. Heading-Grant has over 16 years of experience as a senior-level administrator in higher education. She has spent her career focusing on issues of social justice, education, and equality. Dr. Heading-Grant holds a faculty appointment in the Department of Social Work and is a member of the Graduate College at the University of Vermont.

Richard Greggory Johnson III is Associate Professor of Educational Leadership and Policy Studies and Program Director of Race and Culture at the University of Vermont. Dr. Johnson has published many journal articles and several books addressing social justice and leadership. He holds a doctorate in Public Policy and Administration from Golden Gate University, a M.S. from DePaul University and an M.A. from Georgetown University. Dr. Johnson has been an active member of the American Society for Public Administration since 1991. He is a Life Member of Alpha Phi Alpha Fraternity and is active with the Vermont Alumni Chapter.

Theresa Julnes Kaimanu is a Professor at Portland State University where she has been teaching graduate courses and has conducted research on health policy and other healthcare-related topics since 1988. She holds a Ph.D in public administration.

Adriana Katzew is Assistant Professor in the Art Education Program at Massachusetts College of Art and Design in Boston. She was the Director of the Art Education Program and Assistant Professor in the Art and Art History Department at the University of Vermont from 2005 to 2009. Her research focuses on the intersection between Chicana/os, Latina/os, art, education, social justice, and activism. Dr. Katzew obtained her doctorate from Harvard University Graduate School of Education and a law degree from the University of Pennsylvania Law School. She is an artist working in photography and mixed media and has taught photography and creative writing to immigrant children from Puerto Rico and the Dominican Republic.

Amy Helene Kirschke is Professor of Art History and African American Studies at UNC Wilmington. She is the author of *Aaron Douglas: Art Race and the Harlem Renaissance* (1995), *Art in Crisis: W.E.B. DuBois and the Struggle for African American Identity and Memory* (2007), *Common Joy, Common Sorrow: Women Artists of the Harlem Renaissance* (2010), and *One Hundred Years of Crisis* (2010), co-edited with Phillip Sinitiere. She is currently researching contemporary African art in Senegal, Ghana and South Africa.

Carolyn Bailey Lewis is director and general manager of the WOUB Center for Public Media at Ohio University. She was the first African American woman to provide leadership for a full-power PBS station in the U.S. when she was named General Manager in 1993. She earned B.S. and M.S. degrees from West Virginia University's P. I. Reed School of Journalism, and her Ph.D. from Ohio University's School of Communication Studies, Scripps College of Communication—health communication and organizational communication. She is Adjunct Professor in the School of Media Arts and Studies and an advocate for disability rights.

Evelyn Lewis earned her medical degree from the University of the Health Sciences, Chicago Medical School and completed residency at Naval Hospital Jacksonville. She earned a master's degree in the social and behavioral sciences from Pacific Lutheran University. She served in the Navy as a family physician for 25 years and was Director Medical Policy for Pfizer Pharmaceuticals. She is Deputy Director, National Medical Association/Montague Cobb Research Institute and holds a faculty appointment in the departments of Family Medicine and Medical and Clinical Psychology, Uniformed Services University. She is a nationally recognized expert on Cultural Competency, Health and Healthcare Disparities.

Emma Lucas-Darby is Professor in the Department of Social Work, Carlow University. She holds a Ph.D. in Social Work from the University of Pittsburgh and an M.A. in Political Science from Purdue University. She has published on African women and economic development, gerontology, multiculturalism, alcohol use among pregnant women, and service-learning. She was a National Institutes of Health Fellow at the University of Pittsburgh School of Medicine, was past state president of the National Association of Social Workers. She serves on boards of several community organizations and the PA Board of Social Workers, Marriage and Family Therapists and Professional Counselors.

Cynthia I. Macri grew up in Minnesota, Hawaii, Egypt, Mexico, and Pakistan. At Lehigh University, she majored in Biology and, among other activities, played soccer and ultimate frisbee. She attended Temple University School of Medicine on the Navy's Health Professions Scholarship Program (HPSP), graduating with an M.D. degree in 1983. She is a board-certified gynecologic oncologist, competitive adult women's soccer player, and mother of an aspiring Navy doctor. Her Navy career spans three decades and includes challenging and rewarding assignments, culminating in her current duty as the Special Assistant to the Chief of Naval Operations for Diversity.

Aretha F. Marbley is an Associate Professor of education at Texas Tech. She holds a Ph.D. from the University of Arkansas in Counselor Education & Supervision. Dr. Marbley has published widely in the field of counselor education as well.

Fayneese Sheryl Miller is Dean of the College of Education and Social Services and Professor of Human Development, Educational Leadership and Policy Studies at the University of Vermont. Her research focuses on social and political development of youth, truancy, and leadership in higher education. Dr. Miller is an ACE and Millennium Leadership Fellow. She has also been both a Salzburg and NSF Fellow. She is a member of Alpha Kappa Alpha Sorority.

La Vonne I. Neal is Dean of the College of Education at the University of Colorado at Colorado Springs. Neal is a teacher educator whose work in the design and implementation of culturally responsive teaching methods has earned wide recognition both among educators and in the popular press. For example, her research on the correlation between African American male students' walking styles and their placement in special education courses has been featured in *USA Today*, the *Atlanta Journal-Constitution*, DiversityInc.Com, and radio and television stations across the country.

Karin Pleasant is a native of Flint, MI. She received a bachelor's degree in communications from the University of Michigan, Ann Arbor in 1996, a master of fine arts in writing from California Institute of the Arts in 2001 and a master of business administration from Pepperdine University in 2007. Ms. Pleasant continues the collaboration, M.U.L.E., started in 1999 with artist Isabelle Lutterodt to develop art projects and research cultural ideas. Trade&Row Corp. was formed with designer Aldo Puicon and incorporated in 2008 to create programming that is entertaining and socially relevant.

Christopher Anne Robinson-Easley is an Associate Professor of Management, President of Enlightening Management Consultants, Inc., and a management consultant to government agencies, nonprofits, social service organizations and the private sector. Throughout her career, Chris has worked in managerial and directorship positions in operations, human resources and organization development in the business sector. She has served in the roles of director, dean and assistant provost in higher education. She received her B.A. and master's degrees from Loyola

University of Chicago and her doctoral degree from Benedictine University. She is currently pursuing a master's Degree in Divinity at Chicago Theological Seminary.

E. Renée Sanders-Lawson is Assistant Professor and Director of the Center for Urban School Leadership in the Leadership Department at the University of Memphis. She received her Ph.D. in Educational Administration from Michigan State University and her Bachelor of Arts degree in Psychology and master's of Science degree in Rehabilitation Counseling from The University of North Carolina at Chapel Hill. Her research interests include school leadership, diversity in the administration of K-12 schools, first-year principals, women of color in higher education administration and, Black women superintendents in K-12 urban school settings. She is a member of Alpha Kappa Alpha Sorority.

Pamela C. Smith is an Associate Professor of Accounting at the University of Texas at San Antonio (UTSA). She earned her BS in Commerce, with a concentration in Accounting from the University of Virginia and her M.S. and Ph.D. in accounting from Virginia Tech. Dr. Smith researches how tax policy impacts nonprofit healthcare organizations. She is a member of several professional organizations, including the American Taxation Association and the National Association of Black Accountants. She also serves as a faculty mentor for the PhD Project and is a member of the Virginia Tech Black Cultural Center Alumni Advisory Board. Dr. Smith is a member of Delta Sigma Theta Sorority.

Vidu Soni, Ph.D. is a professor of public administration and a human resources management consultant. Her scholarship and consulting practice involve human capital development, workplace diversity management, and organizational development. Prior to her academic career, Dr. Soni served as a human resource management executive. She is active in various professional organizations and holds leadership positions in them.

Olga M. Welch, a Phi Beta Kappa graduate of Howard University and the University of Tennessee, is Dean of the School of Education at Duquesne University. Before coming to Duquesne, she was Professor Emerita in the College of Education, Health and Human Services at the University of Tennessee. Dr. Welch has authored/co-authored several publications, chapters and books, and serves on several journal editorial boards. Most recently, (with Dr. Diane S. Pollard), she examined the construction of research epistemologies by women of color in their edited volume, *From Center to Margins: The Importance of Self-Definition in Research* (SUNY Press). Dr. Welch is a member of Alpha Kappa Alpha Sorority.

Phyllis M. Wise became Provost and Executive Vice President (EVP) at the University of Washington in August 2005. As the University's chief academic and budgetary officer, the Provost and EVP provides leadership in educational and curriculum development, formulation and allocation of budget and space, long-range strategic planning, and management of the University's research programs. Dr. Wise holds a bachelor's degree from Swarthmore College in biology and a doctorate degree in zoology from the University of Michigan. In 2008 she was awarded an honorary doctor of sciences from Swarthmore College.